Old School Still Matters

Lessons from History to Reform Public Education in America

Brian L. Fife

 PRAEGER

AN IMPRINT OF ABC-CLIO, LLC
Santa Barbara, California • Denver, Colorado • Oxford, England

Library of Congress Cataloging-in-Publication Data

Fife, Brian L.
   Old school still matters : lessons from history to reform public education in America / Brian L. Fife.
      pages cm
   Includes bibliographical references and index.
   ISBN 978–0–313–39809–4 (hardback) — ISBN 978–0–313–39810–0 (ebook)
1. Public schools—United States—History. 2. Education—United States—History. 3. Educational change—United States—History. I. Title.
LA212.F48   2013
371.010973—dc23   2013010545

ISBN: 978–0–313–39809–4
EISBN: 978–0–313–39810–0

17 16 15 14 13   1 2 3 4 5

This book is also available on the World Wide Web as an eBook.
Visit www.abc-clio.com for details.

Praeger
An Imprint of ABC-CLIO, LLC

ABC-CLIO, LLC
130 Cremona Drive, P.O. Box 1911
Santa Barbara, California 93116-1911

This book is printed on acid-free paper ∞

Manufactured in the United States of America

To my former teachers at Central School, Marshwood Junior High School, and Marshwood High School.

Thank you for your dedication, instruction, and guidance.

Contents

Acknowledgments

I must express my gratitude for all of my colleagues at Indiana University–Purdue University Fort Wayne (IPFW) for supporting this effort through a research sabbatical and for providing essential resources in order to complete the project. In addition, a heartfelt thank you to all the wonderful librarians at both the Helmke Library at IPFW and the Allen County Public Library in downtown Fort Wayne for all their assistance. Our community is fortunate to have such stellar public institutions and officials. I am also thankful to have had the opportunity to visit the Olive Kettering Library at Antioch College in Yellow Springs, Ohio, where Horace Mann's papers are housed. It was a fascinating experience for me, and the photographs of Horace Mann utilized in this book were provided by Antiochiana at Antioch. In particular, I appreciate the assistance of Scott Sanders and Nina Myatt.

A book project is obviously a collaborative effort of sorts, and I am fortunate to have had the opportunity to work with Beth Ptalis, who answered many questions and provided sage counsel throughout the process of writing this book. In addition, I am grateful for the assistance of Valentina Tursini in the beginning phases of this project. Finally, I am thankful to have a wonderful family, and I appreciate the presence of my wife, Melissa, and our sons, Sam and Jack, in my life immensely. I also enjoyed many hours spent with our canine friends, Maisy and Lily, throughout this process.

Horace Mann and the Common School Ideology

The idea that free public schools would benefit society as a whole, especially in a republican form of government, has deep antecedents in American history. Under America's first written constitution, the Articles of Confederation and Perpetual Union, the members of the Confederate Congress did not originally endorse Thomas Jefferson's recommendations for the division and government of the western edges of the United States on March 1, 1784.[1] However, when the members revisited the matter on April 23, 1784, the Ordinance of 1784 was approved.[2] This ordinance required that the land west of the Appalachian Mountains, north of the Ohio River, and east of the Mississippi River be divided into separate states. Yet the proposal did not include a mechanism by which the land in question would become states.

Photograph of Horace Mann taken before his years at Antioch College (1853–1859). (Image courtesy of Antiochiana, Antioch College.)

A year later (May 20), the members of the Confederate Congress passed the Land Ordinance of 1785.[3] This ordinance effectively implemented the Ordinance of 1784 by providing a specific manner for selling and settling the land in the Northwest Territory. Each township would be surveyed into square townships, six square miles on each side, totaling 640 acres. Each township would have 36 sections, and section 16 of each township would be dedicated to public schools, which reflected Jefferson's commitment to public education as being essential to democratic governance.[4]

One of the significant accomplishments of the Confederate Congress during the 1780s was passage of the Northwest Ordinance on July 13, 1787.[5] This act provided government for the area north and west of the Ohio River; this area includes the five states of Ohio, Indiana, Illinois, Michigan, and Wisconsin. Ironically, the Confederate Congress passed the Northwest Ordinance while at the same time delegates from 12 of the 13 states were meeting in Philadelphia and ultimately drafted the U.S. Constitution.[6] The Northwest Ordinance of 1787 did not require the states to provide public education, but it was "encouraged" nevertheless: "Religion, morality, and knowledge, being necessary to good government and the happiness of mankind, schools and the means of education shall forever be encouraged."[7] Ironically, in the same article, the following promise was made to Native Americans, a promise that would never be fulfilled:

> The utmost good faith shall always be observed towards the Indians; their lands and property shall never be taken from them without their consent; and, in their property, rights, and liberty, they shall never be invaded or disturbed, unless in just and lawful wars authorized by Congress; but laws founded in justice and humanity, shall from time to time be made for preventing wrongs being done to them, and for preserving peace and friendship with them.[8]

Yet even before the Northwest Ordinance was passed, other leaders in America under the Articles of Confederation and Perpetual Union expressed their endorsement of public education for all citizens.

THE IDEA OF PUBLIC EDUCATION FOR ALL

In an open letter to the citizens of Philadelphia on March 28, 1787, the great American physician, educator, and signer of the Declaration of Independence Benjamin Rush declared,

> Every friend to the prosperity of Pennsylvania must view with pleasure the establishment and success of those seminaries of learning which are

intended to diffuse knowledge through the state; but useful as these colleges and academies are, they are not sufficiently extensive in their objects to spread literature through the humble and indigent classes of the people: they are calculated chiefly for the benefit of the affluent and independent part of the citizens of the state. The blessings of knowledge can be extended to the poor and laboring part of the community only by the means of FREE SCHOOLS. The remote and unconnected state of the settlements in the new counties will forbid the establishment of those schools for some years to come by a general law; but there is nothing to prevent this being set on foot immediately in the city of Philadelphia and in the old and thick-settled counties of the state. To a people enlightened in the principles of liberty and Christianity, arguments, it is to be hoped, will be unnecessary to persuade them to adopt these necessary and useful institutions. The children of poor people form a great proportion of all communities. Their ignorance and vices when neglected are not confined to themselves; they associate with and contaminate the children of persons in the higher ranks of society. Thus they assist after they arrive at manhood in choosing the rulers who govern the whole community. They give a complexion to the morals and manners of the people. In short, where the common people are ignorant and vicious, a nation, and above all a republican nation, can never be long free and happy. It becomes us, therefore, as we love our offspring and value the freedom and prosperity of our country, immediately to provide for the education of the poor children who are so numerous in the thick-settled parts of the state.[9]

Education was a matter of great importance in the new American nation. To Rush, who founded Dickinson College, it was important to educate both young men and young women alike, though his views on gender were not entirely out of context with his era.[10]

Even before the Revolutionary War, Thomas Jefferson had a vision of a system of common schools, which would provide all children in Virginia with an opportunity to secure a formal education. During the war, he became Virginia's second governor in 1779 by succeeding Patrick Henry. Monetary resources, however, were absorbed in the cause for independence, so Jefferson could not pursue the implementation of his vision for education reform.[11]

In a letter to Colonel Charles Yancey dated January 6, 1816, former president Jefferson offered the following prophesy regarding public education in a republic:

I am a great friend to the improvements of roads, canals, and schools. But I wish I could see some provision for the former as solid as that of the latter,—something better than fog. The literary fund is a solid provision, unless lost in the impending bankruptcy. If the legislature would add to that a perpetual tax of a cent a head on the population of the State, it would set agoing at once, and forever maintain, a system of primary or ward schools, and an university where might be taught, it its highest degree, every branch of science useful in our time and country; and it would rescue us from the tax of toryism, fanaticism, and indifferentism to their own State, which we now send our youth to bring from those of New England. If a nation expects to be ignorant and free, in a state of civilization, it expects what never was and never will be. The functionaries of every government have propensities to command at will the liberty and property of their constituents. There is no safe deposit for these but with the people themselves; nor can they be safe with them without information. Where the press is free, and every man able to read, all is safe.[12]

President Jefferson seemingly articulated a vision of common schooling where the good of the many, society as a whole, supersedes the perceived self-interest of any particular individual. The very cause of republicanism, in fact, necessitated the subjugation of individual needs for the greater public interest. In addition, safeguarding democracy required universal education so that the people would be equipped to fend off the forces of tyranny that might arise from time to time.

As historian Frederick Rudolph has noted, there are a number of scholars who touted the idea of free public schools for all children in the American republic. In a book he edited in 1965, he includes essays from seven individuals whose manuscripts were written and published between 1786 and 1799.[13] The previously mentioned Benjamin Rush (1745–1813) offered his "Plan for the Establishment of Public Schools" in 1786.[14] In his plan, he advocated universal education for all and explains how public education should be financed:

But, shall the estates of orphans, bachelors, and persons who have no children be taxed to pay for the support of schools from which they can derive no benefit? I answer in the affirmative to the first part of the objection, and I deny the truth of the latter part of it. Every member of the community is interested in the propagation of virtue and knowledge in the state. But I will go further and add [that] it will be true economy in individuals to support public schools.[15]

His premise was rather simple: all taxpaying citizens are benefited by public education, so all must pay.

Noah Webster (1758–1843) published "On the Education of Youth in America" in 1790.[16] The great American lexicographer offered this sentiment with regard to educating young children: "The education of youth is, in all governments, an object of the first consequence. The impressions received in early life usually form the characters of individuals, a union of which forms the general character of a nation."[17] In extolling the virtues of educating children, his views on the subject are very much in sync with noteworthy modern advocates for children, such as Dr. Benjamin Spock and Dr. T. Berry Brazelton.

Robert Coram (1761–1796), a veteran of the Revolutionary War who served on the *Bonhomme Richard* under John Paul Jones, became a strong Anti-Federalist during the ratification debate following the Philadelphia Convention. After the Revolution, he settled in Wilmington, Delaware, and became the editor of the *Delaware Gazette*. In 1791, he published "Political Inquiries: to Which Is Added, a Plan for the General Establishment of Schools throughout the United States."[18] In his essay, he makes an equalitarian case for free compulsory elementary education:

> It is generally observed that most of the American legislatures are composed of lawyers and merchants. What is the reason? Because the farmer has no opportunity of getting his son instructed without sending him to college, the expense of which is more than the profits of his farm. An equal representation is absolutely necessary to the preservation of liberty. But there can never be an equal representation until there is an equal mode of education for all citizens.[19]

Coram's vision of education is particularly noteworthy given the fact that it was presented to the public after the U.S. Constitution had been in effect for only two years and during the same year that the Bill of Rights was added to the document.

Simeon Doggett (1765–1852) was a New England Unitarian minister who became the principal of Bristol Academy in Taunton, Massachusetts, in 1796. His dedicatory address was delivered on the opening of the Bristol Academy on July 18, 1796. It was published in New Bedford, Massachusetts, in 1797.[20]

In "A Discourse on Education," Doggett expressed his education philosophy in closing:

> Such then, my friends, being the immense value of education, let all embark in its cause. Let government and able individuals offer their patronage and encouragement. Let parents exhaust their tenderest affections in the glorious work. Let teachers realize and carefully

discharge the amazing responsibility which lies upon them. Let both sexes equally share in those exertions; let them be begun early and no time be lost. Let youth be impressed with the value of a good education and the laborious attention necessary to acquire it. Let their exertions be measured by the greatness and value of the work and the brevity and value of the morning of life and correspondent to the anxious wishes, prayers, and exertions of their parents and instructors. As all of us are equally interested in the great and common cause; let us, in heart and hand, unite to advance it, and the blessings of God will attend us.[21]

Even though he was a very spiritual individual, Doggett viewed education as a "common cause," a paradigm that would be fully embraced by many of his successors in the nineteenth-century education reform crusade. Like other liberal thinkers during his time period, Doggett believed that wide dissemination of knowledge is advantageous in a republic and will counteract the forces of tyranny and aristocracy.

Samuel Harrison Smith (1772–1845) was an American journalist and newspaper publisher who shared a prize, along with Samuel Knox, for the best essay on a national system of education by the American Philosophical Society in 1797. His essay was written in 1796 and was published in Philadelphia in 1798. He became the editor of *National Intelligencer* and was closely aligned with the party of Thomas Jefferson.[22]

In his "Remarks on Education," Smith provided an eloquent endorsement for public education:

The acquisition of knowledge is open to all. It injures no one. Its object is disinterested. It delights in distinction only so far as it increases the mass of public good. Here then is an object which all may pursue without the interference of one with another. So far from producing interference, it will constantly tend to destroy it; for the more men think, the more they will resemble each other, and the more they resemble each other, the stronger will their mutual attachment be.[23]

Smith envisioned an enlightened America, through the implementation of free education for all, where peace triumphed over war and where virtue was omnipresent through the diffusion of knowledge.

According to Rudolph, not much is known about Amable-Louis-Rose de Lafitte du Courteil other than he appears to have been a refugee from the French Revolution who had one literary effort while he served as a "professor" at an academy for boys at Bordentown, New Jersey. His essay "Proposal to Demonstrate the Necessity of a

National Institution in the United States of America, for the Education of Children of Both Sexes. To Which Is Joined, a Project of Organization, etc.," was published in Philadelphia in 1797, and it must be understood that his English skills were somewhat challenged.[24]

Lafitte came to the United States in 1796 and traveled until he accepted the position in Bordentown.[25] He offered the following overview of his view of American societal conditions and needs at that time: "The United States of America afford an observer afflicting contrasts. If he first visits the principal cities, from Boston to Charleston, he is astonished at the extent of these cities, their luxury, their commerce, and their population. It does not appear to him that he has left Europe [when he visits]. . . . If after this first examination of the cities, this observer travels through the country, then his heart will be truly wounded."[26] The primary reason that visitors will be disillusioned with American life, according to Lafitte, was because the country lacked public education for all children. In spite of the advancements made in cities such as Philadelphia, New York, Boston, and Charleston, Lafitte counseled citizens, as well as political leaders, to be attentive to the education needs of America's children. He was particularly concerned with his perception that American parents were either too occupied with their affairs, too apathetic, or too misguided and, as a result, that children were woefully neglected. In his travails, he determined that too many American children were running about the streets without any adult supervision.

Samuel Knox (1756–1832) was born in Ireland but came to the United States around 1795. He had a dual career as a clergyman and educator. For many years, he served as the principal of an academy in Frederick, Maryland. In sharing the prize given by the American Philosophical Society in 1797 for the best essay on a national system of education, Knox's "An Essay on the Best System of Liberal Education, Adapted to the Genius of the Government of the United States" was published in Baltimore in 1799.[27]

Knox captured public sentiment on education by stating, "There is no individual in society whom you may not hear ACKNOWLEDGING the great importance of education. Even those who are most ignorant of its advantages are heard to express the highest encomiums on its inestimable value to the state, to the interests of human happiness, social or individual. The learned and unlearned seem equally agreed on this subject."[28] In this essay, directed specifically to the members of the Maryland state legislature, Knox refers to education as a "system for the public good."[29] Thus, a general paradigm had clearly evolved on the part of some education theorists by the late eighteenth century in the United States. All citizens, regardless of their plight, had a right to a public education, and the government had a responsibility to provide it. A more enlightened citizenry, in turn, would be better positioned to be effective contributors to the American republic.

THE IMPORTANCE OF THEORY AND HISTORY IN EDUCATION REFORM

It should be noted that education reform, regardless of one's politics or ideology, is impossible without theory. Plausible theory is essential in the pursuit of more scientific knowledge about education policy. In other words, a better command of ideas will promote the cause of education reform. Reform is not inevitable, and it does not systematically evolve by chance. In this noble campaign that we all universally endorse, our relative success is completely dependent on the human mind, the human spirit, and the political arena. As the great student of law Oliver Wendell Holmes Jr. so eloquently stated in the late nineteenth century,

> Theory is the most important part of the dogma of the law, as the architect is the most important man who takes part in the building of a house. The most important improvements in the last twenty-five years are improvements in theory. It is not to be feared as unpractical, for, to the competent, it simply means going to the bottom of the subject. For the incompetent, it sometimes is true, it has been said, that an interest in general ideas means an absence of particular knowledge. I remember in army days reading of a youth who, being examined for the lowest grade and being asked a question about squadron drill, answered that he never had considered the evolutions of less than ten thousand men. But the weak and foolish must be left to their folly. The danger is that the able and practical minded should look with indifference or distrust upon ideas the connection of which with their business is remote.[30]

When Justice Holmes presented his ideas in an address to aspiring attorneys at Boston University in 1897, he was a justice on the Massachusetts Supreme Judicial Court.[31] He would later be appointed to the U.S. Supreme Court by President Theodore Roosevelt and confirmed by the U.S. Senate, and he served from 1902 to 1932. What Justice Holmes articulated about the law is equally applicable to education reform. Any solution to the challenges in education policy is theoretical in nature. If it is possible to enhance the status quo with regard to K–12 education, then the optimum way to do this is through the concoction of ideas that are reasonable, intuitive, and perhaps just downright common sense. As is true in so many venues, history is an important guide in any attempt at public policy reform.[32]

Technological advancements over the course of American history are well documented and most impressive by many criteria. It is undoubtedly safe to assume that they will continue, perhaps in ways that many of us cannot envision at this time. At the same time, however, many American political, ideological, partisan, and policy debates have been around for some time. While the primary political actors change since human life is a finite entity, many of the issues, including those in education, remain fairly constant. As such, a vast body of knowledge can be extracted from the lessons of history. When identifying the importance of history in the legal field, Justice Holmes opined that

> At present, in very many cases, if we want to know why a rule of law has taken its particular shape, and more or less if we want to know why it exists at all, we go to tradition. We follow it into the Year Books, and perhaps beyond them to the customs of the Salian Franks, and somewhere in the past, in the German forests, in the needs of Norman kings, in the assumptions of a dominant class, in the absence of generalized ideas, we find out the practical motive for what now best is justified by the mere fact of its acceptance and that men are accustomed to it. The rational study of law is still to a large extent the study of history. History must be a part of the study, because without it we cannot know the precise scope of rules which it is our business to know. It is a part of the rational study, because it is the first step toward an enlightened skepticism, that is, toward a deliberate reconsideration of the worth of those rules. When you get the dragon out of his cave on to the plain and in the daylight, you can count his teeth and claws, and see just what is his strength. But to get him out is only the first step. The next is either to kill him, or to tame him and make him a useful animal. For the rational study of the law the black-letter man may be the man of the present, but the man of the future is the man of statistics and the master of economics. It is revolting to have no better reason for a rule of law than that so it was laid down in the time of Henry IV. It is still more revolting if the grounds upon which it was laid down have vanished long since, and the rule simply persists from blind imitation of the past.[33]

It is crucial in any policy area to extract lessons from history as Justice Holmes articulated. Education is not unique in this regard. This does not mean that all past policies need to be continued if applicable or that existing policies need to replicate those implemented by our predecessors. The underlying theory and the ideas on which the policies in question were predicated do merit intense scrutiny. Advocates of education reform, which includes a large and diverse group of people with differing cultural, economic, social, racial, ethnic, religious, and gender backgrounds, deserve nothing less, as the challenges that currently confront citizens can be properly and substantively addressed only by reflecting on America's own history.

PUBLIC VERSUS PRIVATE INSTITUTIONS

In advance of a discussion of the common school movement and the contributions made by Horace Mann, it is necessary to highlight an important early nineteenth-century U.S. Supreme Court case that had the effect of delineating the difference between government-controlled educational institutions and private entities.[34] On February 2, 1819, the Supreme Court justices decided the case of *Dartmouth College v. Woodward*.[35] This important case was adjudicated about a month before one of the most important in U.S. history, *McCulloch v. Maryland*, the celebrated national bank controversy.[36]

In 1816, the legislators in New Hampshire attempted to change Dartmouth College, a privately funded institution, into a state university. A law was passed that changed the school's corporate charter by transferring the control of the trustee appointments to the governor. In an attempt to regain authority over the resources of Dartmouth College, the old trustees filed suit against William Woodward, who sided with the new gubernatorial appointees. Thus, the justices had to determine whether the state legislators had unconstitutionally interfered with Dartmouth College's rights under the contract clause.

Under Article I, Section 10, the contract clause stipulates, "No State shall enter into any Treaty, Alliance, or Confederation; grant Letters of Marque and Reprisal; coin Money; emit Bills of Credit; make any Thing but gold and silver Coin a Tender in Payment of Debts; pass any Bill of Attainder, ex post facto Law, or Law impairing the Obligation of Contracts, or grant any Title of Nobility." The legendary chief justice John Marshall wrote for the Court's majority (himself, Bushrod

Washington, William Johnson, Brockholst Livingston, and Joseph Story). Justice Thomas Todd did not participate in the case, and Justice Gabriel Duvall dissented without providing his reasoning.

Chief Justice Marshall determined that the charter granted by the British Crown to the trustees of Dartmouth College in 1769 constituted a contract within the meaning of the contract clause of the federal Constitution. As a result, the contract could not be altered by the New Hampshire state legislature. In his own words, Chief Justice Marshall declared,

> A corporation is an artificial being, invisible, intangible, and existing only in contemplation of law. Being the mere creature of law, it possesses only those properties which the charter of its creation confers upon it either expressly or as incidental to its very existence. These are such as are supposed best calculated to effect the object for which it was created. Among the most important are immortality, and, if the expression may be allowed, individuality—properties by which a perpetual succession of many persons are considered as the same, and may act as a single individual. They enable a corporation to manage its own affairs and to hold property without the perplexing intricacies, the hazardous and endless necessity, of perpetual conveyances for the purpose of transmitting it from hand to hand. It is chiefly for the purpose of clothing bodies of men, in succession, with these qualities and capacities that corporations were invented, and are in use. By these means, a perpetual succession of individuals are capable of acting for the promotion of the particular object like one immortal being. But this being does not share in the civil government of the country, unless that be the purpose for which it was created. Its immortality no more confers on it political power, or a political character, than immortality would confer such power or character on a natural person. It is no more a state instrument than a natural person exercising the same powers would be. If, then, a natural person, employed by individuals in the education of youth or for the government of a seminary in which youth is educated would not become a public officer or be considered as a member of the civil government, how is it that this artificial being, created by law for the purpose of being employed by the same individuals, for the same purposes, should become a part of the civil government of the country? Is it because its existence, its capacities, its powers, are given by law? Because the government has given it the power to take and to hold property, in a particular form, and for particular purposes, has the government a consequent right substantially to change that form, or to vary the purposes to which the property is to be applied? This principle has never been asserted or recognised, and is supported by no authority.[37]

The impact of this case was significant. Business investment and growth were encouraged, as state officials were now precluded from interfering with charters under the contract clause. This permitted business entrepreneurs to attract more investors, employ more workers, and contribute to overall national economic prosperity.

According to the historian Leon Richardson, an unknown lawyer at that time argued the position of the Dartmouth trustees on March 10, 1818. He was a Dartmouth graduate of the class of 1801 by the name of Daniel Webster. According to some historians, as he drew to a close, Webster broke into tears, as did Chief Justice Marshall, who listened intently.[38] Mr. Webster closed his plea by stating,

> This, sir, is my case. It is the case, not merely of that humble institution, it is the case of every college in the land. It is more. It is the case of every eleemosynary institution throughout our country, of all those great charities founded by the piety of our ancestors to alleviate human misery, and scatter blessings along the pathway of human life. It is more. It is in some sense the case of every man who has property of which he may be stripped—for the question is simply this: Shall our state legislature be allowed to take that which is not their own, to turn it from its original use, and apply it to such ends or purposes as they, in their discretion, shall see fit? Sir, you may destroy this little institution; it is weak; it is in your hands. I know it is one of the lesser lights in the literary horizon of our country. You may put it out, but if you do you must carry through your work! You must extinguish, one after another, all those great lights of science, which, for more than a century, have thrown their radiance over the land! It is, sir, as I have said, a small college, and yet there are those that love it.[39]

The Court's majority determined that Dartmouth College was not a civil or a public institution, nor was its property in the public domain. Dartmouth College was a private eleemosynary institution with an entity (education) of benefit to the public; however, it was not a public institution under government control. As a result of this pivotal case, private institutions were safeguarded from legislative interference. In many ways, it gave greater understanding and a more specific definition of the American corporation.[40]

Dartmouth College was chartered on December 13, 1769. Its first president (and founder) was Eleazor Wheelock.[41] Yet Richardson believed that Dartmouth College was "refounded" by Daniel Webster because of his eloquence and keen intellect as evidenced in the Dartmouth College case. Furthermore, he maintained that the institution was kept intact because of the determination, political acumen, wisdom, and leadership of Chief Justice Marshall.[42]

THE COMMON SCHOOL IDEOLOGY OF THE 1830s AND 1840s

As Joel Spring has contended, the common, or public, school movement of the 1830s and 1840s put into practice many of the educational ideas of previous generations.[43] An absolutely instrumental figure in the evolution of universal public schools in the United States was Horace Mann (1796–1859). According to the prolific author and librarian Robert B. Downs, "The impact of Horace Mann's ideas and achievements has been profoundly felt in the educational world at home and abroad for well over a century. Few figures in our history have made such a pervasive and enduring impression on American culture and civilization. Many of the issues raised by Mann are as live and relevant today as they were in the eighteen-forties, when he was a highly effective missionary for universal public education."[44] While a brief biographical sketch is provided in order to enhance a chronological understanding of Mann's many contributions, it is absolutely essential that the reader understand that the pertinence of Mann to contemporary debates over education reform lies in his theoretical ideas and ideals.[45]

Horace Mann was born in Franklin, Massachusetts, on May 4, 1796. In 1816, he entered Brown University in Providence, Rhode Island, as a sophomore. He did so on the instruction of Samuel John Barrett, an itinerant teacher. In 1819, he graduated with high honors from Brown and entered the law office of J. J. Fiske in Wrentham, Massachusetts, for a few months and then returned to Brown to become a tutor in Latin and Greek. Two years later, he resigned as a tutor to study law under Judge James Gould at Litchfield, Connecticut. In 1823, he was admitted to the Massachusetts bar and entered the law office of James Richardson in Dedham, Massachusetts, a post he continued for the next 14 years. The following year, he began an active interest in public affairs and politics and subsequently was elected to serve in the Massachusetts state legislature (General Court). In 1830, he married Charlotte Messer, the daughter of the president of Brown. His wife died less than two years later. In 1833, Mann was elected to the Massachusetts senate; he served as president of the senate from 1835 to 1837 and was instrumental in the establishment of the

Massachusetts State Hospital for the Insane. In 1837, he resigned from the state legislature to become the first secretary of the newly established Massachusetts Board of Education. He served in this position until 1848. During this time, he wrote 12 annual reports that became highly influential in the common school movement. In 1843, he married Mary Peabody and traveled to Europe to observe the educational systems in several different nations. In 1848, he resigned his position as secretary of the Board of Education to fill a vacant seat in the U.S. House of Representatives caused by the death of John Quincy Adams, the former president. He was active in the abolitionist movement during his tenure in the U.S. House of Representatives. In 1852, Mann was defeated in his bid to become governor of Massachusetts (he was the Free-Soil candidate). After his defeat, he accepted the presidency of Antioch College in Yellow Springs, Ohio. He died on August 2, 1859, at Antioch.[46]

Life and Written Works of Horace Mann

After the Civil War, an initial volume of Horace Mann's life was edited by Mary Peabody Mann. By the end of the nineteenth century, two other editors, George Combe Mann (Horace Mann's son) and Félix Pécaut, would contribute to the development of a five-volume series on Mann's life and his written contributions.[47] A synopsis of Mann's works and an analysis of his experiences is provided so that the reader can familiarize him- or herself with his views on public education in the United States.

While many public school teachers today may be beleaguered and feel somewhat under siege, some reassurance may be found in the reality that Mann had a very positive perception of educators in the nineteenth century. According to Mrs. Mann, he "felt that the vocation of educator was the highest possible one in a republic. He approached it with the deepest awe and a sense of the highest responsibility, gladly relinquishing senatorial honors and wealth for its arduous but interesting duties."[48] When Mann abandoned a promising political career and his law practice to become the first secretary of the Massachusetts Board of Education, many of his peers clearly questioned his wisdom and judgment: "Most of his friends, who thought wealth, the position which it insures, and the prospects of political advancement that lay fairly before him, the most desirable objects of life, considered him foolish and visionary in making the change from a lucrative profession. A few, who knew the spirit he was of, rejoiced in his decision, although his present aim promised no worldly honors."[49] In terms of human values, what has changed in the United States since the 1830s? Some may praise the rising star for abdicating wealth and fame in pursuit of other noble objectives, but most would generally impugn such endeavors as the quest for material items perpetuates in the Western tradition.

Mann was approached by Edmund Dwight to become the first secretary of the new state Board of Education in early 1837.[50] As captured in Mann's own journal on May 6, 1837,

> Dined to-day with Edmund Dwight, Esq., for the purpose of conferring with him on the late law authorizing the appointment of a Board of Education. Mr. Dwight had the civility, or the incivility (I do not doubt that his *motives* would place the act under the former category), to propose that *I* should be Secretary of the Board,—a most responsible and important office, bearing more effectually, if well executed, upon the coming welfare of the State, than any other office in it. For myself, I never had a sleeping nor a waking dream that I should ever think of myself, or be thought of by any other, in relation to that station. Query, therefore, could he have been sincere in his suggestion?[51]

Dwight was persistent in his recruitment of Senator Mann, and he ultimately capitulated.

First Annual Report (1837)

Mann's first annual report as secretary of the Massachusetts Board of Education was written in 1837 and submitted to the members of the board in early 1838.[52] Mann emphasized four essential needs in public education:

> *First* in order is the situation, construction, condition, and *number* of the schoolhouses. I mention the *number* of the schoolhouses under this head, because, in populous places, there is a temptation to build too few, and to compact too many scholars into one house; while towns sparsely populated are beset with the opposite temptation, of making too minute a subdivision of their territory into districts; and thus, in attempting to accommodate all with a schoolhouse near by, the accommodation itself is substantially destroyed. In many cases, this pursuit of the incident works a forfeiture of the principal. A schoolhouse is

erected near by, but it is at the expense of having a school in it, so short, as to be of but little value. *Secondly*, the manner, whether intelligent and faithful, or inadequate and neglectful, in which school-committeemen discharge their duties. *Thirdly*, the interest felt by the community in the education of *all* its children; and the position in which a certain portion of that community stand in relation to the free schools. *Fourthly*, the competency of teachers.[53]

With regard to his initial point about the number of schools in the commonwealth, he cited a statistic from over 175 years ago that is largely intact today. More than five-sixths of all children in Massachusetts attended public schools in 1837, indicating that those children who were not enrolled in public schools at that time attended parochial and/or private schools.[54] Today, about 90 percent of all school-aged children attend public schools across the 50 states and District of Columbia.[55]

To Mann,

the construction of schoolhouses connects itself closely with the love of study, with proficiency, health, anatomical formation, and length of life. These are great interests, and therefore suggest great duties. It is believed that, in some important particulars, their structure can be improved without the slightest additional expense; and that, in other respects, a small advance in cost would be returned a thousand-fold in the improvement of those habits, tastes, and sentiments of our children, which are soon to be developed into public manners, institutions, and laws, and to become unchangeable history.[56]

The Mann philosophy of the past on this issue of tangible physical facilities is still apparent today. Many Americans in the early twenty-first century associate impressive school buildings with quality education. As many would contend regarding the school choice debate, among the most popular schools in the United States today are well-funded, affluent public schools located in the suburbs.[57]

In the early years of universal education for all children, Mann explicitly addressed the role of administration in the deliverance of a common education for all children. The optimum approach to the provision of quality education for children is to ensure that, according to Mann, intelligent, faithful, and ethical people are afforded the opportunity to serve as public administrators in the field of education.

The assembly of a team of prudent administrators enhanced the probability that competent teachers would be employed, and crucial issues, such as textbook selection, would be determined to the benefit of the children served. Make no mistake, however, in the misperception that times have changed greatly since the 1830s on this issue in particular. Reflecting on Mann's own words, "There is a public evil of great magnitude in the multiplicity and diversity of elementary books. They crowd the market, and infest the schools. One would suppose there might be uniformity in rudiments, at least; yet the greatest variety prevails. Some books claim superiority, because they make learning easy, and others because they make it difficult. All decry their predecessors, or profess to have discovered new and better modes of teaching."[58] Mann's description of book-publishing strategies could have been written this year, and his theory would remain intact. Educators in the K–12 system, as well as college and university instructors, could corroborate his views from their own experience as practitioners.

In this first annual address to the Board of Education, Mann determined that two groups exist that plague and challenge the common school ideal. His theory, articulated so long ago, may still resonate with the reader:

> Another topic, in some respects kindred to the last, is the apathy of the people themselves towards our Common Schools. The wide usefulness of which this institution is capable is shorn away on both sides, by two causes diametrically opposite. On one side, there is a portion of the community, who do not attach sufficient value to the system to do the things necessary to its healthful and energetic working. They may say excellent things about it, they may have a conviction of its general utility; but they do not understand, that the wisest conversation not embodied in action, that convictions too gentle and quiet to coerce performance, are little better than worthless. The prosperity of the system always requires some labor. It requires a conciliatory disposition, and oftentimes a little sacrifice of personal preferences.[59]

With regard to the opposing group, Mann offered the following analysis:

> Opposite to this class, who tolerate, from apathy, a depression in the Common Schools, there is another class, who affix so high a value upon the culture of their children, and understand so well the necessity of a skilful preparation of means for its bestowment, that they turn away from the Common Schools, in their depressed state, and seek, elsewhere, the helps of a more enlarged and thorough education. Thus the standard, in descending to a point corresponding with the views and wants of one portion of society, falls below the demands and the regards of another. Out of different feelings grow different plans; and while one remains fully content with the Common School, the other builds up the private school or the academy.[60]

Mann articulated a vision of reality in the Commonwealth of Massachusetts in 1837 that still has broad implications and utility today. Although 9 in 10 school-aged children attend public schools, the contemporary public school advocate would be wise to heed Mann's sage counsel from the nineteenth century. At best, defenders of the common school ideology will extract modest support from the general public under the most optimum of circumstances. This tepid support, however, exists simultaneously in the context of a vocal minority that seeks to undermine public education and promote a private education and/or parochial school agenda.

Public support for common schools is generally passive by definition. Opposition to taxation to fund the public schools is typically poignant. Parents of children enrolled in nonpublic schools are somewhat steadfast in their belief that their children will receive a more qualitative and substantive education through the private sector. This omnipresent, elitist notion should be duly recognized, understood, and addressed in the policy community on an ongoing basis.

Having quality, competent teachers is valued by public school advocates to this day. As Mann articulated in 1837,

> Teaching is the most difficult of all arts, and the profoundest of all sciences. In its absolute perfection, it would involve a complete knowledge of the whole being to be taught, and of the precise manner in which every possible application would affect it; that is, a complete knowledge of all the powers and capacities of the individual, with their exact proportions and relations to each other, and a knowledge, how, at any hour or moment, to select and apply, from a universe of means, the one then exactly apposite to its ever-changing condition. But in a far more limited and practical sense, it involves a knowledge of the principal laws of physical, mental, and moral growth, and of the tendency of means, not more to immediate than to remote results. Hence to value schools, by length instead of quality, is a matchless absurdity. Arithmetic, grammar, and the other rudiments, as they are called, comprise but a small part of the teachings in a school. The rudiments of feeling are taught not less than the rudiments of thinking. The sentiments and passions get more lessons than the intellect. Though their open recitations may be less, their secret rehearsals are more. And even in training the intellect, much of its chance of arriving, in after-life, at what we call sound judgment, or common sense, much of its power of perceiving ideas as distinctly as though they were colored diagrams, depends on the tact and philosophic sagacity of the teacher.[61]

The profession of teaching is multifaceted by definition. An effective teacher is one who has the requisite expertise in given subjects. A sufficient knowledge base is the sine qua non of teaching. However, teachers have to be adept managers as well. In the day-to-day experiences of a teacher, he or she must use reasonable judgment about a wide array of issues, much like Mann delineated in his initial annual report. Teachers are role models for children. They must set an example of civility, respect, fairness, citizenship, discipline, and a host of other important matters for their students.

Ultimately, in the practitioner's profession of teaching, teachers are held to a high standard—and justifiably so, according to Mann and many contemporaries. I am not convinced, however, that we have a comprehensive understanding or definition of effective teaching to this day. More about this subject will be scrutinized at a later time.

Second Annual Report (1838)

Most of Mann's second report was devoted to the subjects of reading, spelling, and composition in the public schools. He offered many recommendations regarding the teaching of reading and spelling as well as a discussion of the place of language in education.[62] To Mann, "Language is not merely a necessary instrument of civilization, past or prospective, but it is an indispensable condition of our existence as rational beings."[63] The use of language—indeed, the art of communication—is crucial in a republic, for, as Mann opined, "For all social purposes, thought and expression are dependent, each upon the other. Ideas without words are valueless to the public; and words without ideas have this mischievous attribute, that they inflict the severest pains and penalties on those who are most innocent of thus abusing them."[64] Theories and ideas are the essence of politics and public affairs. In the American democracy, many citizens focus disproportionately on the horse race of elections, campaign financing, and public opinion polling. It is important for all concerned citizens to focus more on the ideas on which policy preferences are predicated. Yet it is absolutely crucial for the communication of the ideas in question to be clear and coherent so that citizens are better positioned to evaluate them in a manner that they may deem appropriate.

Yet it is the imparting of knowledge that is central to the education enterprise. In today's world, many officials have seemingly forgotten and/or ignored this fundamental truth. The impartation of knowledge cannot be readily measured with one standardized test. Knowledge is gained in two ways from the perspective of the common school idealist:

> We arrive at knowledge in two ways: first, by our own observation of phenomena without, and our own consciousness of what passes within us; and we seek words aptly to designate whatever has been observed, whether material or mental. In this case, the objects and events are known to us, before the names, or phrases, which describe them; or, secondly, we see or hear words, and through a knowledge of their diversified applications we become acquainted with objects and phenomena, of which we should otherwise have remained forever ignorant.[65]

It is the common public school, according to the nineteenth-century reformer, that is the appropriate venue for children to accumulate systematic knowledge that they might not otherwise obtain. In stark terms,

> to prepare children for resembling the philosopher, rather than the savage, it is well to begin early, but it is far more important to begin right; and the school is the place for children to form an invincible habit of never using the organs of speech, by themselves, and as an apparatus, detached from, and independent of, the mind. The school is the place to form a habit of observing distinctions between words and phrases, and of adjusting the language used to various extents of meaning.[66]

It is very important for educators in general to consider Mann's prophecy when it comes to the learning process. He did not envision learning to be a passive enterprise by definition.

Consider the Mann philosophy of 1838 as applied to the contemporary time period in which we live:

> One preliminary truth is to be kept steadily in view in all the processes of teaching, and in the preparation of all its instruments; viz., that, though much may be done by others to aid, yet the effective labor must be performed by the learner himself. Knowledge cannot be poured into a child's mind like fluid from one vessel into another. The pupil may do something by intuition, but generally there must be a conscious effort on his part. He is not a passive recipient, but an active, voluntary agent. He must do more than admit or welcome; he must reach out, and grasp, and bring home. It is the duty of the teacher to bring knowledge within arm's-length of the learner; and he must break down its masses into portions so minute, that they can be taken up and appropriated, one by one; but the final appropriating act must be the learner's.[67]

The highlighting of this theoretical premise is of such importance in today's world. Teaching professionals in the public sector have been largely ostracized by critics of public education for poor student performance on state standardized tests. While the pursuit of reform in teaching must never cease, one wonders to what extent students collectively are maximizing their own efforts in education. Are all students prepared to learn on a given day in school? If not, what proportion may fit this category? Have parents or caregivers ensured that the children for whom they are responsible are amenable to the learning process on a daily basis? In short, have adults in the United States collectively implemented all reasonable measures to enhance the probability that children will have a proactive learning experience in their schools? If not, perhaps students can make their own education more effective and parents and caregivers can do more to advance the cause of education in America. Teachers, of course, will continue to be held accountable as well.

Third Annual Report (1839)

In the third annual report, Mann argued that free public libraries are needed to coincide with free public schools. For students to flourish in terms of reading, they need a supply of worthy reading materials. As Mann pragmatically asserted,

> After the rising generation have acquired habits of intelligent reading in our schools, *what shall they read?* for, with no books to read, the power of reading will be useless; and, with bad books to read, the consequences will be as much worse than ignorance as wisdom is better. What books, then, are there accessible to the great mass of the children in the State, adapted to their moral and intellectual wants, and fitted to nourish their minds with the elements of uprightness and wisdom?[68]

Apparently, this wisdom as it pertains to public libraries is still in vogue today. A cursory examination of the top 100 public libraries, for example, suggests that citizens in communities all across the nation perceive that funding public libraries is an important investment at the local level in the United States. In the 2010 edition of Hennen's American Public Library Ratings, libraries in 26 states are included. There is ample representation of urban and rural states in the survey. Clearly, a value exists in the United States that public libraries are worth funding and have intrinsic value for communities.

Why is this the case? Undoubtedly, this policy reality is a reflection of a basic theoretical premise that Mann and other education advocates communicated some time ago.[69]

Fourth Annual Report (1840)

In the fourth report, Mann addressed a variety of issues, including the training of common school teachers, a subject that is still debated today. What qualifications should be essential to the profession of teaching? Mann shared his thoughts on the subject in 1840, the year in which William Henry Harrison was elected president.[70]

Substantive knowledge is the first qualification that Mann emphasized in teaching in his report:

> One requisite is a knowledge of Common-school studies. Teachers should have a perfect knowledge of the rudimental branches which are required by law to be taught in our schools. They should understand, not only the rules, which have been prepared as guides for the unlearned, but also the principles on which the rules are founded,— those principles which lie beneath the rules, and supersede them in practice, and from which, should the rules be lost, they could be framed anew. Teachers should be able to teach *subjects*, not manuals merely. This knowledge should not only be thorough and critical, but it should be always ready at command for every exigency,—familiar like the alphabet, so that, as occasion requires, it will rise up in the mind instantaneously, and not need to be studied out with labor and delay.[71]

Mann did not envision teachers to be passive entities who simply taught out of prescribed manuals. Teachers had to be trained professionals themselves since they were entrusted with the education of children. Thus, teachers had to accumulate a sufficient knowledge base themselves, for without it, they could not hope to impart the same information to the children in their classrooms.

A second essential qualification in teaching is learning how to teach in the first place. According to the author of the fourth report,

> The next principal qualification in a teacher is the *art of teaching*. This is happily expressed in the common phrase, *aptness to teach*, which in a few words comprehends many particulars. The ability to acquire, and the ability to impart, are wholly different talents. The former may exist in the most liberal measure without the latter. It was a remark of Lord Bacon, that "the art of well-delivering the knowledge we possess is

among the secrets left to be discovered by future generations." Dr. Watts says, "There are some very learned men who know much themselves, but who have not the talent of communicating their knowledge." Indeed, this fact is not now questioned by any intelligent educationist. Hence we account for the frequent complaints of the committees, that those teachers who had sustained an examination in an acceptable manner failed in the schoolroom through a want of facility in communicating what they know. The ability to acquire is the power of understanding the subject-matter of investigation. Aptness to teach involves the power of perceiving how far a scholar understands the subject-matter to be learned, and what, in the natural order, is the next step he is to take. It involves the power of discovering and of solving at the time the exact difficulty by which the learner is embarrassed.[72]

Effective teaching can be manifested in different ways, but one inherent reality has persisted over time. In this continuing evolution of electronic technology, human judgment is still a necessary factor in the teaching profession. Teachers must ultimately rely on their own judgment as well as intuition. In addition, it may very well be the case that no singular solution regarding common challenges applies in all cases. Students are individuals, and not all people respond to a similar series of vexing issues in the same manner. Thus, while effective teaching may have numerous components, sound judgment is absolutely essential in order to address the needs of all children in a classroom environment.

Education policy is not unique, according to Mann. Not all things can be measured in a quantitative manner:

Experience has also proved that there is no necessary connection between literary competency, aptness to teach, and the power to manage and govern a school successfully. They are independent qualifications; yet a marked deficiency in any one of the three renders the others nearly valueless. In regard to the ordinary management or administration of a school, how much judgment is demanded in the organization of classes, so that no scholar shall either be clogged and retarded, or hurried forward with injudicious speed, by being matched with an unequal yoke-fellow! Great discretion is necessary in the assignment of lessons, in order to avoid, on the one hand, such shortness in the tasks as allows time to be idle; and, on the other, such over-assignments as render thoroughness and accuracy impracticable and thereby so habituate the pupil to mistakes and imperfections, that he cares little or nothing about committing them. Lessons, as far as it is possible, should be so adjusted to the capacity of the scholar, that there should be no failure in a recitation not occasioned by culpable neglect.[73]

To Mann, a third necessary qualification for teaching entails not only the requisite expertise in academic subjects and the ability to impart the knowledge gained by the teacher to a classroom of children but also the management, government, and discipline of a school. He emphasizes the need, on the part of teachers, to utilize punishments whenever necessary, but he nevertheless highlighted the importance of being consistent over time and not succumbing to being overly strict on the one hand or too dismissive of unruly behavior on the other.[74]

A fourth qualification for teaching in the public schools is the ability to teach children to engage in good behavior. According to Mann,

> In two words the statute opens to all teachers an extensive field of duty, by ordaining that all the youth in the schools shall be taught *"good behavior."* The framers of the law were aware how rapidly good or bad manners mature into good or bad morals; they saw that good manners have not only the negative virtue of restraining from vice, but the positive one of leading, by imperceptible gradations, towards the practice of almost all the social virtues. The effects of civility or discourtesy, of gentlemanly or ungentlemanly deportment, are not periodical or occasional, merely, but of constant recurrence; and all the members of society have a direct interest in the manners of each of its individuals; because each one is a radiating point, the centre of a circle which he fills with pleasure or annoyance, not only for those who voluntarily enter it, but for those, who, in the promiscuous movements of society, are caught within its circumference.[75]

In the contemporary era of the early twenty-first century, many citizens would likely concur with the premise that teachers set an example, on a regular basis, for their students. The role that teachers play in the lives of children, especially for those in single-parent homes or where caregivers are utilized extensively, is immeasurable by definition.

Finally, Mann maintained that teachers should be held accountable to a high standard and should conduct themselves in a morally prudent manner:

> On the indispensable, all-controlling requisite of moral character, I have but a single suggestion to make in addition to those admirable views on this subject which are scattered up and down through the committees' reports. This suggestion relates to the responsibility resting on those individuals who give letters of recommendation or certificates of character to candidates for schools. Probably one-half, perhaps more,

of all the teachers in the State are comparatively strangers in the respective place where they are employed. Hence the examining committee, in the absence of personal knowledge, must rely upon testimonials exhibited before them. These consist of credentials brought from abroad, which are sometimes obtained through the partialities of relationship, interest, or sect; or even given lest a refusal should be deemed an unneighborly act, and the applicant should be offended or alienated by a repulse. But are interests of such vast moment as the moral influence of teachers upon the rising generation to be sacrificed to private considerations of relationship or predilection, or any other selfish or personal motive whatever? It may be very agreeable to a person to receive the salary of a teacher, but this fact has no tendency to prove his fitness for the station: if so, the poorhouse would be the place to inquire for teachers; and what claim to conscience or benevolence can that man have who jeopards the permanent welfare of fifty or a hundred children for the private accommodation of a friend?[76]

In an operational sense today, many citizens would agree that convicted felons should not be eligible to teach children in the public schools. I suspect that the Mann philosophy on teaching qualifications would garner a good deal of popular support today even though it was articulated in 1840.

Fifth Annual Report (1841)

The fifth report included reiterations about the qualifications of teachers, schoolhouses, and the threat of religious discord in the public schools. But the main emphasis of this particular report was really political salesmanship. Mann contended that businessmen should support public education if for no other reason than pure self-interest. A more educated citizenry would result in a more productive workforce; thus, he clearly succeeded in mobilizing business interest in the public schools.[77] The following argument was offered by Mann in this report:

The capitalist and his agents are looking for the greatest amount of labor, or the largest income in money from their investments; and they do not promote a dunce to a station where he will destroy raw material, or slacken industry, because of his name or birth or family connections. The obscurest and humblest person has an open and fair field for competition. That he proves himself capable of earning more money for his employer is a testimonial better than a diploma from all the colleges.

Now, many of the most intelligent and valuable men in our community, in compliance with my request,—for which I tender them my public and grateful acknowledgments,—have examined their books for a series of years, and have ascertained both the quality and the amount of work performed by persons in their employment; and the result of the investigation is a most astonishing superiority, in productive power, on the part of the educated over the uneducated laborer. The hand is found to be another hand when guided by an intelligent mind. Processes are performed, not only more rapidly, but better, when faculties which have been exercised in early life furnish their assistance. Individuals who, without the aid of knowledge, would have been condemned to perpetual inferiority of condition, and subjected to all the evils of want and poverty, rise to competence and independence by the uplifting power of education. In great establishments, and among large bodies of laboring men, where all services are rated according to their pecuniary value; where there are no extrinsic circumstances to bind a man down to a fixed position, after he has shown a capacity to rise above it; where, indeed, men pass by each other, ascending or descending in their grades of labor, just as easily and certainly as particles of water of different degrees of temperature glide by each other,—there it is found as an almost invariable fact, other things being equal, that those who have been blessed with a good common-school education rise to a higher and a higher point in the kinds of labor performed, and also in the rate of wages paid, while the ignorant sink like dregs, and are always found at the bottom.[78]

This theory articulated by Mann has been a dominant paradigm in education policy in the United States for well over 170 years. It is an ideal that has remained largely intact in spite of a number of contemporary challenges to public education in America that will be addressed shortly. Suffice it to say, however, that it is under attack by conservative political forces at the present time.

Sixth Annual Report (1842)

The consumer of Mann's sixth report will likely conclude that very little has changed in the United States since the 1840s in the sense that a number of health challenges still exist when it pertains to children in contemporary society. He presents a passionate advocacy for health and physical education in the common schools. His bold declaration about the public's knowledge of human health issues may still resonate today: "There is a frightful extent of ignorance on the subject of the physical laws, as they appertain to the human constitution (and in this sense only I use the phrase), pervading the whole community. Even educated men, who are not physicians, are rare exceptions to this remark."[79] While Mann was particularly concerned with mortality rates among infants and young children, his basic premise is still relevant today. The children of modern America are still plagued by the ravages of poverty and basic ignorance when it comes to matters of public health.

With regard to physical exercise, Mann offered this by way of his own observations while performing the tasks associated with his job:

> I hope to be pardoned for evincing a feeling and a conviction on this subject more deep and strong than will meet with the sympathy or concurrence of others. Within the last six years I have visited schools in every section of the Commonwealth, seaboard and inland, city and country. Every day's observations has added proof to proof, and argument to argument, respecting the importance of physical training. Were I to be carried blindfold, and set down in any school in the State, I could tell at a glance, by seeing the mere outline of the bodies and limbs, without referring to face or hands as a test, what had been the habits of the children composing it. Such as have been accustomed to live in the open air, such as have been subjected to the exposures and the hardy exercises of the farm or the mechanical trade, appear almost like a different race of beings when compared with those who suffer under the amazing parental folly of being delicately brought up. As a general fact, the children of the rural population, and of those who live in sparsely-settled towns upon the seaboard, have double the bodily energy, the vital force, the stamina of constitution, which belong to the children of cities and of crowded towns. A fuller development of body, of limbs, and of brow; a firmer texture of muscle; motions evincive, not only of great vigor, but of longer endurance; in fine, the whole bodily appearance indicating that they have been laid out by Nature on an ampler scale,—characterize the former as compared with the latter.[80]

Obviously much has changed in the United States demographically since the days of Mann. Rural dwellers are in the vast minority compared to their urban and suburban counterparts. However, his premise is still applicable today. Many American children do not get proper exercise and nutrition, and the obesity rate among children in the United States is nothing less than a national crisis. According to the Centers for Disease Control and Prevention, about 17 percent of children and adolescents ages 2 to 19 years are obese. Moreover, this rate has almost tripled in the last 30 years.[81]

Seventh Annual Report (1843)

At his own expense, Mann was permitted by the members of the Board of Education to travel to Europe to engage in systematic comparative education.[82] As such, he traveled to England, Ireland, Scotland, Germany, Holland, Belgium, and France.[83] According to Lawrence Cremin, this report was the most well known of the 12 that Mann authored because it was the most controversial. In it, he praised student–teacher relationships in Prussian (German) schools, prompting many school officials to question Mann's ability to lead the education reform movement.[84]

In praising the Prussian mode of teaching, Mann appeared to be critical of at least some teachers in America:

> The third circumstance I mentioned above was the beautiful relation of harmony and affection which subsisted between teacher and pupils. I cannot say that the extraordinary fact I have mentioned was not the result of chance or accident. Of the probability of that, others must judge. I can only say, that, during all the time mentioned, I never saw a blow struck, I never heard a sharp rebuke given, I never saw a child in tears, nor arraigned at the teacher's bar for any alleged misconduct. On the contrary, the relation seemed to be one of duty first, and then affection, on the part of the teacher; of affection first, and then duty, on the part of the scholar. The teacher's manner was better than parental; for it had a parent's tenderness and vigilance without the foolish dotings or indulgences to which parental affection is prone. I heard no child ridiculed, sneered at, or scolded, for making a mistake. On the contrary, whenever a mistake was made, or there was a want of promptness in giving a reply, the expression of the teacher was that of grief and disappointment, as though there had been a failure, not merely to answer the question of a master, but to comply with the expectations of a friend. No child was disconcerted, disabled, or bereft of his senses, through fear.[85]

Later in the report, the common school reformer declared that he was not being critical of common school teachers in Massachusetts:

> I mean no disparagement of our own teachers by the remark I am about to make. As a general fact, these teachers are as good as public opinion

has demanded; as good as the public sentiment has been disposed to appreciate; as good as public liberality has been ready to reward; as good as the preliminary measures taken to qualify them would authorize us to expect. But it was impossible to put down the questionings of my own mind,—whether a visitor could spend six weeks in our own schools without ever hearing an angry word spoken, or seeing a blow struck, or witnessing the flow of tears?[86]

Clearly, however, some professionals in Massachusetts took exception with the secretary's positive comments on Pestalozzian methods in the Prussian schools. Sharp criticism was evoked from an ad hoc association of Boston schoolmasters, and throughout the following year Mann was involved in an ongoing battle of rejoinders and rejoinders to rejoinders.[87]

Eighth Annual Report (1844)

The eighth annual report lacks a central theme, and instead Mann presented his views on a variety of subjects, including private schools, school appropriations, the employment of female teachers, the beneficial effects of teacher institutes, and the positive aspects of music in the common schools. His views regarding women in the teaching profession are intriguing for his time yet reflective of nineteenth-century romantic paternalistic values at the same time:[88]

This change in public sentiment, in regard to the employment of female teachers, I believe to be in accordance with the dictates of the soundest philosophy. Is not woman destined to conduct the rising generation, of both sexes, at least through all the primary stages of education? Has not the Author of nature preadapted her, by constitution, and faculty, and temperament, for this noble work? What station of beneficent labor can she aspire to, more honorable, or more congenial to every pure and generous impulse? In the great system of society, what other part can she act, so intimately connected with the refinement and purification of the race? How otherwise can she so well vindicate her right to an exalted station in the scale of the being; and cause that shameful sentence of degradation by which she has so long been dishonored, to be repealed? Four fifths of all women who have ever lived, have been the slaves of man,—the menials in his household, the drudges in his field, the instruments of his pleasure; or, at best, the gilded toys of his leisure days in court or palace. She has been outlawed from honorable service, and almost incapacitated, by her servile condition, for the highest aspirations after usefulness and renown. But a noble revenge awaits her. By a manifestation of the superiority of moral power, she can triumph over that physical power which has hitherto subjected her to bondage. She can bless those by whom she has been wronged. By refining the tastes and sentiments of man, she can change the objects of his ambition; and, with changed objects of ambition, the fields of honorable exertion can be divided between the sexes. By inspiring nobler desires for nobler objects, she can break down the ascendancy of those selfish motives that have sought their gratification in her submission and inferiority. All this she can do, more rapidly, and more effectually than it can ever be done in any other way, unless through miracles, by training the young to juster notions of honor and duty, and to a higher appreciation of the true dignity and destiny of the race.[89]

While Mann certainly had many progressive viewpoints for his era, it is incumbent on all students of history to understand the premise that historical figures should be analyzed and judged for their contributions within the context of their time periods. Affixing the dominant realities, mores, and values of the contemporary world to a distant historical time period is a practice that has utility but is certainly limited by definition.

Ninth Annual Report (1845)

Mann argued, for the first time, that education could serve as an economic equalizer in the United States so that poor people could become wealthy. In other words, he argued that the vicissitudes of poverty could be eradicated by formal education. To him, common schools would result in a more democratic and egalitarian society. Based on American history, Mann offered the following prophecy in this report:

> One of the highest and most valuable objects to which the influences of a school can be made conducive consists in training our children to self-government. The doctrine of no-government, even if all forms of violence did not meet the first day to celebrate its introduction by a jubilee, would forfeit all the power that originates in concert and union. So tremendous, too, are the evils of anarchy and lawlessness, that a government by mere force, however arbitrary and cruel, has been held preferable to no-government. But self-government, self-control, a voluntary compliance with the laws of reason and duty, have been justly considered as the highest value of excellence attainable by a human being. No one, however, can consciously obey the laws of reason and

duty, until he understands them. Hence the preliminary necessity of their being clearly explained, of their being made to stand out, broad, lofty, and as conspicuous as a mountain against a clear sky. There may be blind obedience without a knowledge of the law, but only of the will of the lawgiver; but the first step towards rational obedience is a knowledge of the rule to be obeyed, and of the reasons on which it is founded.

The above doctrine acquires extraordinary force, in view of our political institutions, founded, as they are, upon the great idea of the capacity of man for self-government,—an idea so long denounced by the State as treasonable, and by the Church as heretical. In order that men may be prepared for self-government, their apprenticeship must commence in childhood. The great moral attribute of self-government cannot be born and matured in a day; and if school-children are not trained to do it, we only prepare ourselves for disappointment if we expect it from grown men. Everybody acknowledges the justness of the declaration, that a foreign people, born and bred and dwarfed under the despotisms of the Old World, cannot be transformed into the full stature of American citizens merely by a voyage across the Atlantic, or by subscribing the oath of naturalization. If they retain the servility in which they have been trained, some self-appointed lord or priest, on this side of the water will succeed to the authority of the master whom they have left behind them. If, on the other hand, they identify liberty with an absence from restraint and an immunity from punishment, then they are liable to become intoxicated and delirious with the highly-stimulating properties of the air of freedom; and thus, in either case, they remain unfitted, until they have become morally acclimated to our institutions, to exercise the rights of a freeman. But can it make any substantial difference whether a man is suddenly translated into all the independence and prerogatives of an American citizen, from the bondage of an Irish lord or an English manufacturer, or from the equally rigorous bondage of a parent, guardian or school-teacher? He who has been a serf until the day before he is twenty-one years of age cannot be an independent citizen the day after; and it makes no difference whether he has been a serf in Austria or in America. As the fitting apprenticeship for despotism consists in being trained to despotism, so the fitting apprenticeship for self-government consists in being trained to self-government; and the law of force and authority is as appropriate a preparation for the subjects of an arbitrary power as liberty and self-imposed law are for developing and maturing those sentiments of self-respect, of honor and of dignity, which belong to a truly republican citizen. Were we hereafter to govern irresponsibly, then our being forced to yield implicit obedience to an irresponsible governor would prepare us to play the tyrant in our turn; but if we are to govern by virtue of a law which embraces all, which overlies all, which includes the governor as well as the governed, then lessons of obedience should be inculcated upon childhood, in reference to that sacred law. If there are no two things under wider asunder than freedom and slavery, then must the course of training which fits children for these two opposite conditions of life be as diverse as the points to which they lead. Now, for the high purpose of training an American child to become an American citizen,—is it not obvious that, in all cases, the law by which he is to be bound should be made intelligible to him; and as soon as his capacity will permit, that the reasons on which it is founded, should be made as intelligible as the law itself?[90]

The optimism and idealism that Mann possessed with regard to the vital roles that the common schools would perform in the American democracy are apparent in this passage. He envisioned a proactive citizenry charged with making important decisions about politics and public policy. The key to enlightening the masses to fulfill their civic obligations in a democracy would be public education, funded by taxpayers for the betterment of society, and it would be universal for all citizens regardless of social or economic class.

Tenth Annual Report (1846)

In this report, Mann argued that education is a natural right for every child and each state should provide it for all children. This report led to the first compulsory school attendance law in the country in Massachusetts in 1852. By 1918, all states required children to receive an education.[91] According to Mann,

I believe that this amazing dereliction from duty, especially in our own country, originates more in the false notions which men entertain *respecting the nature of their right to property* than in any thing else. In the district-school-meeting, in the town-meeting, in legislative halls, everywhere, the advocates for a more generous education could carry their respective audiences with them in behalf of increased privileges for our children, were it not instinctively foreseen that increased privileges must be followed by increased taxation. Against this obstacle, argument falls dead. The rich man who has no children declares that the exaction of a contribution from him to educate the children of his neighbor is an invasion of his rights of property. The man who has reared and educated a family of children denounces it as a double tax when he is called upon to assist in educating the children of others also;

or, if he has reared his own children without educating them, he thinks it peculiarly oppressive to be obliged to do for others what he refrained from doing even for himself. Another, having children, but disdaining to educate them with the common mass, withdraws them from the public school, puts them under what he calls "selecter influences," and then thinks it a grievance to be obliged to support a school which he contemns. Or if these different parties so far yield to the force of traditionary sentiment and usage, and to the public opinion around them, as to consent to do something for the cause, they soon reach the limit of expense at which their admitted obligation or their alleged charity terminates.[92]

Mann embraced a communitarian view of education in a distant era. Since citizens in a democracy benefit economically and otherwise with a more educated populace, all adults must contribute to the cause of funding public education, whether they have children currently attending common schools or not. Furthermore, he contended that

I believe in the existence of a great, immortal, immutable principle of natural law, or natural ethics,—a principle antecedent to all human institutions, and incapable of being abrogated by any ordinance of man,—a principle of divine origin, clearly legible in the ways of Providence as those ways are manifested in the order of Nature and in the history of the race, which proves the *absolute right* to an education of every human being that comes into the world; and which, of course, proves the correlative duty of every government to see that the means of that education are provided for all.[93]

This theoretical premise was truly progressive given the time period in question. At this point in American history, formal education was dominated by social and economic elites who had the requisite means by which to finance the education for their own children. In spite of the dominant paradigm and mores of the mid-nineteenth century, this contributor to the development of the American republic offered an idea in this report that would affect education policy and public budgeting in a profoundly substantive manner.

Eleventh Annual Report (1847)

Mann published the average salaries of public school teachers in this report. His commentary on providing this information may still be applicable today:

Look at the average rate of wages paid to teachers in some of the pattern States of the Union. In Maine, it is $15.40 per month to males, and $4.80

to females. In New Hampshire, it is $13.50 per month to males, and $5.65 to females. In Vermont, it is $12.00 per month to males, and $4.75 to females. In Connecticut, it is $16.00 per month to males, and $6.50 to females. In New York, it is $14.96 per month to males, and $6.69 to females. In Pennsylvania, it is $17.02 per month to males, and 10.09 to females. In Ohio, it is $15.42 per month to males, and $8.73 to females. In Indiana, it is $12.00 per month to males, and $6.00 to females. In Michigan, it is $12.71 per month for males, and $5.36 for females. Even in Massachusetts, it is only $24.51 per month to males, and $8.07 to females. All this is exclusive of board; but let it be compared with what is paid to cashiers of banks, to secretaries of insurance-companies, to engineers upon railroads, to superintendents in factories, to custom-house officers, navy agents, and so forth, and so forth, and it will then be seen what pecuniary temptations there are on every side, drawing enterprising and talented young men from the ranks of the teacher's profession.[94]

Bear in mind that the Equal Pay Act would not become federal law until 1963.[95] The premise that Mann highlighted, however, is still debated today in the education community, where officials have long posited that many talented students avoid focusing on education as a career because they can command much higher salaries in other professional fields.

Twelfth Annual Report (1848)

This final report by Mann was in fact a summary of his earlier reports as he wrote it after he had won a seat in the U.S. House of Representatives. It is the most inclusive and encompassing of all the previous reports, as he presents a theory of public education in this work.[96] In it, he advocated nonsectarian schools so that taxpayers would not be forced to support any established religion with which they might disagree. Here is part of the education vision that Mann shared with his contemporaries:

Under the providence of God, our means of education are the grand machinery by which the "raw material" of human nature can be worked up into inventors and discoverers, into skilled artisans and scientific farmers, into scholars and jurists, into the founders of benevolent institutions, and the great expounders of ethical and theological science. By means of early education, those embryos of talent may be quickened which will solve the difficult problems of political and economical

law; and by them, too, the genius may be kindled which will blaze forth
in the poets of humanity. Our schools, far more than they have done,
may supply the presidents and professors of colleges, and superintendents of public instruction, all over the land; and send, not only into
our sister States, but across the Atlantic, the men of practical science to
superintend the construction of the great works of art. Here, too, may
those judicial powers be developed and invigorated which will make
legal principles so clear and convincing as to prevent appeals to force;
and, should the clouds of war ever lower over our country, some hero
may be found—the nursling of our schools, and ready to become the
leader of our armies, that best of all heroes—who will secure the glories
of a peace, unstained by the magnificent murders of the battle-field.[97]

Suffice it to say that this vision of public education is a bit more opti-
mistic and hopeful than its critics would emphasize today.

In spite of Mann's praise for the Prussian schools, he envisioned a
dichotomy when it came to public comparative education:

According to the European theory, men are divided into classes,—some
to toil and earn; others to seize and enjoy. According to the Massachusetts
theory, all are to have an equal chance for earning, and equal security in
the enjoyment of what they earn. The latter tends to equality of condition;
the former, to the grossest inequalities. Tried by any Christian standard of
morals, or even by any of the better sort of heathen standards, can any
one hesitate, for a moment, in declaring which of the two will produce
the greater amount of human welfare, and which, therefore, is the more
conformable to the divine will? The European theory is blind to what
constitutes the highest glory as well as the highest duty of a State. Its
advocates and admirers are forgetful of that which should be their
highest ambition, and proud of that which constitutes their shame.[98]

The most important task for officials in the American states, according
to Mann, is to educate their people so that not only the masses but also
the other members of society will have a better life. The more enlightened people will be better positioned to fulfill their roles in a
democracy.

Mann made the following speculation about education in his final
report to the Board of Education:

Education, then, beyond all other devices of human origin, is the great
equalizer of the conditions of men,—the balance-wheel of the social
machinery. I do not here mean that it so elevates the moral nature as to
make men disdain and abhor the oppression of their fellow-men. This
idea pertains to another of its attributes. But I mean that it gives each

man the independence and the means by which he can resist the selfishness of other men. It does better than to disarm the poor of their hostility
towards the rich: it prevents being poor. Agrarianism is the revenge of
poverty against wealth. The wanton destruction of the property of
others—the burning of hay-ricks and corn-ricks, the demolition
of machinery because it supersedes hand-labor, the sprinkling of vitriol
on rich dresses—is only agrarianism run mad. Education prevents both
the revenge and the madness. On the other hand, a fellow-feeling for
one's class or caste is the common instinct of hearts not wholly sunk in
selfish regards for person or for family. The spread of education, by
enlarging the cultivated class or caste, will open a wider area over
which the social feelings will expand; and, if this education should be
universal and complete, it would do more than all things else to obliter-
ate factitious distinctions in society.[99]

Thus, education would be the great equalizer in society. It would do
more to minimize conflict and strife between the social classes than
anything else. This ideal is undoubtedly not measurable in any exact
quantitative sense; its attractiveness depends on one's intuition and
the importance of theory in education and public affairs. More will
be discussed regarding this matter in subsequent chapters.

With regard to the topic of political education, Mann was a republican
in the mode of James Madison, George Washington, Alexander
Hamilton, Benjamin Franklin, Gouverneur Morris, and James Wilson,
as well as many of the other framers of the U.S. Constitution.[100]
He embraced the possibilities inherent in a representative democracy.
He made an important link between republicanism and common
schools for all in this final report:

And hence it is, that the establishment of a republican government,
without well-appointed and efficient means for the universal education
of the people, is the most rash and fool-hardy experiment ever tried by
man. Its fatal results may not be immediately developed, they may not
follow as the thunder follows the lightning; for time is an element in
maturing them, and the calamity is too great to be prepared in a day:
but, like the slow-accumulating avalanche, they will grow more terrific
by delay, and at length, though it may be at a late hour, will overwhelm
with ruin whatever lies athwart their path. It may be an easy thing to
make a republic; but it is a very laborious thing to make republicans;
and woe to the republic that rests upon no better foundations than ignorance, selfishness, and passion! Such a republic may grow in numbers
and in wealth. As an avaricious man adds acres to his lands, so its rapa-
cious government may increase its own darkness by annexing

provinces and states to its ignorant domain. Its armies may be invincible, and its fleets may strike terror into nations on the opposite sides of the globe at the same hour. Vast in its extent, and enriched with all the prodigality of Nature, it may possess every capacity and opportunity of being great and of doing good. But, if such a republic be devoid of intelligence, it will only the more closely resemble an obscene giant who has waxed strong in his youth, and grown wanton in his strength; whose brain has been developed only in the region of the appetites and passions, and not in the organs of reason and conscience; and who, therefore, is boastful of his bulk alone, and glories in the weight of his heel, and in the destruction of his arm. Such a republic, with all its noble capacities for beneficence, will rush with the speed of a whirlwind to an ignominious end; and all good men of after-times would be fain to weep over its downfall, did not their scorn and contempt at its folly and its wickedness repress all sorrow for its fate.[101]

Mann's theory of republicanism and education is reminiscent of Benjamin Franklin's view of the U.S. Constitution right after it was signed by the framers remaining in Philadelphia who supported it on September 17, 1787. On leaving the Philadelphia Convention, he was approached by a citizen who asked, "What have you wrought in this meeting?"[102] The great inventor replied, "A Republic, if you can keep it."[103] To the nineteenth-century education reformer, the best way to keep republicanism intact is through systematic education and ensuring that citizens do not compromise the promise and hope of democracy by their own ignorance.

On the subject of moral education, the very spiritual Mann determined that it was absolutely essential in modern society:

Moral education is a primal necessity of social existence. The unrestrained passions of men are not only homicidal, but suicidal; and a community without a conscience would soon extinguish itself. Even with a natural conscience, how often has evil triumphed over good! From the beginning of time, wrong has followed right, as the shadow the substance. As the relations of men became more complex, and the business of the world more extended, new opportunities and new temptations for wrong-doing have been created. With the endearing relations of parent and child came also the possibility of infanticide and parricide; and the first domestic altar that brothers ever reared was stained with fratricidal blood. Following close upon the obligations of truth came falsehood and perjury, and closer still upon the duty of obedience to the divine law came disobedience. With the existence of private relations between men came fraud; and with the existence of public relations between nations came aggression, war, and slavery. And so, just in proportion as the relations of life became more numerous, and the interests of society more various and manifold, the range of possible and of actual offences has been continually enlarging.[104]

In a practical sense, could a sizable population be taught moral education? If so, how could it be accomplished? Mann's response to these questions was as follows:

> But to all doubters, disbelievers, or despairers in human progress, it may still be said, there is one experiment which has never yet been tried. It is an experiment, which, even before its inception, offers the highest authority for its ultimate success. Its formula is intelligible to all; and it is as legible as though written in starry letters on an azure sky. It is expressed in these few and simple words: *"Train up a child in the way he should go; and, when he is old, he will not depart from it."* This declaration is positive. If the conditions are complied with, it makes no provision for a failure. Though pertaining to morals, yet, if the terms of the direction are observed, there is no more reason to doubt the result than there would be in an optical or a chemical experiment. But this experiment has never yet been tried. Education has never yet been brought to bear with one-hundredth part of its potential force upon the natures of children, and, through them, upon the character of men and of the race. In all the attempts to reform mankind which have hitherto been made, whether by changing the frame of government, by aggravating or softening the severity of the penal code, or by substituting a government-created for a God-created religion,—in all these attempts, the infantile and youthful mind, its amenability to influences, and the enduring and self-operating character of the influences it receives, have been almost wholly unrecognized. Here, then, is a new agency, whose powers are but just beginning to be understood, and whose mighty energies hitherto have been but feebly invoked; and yet, from our experience, limited and imperfect as it is, we do know, that, far beyond any other earthly instrumentality, it is comprehensive and decisive.[105]

Clearly, Mann had a vision that common schools could promote the greater public good in a number of discernible ways. He would undoubtedly be considered a communitarian in contemporary society.

Although he was very religious, Mann advocated nonsectarian schools so that the taxpayer would not be forced in the position of supporting any established religion with which he or she might disagree in conscience:

> The very terms "public school" and "common school" bear upon their face that they are schools which the children of the entire community

may attend. Every man not on the pauper-list is taxed for their support; but he is not taxed to support them as special religious institutions: if he were, it would satisfy at once the largest definition of a religious establishment. But he is taxed to support them as a *preventive* means against dishonesty, against fraud, and against violence, on the same principle that he is taxed to support criminal courts as a *punitive* means against the same offences. He is taxed to support schools, on the same principle that he is taxed to support paupers,—because a child without education is poorer and more wretched than a man without bread. He is taxed to support schools, on the same principle that he would be taxed to defend the nation against foreign invasion, or against rapine committed by a foreign foe,—because the general prevalence of ignorance, superstition, and vice, will breed Goth and Vandal at home more fatal to the public well-being than any Goth or Vandal from abroad. And, finally, he is taxed to support schools, because they are the most effective means of developing and training those powers and faculties in a child, by which, when he becomes a man, he may understand what his highest interests and his highest duties are, and may be in fact, and not in name only, a free agent. . . . But if a man is taxed to support a school where religious doctrines are inculcated which he believes to be false, and which he believes that God condemns, then he is excluded from the school by the divine law, at the same time he is compelled to support it by the human law. This is a double wrong. It is politically wrong, because, if such a man educates his children at all, he must educate them elsewhere, and thus pay two taxes, while some of his neighbors pay less than their due proportion of one; and it is religiously wrong, because he is constrained by human power to promote what he believes the divine power forbids. The principle involved in such a course is pregnant with all tyrannical consequences.[106]

The framers of the Constitution, based in part on their experience with Great Britain, did not create a specific church of the U.S. government. Instead, they supported the premise that people should be able to worship as they may please. Mann argued that the same principle must be upheld with regard to public, or common, education and the issue of taxation. The state should not endorse a specific religious denomination per se. Although his beliefs with regard to teaching religion in the common schools are at odds with modern approaches, he argued some time ago that taxpayer money should not be utilized in order to subsidize parochial education. Today's advocates of school vouchers may be enlightened to know that one of the great education crusaders in American history was opposed to the concept a long time ago.

HORACE MANN'S COMMON SCHOOL IDEOLOGY IN THE CONTEMPORARY WORLD AND BEYOND

Some of Mann's ideas have endured the generations that have passed since he wrote his annual reports as secretary of the Board of Education in Massachusetts. He believed that the common school is a public institution capable of preparing America's youth to contribute to the community in a positive manner. In order to accomplish this feat, Mann articulated three primary ideas, two of which are still relevant and necessary today. First, he maintained that the community should be taxed to support the school to ensure the existence of a positive bond between the school and the greater community. Second, he believed that men and women should be professionally trained who would be committing their professional lives to educating children. His other primary belief, emphasizing Protestant virtues to students while advocating nonsectarian schools at the same time, is not relevant today, nor should it be touted for two primary reasons. First, doing so would be a clear violation of the establishment clause of the First Amendment. Second, advocating any particular faith in a multicultural society is counterintuitive and would likely exacerbate conflict between and among groups in society. In short, Mann viewed education as a truly public good, one in which students from diverse backgrounds would assemble in the same building for a common purpose. He was an unapologetic advocate for schools run by public sector (government) entities.

The ideals that Mann communicated in his reports are still very important today, particularly since public education has been heavily criticized and under political attack at least since the publication in 1983 of *A Nation at Risk: The Imperative for Educational Reform.*[107] A scathing critique of public education was promulgated by the National Commission on Excellence in Education, which was created by Terrel Bell, the second U.S. secretary of education, who served during President Ronald Reagan's first term and was succeeded by William Bennett. For at least 30 years in a systematic manner, officials from the conservative political right in the United States have consistently maintained that public education is failing and should therefore be subject to "reform." The types of changes in education that have been touted and, in some areas, implemented have been charter schools and education vouchers. Conservatives typically argue that market-based competition will enhance public education, with the obvious assumption being that public schools are deficient when compared to private and/or parochial schools. Citizens across the United States today owe it to Mann to investigate and analyze this premise a bit more carefully.

2

The Market-Based Ideology and Politics of the Conservative Right

The year 1776 was particularly prominent in the annals of American history. Thomas Jefferson and his colleagues drafted the Declaration of Independence, and the Revolutionary War began in earnest against Great Britain. In Scotland, a social philosopher by the name of Adam Smith published *The Wealth of Nations*.[1] The economic and political ideology espoused in this influential book has had a substantial impact on American history and politics and is still a core philosophical foundation of the conservative right in contemporary U.S. politics. Adam Smith articulated the following vision of laissez-faire economics: "As it is the power of exchanging that gives occasion to the division of labour, so the extent of this division must always be limited by the extent of that power, or, in other words, by the extent of the market."[2] The conservative premise that

Photograph of Horace Mann taken before his years at Antioch College (1853–1859). (Image courtesy of Antiochiana, Antioch College.)

the private marketplace, with limited interference through regulation from government officials, adjusts to most economic realities in a plausible manner has been a mainstay in American history. Laissez-faire capitalism, often known as classical economic theory today, was the dominant economic paradigm from the founding of the republic until the New Deal policies of Franklin Roosevelt in the 1930s. Even though the size and scope of the federal government has expanded and broadened during the modern era, conservatives still adhere to their central belief that the federal government can impede entrepreneurialism and economic growth by imposing burdensome regulations and high taxes.

During the nineteenth century, the dominant philosophy about the involvement of the federal government in public policy and society was articulated by the New England transcendentalist Henry David Thoreau. In his essay titled "Resistance to Civil Government," Thoreau declared that

> I HEARTILY accept the motto,—"That government is best which governs least;" and I should like to see it acted up to more rapidly and systematically. Carried out, it finally amounts to this, which also I believe,—"That government is best which governs not at all;" and when men are prepared for it, that will be the kind of government which they will have. Government is at best but an expedient; but most governments are usually, and all governments are sometimes, inexpedient. The objections which have been brought against a standing army, and they are many and weighty, and deserve to prevail, may also at last be brought against a standing government. The standing army is only an arm of the standing government. The government itself, which is only the mode which the people have chosen to execute their will, is equally liable to be abused and perverted before the people can act through it. Witness the present Mexican war, the work of comparatively a few individuals using the standing government as their tool; for, in the outset, the people would not have consented to this measure.[3]

Thoreau was a vehement opponent not only of the Mexican War but of the institution of slavery as well. His views about the government are reflective of these important issues but are also contextual as well. Simply put, the federal government, through its public policies, did not have much of an impact on the daily lives of most citizens, and this reality was perceived to be preferable by Americans at that time in history.

It is important to note that the famous motto articulated by Thoreau, "That government is best which governs least," has historically been credited erroneously to Thomas Jefferson. Researchers at Monticello, the residence of President Jefferson and now a national historic landmark outside of Charlottesville, Virginia, have not found this statement in any of Jefferson's writings. Although the ideas expressed in the statement are Jeffersonian in nature, the exact phrasing is almost certainly not attributed to the former president.[4] However, many historians today believe that Thoreau was simply paraphrasing the motto of *The United States Magazine and Democratic Review,* a periodical published from 1837 to 1859 by John L. O'Sullivan.[5]

TWENTIETH-CENTURY CONSERVATIVE PHILOSOPHERS

Although it is always somewhat subjective in nature to contend that certain individuals were more profound in their impact on social movements than others, clearly Friedrich Hayek ranks among the most important contributors to conservative political philosophy and the laissez-faire ideology in the modern era. He is perhaps the best-known advocate for the Austrian school of economics.[6] Hayek believed, in the tradition of Adam Smith, that free markets, not government intervention, largely coordinated people's actions even though coordination was not planned or intended. The market, to the economics professor, was a spontaneous order. The spontaneity in question was not the result of anything akin to strategic planning; rather, the market evolved slowly as a result of human actions. Although the eminent British economist John Maynard Keynes was an advocate of free markets, his views on fiscal policy would provide a juxtaposition between his economic views and those of Hayek.[7] The intellectual debate, however, would curtail somewhat as Keynes passed away shortly after World War II, though Hayek would live into the 1990s.[8]

Friedrich Hayek

In *The Road to Serfdom* (1944), Hayek determined that the abandonment of values, including individualism, freedom, and laissez-faire capitalism, inevitably leads to socialist or fascist oppression and tyranny and ultimately results in the serfdom of the individual citizen. A year before the Allies secured victory in World War II, Hayek lamented that when the course of civilization takes an unexpected turn—when, instead of the continuous progress which we have come to expect, we find ourselves threatened by evils associated by us with past ages of barbarism—we naturally blame anything but ourselves. ... Have not all our efforts and hopes been directed toward greater freedom, justice, and prosperity? If the outcome is so different from our aims—if, instead of freedom and prosperity, bondage and misery stare us in the face—is it not clear that sinister forces must have foiled our intentions, that we are the victims of some evil power which must be conquered before we can resume the road to better things? However much we may differ when we name the culprit—whether it is the wicked capitalist or the vicious spirit of a particular nation, the stupidity of our elders, or a social system not yet, although we have struggled against it for half a century, fully overthrown—we all are, or at least were until recently, certain of one thing: that the leading ideas which during the last generation have become common to most people of good will and have determined the major changes in our social life cannot have been wrong. We are ready to accept almost any explanation of the present crisis of our civilization except one: that the present state of the world may be the result of genuine error on our own part and that the pursuit of some of our most cherished ideals has apparently produced results utterly different from those which we expected.[9]

To this conservative philosopher, progressives in Western Europe and America had succumbed to a false notion that government intervention could result in more utopian policies. The path to socialism, as Hayek perceived it, was full of honorable intentions but would result in an oppressive state where individual freedom was compromised and even sacrificed to a significant extent.

Hayek envisioned a stark difference between a free market economy and one which is socialistic and heavily regulated:

The choice open to us is not between a system in which everybody will get what he deserves according to some absolute and universal standard of right, and one where the individual shares are determined partly by accident or good or ill chance, but between a system where it is the will of a few persons that decides who is to get what, and one where it depends at least partly on the ability and enterprise of the people concerned and partly on unforeseen circumstances.[10]

Hayek espoused the idea of market forces determining economic, social, and political outcomes; such matters should not be the result of intervention by government officials. In such a manner, the people can experience more freedom from government interference in the pursuit of their own self-interest.

Hayek strongly endorsed the nineteenth-century vision of liberalism that prevailed in European and American politics. He believed that the essence of a good society stemmed from limited government:

> If we are to build a better world, we must have the courage to make a new start—even if that means some *reculer pour mieux sauter.* It is not those who believe in inevitable tendencies who show this courage, not those who preach a "New Order" which is no more than a projection of the tendencies of the last forty years, and who can think of nothing better than to imitate Hitler. It is, indeed, those who cry loudest for the New Order who are most completely under the sway of the ideas which have created this war and most of the evils from which we suffer. The young are right if they have little confidence in the ideas which rule most of their elders. But they are mistaken or misled when they believe that these are still the liberal ideas of the nineteenth century, which, in fact, the younger generation hardly knows.[11]

During the World War II, Hayek envisioned a causal relationship between extensive government intervention in the economy and society and an increase in tyranny and a corresponding decline in individual freedom. To him, a strict laissez-faire approach to the marketplace was not only prudent economically but also essential to a more free and democratic society.

A number of years later, the Nobel laureate published another prominent book, *The Constitution of Liberty* (1960).[12] In this work, he contended that extensive government intervention into the marketplace, especially through social programs for the indigent, often produced unintended consequences that were negative. This premise would be a central component of the conservatism of Ronald Reagan in the United States and Margaret Thatcher in Great Britain in the 1980s and 1990s.[13] Hayek provided a lamentation of sorts when he offered the following insight:

> It has been a long time since that ideal of freedom which inspired modern Western civilization and whose partial realization made possible the achievements of that civilization was effectively restated. In fact, for almost a century the basic principles on which this civilization was built have been falling into increasing disregard and oblivion. Men have sought for alternative social orders more often than they have tried to improve

their understanding or use of the underlying principles of our civilization. It is only since we were confronted with an altogether different system that we have discovered that we have lost any clear conception of our aims and possess no firm principles which we can hold up against the dogmatic ideology of our antagonists.[14]

To him, the rise in "big government," as American conservatives typically describe the increase in government activism and the rise of the modern administrative state, has resulted in the concomitant decline in individual freedom. He believed in a market economy, where decentralized decisions made by buyers and sellers resulted in not only the allocation of resources in society but also enhanced individual freedom (i.e., freedom from government interference). Hayek rejected the socialistic premise that government decision makers, or central planners, could create more equitable laws and implement them on an equal basis as opposed to free individuals making free choices in the marketplace. From his perspective, it was far more preferable to promote the spontaneous interactions of individual citizens and not try to engage in a decision-making process that may limit and even undermine the freedom to choose for oneself in a capitalist society.

Hayek envisioned a modest role for the federal government in the domestic economy. It was incumbent on government officials to create general laws that are both reasonable and fair. As he contended,

> All these activities of government are part of its effort to provide a favorable framework for individual decisions; they supply means which individuals can use for their own purposes. Many other services of a more material kind fall into the same category. Though government must not use its power of coercion to reserve for itself activities which have nothing to do with the enforcement of the general rules of law, there is no violation of principle in its engaging in all sorts of activities on the same terms as the citizens. If in the majority of fields there is no good reason why it should do so, there are fields in which the desirability of government action can hardly be questioned.[15]

This libertarian philosopher believed that too much government policymaking in the economy—as well as a host of other policy matters, including social welfare, housing, agriculture, education, and research—results in an oppressive state that thwarts the very values of nineteenth-century classical liberalism.

Leo Strauss

Another significant contributor in the evolution of modern conservative political philosophy was Leo Strauss.[16] One researcher contended that

> a central figure in the debates surrounding neoconservatism is Leo Strauss. A German Jew émigré from Nazi Germany, Strauss eventually became a professor of political science at the University of Chicago after escaping to the US, where he served as a faculty member from 1949–1968. It was during his tenure there that some claim Strauss influenced the founding thinkers of neoconservatism, at least in the United States, such as Irving Kristol, Gertrude Himmelfarb, Joseph Cropsey and Allan Bloom. Through Strauss's students (and the students of his students), his influence spreads out to such current conservatives as William Kristol, Paul Wolfowitz, and even, some claim ... to the US's Supreme Court Justice Clarence Thomas and former Speaker of the House Newt Gingrich.[17]

Strauss reflected on an important reality in the discipline of Political Science in *On Tyranny* (1963):

> It is no accident that present-day political science has failed to grasp tyranny as what it really is. Our political science is haunted by the belief that "value judgments" are inadmissible in scientific considerations, and to call a regime tyrannical clearly amounts to pronouncing a "value judgment." The political scientist who accepts this view of science will speak of the mass-state, of dictatorship, of totalitarianism, of authoritarianism, and so on, and as a citizen he may wholeheartedly condemn these things; but as a political scientist he is forced to reject the notion of tyranny as "mythical." One cannot overcome this limitation without reflecting on the basis, or the origin, of present-day political science. Present-day political science often traces its origin to Machiavelli. There is truth in this contention. To say nothing of broader considerations, Machiavelli's *Prince* (as distinguished from his *Discourses on Livy*) is characterized by the deliberate indifference to the distinction between king and tyrant; the *Prince* presupposes the tacit rejection of that traditional distinction. Machiavelli was fully aware that by conceiving the view expounded in the *Prince* he was breaking away from the whole tradition of political science; or, to apply to the *Prince* an expression which he uses when speaking of his *Discourses*, that he was taking a road which had not yet been followed by anyone. To understand the basic premise of present-day political science, one would have to understand

the meaning of the epoch-making change effected by Machiavelli; for that change consisted in the discovery of the continent on which all specifically modern political thought, and hence especially present-day political science, is at home.[18]

Strauss provided a most insightful analysis when it pertains to this academic discipline. It is inherently crucial to understand the premise that politics, ultimately, is about ideas. No human being, academician and nonacademician alike, is somehow neutral or value free; we all undergo the process of political socialization and are duly impacted accordingly. No one is above this omnipresent reality.[19]

As Nasser Behnegar indicated, Strauss rejected the "value-free" social science of his time period. In so doing, he sought a genuine social science through classical political philosophy.[20] When addressing the tyrannical regimes of Adolf Hitler and Joseph Stalin, Strauss declared,

> A social science that cannot speak of tyranny with the same confidence with which medicine speaks, for example, of cancer, cannot understand social phenomena as what they are. It is therefore not scientific. Present-day social science finds itself in this condition. If it is true that present-day social science is the inevitable result of modern social science and of modern philosophy, one is forced to think of the restoration of classical social science. Once we have learned again from the classics what tyranny is, we shall be enabled and compelled to diagnose as tyrannies a number of contemporary regimes which appear in the guise of dictatorships. This diagnosis can only be the first step toward an exact analysis of present-day tyranny, for present-day tyranny is fundamentally different from the tyranny analyzed by the classics.[21]

While it is not clear why a return to classical political philosophy will inevitably correct the problems associated with a value-free social science, the Straussian perspective that the scientific method is not necessarily a prudent standard by which scientific inquiry ought to be judged is intuitive.[22]

Yet a great deal of criticism of Strauss from the American left continues with regard to his emphasis on classical political philosophy. While other academicians were focused on advancing political science and political philosophy in the 1950s, the conservative philosopher was instead attempting to reactivate the legitimacy of ancient political philosophy in the modern world. This is where some accuse the late professor of engaging in the politics of deception. According to Shadia Drury, Strauss advocated the utilization of deception, religion, and aggressive nationalism in order to pursue his own conservative agenda. She argued that Strauss believed that political leaders needed to practice deception in order to maintain public order. These leaders (e.g., George W. Bush, Richard Cheney, Donald Rumsfeld, Paul Wolfowitz, and Condoleezza Rice) did not need to be moral; they had the right to deceive simply because they were leaders, and those in power have the right to rule over the masses. Drury also maintains that Strauss had contempt for secular democracy. In fact, she suggests that Strauss believed that religion was absolutely essential in order to impose morality on the people who might otherwise be prone to extremism and violence. Finally, in advocating for a return to classical philosophy, Strauss, like Thomas Hobbes, believed that most people were inherently aggressive and therefore had to be restrained and held accountable by a powerful nationalistic state. Such conservative beliefs, sometimes referred to as neoconservative ideals today, are undemocratic and run antithetical to the principle of accountability from the perspective of those on the left side of the ideological spectrum.

Drury provided a succinct summary of the Straussian impact on American politics and society:

> Strauss's impact on academic life in North America has been something of a phenomenon; historian Gordon S. Wood described it as the largest academic movement in the twentieth century. Nor is this influence confined to political philosophy. It extends into religious studies, literary criticism, intellectual history, classics, American history, and American constitutional law. In 1987, the year of the two-hundredth anniversary of the US Constitution, Wood observed that the Straussians, as they are known in the academy, dominated the conferences; they were well-organized and well-funded. And even though most of them were political scientists by training, they outnumbered historians when it came to giving papers and organizing conferences on the American founding, which is a topic of great *political* and not just historical significance for the Straussians.[23]

The impact of Strauss's neoconservative movement has been well documented in American politics since the 1980s. The Grand Old Party has been dominated by the conservative wing to the point that the liberal wing of the Republican Party has become extinct and moderates have had minimal influence in that party for over 30 years. Professor Drury provided the following assessment in the late 1990s:

> What seems more surprising than his influence inside the academy is the influence that Strauss has exerted on American politics. Strauss's students and their students have occupied important positions in the

Reagan and Bush administrations and continue to play a significant role within the Republican Party. Prominent figures on the American political scene include Reagan's ambassador to Indonesia, Paul Wolfowitz; Caspar Weinberger's former speechwriter, Seth Cropsey; National Endowment for the Humanities Deputy Chairman, John T. Agresto; National Security Council advisor Carnes Lord; Assistant Secretary of State for International Organization Affairs, Alan Keyes; legal scholar and judge Robert Bork (whose nomination to the Supreme Court by former president [Ronald Reagan] was defeated by the Democratic majority in the Senate); Justice Clarence Thomas of the Supreme Court; former Secretary of Education William Bennett; former Education Department Chief of Staff, William Kristol (later former vice-president Dan Quayle's chief of staff and then the chief pundit and policy maker of the Republican party). Journalists have been fully cognizant of this influx of Straussians into Washington and of the power they have within the Republican Party. So much so that the *New York Times* has dubbed Leo Strauss the godfather of the Republican party's 1994 Contract with America.[24]

Although I am focused on public education in this book, I believe that Drury's conclusion about the Straussians is entirely accurate in contemporary America:

In short, neoconservatism is the legacy of Leo Strauss. It echoes all the dominant features of his philosophy—the political importance of religion, the necessity of nationalism, the language of nihilism, the sense of crisis, the friend/foe mentality, the hostility toward women, the rejection of modernity, the nostalgia of the past, and the abhorrence of liberalism. And having established itself as the dominant ideology of the Republican party, it threatens to remake America in its own image.[25]

The neoconservatives, while embracing the marketplace theory of the Austrian economists, simultaneously believe that the federal government should impose its will on the citizenry via elected and appointed officials in order to promote a more moral society, at least in terms of their conception of morality. They perceive this crusade to be justified and any means to implement their agenda as reasonable (such as the cessation of the examination of legally cast votes in the 2000 presidential election).[26] Government efforts in order to impose a moral character on the masses are thought by many neoconservatives to be positive and even necessary in order to promote a more stable society. As the conservative commentator George Will noted in the 1980s,

To say that statecraft is soulcraft is not to say that government should be incandescent with ardor for excellence in everyone and everything at all times. That would be tiresome. Statecraft as soulcraft should mean only a steady inclination, generally unfelt and unthought. It should mean a disposition, in the weighing of political persons and measures, to include consideration of whether they accord with worthy ends for the polity. Such ends conduce—that word is strong enough—to the improvement of persons. When this political inclination is a community instinct, there is no question of a particular arm or agency of government's being restlessly responsible for civic virtue. A particular institution charged with the routinized planning of virtue, the way the Federal Highway Administration plans highways, would be ominous and would deserve the ridicule it would receive. A polity which understands that statecraft is soulcraft is not a polity with a distinctive branch grafted on to the trunk of government. It is a polity not with a particular institutional framework, but with a particular frame of mind.[27]

In his book published during the Reagan presidency, Will contended that Americans have become more self-indulgent, which obviously would be difficult to measure empirically with past historical time periods. According to him, federal officials need to cultivate the moral character of its citizens. Consequently, he maintained that conservatives should not abhor the government, for conservatism has a greater purpose than simply the promotion of limited government in the marketplace. To him, government should not just be loathed by conservatives but should be structured more effectively so as to encourage citizens to be more moral and virtuous and not simply focus on economics.

When discussing the conservative movement half a century ago, an avowed conservative, Willmoore Kendall, made this declaration concerning Strauss and his academic institution, the University of Chicago:

The old breed are obtainable in quantity, any June, at any of the nation's Ph.D. factories; the new breed are still *rara avis*, and come, for the most part, from a single institution, namely the University of Chicago, and for a good reason. Most of them are pupils of one of the two or three great teachers of politics of our day, Professor Leo Strauss, who communicates to them, as if by magic, his own love of learning, his own sense of the gravity of the great problems of politics, and his own habit of thinking deeply about a problem before rushing into print. The old breed are riding high, and make and unmake reputations for professional achievements; the new breed are unlikely, for a good long while anyhow, to cut much ice on the political science profession's most exalted counsels. But they may well do something far more important—namely, to revive the habit of political thought in the United States, to set standards for it that the old breed (because of the patent inadequacy of their training) cannot live up to, *and* bring under challenge the Liberal orthodoxy that is the main burden of the bulk of our current political science literature.[28]

Kendall maintained a lengthy friendship with Strauss and is considered by many to be a prominent conservative philosopher in the post–World War II era in his own right.[29] To critics of the political right, the followers of Leo Strauss were cultish in nature and believed that they received a much more intellectual and sophisticated graduate education at the University of Chicago than their predecessors did in political philosophy elsewhere in the country.

Barry Goldwater

Barry Goldwater was a U.S. senator for 30 years (1953–1965 and 1969–1987) from Arizona.[30] In 1964, he was the Republican nominee for president but lost handily to the Democratic incumbent, Lyndon B. Johnson.[31] In his influential book titled *The Conscience of a Conservative* (1960), Goldwater outlined his fundamental philosophical views about politics and public affairs: "Thus, for the American Conservative, there is no difficulty in identifying the day's overriding political challenge: it is *to preserve and extend freedom*. As he surveys the various attitudes and institutions and laws that currently prevail in America, many questions will occur to him, but the Conservative's first concern will always be: *Are we maximizing freedom?*"[32] The top priority for contemporary conservatives, as delineated by the late senator, is the pursuit of individual freedom. Typically for conservatives, this generally entails freedom from government intervention, based on the ideology of marketplace capitalism.

When discussing states' rights in this book, Goldwater captured the essence of the modern conservative philosophy and the values inherent in it:

Franklin Roosevelt's rapid conversion from Constitutionalism to the doctrine of unlimited government, is an oft-told story. But I am here concerned not so much by the abandonment of States' Rights by the national Democratic Party—an event that occurred some years ago when that party was captured by the Socialist ideologues in and about the labor movement—as by the unmistakable tendency of the Republican Party to adopt the same course. The result is that today *neither* of our two parties maintains a meaningful commitment to the principle of States' Rights. Thus, the cornerstone of the Republic, our chief bulwark against the encroachment of individual freedom by Big Government, is fast disappearing under the piling sands of absolutism.[33]

Today, conservatives consistently bemoan the usurpation of individual freedom by an entity they generally refer to as "big government." However, the states' rights ideology, if taken to an extreme level, can result in undemocratic, immoral, and unjust outcomes. By way of illustration, reflect on these words of a political opponent of Barry Goldwater, Vice President Hubert Humphrey, in 1948, when he was the mayor of Minneapolis:[34] "My friends, to those who say that we are rushing this issue of civil rights, I say to them we are 172 years late. To those who say that this civil rights program is an infringement on states' rights, I say this: The time has arrived in America for the Democratic Party to get out of the shadow of states' rights and to walk forthrightly into the bright sunshine of human rights."[35] The states' rights ideology in American history perpetuated slavery and the suppression of equal rights for women and for African Americans in particular, precluded many citizens from exercising their right to vote, and today is being utilized to deprive gay and lesbian Americans from having the same rights and privileges as their heterosexual peers in society. This mind-set is profoundly disturbing and has many substantive implications in the American democracy. At times in American history, as Jennifer Hochschild has documented, when incremental and participatory methods were used to desegregate the public schools, for example, both African Americans and Caucasians were worse off than if desegregation had been imposed by nonelected officials without citizen involvement.[36] Thus, should we allow the majority to dictate public policy outcomes to those in the minority, even though the policies in question may be undemocratic in nature, or should we focus more on the substantive policy outcomes and what may be gained by focusing less on process issues (e.g., centralized bodies that are not directly accountable to the people controlling policy outcomes, such as federal judges or unelected public servants)? Which approach is more democratic? Perhaps we should reflect back on the work of the framers of the U.S. Constitution in 1787 in Philadelphia. Students of history must note that the framers sought to prevent the tyranny of the majority and generally sought to protect the rights of those in the minority on a given policy issue. By minority,

I am referring not to women, African Americans, or Native Americans but simply to those citizens who may find their beliefs to be in the vast minority but arguably in sync with the federal Constitution, the supreme law of the land, nevertheless.[37]

Goldwater articulated other important aspects of the neoconservative philosophy, especially with regard to the appropriate policy realms of the federal government and the matter of the original intent of the framers and members of Congress at the time amendments were added to the federal Constitution. First, with regard to the U.S. Supreme Court's decision in *Brown v. Board of Education of Topeka, Kansas*.[38] Goldwater shared his views on federal intervention in the field of public education:

> It so happens that I am in agreement with the *objectives* of the Supreme Court as stated in the *Brown* decision. I believe that it *is* both wise and just for negro children to attend the same schools as whites, and that to deny them this opportunity carries with it strong implications of inferiority. I am not prepared, however, to impose that judgment of mine on the people of Mississippi or South Carolina, or to tell them what methods should be adopted and what pace should be kept in striving toward that goal. That is their business, not mine. I believe that the problem of race relations, like all social and cultural problems, is best handled by the people directly concerned. Social and cultural change, however desirable, should not be effected by the engines of national power. Let us, through persuasion and education, seek to improve institutions we deem defective. But let us, in doing so, respect the orderly process of the law. Any other course enthrones tyrants and dooms freedom.[39]

Again, these beliefs are particularly disturbing in terms of democratic theory. To argue that we should try to educate and persuade majoritarian populations so that they will acknowledge the constitutional, legal, ethical, and even moral rights and responsibilities of their fellow citizens is a philosophy that is fundamentally flawed and is downright unacceptable. There is no first and second-class citizenship under the Constitution. Intrinsically, we are all the same and should be treated as such.

There is a rich intellectual debate in terms of the appropriate manner in which to interpret the federal Constitution. In the history of the American republic, there has always been a different approach to constitutional interpretation. Those who supported Thomas Jefferson in the early nineteenth century generally favored a strict interpretation of the Constitution and maintained that Congress had enumerated powers in the Constitution and that anything not mentioned in that document was a states' rights matter. The followers of Alexander Hamilton, however, typically favored a broad interpretation of the Constitution and believed that Congress was given broad authority to regulate the domestic economy under the Constitution and that Congress had not only enumerated powers but implied powers as well.[40] Goldwater was unequivocal in presenting his beliefs with regard to constitutional interpretation:

> I am therefore not impressed by the claim that the Supreme Court's decision on school integration is the law of the land. *The Constitution, and the laws "made in pursuance thereof," are the "supreme law of the land."* The Constitution is what its authors intended it to be and said it was— not what the Supreme Court says it is. If we condone the practice of substituting our own intentions for those of the Constitution's framers, we reject, in effect, the principle of Constitutional Government: we endorse a rule of men, not of laws.[41]

Two of the justices on the Supreme Court have offered their beliefs with regard to the debate of how to plausibly and appropriately interpret the federal Constitution. Justice Antonin Scalia is an avowed textualist, one who believes that federal judges are fairly bound by the authors of the original Constitution (members of Congress when the Constitution was amended) or by the drafters of legislation in Congress. Scalia argues against strict constructionism, but he maintains that the interpretation of the Constitution or a law should not go beyond a reasonable limit. Federal judges should not usurp the task of legislators but should simply adhere to the legislative intent of the framers or members of Congress if discernible.[42] In his own words, "In textual interpretation, context is everything, and the context of the Constitution tells us not to expect nit-picking detail, and to give words and phrases an expansive rather than narrow interpretation— though not an interpretation that the language will not bear."[43] To Scalia, there is too much subjectivity involved for those who believe that the Constitution is, in fact, evolutionary in nature:

> In the last analysis, however, it probably does not matter what principle, among the innumerable possibilities, the evolutionist proposes to determine in what direction The Living Constitution will grow. Whatever he might propose, at the end of the day an evolving constitution will evolve the way the majority wishes. The people will be willing to leave

interpretation of the Constitution to lawyers and law courts so long as the people believe that it is (like the interpretation of a statute) essentially lawyers' work—requiring a close examination of the text, history of the text, traditional understanding of the text, judicial precedent, and so forth. But if the people come to believe that the Constitution is *not* a text like other texts; that it means, not what it says or what it is understood to mean, but what it *should* mean, in light of the "evolving standards of decency that mark the progress of a maturing society"— well, then, they will look for qualifications other than impartiality, judgment, and lawyerly acumen in those whom they select to interpret it. More specifically, they will look for judges who agree with *them* as to what the evolving standards have evolved to; who agree with *them* as to what the Constitution *ought* to be.[44]

Justice Stephen Breyer is critical of his colleague's theoretical framework as well as the harmful effect it has on citizens in a democratic republic. As opposed to textualism, Breyer advocates "active liberty." He believes that the Constitution was never intended by the framers to be a static document. In fact, he argues that the genius of the framers of the Constitution is that they created a living document that was intended to be a framework for the application of basic democratic principles applied to a changing society rather than a rigid document that restricted civil liberties to its citizens.[45]

Whether one promotes textualism, as is the case with Scalia, or originalism, sometimes referred to as the theory of original intent, or literalism, Breyer believes that this general approach to constitutional interpretation is too narrow in scope and results in policies that run counter to the general aims of democratic governance. Breyer declared that

the answer, in my view, lies in the unsatisfactory nature of that interpretive approach. First, the more "originalist" judges cannot appeal to the Framers themselves in support of their interpretive views. The Framers did not say specifically what factors judges should take into account whey they interpret statutes or the Constitution. This is obvious in the case of statutes. Why should the Framers have preferred (1) a system of interpretation that relies heavily on linguistic canons to (2) a system that seeks more directly to find the intent of the legislators who enacted the statute? It is close to obvious in respect to the Constitution. Why would the Framers, who disagreed even about the necessity of *including* a Bill of Rights in the Constitution, who disagreed about the *content* of that Bill of Rights, nonetheless have agreed about *what school of interpretive thought* should prove dominant in interpreting that Bill of Rights in the centuries to come?[46]

Breyer has a valid point. The framers did not have all the answers to the perplexing quandaries of their time. They nevertheless wrote a document that was intended to create a stable government, as chaos was the norm under the Articles of Confederation and Perpetual Union. The daily debates of the Philadelphia Convention bear testimony to the premise that the framers did not have all the answers to the political and societal challenges of their time. The framers who did sign and endorse the final Constitution in 1787 agreed to compromise on a number of divisive issues. The framers understood that the first experiment in democracy in America failed. They could not have known at the time whether the document would be ratified (which did occur successfully in 1788), and they could not have known that the document would still be functional in the early twenty-first century.[47] The nationalists in Philadelphia did agree to create a stronger national government in the context of a democratic republic. In this aspect, James Madison, in particular, was enormously successful in Philadelphia.

Breyer, it seems to me, is highlighting the reality that constitutions tend to be broad and somewhat vague by definition. It is perhaps easier, during the legislative process, to attract more supporters by avoiding specificity. Human history and the study of political science are definitive in one aspect: no singular generation of people has demonstrated mastery in the sense of resolving all the policy challenges of present and future societies. Why, then, would a group of mostly learned elites presume that they would have all the answers for future generations? Why would they have presumed that their intent should be entirely binding on people hundreds and perhaps thousands of years into the future? The fact that they created a mechanism, albeit a challenging one to be sure, to change the very document that they created suggests that the framers were not unlike leaders past and present who know for sure that they do not have all the answers to society's vexing quandaries. Although amending the Constitution is a difficult process and requires supermajorities at both the national and the state level, the process, it is reasonable to assume given the great political debates in Philadelphia, allows future generations to undo the work of the framers if they believe that certain aspects of the Constitution are flawed in any manner. Amending the Constitution has also obviously allowed civil liberties and democracy to expand in U.S. history.

Breyer provided a theoretical refutation to Scalia's textualist approach to statutory interpretation:

> In sum, a "reasonable legislator" approach is a workable method of implementing the Constitution's democratic objective. It permits ready translation of the general desire of the public for certain ends, through the legislator's efforts to embody those ends in legislation, into a set of statutory words that will carry out those general objectives. I have argued that the Framers created the Constitution's complex governmental mechanism in order better to translate public will, determined through collective deliberation, into sound public policy. The courts constitute part of that mechanism. And judicial use of the "will of the reasonable legislator"—even if at times it is a fiction—helps statutes match their means to their overall public policy objectives, a match that helps translate the popular will into sound public policy. An overly literal reading of a text can too often stand in the way.[48]

Breyer argued that there are real-world consequences to judicial decision making. The contention by Scalia that judges should rely on textualism or originalism and somehow as a result avoid judicial policymaking is truly a subterfuge and does not reflect the reality that in deciding disputes among two or more parties in our adversarial system of justice, federal judges have always made public policy and will continue to do so regardless of theories of constitutional interpretation.[49]

Milton Friedman

Milton Friedman (1912–2006) was widely regarded as the leader of the Chicago school of monetary economics, which stressed the importance of the quantity of money as an instrument of government fiscal policy and as a determinant of business cycles and inflation. He was a member of President Reagan's Economic Policy Advisory Board.[50] In 1976, he was awarded the Nobel Prize in Economic Sciences.[51] According to the 2008 winner of the same prize, Paul Krugman, "A number of economists played important roles in the great revival of classical economics between 1950 and 2000, but none was as influential as Milton Friedman."[52] During the comparatively high inflation, unemployment, interest rates, and budget deficits era of the 1970s, Keynesian economic philosophy was under assault. Clearly, government leaders, especially President Reagan, were more amenable to laissez-faire economic policies once again. According to Krugman,

The odds are that the great swing back toward *laissez-faire* policies that took place around the world beginning in the 1970s would have happened even if there had been no Milton Friedman. But his tireless and brilliantly effective campaign on behalf of free markets surely helped accelerate the process, both in the United States and around the world. By any measure—protectionism versus free trade; regulation versus deregulation; wages set by collective bargaining and government minimum wages versus wages set by the market—the world has moved a long way in Friedman's direction. And even more striking than his achievement in terms of actual policy changes has been the transformation of the conventional wisdom: most influential people have been so converted to the Friedman way of thinking that it is simply taken as a given that the change in economic policies he promoted has been a force for good.[53]

The Friedman philosophy of economics is clearly articulated in an important book he published in 1962.

In *Capitalism and Freedom*, Friedman presented a defense of laissez-faire capitalism. He maintained that private enterprise operating in a free market system not only results in economic freedom but is a necessary condition for political freedom as well. In this work, he contended that government should have two primary functions:

First, the scope of government must be limited. Its major function must be to protect our freedom both from the enemies outside our gates and from our fellow-citizens: to preserve law and order, to enforce private contracts, to foster competitive markets. Beyond this major function, government may enable us at times to accomplish jointly what we would find it more difficult or expensive to accomplish severally. However, any such use of government is fraught with danger. We should not and cannot avoid using government in this way. But there should be a clear and large balance of advantages before we do. By relying primarily on voluntary co-operation and private enterprise, in both economic and other activities, we can insure that the private sector is a check on the powers of the governmental sector and an effective protection of freedom of speech, of religion, and of thought. The second broad principle is that government power must be dispersed. If government is to exercise power, better in the county than in the state, better in the state than in Washington. If I do not like what my local community does, be it in sewage disposal, or zoning, or schools, I can move to another local community, and though few may take this step, the mere possibility acts as a check. If I do not like what my state does, I can move to another. If I do not like what Washington imposes, I have few alternatives in this world of jealous nations.[54]

Friedman, in theoretical agreement with the classical economic philosophers, envisioned a very limited role for the federal government in the domestic economy and clearly had a suspicious and negative view of government intervention in general. His perspective on the private marketplace, on the contrary, was hopeful and positive, and he envisioned that voluntary exchanges in a capitalist economy had the tangible result of enhancing individual freedom in the United States.[55]

In a book published almost 20 years later, both Milton and Rose Friedman extolled the virtues of the free market system:

> The two ideas of human freedom and economic freedom working together came to their greatest fruition in the United States. Those ideas are still very much with us. We are all of us imbued with them. They are part of the very fabric of our being. But we have been straying from them. We have been forgetting the basic truth that the greatest threat to human freedom is the concentration of power, whether in the hands of government or anyone else. We have persuaded ourselves that it is safe to grant power, provided it is for good purposes. Fortunately, we are waking up. We are again recognizing the dangers of an overgoverned society, coming to understand that good objectives can be perverted by bad means, that reliance on the freedom of people to control their own lives in accordance with their own values is the surest way to achieve the full potential of a great society. Fortunately, also, we are as a people still free to choose which way we should go—whether to continue along the road we have been following to ever bigger government, or to call a halt and change direction.[56]

In providing lavish praise on the free market, the Friedmans simultaneously condemned the growth in size and scope of the federal government. They associated this growth with a corresponding decrease in individual freedom. I can only wonder at this juncture if some philosophers conveniently ignore an important variable in both quantitative and qualitative research: history. Why has the size and scope of government increased? This growth did not occur simply as a result of the Great Depression and corresponding New Deal economic and social policies. Obviously, the government's regulatory authority was utilized much more extensively by President Franklin Roosevelt and members of Congress as a reaction to the great economic calamity of the twentieth century, but the exponential growth of federal authority had already commenced during the Progressive Era, often defined by historians as the 1870–1920 time period.[57] Many citizens demanded more government oversight in the railroad and oil industries, in particular, during the decades of the late nineteenth and early twentieth centuries. Some of the wealthiest Americans in history amassed their fortunes during much of this half-century span of time, including John D. Rockefeller Sr., Andrew Carnegie, Henry Ford, and, to a lesser extent since he was born in the late eighteenth century, Cornelius Vanderbilt.[58] The reality is that the gap between rich and poor was historically expansive during this time period, and some people got wealthy not necessarily because they were more entrepreneurial, clever, or hardworking than others but simply because they exploited a deregulated capitalist economy to their advantage. This was likely the case with regard to arguably the wealthiest person in U.S. history, John D. Rockefeller Sr.[59] The romantic libertarian perspective that the free enterprise system will maximize consumer choices and maintain freedom seemingly ignores the reality that, in a historical sense, Americans have typically demanded government intervention to help curb some of the excesses of capitalism.

THE IMPACT OF CONSERVATISM ON AMERICAN POLITICS SINCE 1980

Republican challenger Ronald Reagan won the 1980 presidential election decisively over the Democratic incumbent, Jimmy Carter. He received 51 percent of the popular vote to 41 percent for Carter and 7 percent for Independent John Anderson. In the Electoral College tally, he captured the popular vote in 44 states, resulting in 489 electoral votes. President Carter prevailed in Minnesota, Georgia, West Virginia, Maryland, Rhode Island, Hawaii, and the District of Columbia for a total of 49 votes.[60] Incidentally, four years later, President Reagan won 59 percent of the popular vote to 41 percent for the Democratic candidate, former vice president Walter Mondale. The vice president won his home state of Minnesota and the District of Columbia. The incumbent was victorious in the rest of the country, resulting in a 525–13 Electoral College landslide.[61] The conservative Reagan achieved what was elusive to his philosophical predecessor, Barry Goldwater. Americans were much more amenable to supporting a very conservative presidential candidate in 1980 than they were in the mid-1960s, when many progressive movements (e.g., civil rights, anti–Vietnam War, women's, environmental, and consumer rights) were evolving simultaneously in American society.

According to political scientist William Hudson, many of the conservative economic ideals in post–World War II America were based on the libertarian philosophy. Those who embrace the unbridled laissez-faire beliefs of Professor Hayek have found an intellectual home in the Grand Old Party for over 30 years. While the libertarian beliefs, particularly with regard to the domestic economy, were perceived as fringe or even radical in the past, this is no longer the case in contemporary America. The Republican Party supporters have embraced the libertarian economic philosophy for over 30 years, and the tangible result is that the ideas in question are perceived by many to be mainstream in nature when they are, indeed, radical and downright harmful to the greater public good. To Hudson, the libertarian ideals are nothing more than an illusion.[62] As Hudson astutely observed,

> Eventually politicians would integrate libertarian-based policy proposals into their campaign platform. Conservative Republican presidential candidate Barry Goldwater translated his personal libertarian outlook into major themes in his 1964 campaign. Although Goldwater endured a massive repudiation at the polls, the conservative activists he inspired and other politicians, such as Ronald Reagan, carried forward the conservative dream and the libertarian ideas that formed a part of it. By the 1970s, libertarian proposals were taken seriously in political debate and well represented in policy discussions in Washington. At this time, policy think tanks like the Cato Institute and the Heritage Foundation were founded to promote these policy ideas. . . . So when Ronald Reagan took the presidential oath in 198[1], libertarianism was no longer an obscure doctrine of eccentric émigré thinkers but a coherent and influential set of ideas that would guide one side of the public policy debate into the next century.[63]

Hudson contends that contemporary conservatives have embraced the libertarian ideals of the Austrian economists. Although the Libertarian Party has a relatively small number of adherents as measured by electoral success, the professor makes an important substantive point. The highly conservative policies of the libertarian philosophers have been successfully absorbed by the right wing of the Grand Old Party. This has been true since Ronald Reagan was first elected president in 1980. In Hudson's own words,

> The libertarian outlook gained adherents. Sentiments like Friedman's have gained currency, and by the 1980s many of his specific policy recommendations were being adopted. Today, libertarian solutions are invariably major contenders when any policy problem reaches the public agenda, and many have been implemented, transforming profoundly

the character of American life. No matter what the issue, proponents of providing individuals with freedom of choice on the matter—an ability to determine for themselves what they want free from governmental interference—will make themselves heard.[64]

Thus, the libertarians have been enormously successful at promoting their ideas through the mainstream Republican Party. Presidents such as Ronald Reagan and George W. Bush promoted the libertarian economic agenda under the banner of the Republican Party.

Ronald Reagan

Ronald Reagan (1911–2004) was the fortieth president of the United States and served from 1981 to 1989. Prior to being president, he was the governor of California from 1967 to 1975. He is a fascinating president to study in an ideological sense, as he evolved from being a supporter of Franklin D. Roosevelt and the New Deal in the 1930s and 1940s to a stalwart conservative Republican president in the 1980s.[65] According to Thomas Evans, Ronald Reagan, once a Hollywood liberal and president of the Screen Actors Guild, changed his political ideology as a result of his experience as a General Electric employee from 1954 to 1962.[66] In his book, Evans argues that a General Electric executive, Lemuel Boulware (1895–1990), became Ronald Reagan's political and ideological mentor. The years that the future president spent at General Electric were transformational, as Mr. Boulware had a profound influence on the worldview of Ronald Reagan. Boulware was an avowed subscriber to the philosophy of laissez-faire capitalism, limited government, lower taxes, anticommunism, and antiunionism. These fundamental conservative ideals would later become the foundation of the Reagan agenda in the White House.[67]

On October 27, 1964, Reagan delivered a televised speech in support of Barry Goldwater's presidential candidacy. His speech was titled "A Time for Choosing" but later became known as "The Speech."[68] This speech made Reagan a national figure in American politics, and even though Barry Goldwater lost decisively in 1964, Reagan would be elected governor of California two years later. The Reagan conversion to political conservatism is apparent:

> Another articulate spokesman for the welfare state defines liberalism as meeting the material needs of the masses through the full power of centralized government. I for one find it disturbing when a representative

refers to the free men and women of this country as the masses, but beyond this the full power of centralized government was the very thing the Founding Fathers sought to minimize. They knew you don't control things; you can't control the economy without controlling people. So we have come to a time for choosing. Either we accept the responsibility for our own destiny, or we abandon the American Revolution and confess that an intellectual belief in a far-distant capitol can plan our lives for us better than we can plan them ourselves. Already the hour is late. Government has laid its hand on health, housing, farming, industry, commerce, education, and, to an ever increasing degree, interferes with the people's right to know. Government tends to grow; government programs take on weight and momentum, as public servants say, always with the best of intentions, "What greater service we could render if only we had a little more money and a little more power." But the truth is that outside of its legitimate function, a government does nothing as well or as economically as the private sector of the economy.[69]

Reagan began this famous speech by saying, "I am going to talk of controversial things. I make no apology for this."[70] His own personal ideological conversion was therefore complete by 1964.

In this speech, the Reagan ideology was unambiguous and uncompromising. He offered his listeners the following dichotomy:

It's time we asked ourselves if we still know the freedoms intended for us by the Founding Fathers. James Madison said, "We base all our experiments on the capacity of mankind for self-government." This idea that government was beholden to the people, that it had no other source of power except the sovereign people, is still the newest most unique idea in all the long history of man's relation to man. For almost two centuries we have proved man's capacity for self-government, but today we are told we must choose between a left and right or, as others suggest, a third alternative, a kind of safe middle ground. I suggest to you there is no left or right, only an up or down. Up to the maximum of individual freedom consistent with law and order, or down to the ant heap of totalitarianism; and regardless of their humanitarian purpose those who would sacrifice freedom for security have, whether they know it or not, chosen this downward path.[71]

As the former president would reiterate in many speeches, he equated the pursuit of more individual freedom with less government intervention in the economy in particular. This is undoubtedly why his economic philosophy and subsequent policies would be the most significant defining feature of the Reagan presidency.

As Robert Collins declared,

> President Ronald Reagan's most profound impact on public policy
> came in the realm of political economy. This was the area in which his
> intentions were most radical, and where his radical intentions coincided
> with the collapse of the old Keynesian order that had dominated policy
> throughout the postwar era and the resulting reorientation of economic
> thought. Economists refer to such changes as inflection points, shifts in
> direction; historians speak of watersheds. Whatever the particular term,
> the label fits the 1980s. The changes in economic thought and economic
> policy that took hold in the 1980s were substantial and, as such matters
> go, long-lasting, continuing at least into the early years of the new mil-
> lennium. The economist Lawrence B. Lindsey has observed that "in
> terms of economic performance, government policy, and the effect on
> the thinking of professional economists, the 1980s and 1990s form a con-
> tinuous era radically different from what preceded it." What contempo-
> raries somewhat derisively called "Reaganomics" cast a long shadow.[72]

President Reagan had a number of economic objectives. He wanted to
create the conditions, especially with deregulation, to spur economic
growth and individual entrepreneurialism. He also wanted to reduce
the rate of inflation and unemployment and promote policies that
would lower interest rates for those borrowing money. The president
became the central figure in the supply-side revolution.[73]

Collins provided a basic summary of the supply-side economic
approach in the 1980s:

> First, the supply-siders emphasized that supply matters greatly, an eco-
> nomic truism that had been under-appreciated since the triumph of
> Keynes, who had emphasized the maintenance of sufficiently high
> aggregate demand to keep pace with the economy's recurrent tendency
> toward overproduction. Supply-siders shifted attention back to the
> problem of productivity and how to raise it. Second, in achieving this
> rediscovery of the relative significance of supply, the supply-siders also
> necessarily shifted attention away from macroeconomics, with its con-
> cern for aggregate behavior, and back to the behavior of discrete eco-
> nomic actors—individuals and firms. Third, following the logic of
> their broad suppositions, the supply-siders believed that the way to
> achieve prosperity without inflation was to expand supply by increas-
> ing the incentives for individuals to work, save, and invest. The surest
> way to achieve such results was to cut taxes, especially the existing high
> marginal rates—those tax rates that applied to the last dollar of income
> and that therefore most discouraged extra effort and enterprise. Such a
> tax reduction, they claimed, would raise real output—not by increasing

demand but by operating on the supply side of the economy. Full-bore supply-siders went so far as to assert that such tax cuts would be so powerful as to actually generate more revenue than would be lost by the cuts themselves.[74]

The intellectual debate about the plausibility of President Reagan's economic policies is important even today because the ideas on which they are predicated are still prominent with contemporary conservatives. Yet as Collins indicated, there are two primary indictments against Reaganomics that still impact Americans today: the U.S. national debt increased dramatically during the 1980s, and the president's policies caused a dramatic rise in income inequality.[75]

Reagan delivered his farewell address on January 11, 1989. In it, he reemphasized his conservative belief that the pursuit of individual freedom generally entails a limited centralized government:

> Ours was the first revolution in the history of mankind that truly reversed the course of government, and with three little words: "We the People." "We the People" tell the government what to do; it doesn't tell us. "We the People" are the driver; the government is the car, and we decide where it should go, and by what route, and how fast. Almost all the world's constitutions are documents in which governments tell the people what their privileges are. Our Constitution is a document in which "We the People" tell the government what it is allowed to do. "We the People" are free. This belief has been the underlying basis for everything I've tried to do these past 8 years.[76]

The philosophical premise that President Reagan communicated throughout the 1980s was consistent, clear, and unwavering. Government was not the solution to the economic and public policy challenges of contemporary America—it was the problem. The path to economic prosperity came through deregulation and allowing citizens, as much as possible, to pursue their own self-defined objectives with limited government interference.

Historian David Farber has provided a succinct summary of the Reagan years in the context of U.S. history:

> Ronald Reagan ended his presidency on a wave of popularity equaled in the twentieth century only by his former idol, Franklin Roosevelt. A leading expert on the American presidency, Stephen Skowronek, places Reagan in the rich company of the presidents who transformed the United States: Thomas Jefferson, Andrew Jackson, Abraham Lincoln, and Franklin Roosevelt. ... Reagan took the dreams and ideas of the

conservative movement that had been in the works for decades and made them, in many cases, the law of the land—and, just as telling, conventional wisdom. By no means did all Americans accept his conservative plan for the United States. At the end of his presidency, Reagan's social policies remained enormously divisive, and in many cases a majority rejected his attempts to rollback the government-assisted struggles for racial justice, gender equity, and equal opportunity in American life. Liberals believed his indifference to the plight of the poor and to growing economic inequality in the United States were terrible wounds in the body politic, and they vowed to heal them. Reagan transformed American politics, but he also contributed to the growing polarization of the American people. When he left office, just as when he gained it, liberals despised him. But conservatives, even more, loved him for what he had accomplished. Reagan's electoral coattails remained long. Reagan's vice president, George H.W. Bush, who once scorned Reaganomics as "voodoo economics," had refashioned himself as a Reagan acolyte and won the 1988 election. Much of what Reagan had created would be continued.[77]

Indeed, the first Republican president by the name of George Bush garnered 53 percent of the popular vote to 46 percent for the Democratic nominee, Michael Dukakis. The Bush ticket prevailed in 40 states, whereas the Democratic ticket carried 10 states (Massachusetts, Rhode Island, New York, West Virginia, Wisconsin, Minnesota, Iowa, Washington, Oregon, and Hawaii) as well as the District of Columbia.[78] The margin of victory in the Electoral College was 426 to 111 for the Republicans.[79]

However, George H. W. Bush was denied a second term by the electorate in 1992. The Democratic nominee, Bill Clinton, won the popular vote with 43 percent to 38 percent for the incumbent president and 19 percent for the Independent candidate, H. Ross Perot. The Democrats prevailed in 32 states and the District of Columbia, while the Republicans carried the remaining 18 states, resulting in a 370–168 margin of victory in the Electoral College.[80] Four years later, Bill Clinton became the first Democratic president to be reelected since Franklin Roosevelt. The election results were similar to 1992. While President Clinton received 49 percent of the popular vote, the Republican nominee, Robert Dole, secured 41 percent to 8 percent for the Reform Party nominee, Perot. The Democratic ticket prevailed in 31 states and the District of Columbia, resulting in 379 electoral votes; the Republicans won 19 states and 159 votes in the Electoral College.[81]

While the Democratic nominee, Al Gore, won the popular vote in 2000 with 48.4 percent of the vote to 47.9 percent for the Republican nominee, George W. Bush, he lost the presidency in the Electoral College by a 271–266 margin. The Republicans won 30 states; the Democrats prevailed in the remaining 20 states and the District of Columbia.[82] In 2004, George W. Bush was reelected over the Democratic nominee, John Kerry, by a popular vote tally of 51 to 48 percent. His margin of victory in the Electoral College increased slightly from four years earlier: 286 to 251. The Republicans won 31 states, while the Democrats carried 19 states and the District of Columbia.[83]

George W. Bush

George W. Bush was the forty-third president of the United States and served from 2001 to 2009. Prior to his federal service, he was governor of Texas from 1995 to 2000. While he was a self-proclaimed "compassionate conservative," his brand of conservatism was rather unique when compared to Reagan. According to Farber,

> Bush was an unusual conservative leader. He had not come of age intellectually in conservative institutions or organizations, nor was he well-schooled in the conservative intellectual tradition. His conservatism came from a different set of experiences. It was roughly forged in his disgust with the left-wing, sixties campus political culture he endured as an undergraduate at Yale University. While others protested the war in Vietnam and struggled for racial justice, young George embraced the conventional role of hard-drinking, fun-loving fraternity boy. ... Finally, and unlike Ronald Reagan, Bush found the core of his conservative values not in his readings in free-market economics or anticommunist treatises but, he said, in the words of God as revealed in the Bible. Like Barry Goldwater, Bush was an instinctual conservative. More than any other democratically elected conservative profiled here, Bush found his conservative anchor in his spiritual and not his intellectual life. That spiritual life had brought order to his troubled soul, and Bush believed that a religiously infused public life was a vital ingredient in bringing order and moral discipline to American society.[84]

There are some similarities between the fortieth and forty-third presidents. Both were avowed conservatives, and both served two terms in office. However, while Reagan won two electoral landslides over his two opponents, Bush lost the popular vote in 2000 and ascended to the presidency through a somewhat unique court battle in the Supreme

Court.[85] A divided electorate kept him in office, perhaps in large part due to the administration's ongoing war on terrorism in the aftermath of the terrorist attacks in the United States on September 11, 2001.

In terms of public opinion, using the Gallup Poll as a constant benchmark, Reagan had an overall average approval rating of 52.8 percent during his two terms, and Bush had a 49.4 percent average during his tenure. During his first term, President Reagan had a 50.3 percent average approval rating and a 55.3 percent average in his second term. President Bush had a 62.2 percent average approval rating in his first term and a 36.5 percent average rating in his second. President Reagan's highest approval rating during his tenure was 68 percent (in May 1981 and May 1986). His lowest approval rating was 35 percent (January 1983). Thus, his range of popular approval was 33 percent. Bush has the single highest popular approval rating in Gallup history— 90 percent. This occurred in September 2001 shortly after the terrorist attacks. His lowest approval rating was 25 percent (October 2008). Thus, his range of popular approval was considerably high at 65 percent.[86]

Before examining his brand of conservatism, it should be noted that political scientists often categorize elected officials on a continuum when it pertains to such matters as ideology. Simply put, there is diversity between and among individuals who may classify themselves as liberals, moderates, or conservatives. By way of illustration, Tim Conlan and John Dinan contend that there are several different types of conservatives in American politics today:

> There are several different strains of conservatism in the United States, and four somewhat overlapping strains are especially relevant to contemporary issues of federalism and the vertical distribution of power. What might be termed institutional conservatism aims to preserve traditional and customary roles among the different levels of government. Economic conservatives hold libertarian beliefs and advocate small government, low taxes, and free markets. Social conservatives are more apt to be supportive of active government involvement in support of traditional social norms and roles. Neoconservatism overlaps with social conservatism in its distrust of cultural liberalism, but it emphasizes a more active, interventionist approach to foreign policy and a greater skepticism of government action domestically. The relative significance of these different strands of thought, and the ways in which they are melded together, have changed over time, and such changes are important for understanding the design of administration policies and their implications for federalism.[87]

Clearly, conservatives tend to support varying levels of intervention by the federal government through its officials. Decentralized governance is championed by institutional conservatives. The economic conservatives are classical (eighteenth-century) liberals who advocate small government, libertarian values, and laissez-faire capitalism. The social conservatives are much more amenable to activist governmental policies as long as they are designed to promote a more moralistic society in sync with their own religious and social belief systems. The neoconservatives are similar to the social conservatives in that both have disdain for social liberalism in contemporary society. At the same time, however, neoconservatives tend to oppose federal intervention in domestic policy issues.[88]

Another scholar, Adam Wolfson, wrote about the increasing intellectual and media attention dedicated to neoconservatism during Bush's presidency. His labels for the varying strands of conservatism were slightly different than the previously mentioned researchers:

> The basic contours of neoconservatism most readily emerge against the backdrop of its two main conservative rivals: libertarianism and traditionalism. (I will have little to say of religious conservatives and Straussians, since they are frequently allied with neocons and have moreover helped shape the neocon impulse.) These three conservative approaches—traditionalism, libertarianism, and neoconservatism—have distinct historical and philosophic roots. Generally speaking, traditionalists look to Edmund Burke, libertarians to Friedrich Hayek, and neocons to Alexis de Tocqueville. However, each finds its origins in something more elemental. Anyone of us can't help but have a gut feeling about modern American life—its possibilities and limits, whether it is humane and decent or alienating and corrupting. Those of us who regret much of modern American life and find solace in old, inherited ways will cling to traditionalism. Others, who celebrate the new freedoms and new technologies, will turn to libertarianism. As for those who see in modernity admirable principles but also worrisome tendencies, their persuasion will be neoconservatism.[89]

In highlighting the intellectual diversity within the conservative political community, I am not seeking to label or categorize influential thinkers and elected officials. Clearly, there are some fundamental core beliefs among conservatives. These core beliefs affect the views that conservatives have about public policy issues, including education and the appropriate role of the federal government in society, and provide an important context for understanding why they advocate what they do by way of policies and why they believe that the pursuit of individual freedom, as they define it, is a top priority.

In 1999, the year before he would prevail in the Electoral College in the presidential election, Bush delineated his own political philosophy in *A Charge to Keep*. In his own words,

> I am a conservative because I believe in the worth and dignity and power of each individual. My philosophy trusts individuals to make the right decisions for their families and communities, and that is far more compassionate than a philosophy that seeks solutions from distant bureaucracies. I am a conservative because I believe government should be limited and efficient, that it should do a few things and do them well. I am a conservative because I believe in strong national defense to keep the peace. I am a conservative because I support free markets and free trade. I am a conservative because I believe government closer to the people governs best. I am a fiscal conservative and a family conservative. And I am a compassionate conservative, because I know my philosophy is optimistic and full of hope for every American. Compassionate conservatism outlines a new vision of the proper role for the American government. Government must be limited and focused, but it has an important job within its bounds. Government is too often wasteful and overreaching. But we must correct it and limit it, not disdain it. I differ from those who want to dismantle government down to the last paper clip—and with those who want to extend its reach. Government is neither the enemy or the answer. The federal government has some compelling purposes: to defend our homeland, to help keep peace in the world, to help secure the retirement and health needs of our senior citizens, and to help our society confront human suffering. State and local government must educate children, put criminals behind bars, and maintain roads and basic services. But in some cases, the job is best done not by government itself, but by directing government resources to neighborhoods and parents and schools and faith-based institutions that shape values and change lives.[90]

As Farber detailed, Bush's religious faith had a fundamental influence on his life in public service. By his own admission, when he quit drinking alcohol after he turned 40 years of age, the president turned to his faith for guidance not only in his personal life but in the public sector as well.[91] Critics such as Esther Kaplan believe that Bush and his supporters in the Christian fundamentalist community used religion to promote a radical policy agenda that undermined basic American democratic principles.[92] Charles Tiefer maintained that Bush systematically manipulated American law to promote the

political agenda of right-wing extremists in the United States.[93] The
political commentator Paul Waldman was particularly poignant in
his assessment of the Bush presidency:

> While liberals may find George W. Bush's presidency distressing
> because they disagree with the policies he pursues, there is much more
> to despise than his ideology. Each of us in our lifetimes will live under
> presidents both Democrat and Republican, liberal and conservative.
> What is so pernicious about the Bush presidency is not its hard-right
> agenda but the fact that it is built on and maintained by an endless pro-
> cession of lies, each more brazen and sweeping than the last. American
> citizens have been lied to before by their presidents, and those lies have
> inspired everything from utter indifference to constructive outrage. But
> long ago, George W. Bush moved well past the amount of deceit we can
> reasonably be expected to bear.[94]

While there are many critics of the forty-third president from a variety
of perspectives, not all the criticism of Bush's presidency emanates
from political liberals.[95]

John Dean, former White House counsel to President Richard
Nixon from 1970 to 1973, argued that Bush's presidency was worse
than that of his former boss during Watergate in terms of secrecy.[96]
In addition, he also questions the political strategy employed by Bush
and his vice president, Dick Cheney:

> Among the most troubling of the authoritarian and radical tactics being
> employed by Bush and Cheney are their politics of fear. A favorite gam-
> bit of Latin American dictators who run sham democracies, fear-
> mongering has generally been frowned upon in American politics.
> Think of the modern presidents who have governed our nation—
> Roosevelt, Truman, Eisenhower, Kennedy, Johnson, Ford, Carter,
> Reagan, Bush I, and Clinton—and the various crises they confronted—
> the Great Depression, World War II, the Korean war, the cold war, the
> Cuban missile crisis, the war in Vietnam, Iran's taking of American hos-
> tages, the danger of American students in Grenada, Saddam's invasion
> of Kuwait, the terrorist bombings at the World Trade Center in 1993, and
> Timothy McVeigh's 1995 bombing of the federal building in Oklahoma.
> None of these presidents resorted to fear in dealing with these situa-
> tions. None of these presidents made the use of fear a standard pro-
> cedure or a means of governing (or pursuing office or political goals).
> To the contrary, all of these presidents sought to *avoid* preying on the
> fears of Americans. (It will be noted that Nixon is not included in this
> list because he did use fear in both his 1968 and 1972 presidential cam-
> paigns, and he continued to use this tactic once in office.) Frightening

Americans, nonetheless, has become a standard ploy for Bush, Cheney, and their surrogates. They add a fear factor to every course of action they pursue, whether it is their radical foreign policy of preemptive war, or their implementation of a radical new health care scheme.[97]

Dean contends that a number of prominent contemporary conservatives, including Bush and Cheney, have undermined the conservative cause by engaging in authoritarian power politics. To him, such officials have been indifferent to the American founding principles of liberty and equality and have seemingly justified their actions and decisions on moral grounds when in reality they have subverted the very constitutional principles they were supposed to defend.[98]

Bruce Bartlett worked in the Reagan White House as a senior policy analyst and was deputy assistant secretary for economic policy at the Department of the Treasury during the presidency of George H. W. Bush. The longtime conservative columnist was a senior fellow at the National Center for Policy Analysis from 1995 to 2005 but was fired for writing a book critical of George W. Bush titled *Impostor: How George W. Bush Bankrupted America and Betrayed the Reagan Legacy.*[99] Bartlett is a staunch conservative who believed that the junior Bush sacrificed conservative causes in order to advance his own agenda in a Nixonian manner:

> George W. Bush is widely considered to be one of the most politically conservative presidents in history. His invasion of Iraq, his huge tax cuts, and his intervention in the Terri Schiavo case are among the issues where those on the left view him as being to the right of Attila the Hun. But those on the right have a different perspective—mostly discussed among themselves or in forums that fly below the major media's radar. They know that Bush has never really been one of them the way Ronald Reagan was. Bush is more like Richard Nixon—a man who used the right to pursue his agenda, but was never really part of it. In short, he is an impostor, a pretend conservative. I write as a Reaganite, by which I mean someone who believes in the historical conservative philosophy of small government, federalism, free trade, and the Constitution as originally understood by the Founding Fathers. On that basis, Bush clearly is not a Reaganite or "small c" conservative. Philosophically, he has more in common with liberals, who see no limits to state power as long as it is used to advance what they think is right. In the same way, Bush has used government to pursue a "conservative" agenda as he sees it. But that is something that runs totally contrary to the restraints and limits to power inherent in the very nature of traditional conservatism. It is inconceivable to traditional conservatives that there could

ever be such a thing as "big government conservatism," a term often used to describe Bush's philosophy.[100]

Richard Viguerie made the same argument (that George W. Bush sacrificed the conservative political cause) in a book published the same year (2006).[101]

Viguerie transformed American politics in the 1960s and 1970s by pioneering the use of computerized direct-mail fund-raising in the political and ideological arenas. He helped to build the conservative movement that culminated in the election of Reagan. In his book, he presented 27 "Conservative Articles of Indictment against President George W. Bush."[102] One of his most substantive criticisms levied against George W. Bush is that the size of the federal government, adjusted for inflation, grew more under him than any other president dating back to Lyndon Johnson in the 1960s.[103]

POLICY IMPLICATIONS OF THE MARKET-BASED IDEOLOGY AND CONSERVATIVE POLITICAL PHILOSOPHY

However conservatism may be manifested in public policy terms, the market-based ideology has some important implications in the arena of education policy. In the economic sphere, conservatives operate largely on the assumption that private and parochial schools are "better" than their traditional public school counterparts, though they rarely identify and define an effective school in a clear and measurable manner. An inherent assumption therefore exists. If public schools had to compete with nonpublic schools, charter schools, and even home schooling, the overall quality of public K–12 education will be enhanced. Although this point is often subtle in nature, the theoretical assumptions made by many conservatives are of fundamental importance because public policies have been enacted all across the country that are reflective of the conservative ethos. It is akin to the assumption of the superiority of private corporations over government bureaucracies on various performance measures. Many conservatives routinely accept the premise that private companies outperform government entities without engaging in a systematic analysis. But are these theoretical assumptions always valid? Are they valid the majority of the time? Are they mostly invalid? These questions cannot be addressed in a tangible manner without more scientific research. Researchers and citizens alike have much in common. All of us should conduct more investigations before accepting and embracing theoretical premises that may, in fact, be dubious.

Ideas are the central and most important elements of politics. This was as true during Horace Mann's time as it is now. The great crusader for public education had a vision. He believed in the necessity and plausibility of schools run by public sector entities otherwise known as government bureaucracies. He viewed an educated citizenry, subsidized by taxes paid by citizens, as an essential condition in a republican form of government. An educated populace would be much more inclined to promote the conditions for economic prosperity. Educated citizens would be less likely to engage in the politics of extremism, and they would be less likely to embrace to engage in criminal activity. Educated Americans would seek to make their communities better places for themselves, for their children, and for their fellow citizens. Perhaps most important in a diverse republic like the United States, bringing citizens from different social classes, religious backgrounds, and racial and ethnic groups together for a common purpose was worthwhile in the first place. It would result in children accumulating knowledge so as to be contributing members of society as adults, yet it would also have the corollary effect of teaching children to get along with another and to practice civility in a microcosm of the greater society. What if Mann's vision, which was initially implemented into concrete public policy in the mid-nineteenth century and was largely upheld for most of U.S. history until the past few decades, is still astute, viable, and plausible today? What if the conservative backlash against public education in contemporary America is misguided and harmful and runs counter to core republican ideals? What if the conservative, market-driven ideology, particularly prominent in American politics since the initial election of Reagan, contributes to the demise of a public policy that was admittedly imperfect, as all human-driven enterprises are destined to be, but worth improving and worth reforming in order to pursue the vision so eloquently articulated by Mann some time ago? Perhaps delving more into our own history will prove facilitative when pondering this particular quandary.

Education and the Politics of Federalism

Federalism is a very important subject within American politics and public affairs. It is a topic that citizens generally do not identify by name but is a matter that Americans have debated since the Philadelphia Convention and will continue to do so without necessarily using the term "federalism" in their discourse.[1] By definition, federalism is the constitutional division of power between the national government and the subnational governments or, in the case of the United States, the state governments. The national government and the state governments are recognized in the federal Constitution. There is no specific reference to local governments in the U.S. Constitution. Local governments did exist in 1787, when the framers drafted the Constitution, but, legally, local governments are appendages of their states. Thus, there was no need to formally mention local governments in the federal document. In pragmatic terms, federalism is the relationship

Photograph of a bespectacled Horace Mann taken before his years at Antioch College (1853–1859). (Image courtesy of Antiochiana, Antioch College.)

between the national government and state and local governments. As Robert Goldwin noted in the early 1960s,

Perhaps no other aspect of American politics is so much discussed in theoretical and historical terms as is our federal system. The question of the legitimate powers of the respective governments—national, state, and local—arises in an amazing variety of political debates in the course of the day-to-day work of governing the United States. It appears in many guises, but federalism's presence is nonetheless unmistakable when we debate such diverse matters as civil rights, sharing of tax revenues, highway construction programs, labor laws, race relations, the farm problem, legislative redistricting, school construction, welfare programs—and so on in an interminable list.[2]

Thus, even though most Americans do not utilize the term "federalism" in their political discussions, debating how much power the national government should have versus state and local governments has been a central feature of American politics throughout the history of this country.

THE ABSTRACT NATURE OF THE FEDERALISM DEBATE

Federalism is an ambiguous topic in the federal Constitution as articulated by Chief Justice John Marshall in the early nineteenth century:

This Government is acknowledged by all to be one of enumerated powers. The principle that it can exercise only the powers granted to it would seem too apparent to have required to be enforced by all those arguments which its enlightened friends, while it was depending before the people, found it necessary to urge; that principle is now universally admitted. But the question respecting the extent of the powers actually granted is perpetually arising, and will probably continue to arise so long as our system shall exist. In discussing these questions, the conflicting powers of the General and State Governments must be brought into view, and the supremacy of their respective laws, when they are in opposition, must be settled. If any one proposition could command the universal assent of mankind, we might expect it would be this—that the Government of the Union, though limited in its powers, is supreme within its sphere of action. This would seem to result necessarily from its nature. It is the Government of all; its powers are delegated by all; it represents all, and acts for all. Though any one State may be willing to control its operations, no State is willing to allow others to control them. The nation, on those subjects on which it can act, must necessarily bind its component parts. But this question is not left to mere reason; the people have, in express terms, decided it by saying, "this Constitution, and the laws of the United States, which shall be made in pursuance thereof," "shall be the supreme laws of the land."[3]

The framers of the Constitution did not provide a finite list of the enumerated powers of Congress. As Chief Justice Marshall indicated in his opinion in *McCulloch v. Maryland*, Congress has not only enumerated powers but implied powers as well. The nation's fourth chief justice emphasized the importance of language in the drafting of constitutional law in his opinion in *McCulloch*.[4] In the context of the *McCulloch* case, Chief Justice Marshall highlighted Article I, Section 8, Paragraph 18, the necessary and proper clause (also known as the elastic clause): "To make all Laws which shall be necessary and proper for carrying into Execution the foregoing Powers, and all other Powers vested by this Constitution in the Government of the United States, or in any Department or officer thereof." What did the framers of the Constitution mean by the necessary and proper clause?

In reality, the necessary and proper clause is subject to interpretation. There is no definitive record of the intent of the framers when it pertains to this section of the Constitution. As is commonly the case in constitutional law, federal judges are often put in a position to determine the meaning of the law. This is clearly what transpired in *McCulloch*, the great federalism case in American history. Chief Justice Marshall highlighted the role that federal judges perform in our system of government with the interpretation of the necessary and proper clause:

> But the argument on which most reliance is placed is drawn from that peculiar language of this clause. Congress is not empowered by it to make all laws which may have relation to the powers conferred on the Government, but such only as may be "necessary and proper" for carrying them into execution. The word "necessary" is considered as controlling the whole sentence, and as limiting the right to pass laws for the execution of the granted powers to such as are indispensable, and without which the power would be nugatory. That it excludes the choice of means, and leaves to Congress in each case that only which is most direct and simple. Is it true that this is the sense in which the word "necessary" is always used? Does it always import an absolute physical necessity so strong that one thing to which another may be termed necessary cannot exist without the other? We think it does not. If reference be had to its use in the common affairs of the world or in approved

authors, we find that it frequently imports no more than that one thing is convenient, or useful, or essential to another. To employ the means necessary to an end is generally understood as employing the means calculated to produce the end, and not as being confined to those single means without which the end would be entirely unattainable. Such is the character of human language that no word conveys to the mind in all situations one single definite idea, and nothing is more common than to use words in a figurative sense. ... The word "necessary" is of this description. It has not a fixed character peculiar to itself. It admits to all degrees of comparison, and is often connected with other words which increase or diminish the impression the mind receives of the urgency it imports. A thing may be necessary, very necessary, absolutely or indispensably necessary.[5]

In the context of the *McCulloch* case, Chief Justice Marshall determined that since Congress had the authority to coin and borrow money and to lay and collect taxes under the Constitution, Congress could therefore create a national banking system in order to manage the people's money. Although the word "bank" does not appear in the enumerated powers of Congress in Article I, Section 8, Congress had the authority to create a national bank under its implied powers granted to it by the framers of the Constitution under the necessary and proper clause.[6]

Although the Constitution that the framers wrote in 1787 is still in effect, it has obviously changed in some ways, particularly through the inclusion of amendments. But perceptions about the proper role of the national government in people's daily lives have also evolved since the late eighteenth century. The national government is much larger today than during the presidency of George Washington not only in size but in the scope of its activities as well. Simply put, the America of yesteryear has vanished, and the level of policymaking and regulatory activity at the national level of government is reflective of the demographic, societal, cultural, political, economic, and social changes that have occurred throughout American history.

THE EVOLUTION OF FEDERALISM IN THE UNITED STATES

As the bicentennial of the drafting of the U.S. Constitution was approaching in 1987, many scholars had renewed interest in a vital constitutional debate—federalism.[7] The extent to which national power supersedes state sovereignty, or whether the doctrine of states' rights should be preserved, has a well-documented history during the

time period between 1620 (the Mayflower Compact) and the ratification and ensuing implementation of the federal Constitution (1789),
debates over the meaning of the Tenth Amendment (1791–1835), disputes over states' rights in the antebellum period and during the Civil
War (1828–1865), changes involving states' rights and federalism from
the Civil War to the New Deal (1865–1940), and states' rights and
American federalism after the New Deal (1940 to the present).[8] Yet
one person is acknowledged perhaps more than any other with regard
to the forging of American federalism, James Madison.[9]

James Madison

In a letter written to George Washington on April 16, 1787 (the
Philadelphia Convention would commence in May 1787), Madison
shared his vision of federalism with General Washington: "Conceiving
that an individual independence of the States is utterly irreconcilable
with their aggregate sovereignty, and that a consolidation of the whole
into one simple republic would be as expedient as it is unattainable,
I have sought for middle ground, which may at once support a due
supremacy of the national authority, and not exclude the local authorities wherever they can be subordinately useful."[10] When Madison
wrote this letter to his esteemed friend and colleague, he knew that
the states had been historically entrenched in America's colonization
and history. Dissolving state boundaries with the intent of creating
one large republic was not politically possible at that time and is still
not to this day. Madison was a political pragmatist; he respected state
boundaries but sought to create a federal republic in the upcoming
Philadelphia Convention. Obviously, he was very successful in this
endeavor.

Later, during the debate over ratification of the Constitution,
Madison participated in the drafting of *The Federalist*.[11] He was assisted
in this project by Alexander Hamilton and John Jay. *The Federalist* was literally a series of 85 essays explaining why the Constitution should be
ratified in the state of New York. All essays were addressed "To the
People of the State of New York."[12] All of them were published anonymously at the time under the pseudonym "Publius." The authors of
these essays chose the name Publius because it was the first name of
an important supporter of the Roman republic, Publius Valerius
Publicola.[13] As Gregory Maggs indicated,

Why the authors thought that signing their own names would have less
political advantage than using a pseudonym remains unclear. Perhaps
Hamilton and Madison felt that praising a Constitution that they had
helped to write would appear immodest. Maybe they wanted to make
arguments that they later could distance themselves from. They might
have wanted to avoid accusations that they were violating the confiden-
tiality of the Constitutional Convention. Or they could have decided
that their group should use just one name to cover the work of all three
authors. But whatever their reason, their use of a pseudonym probably
did not stand out as unusual; political writers of the time commonly
used pseudonyms in essays published in newspapers.[14]

The essays were designed to promote the Madisonian cause of
republicanism, or a representative democracy, to replace the confed-
eral form of government under the Articles of Confederation.

The Federalist began appearing in New York City newspapers
during the fall of 1787 and the spring of 1788. The nationalists at the
time (Madison, Hamilton, and Jay) made the political calculation that
New York would be the pivotal state in the ratification debate. Under
the Constitution, 9 of the 13 states needed to ratify the document for
it to become the new supreme law in the United States. This rationale
was intuitive given the context of America in 1787. New York was a
populous state geographically in the middle of the proposed republic.
New York City had already become the most important commercial
center in the country. In short, New York would have to be included
in the new union for it to succeed.[15] Over time, *The Federalist* became
known as *The Federalist Papers*, though it is important to note that the
original authors of the essays did not refer to the collection in this
manner.[16]

Madison penned *The Federalist* No. 46. In it, he delineated his vision
of American federalism:

I proceed to inquire whether the federal government or the State governments will have the advantage with regard to the predilection and
support of the people. Notwithstanding the different modes in which
they are appointed, we must consider both of them as substantially
dependent on the great body of citizens of the United States. I assume
this position here as it respects the first, reserving the proofs for another
place. The federal and State governments are in fact different agents and
trustees of the people, constituted with different powers, and designed
for different purposes. The adversaries of the Constitution seem to have
lost sight of the people altogether in their reasonings on this subject; and

to have viewed these different establishments, not only as mutual rivals and enemies, but as uncontrolled by any common superior in their efforts to usurp the authorities of each other. These gentlemen must here be reminded of their error. They must be told that the ultimate authority, wherever the derivative may be found, resides in the people alone, and that it will not depend merely on the comparative ambition or address of the different governments, whether either, or which of them, will be able to enlarge its sphere of jurisdiction at the expense of the other.[17]

The Articles of Confederation failed because insufficient authority was assigned to the national government. Instead of having a sovereign nation-state, the 13 states that existed at the time operated as separate countries and pursued policies that promoted their own self-interest, often to the detriment of peer citizens in the other states. Thus, Madison understood that the only way that democracy could succeed in America was contingent on the assignment of more substantive powers and authority to the national government.

As Duane Lockard explained in the late 1960s,

The work of forming a federal system was far from over when the Constitution was ratified. Indeed it was only a beginning. As mentioned previously, the Constitution was vague in many respects and only time and trial would tell what pattern of federal relationships would emerge. Men who agreed in the Convention on what the Constitution meant became bitter antagonists as they fought over the application of the Constitution in practice. Madison and Hamilton were both strong nationalists in the Convention and shared in the writing of *The Federalist* in support of its ratification. Hamilton remained a strong nationalist while Madison shifted to a states-rights position. Unhappy with the Adams administration's use of national power, Madison became a leader of the anti-Federalist party which took a strong states-rights position.[18]

The sheer reality of federalist systems is that there is omnipresent tension between the national and subnational levels of government. This situation has occurred since the Constitution and the new federal republic were put into effect in 1789. During the first few decades of the republic, this tension between competing views of federalism existed between the Federalist Party and the Democratic-Republican Party. America had no political parties when the Constitution was written. By 1800, however, Hamilton and Thomas Jefferson, two prominent members of President George Washington's cabinet, were instrumental in the creation of these two parties.[19] The Hamiltonians (Federalists) believed in a strong national government and a broad interpretation of the Constitution. The Jeffersonians (Democratic-Republicans) embraced the states' rights philosophy and a strict interpretation of the Constitution.

It is important to note, however, that Washington was the only U.S. president without a political party affiliation. He had great disdain for parties and warned Americans against their evil effects in his farewell address in September 1786 (his term expired on March 4, 1797, and he decided to retire, thereby establishing the precedent of serving two terms as president):

> There is an opinion that parties in free countries are useful checks upon the administration of the government and serve to keep alive the spirit of liberty. This within certain limits is probably true; and in governments of a monarchical cast, patriotism may look with indulgence, if not with favor, upon the spirit of party. But in those of the popular character, in governments purely elective, it is a spirit not to be encouraged. From their natural tendency, it is certain there will always be enough of that spirit for every salutary purpose. And there being constant danger of excess, the effort ought to be by force of public opinion, to mitigate and assuage it. A fire not to be quenched, it demands a uniform vigilance to prevent its bursting into a flame, lest, instead of warming, it should consume.[20]

Washington's successor in 1797 was Vice President John Adams, an avowed Federalist. The first president's warning would go unheeded by those who followed him.

The Doctrine of Dual Federalism

Shortly after John Marshall's death, a new theory became prominent in the evolution of American federalism. This theory was first associated with Chief Justice Marshall's successor, Roger Taney.[21] The basic premise of dual federalism is that the states and the national government are coequal levels of government under the Constitution. Under this belief system, the structure of government was akin to a layer cake, where state governments maintain their spheres of public policymaking under an interpretation of the Tenth Amendment and national officials focus exclusively on the enumerated powers of Congress in particular and leave just about all other matters to state officials. The different layers of government in this metaphor are separated by frosting, meaning that they do not interact, nor do they work together when addressing public policy challenges. This was perceived by many to be a plausible and desirable approach toward public policymaking at the time.

Chief Justice Taney articulated his vision of federalism in the *License Cases* in 1847.[22] The cases emanated from Massachusetts, New Hampshire, and Rhode Island and involved antiliquor regulations passed in these states. The merchants in particular determined that only Congress could regulate commerce under the Constitution. Taney and his colleagues did not concur, maintaining that states may regulate their own internal affairs as long as state officials did not ban the importation of liquor:

> It is equally clear that the power of Congress over this subject does not extend further than the regulation of commerce with foreign nations and among the several states, and that beyond these limits the states have never surrendered their power over trade and commerce, and may still exercise it free from any controlling power on the part of the general government. Every state, therefore, may regulate its own internal traffic, according to its own judgment and upon its own views of the interest and wellbeing of its citizens.[23]

It would be his views in another case, however, that would make Taney infamous in historical terms.

In *Dred Scott v. Sandford*, Taney wrote the opinion of the Court in a 7–2 decision. The other eight justices wrote separate opinions. Dred Scott, a Missouri slave, sued for his freedom. He argued that he had previously lived in Illinois, a free state, and Wisconsin, a free territory, so that entitled him to be absolved of his slave status. In a strong proslavery decision, the Court's majority determined that Dred Scott lacked standing to sue in federal court because he was the property of his owner and not a human being under the law. Furthermore, the justices determined that the Missouri Compromise of 1820 was unconstitutional because under the Constitution, Congress lacked the authority to determine whether states or territories could abolish slavery within their borders.[24] The *Dred Scott* decision was the first time since *Marbury v. Madison* (1803) that the Supreme Court justices declared an act of Congress unconstitutional.[25] In its decision, the justices determined to solve the slavery debate and cease internal strife in the United States. The Court's majority was not successful in this objective and instead intensified the divide between North and South and made the Civil War all but inevitable.

Marshall was a key intellectual leader to those who believed in nation-centered federalism. Federalists embraced this philosophy based, in part, on their belief that a stable and prosperous democracy could be achieved only with the assignment of sufficient authority to Congress.[26] Taney believed in state-centered federalism, but by this time in history the Democratic-Republican Party dissolved and a new party emerged, Andrew Jackson's Democratic Party. The Federalist Party also ended, and the Whig Party was formed. Horace Mann was one of its adherents. As Richard Leach noted over 40 years ago,

> In one sense, the Civil War was fought between the proponents of nation-centered and state-centered federalism. With the victory of the North, it might be assumed that the nationalist concept became the dominant and unchallenged interpretation of federalism in the United States. In fact, this was not the case. Even before the war, the Taney Court had begun to develop the concept of dual federalism, which the Supreme Court after the war embellished and utilized well into the twentieth century; and it gained adherents outside the bar and the judiciary as the corporation, which sought freedom from the restraints of both national and state government, came fully into its own. Proponents of dual federalism profess to believe that the Constitution created a governmental system with "collateral political spheres." ... The national and state governments form two separate centers of power, from each of which the other is barred and between which is something like a jurisdictional no-man's land, into which both are barred from entering.[27]

In terms of federalism, the Union's victory in the Civil War provided clarity regarding two issues in federalism. In December 1828, John C. Calhoun, the vice president of the United States at the time, anonymously authored *Exposition and Protest* and gave it to a committee in the South Carolina House of Representatives. Although the house did not adopt this resolution, copies were printed and circulated throughout the state. In this resolution, Vice President Calhoun articulated his belief in the doctrine of nullification and argued that states had the authority under the Constitution to nullify federal laws within their own borders. He was protesting a tariff passed by Congress that raised the price of manufactured American goods. This tariff helped manufacturers in the North but hurt citizens in the South, who did not produce a lot of their goods. British manufacturers were also hurt by the tariff, thus making it difficult for them to purchase southern cotton.[28] President Abraham Lincoln's steadfast leadership during the Civil War rejected not only the nullification doctrine but also the premise that states could secede from the Union without the approval of Congress.

Vice President Calhoun's nullification idea was nothing new in America at the time. In a collaborative effort in the late eighteenth century, Madison and Jefferson presented the same basic argument in the Virginia Resolution (1798) and the Kentucky Resolution (1799). These two future presidents at this time believed that since the national government was created by a compact of the states, all powers not expressly granted to Congress were retained by the individual states or by the people. Thus, state legislatures reserved the right to determine the constitutionality of federal legislation. These two famous Americans opposed the Federalist Alien and Sedition Acts.[29] In the Virginia Resolution, Madison and Jefferson declared,

> That the good people of this commonwealth, having ever felt, and continuing to feel, the most sincere affection for their brethren of the other states; the truest anxiety for establishing and perpetuating the union of all; and the most scrupulous fidelity to that constitution, which is the pledge of mutual friendship, and the instrument of mutual happiness; the General Assembly doth solemnly appeal to the like dispositions of the other states, in confidence that they will concur with this commonwealth in declaring, as it does hereby declare, that the acts aforesaid, are unconstitutional; and that the necessary and proper measures will be taken by each, for co-operating with this state, in maintaining the Authorities, Rights, and Liberties, referred to the States respectively, or to the people.[30]

Like Calhoun, Jefferson was the vice president of the United States at the time he drafted this statement. Almost a year later in Kentucky, Madison and Jefferson determined

> that the several states who formed that instrument, being sovereign and independent, have the unquestionable right to judge of its infraction; and that a nullification, by these sovereignties, of all unauthorized acts done under colour of that instrument, is the rightful remedy: That this commonwealth does upon the most deliberate reconsideration declare, that the said alien and sedition laws, are in their opinion, palpable violations of the said constitution; and however cheerfully it may be disposed to surrender its opinion to a majority of its sister states in matters of ordinary or doubtful policy; yet, in momentous regulations like the present, which so vitally wound the best rights of the citizen, it would consider a silent acquiescence as highly criminal: That although this commonwealth

as a party to the federal compact; will bow to the laws of the Union, yet it does at the same time declare, that it will not now, nor ever hereafter, cease to oppose in a constitutional manner, every attempt from what quarter soever offered, to violate that compact.[31]

These Madisonian and Jeffersonian ideas of federalism would be utilized to justify southern secession following Lincoln's victory in the 1860 presidential election. Thus, whereas nullification and secession were disregarded by most as reasonable options following the Civil War, the doctrine of dual federalism remained intact after 1865.

Edward Corwin was the first person to use the term "dual federalism" to describe the American federal system.[32] In 1934, the year after Franklin Roosevelt assumed the presidency during the Great Depression, Corwin offered this analysis of American federalism:

> From the *Federalist* itself issue the first beginnings of two divergent theories of national power, the contributions of Hamilton and Madison, respectively. By the Hamiltonian theory, the national government, although a government of enumerated powers, is within the range of these powers a truly sovereign government, and so is under no constitutional compulsion, either in the selection of means whereby to make its powers effective or in the selection of objects to be attained by their exercise, to take account of the coexistence of the states or to concern itself to preserve any particular relationship of power between itself and the states. And this also was the theory of the men who "put across" the Constitution and who set the national government going. Also it is the theory which underlies Chief Justice Marshall's famous decisions. For all that, the outlook embodied in the theory was not that of the great mass of the American people either in 1789 or even three quarters of a century later. Their experience was local, their immediate interest local, and through Jefferson and Madison this localistic outlook found expression in a far different version of the Constitution, one which treated it as resulting primarily from a compact among the states and which required that its interpretation be directed to the preservation in the states of their accustomed powers and to the maintenance of that greatest of constitutional contrivances, dual federalism. And in fact the constitutional jurisprudence of the Court conformed largely to these objectives for a full half century succeeding Marshall's death, save as it made accommodation for the more evident lessons of the Civil War.[33]

It is important to note that dual federalism was a theory that was perceived to be plausible by Hamiltonians and Madisonians alike but for different reasons. Daniel Elazar explained this historical reality succinctly:

This concept of demarcation became the key to the entire concept of dual federalism. Dualism came to mean separation between the various levels of government in their dealings with governmental problems. Each level had, according to this theory, its own particular responsibilities, which were generally its exclusive province. While this theory was most often espoused by those advocating states' rights, nationalists also maintained its basic validity. Thus, Madison could demand that the federal government confine itself to its limited, enumerated powers, and leave the rest to the states; and Hamilton could demand that the states refrain from usurping those powers which his broad construction of the Constitution allotted to the federal government. In this way dualism and demarcation were inseparably linked in American federalist theory throughout the nineteenth century, though, in reality, a system of shared activities was developing that embodied its own type of dualism in which co-operation between governments, not demarcation of spheres of action, was the key.[34]

Although Corwin coined the term "dual federalism," many changes were occurring in the United States in the early decades of the twentieth century that affected the relationship between the national and state governments. The United States underwent rapid industrialization and became a prominent economic power, and the size and scope of the national government increased accordingly.[35] The doctrine of dual federalism was no longer an accurate description for federalism in America. Its fate was seemingly determined with the unraveling of some dramatic events in U.S. history, such as the Great Depression, the New Deal policies of President Roosevelt, and the changing global status of the United States following the end of World War II.

The Emergence of Cooperative Federalism

Corwin published a pivotal essay in 1950 titled "The Passing of Dual Federalism."[36] In it, he described how federalism had fundamentally changed in the United States:

Within the generation now drawing to a close this nation has been subjected to the impact of a series of events and ideological forces of a very imperative nature. We have fought two world wars, the second of which answered every definition of "total war," and have submitted to the regimentation which these great national efforts entailed. We have passed through an economic crisis which was described by the late President as "a crisis greater than war." We have become the exclusive custodian of technology's crowning gift to civilization, an invention capable of blowing it to smithereens, and we greatly hope to retain that honorable trusteeship throughout an indefinite future. Meantime we have elected ourselves the head and forefront of one of two combinations of nations which together embrace a great part of the Western World and in this capacity are at present involved in a "cold war" with the head of the opposing combination; and as one phase of this curious and baffling struggle we find ourselves driven to combat at obvious risk to certain heretofore cherished constitutional values, the menace of a hidden propaganda which is intended by its agents to work impairment of the national fiber against the time when the "cold war" may eventuate in a "shooting war." Lastly, though by no means least, the most wide-spread and powerfully organized political interest in the country, that of organized labor, has come to accept unreservedly a new and revolutionary conception of the role of government. Formerly we generally thought of government as primarily a policeman, with an amiable penchant for being especially helpful to those who knew how to help themselves. By the ideological revolution just alluded to, which stems from the Great Depression and the New Deal, it becomes the duty of government to guarantee economic security to all as the indispensable foundation of constitutional liberty. ... In general terms, our system has lost resiliency and what was once vaunted as a Constitution of Rights, both State and private, has been replaced by a Constitution of Powers. More specifically, the Federal System has shifted base in the direction of a consolidated national power, while within the National Government itself an increased flow of power in the direction of the President has ensued.[37]

A new conception of federalism had emerged in the mid-twentieth century in the United States. Morton Grodzins provided a new cake metaphor to describe American federalism, the marble cake:

> The American form of government is often, but erroneously, symbolized by a three-layer cake. A far more accurate image is the rainbow or marble cake, characterized by an inseparable mingling of differently colored ingredients, the colors appearing in vertical and diagonal strands and unexpected whirls. As colors are mixed in the marble cake, so functions are mixed in the American federal system.[38]

Dual federalism, or the layer cake metaphor, had become extinct. Now, cooperative federalism, or the marble cake metaphor, most accurately depicted the state of federalism in America.[39] Government officials at all three levels of government work together and intermingle for a common purpose; within the spirit of cooperation between and among the different levels of government, there is a clear comprehension that the national government is supreme over the state and local governments.[40]

Beyond Cooperative Federalism or Not?

There are a plethora of scholarly accounts regarding the evolution of American federalism since the 1960s.[41] Whatever theoretical approach one may find more tenable than another, it is important to remember Nelson Rockefeller's words in 1962:

> The truth, in short, is that the federal idea—like the whole American experience—is a political adventure. It is no static thing, no dead definition, no dogmatic proclamation. Old as it is in our history, its secret strength is that it forever summons a free people to learn and try the new. It requires us, I believe, to imitate its authors in only one respect: to be, like them, unchained to the past and unfearful of the future, to be—in our time as they were in theirs—political pioneers.[42]

This further reinforces the notion that federalism is a challenging concept to grasp, as it is premised on an idea that often juxtaposes people's basic philosophy about government and its proper roles with more pragmatic day-to-day governance issues.

Some contend that in the 1960s, cooperative federalism gave way to a new approach to federalism utilized by President Lyndon Johnson during the Great Society era commonly known as creative federalism.[43] In his attempt to declare war on poverty, Johnson and Congress provided states with financial assistance, particularly through categorical grants, in order to provide social services to citizens in need. Ironically, it was then Governor Rockefeller who was credited with coining the phrase during the Godkin Lectures at Harvard University in 1962.[44] As David Walker noted about the Johnson administration:

> Creative federalism ... moved beyond the federal efforts in traditionally aided program areas (largely certain state functions) into new state efforts, a range of novel and familiar local services, as well as activities previously provided by the private sector. Many, though not all, of these new grant programs reflected an attempt to move state and local governments into new fields in light of what was deemed a national need. National purpose, of course, had always been a rationale for launching grants, but with Johnson's Creative Federalism it extended to so many

new areas—in economic and regional development, transportation (especially urban mass transit), community development and housing (notably water and sewer facilities and model cities), dozens of education and manpower programs, health (particularly mental health, health services delivery, manpower, and medical assistance), and income security (with Medicaid, child nutrition, special milk and food stamps predominating) that the concept bore little relationship to the one that had been applied previously.[45]

During the context of the time period, Johnson and his political allies clearly viewed the federal government in terms of federalism as a proactive entity that could help alleviate many of the policy challenges at the state and local levels of government.

President Richard Nixon had a different approach to federalism when he assumed the presidency following his narrow victory in the 1968 presidential election.[46] According to Walker,

> With Nixon's New Federalism, a reaction set in to many of the thrusts of Creative Federalism. It was ostensibly anticentralization, anticategorical, and anti-administrative confusion. In positive terms, it supported: greater decentralization within the federal departments to their field units; a devolution of more power and greater discretion to recipient units; a streamlining of the service delivery system generally; a definite preferring of general governments and their elected officials; and some sorting out of some servicing responsibilities by governmental levels. Moreover, there was some relationship between the theory and practice of the New Federalism, though less than was the case with Creative Federalism.[47]

Based on his conservative political philosophy, Nixon believed in devolving some political authority from the national to the subnational levels of government. The Nixon administration's approach to devolution often took the form of general revenue sharing, where state and local officials were afforded greater levels of discretion in terms of how they allocated funds appropriated by the national government.[48] When Nixon left office, many scholars and practitioners believed that the use of categorical grants at the national level would greatly curtail and that the shift toward revenue sharing would accelerate.[49] This did not occur to any significant extent during the administrations of Gerald Ford and Jimmy Carter.[50]

President Ronald Reagan's vision of federalism was similar to that of the Nixon White House. As Timothy Conlan has noted,

When Ronald Reagan entered the White House, he and his entourage of close aides brought with them a radical intergovernmental agenda cloaked in continuities from the past. In the realm of intergovernmental spending, for example, Reagan's budgets did not mark an absolute reversal of past policies; rather, they rapidly accelerated the downward trends in the growth and relative significance of federal aid that had begun during the Carter administration. With respect to policy instruments, Reagan relied even more heavily than Nixon on block grants to promote his New Federalism. These continuities, however, disguised fundamental differences with the first New Federalism as well as the Great Society. That Reagan's budgets should conduct a frontal assault on the programmatic heritage of Lyndon Johnson should come as no surprise. Reagan's hostility to programs like community action services went back to his days as governor of California. The extent of his attack was less predictable, however, particularly for state and local governments and their associations in Washington. At the core of the Great Society was the service strategy, which the Reagan administration frowned upon in virtually all respects. Both the traditionalist and libertarian factions of modern conservatism opposed the service strategy because they believed it drained public resources and sponsored dependency on government by establishing elite cadres of social engineers who reject traditional social values. The greatest impact of the administration's numerous initiatives to reverse or eliminate such policies was felt by state and local governments. With their large educational and social service bureaucracies, state and local governments had become the foot soldiers of the service strategy. They suffered accordingly when federal grants for education, training, and social services were reduced between 1980 and 1985 by as much as 33 percent, which is far in excess of the cuts incurred by all federal aid or domestic spending in those years.[51]

Yet it is important to note a couple of things. For most presidents, reforming federalism, ultimately, is not a high priority. Presidents typically focus on major public policy issues, such as the domestic economy, foreign affairs, and national security. Perhaps in a pragmatic way, presidential candidates and incumbent presidents seeking a second term do not make reforming intergovernmental relations a high priority because they know that past efforts have generally met with incremental success at best and because they know that this is not that important to the general public. Presidents who followed Reagan have not dramatically changed the nature of federalism, either.[52] Yet in the context of the post–New Deal time period, it is still important to consider Walker's basic premise about federalism in the last 50 years:

All of the dominant theories of federalism of these years were enunciated by or derived from the actions of leaders in the government's political branches (chiefly at the national level). They constitute a variation, but only a variation, on the cooperative federal theme. Despite their many differences in emphases, methods, and goals, the Creative Federalism of Lyndon B. Johnson, the "New Federalism" of Richard M. Nixon, the Congressional Federalism of the nation's legislature in the seventies, and the "New Partnership" of Jimmy Carter must be considered as subspecies of the generic cooperative federal concept. All of them were functional theories that stressed governmental activism as well as intergovernmental collaboration, "sharing," and intricate inter-level linkages. Even the "picket-fence" and related operational concepts of the system that emerge from surveys of federal administrators indicate no real departure from these norms, but only other perspectives and approaches toward achieving them.[53]

The reality about the modern era is that the size and scope of the national government has increased. This has been true whether or not a Democrat or a Republican has served as president and whether or not one party has had a numeric majority in one or both chambers of Congress. While it is clear that the doctrine of dual federalism has been extinct for over 80 years, approaches to federalism over the last 50 years have varied somewhat, depending on the outcomes of federal elections. Different philosophical inclinations regarding federalist relations on the part of powerful politicians have nevertheless existed during a time when cooperative federalism has been the dominant paradigm in American society.

THE WHIG PARTY OF THE NINETEENTH CENTURY

The Whig Party leaders fielded presidential candidates from 1836 to 1856. Following the reelection of the Democratic president Andrew Jackson in 1832, the Whigs formally organized and become the primary opposition to the Jacksonian Democrats. In 1836, Democratic candidate Martin Van Buren defeated three Whig candidates (William H. Harrison, Hugh White, and Daniel Webster).[54] Four years later, Harrison defeated President Van Buren in a rematch. In this election, the Whigs were unified behind one candidate.[55] In 1844, the Whigs nominated Henry Clay, but he lost to the Democratic nominee, James K. Polk.[56] Zachary Taylor was the last Whig to be elected president of the United States (1848). He defeated Lewis Cass, the Democratic candidate.[57] In 1852, the Democratic candidate, Franklin Pierce, defeated the Whig nominee, Winfield Scott.[58] The last Whig nominee for president in history (1856), Millard Fillmore, lost to his Democratic opponent, James Buchanan.[59] Thus, four Whigs served as president in American history: William Henry Harrison (1841), John Tyler (1841–1845), Zachary Taylor (1849–1850), and Millard Fillmore (1850–1853). Presidents Tyler and Fillmore assumed the presidency during their respective eras because the elected president in each case died before the end of his term, and both were serving as vice president at the time.[60]

The Whigs organized as a reaction to the authoritarian policies of Andrew Jackson. Critics called him "King Andrew" during this time period. They opposed his policies regarding the Bank of the United States, Native Americans, the Supreme Court, and his use of presidential war powers.[61] In many ways, the Whigs were descendants of the old Federalist Party.[62] They believed that the national government and its officials could create more effective public policies to promote the greater public good. Horace Mann was a Whig originally, and he very much embraced the Whig philosophy of federalism. Mark Groen indicated as much when he noted that "the question of how Whig policies affected the early development of common schools has received little examination in either political or educational histories. There is evidence, however, that Whig party politics did influence early educational reformers."[63] This was particularly true in the case of Mann.[64]

Groen believes that Mann is the most famous of the early common school reformers in the nineteenth century.[65] He contrasted Mann's beliefs with those of his Democratic rivals:

> As a Whig, Mann believed that government had a role to play in providing "internal improvements" as government aided economic development projects were then called. While both Whigs and Democrats perceived that the emerging capitalist social order required a disciplined and literate population, and common schools supported those ends, they differed over the role of government in implementing that policy. Democrats supported free trade and a laissez-faire approach to civic institutions, such as schools. Democrats preferred to leave such concerns to local communities. Whigs embraced a more centralized approach to social policy. As a Whig, Mann endorsed not only a state board of education but also sought legislation creating "a Department of Public Instruction in the National Government."[66]

Ironically, Mann's vision of federalism is similar to today's Democratic Party in this sense. While the adherents of both the contemporary

Republican and Democratic parties advocate state and local control of public schools, Democrats are generally more amenable to utilizing the national government to advance educational objectives, and Republicans are typically resistant to the concept and practice.

In 1848, the Whigs nominated Mann for Congress from the eighth district in Massachusetts. He won easily with over 80 percent of the vote. He succeeded John Quincy Adams. In an expedient manner, he became one of the most outspoken opponents of slavery. His steadfast position on the issue caused opposition within his own party from southern Whigs and from compromise Whigs in New England.[67] As Michael Holt described,

> He had infuriated Southerners by his repeated tirades against slavery and slaveholding as sinful. Applauding this record, the district's Free Soilers nominated Mann as their own candidate in 1850. The question was whether its Whigs would also renominate him. To do so would signal their contempt for Webster, the Fillmore administration, the South, and the Compromise. Anti-Webster Whigs on the state committee and in Boston urged Whigs to choose Mann to keep the seat in Whig hands. The district's Websterites, insisting on a pro-Compromise administration loyalist, surprisingly secured the nomination of Samuel Walley instead.[68]

Mann was reelected to his seat in the U.S. House of Representatives as a member of the Free Soil Party with the support of anti-Webster Whigs. Two years later, he was nominated to be governor of the Commonwealth of Massachusetts by the Free Soil Party. As George Hubbell described the situation over a century ago,

> In 1852 Mr. Mann was nominated by the Free-soil Party for Governor of Massachusetts. There was great interest in the Free-soil movement, but it was yet in the early stages and there was no hope of any immediate success. Men looked to the future for the achievement of great political triumphs, but there was no triumph for freedom in that hour. The slow drag of practical politics was wearing on Mr. Mann's spirit; the state was not ripe for the development of his work, and the hour of human liberty must still wait. Always devoted to those fields where philanthropy and benevolence could have full scope, and mightily biased toward the work of education by his efforts for twelve years as its advocate in Massachusetts, it was the most natural thing in the world for him to turn again in that direction.[69]

John Henry Clifford (Whig) won the governor's race in Massachusetts, and the Democratic candidate, Henry W. Bishop, was the runner-up in the election. Mann finished in third place. As Hubbell indicated, he would return to the education arena following his political defeat and accepted the presidency of Antioch College in 1853.[70] More discussion about Mann's time at Antioch will ensue.

Groen provides a concise summary about the state of American politics in the 1850s:

> The 1850s were a time of rapid expansion for schools and a time of political tumult over slavery. The decade saw the rise of sectionalism, North against South, the rise of new political parties; Know-nothings, Free-Soilers, and finally Republicans, as well as, the demise of the Whig party. During this same period, the common school became an institution in nearly every northern town. It may seem odd that common schools should emerge as a sectional issue, yet here too Horace Mann played a leading role. Common schooling, as Mann noted, tended to be inimical to slavery. Pro-slavery Southerners meanwhile, referred to "that peculiar system of free schools in New England." . . . By 1850, most of the early Whig school reformers, such as [Henry] Barnard and Mann, and later champions of schooling such as George Hoar, Henry Wilson, and Charles Sumner had already begun a political journey through the Free Soil Party toward anti-slavery. Yet, the statewide systems of free common schools remain perhaps the Whig's most enduring legacy.[71]

While the Whig Party has been extinct for over 150 years, the idea of common schooling still exists. It is a powerful idea and premise that has withstood the passage of time, even though most Americans know little of either the nineteenth century Whigs or Mann today. What a remarkable accomplishment, indeed. Perhaps reforming public education in America requires an examination of its own history as a basic starting point. In other words, citizens and policymakers should at least have sufficient curiosity to reflect back on the history and evolution of common schools before the continuance of programs and policies that will certainly have the effect of dismantling them altogether.

Mann and the Whigs had a vision that state and local governments could create a public good, the common school, in order to create a more perfect union. Because it was important to them and because education involves all aspects of society, common school philosophers believed that government intervention, when it came to educating children, was both prudent and justified. Since we all benefit from a more educated populace, we all contribute to schooling through taxation. The basic idea is communitarian in nature.

Since Mann's time, the size and scope of the federal government has changed. The America of the early twenty-first century has obviously changed substantially since Mann died in 1859. Nuances of federalism have changed. The fact that federal officials are more prominent participants in K–12 public education policy today than at that time, however, does not mitigate the importance of the common school philosophy. The educator Joy Elmer Morgan offered this observation in 1936:

> FAITH in the common man and a determination to give him equality of opportunity is America's unique contribution to history. This desire has been called the American Dream. Because of our efforts at equality of opportunity our country has developed faster and farther than any other in all history. The major factor in this development has been the common school, the living embodiment of the spirit that made us a nation, the very symbol of our freedom. The school has awakened aspiration, established ideals, trained skills, and formed character. It is of the people, by the people, and for the people. The contribution of Horace Mann in establishing the schools was so fundamental that he is known as the Father of the American Public School. Colonel F. W. Parker, himself one of the major prophets of American education, held a firm conviction that Horace Mann ranks with Washington and Lincoln as one of the greatest builders of the nation. "Washington and Lincoln," he wrote, "represent the highest types of heroism, patriotism, and wisdom in great crises of republic-building; Horace Mann, the quiet inner building, the soul development of the nation."[72]

Since the era of dual federalism is over, it is important to trace the extent to which federal officials have shaped K–12 public education. While public education is still perceived to be primarily a state and local issue by many to this day and the funding of public schools is reflective of this reality, to what extent, if any, can representatives of the national government contribute to the enterprise of educating America's youth? A brief historical overview may prove illuminating.

NATIONAL INTERVENTION IN K–12 PUBLIC EDUCATION

During the 2011–2012 school year, 87.7 percent of the total funding of public education at the elementary and secondary levels came from state and local governments and private sources. The remaining 12.3 percent came from the federal government.[73] In 1990–1991, the federal share of K–12 was 5.7 percent, and by 2004–2005, it was

8.3 percent. State and local governments have been the primary sources of K–12 education funding and always have been, even though the federal share has increased very incrementally over the last 20 years.[74] Yet there has been federal involvement in public education throughout American history, even before the Constitution was ratified and initially implemented in 1789.

According to researchers at the Center on Education Policy, federal officials have become involved in education for four primary reasons: to promote democracy, to ensure equality of educational opportunity, to enhance national productivity, and to strengthen national defense.[75] Democratic systems require a well-educated and proactive citizenry in order to flourish. Educated citizens are inclined to acquire civic values, civic virtue, and a sense of common national identity. To Mann, the common school experience would create the conditions for less social strife and conflict and enhance the likelihood of greater citizen compassion for one another.[76] Since the members of the Confederate Congress created the Northwest Ordinance of 1787, federal law was created even before the Constitution was ratified in order to encourage the creation of public schools.[77] Since the publication of *A Nation at Risk*, federal legislators have attempted to assist state and local officials at increasing student achievement.[78] This objective was highly emphasized during the lengthy struggle that led to the passage of the Goals 2000: Educate America Act.[79] Enhancing student achievement was also an objective of the much-debated No Child Left Behind (NCLB), Act, though more discussion on this matter is forthcoming.[80]

Providing equal educational opportunities was a significant emphasis on the part of many federal officials during the civil rights movement of the 1950s and 1960s. In some cases, federal intervention was initiated by members of Congress, by actions taken within the executive branch, or by federal judges through court cases. The landmark achievement during this time period was ending segregation in the public schools through *Brown v. Board of Education of Topeka, Kansas* in 1954. Laws and policies that promoted the racial segregation of children in the public schools were declared unconstitutional by the justices on the Supreme Court.[81]

Later, as part of his strategy to declare war on poverty, President Lyndon Johnson persuaded his colleagues in Congress to pass a major bill in education policy in American history, the Elementary and Secondary Education Act (ESEA) of 1965.[82] Members of Congress believed in the 1960s that the federal government could assist state and local policymakers by providing assistance to low-income families in order to enhance public education.[83]

Around the time when Mann was alive, federal officials began to take actions that were designed to prepare citizens for the workforce and to expand their opportunities beyond senior high school. When state leaders began to establish public colleges and universities, their colleagues at the national level passed the Morrill Act in 1862.[84] Grants of federal land were made available to the states in order to establish "land-grant colleges" offering agricultural and engineering courses. Many institutions benefited from this new law, including Cornell University, Pennsylvania State University, Purdue University, the University of California, and the Massachusetts Institute of Technology.[85]

In the early twentieth century, many leaders in the United States concluded that the nation lacked skilled workers to fill new jobs in the manufacturing sector in particular. As a result, federal funds were appropriated through a series of measures to assist state and local officials in the creation of vocational education. In addition, federal programs were created to expand access to higher education.[86] The most recognizable program in question was the Servicemen's Readjustment Act of 1944, otherwise known as the G.I. Bill. [87] Another important federal initiative was passed by Congress and signed by President Lyndon Johnson during the Great Society years, the Higher Education Act of 1965.[88] Later, when the Higher Education Act was reauthorized in 1972, Basic Educational Opportunity Grants were established and were later renamed Pell Grants after Senator Claiborne Pell (D–RI), who was a leading advocate for providing students from indigent backgrounds with financial assistance so that they could pursue opportunities in higher education.[89]

With regard to the strengthening of national defense, federal officials have attempted to improve national defense strategies for decades. In 1957, the Soviets launched the satellite *Sputnik*. A year later, members of Congress responded by passing the National Defense Education Act (NDEA).[90] During the Cold War, national officials in the United States wanted to ensure that highly trained, skilled professionals would be available so that this country could compete with the Soviet Union in highly technical fields. The NDEA included provisions for loans to college students; funds to assist in improving science, mathematics, and foreign-language training in elementary and secondary schools; graduate fellowships; funds to assist in foreign-language training and area studies in higher education; and funds to enhance vocational-technical training.[91]

In a fairly consistent manner since 1945, federal officials have attempted to promote mathematics and science, not only during the Cold War era but in the post–September 11, 2001, period as well. Policymakers have operated on a similar paradigm for decades: the national security needs of the United States can be partly addressed through public education. This phenomenon is evidenced through the very existence of the National Science Foundation, which has offered programs for 60 years in order to improve student performance in science and mathematics and to enhance teacher skills in these areas.[92]

The First Major Federal Intervention in K–12 Public Education: The ESEA of 1965

On April 11, 1965, President Johnson signed the ESEA into law. The ceremony was held in Stonewall, Texas, at the former Junction Elementary School, a one-room schoolhouse where the president went to school as a young boy. His first teacher, Kate Deadrich Loney, taught eight grades simultaneously and was in attendance on this occasion.[93] President Johnson reflected on the events leading up to passage of the ESEA:

> Now, within the past 3 weeks, the House of Representatives, by a vote of 263 to 153, and the Senate, by a vote of 73 to 18, have passed the most sweeping educational bill ever to come before Congress. It represents a major new commitment of the Federal Government to quality and equality in the schooling that we offer our young people. I predict that all of those of both parties of Congress who supported the enactment of this legislation will be remembered in history as men and women who began a new day of greatness in American society.[94]

The ESEA was a significant piece of legislation in education history and federalism because ever since 1965, the federal government's involvement in K–12 public education had been perceived by many as a relative given; this was definitely not the case in U.S. history prior to this important intervention.[95] As one practitioner noted,

> The Elementary and Secondary Education Act (ESEA) was passed in 1965 under the Johnson Administration. Before that, federal legislation dealing with education provided funding or land for schools and

special programs but was careful not to intrude on states' rights to make decisions on curriculum and the general operations of schools. By limiting the federal funds provided under ESEA to only those schools that had extra needs because of the socioeconomic status of their students, there seemed to be the promise that the federal role in education would lessen the achievement gap between students of different backgrounds without intruding on those schools that were doing well without federal mandates.[96]

Federal intervention in public education did not begin with the ESEA. However, the elevated role of the federal government in public education as a result of the passage of this act is well documented. As Eugene Eidenberg and Roy Morey duly noted with regard to the legislative process at the national level,

> As one might imagine, conflict on the floors of Congress is more intense during the authorization process than during the appropriation phase. This does not mean that once a program is authorized, opposition evaporates. Conflict may continue, but much of it is internalized within the appropriations committees and is usually not allowed to spread to the floor. Most members of Congress recognize the fact that once a program has been authorized the odds are overwhelming that it will be given at least partial funding. If a program is especially controversial and is authorized by a narrow vote ... the opposition may successfully block its appropriation. But such a case is unusual. Moreover, a bill becomes less controversial as it passes through the appropriation process itself.[97]

The passage of the ESEA, even as President Johnson signed it into law, meant that the national government would still be a distant third in terms of the financing of public education but that it would be more proactive than in previous time periods when it came to the issue of educating America's children.

The most explicit objective of the ESEA was part of a more grandiose vision of President Johnson. As part of his War on Poverty, he believed that federal funds could improve education for poor children, thereby providing indigent children with the opportunity to escape a future of deprivation and destitution that would perpetuate over generations without federal assistance.[98] The ESEA also authorized grants to acquire library resources, textbooks, and other instructional materials; to establish supplementary education centers; to stimulate educational research and training; and to strengthen state departments of education.[99] The most important part of the bill, where most of the money was concentrated, was Title I: Financial Assistance to Local Educational Agencies for the Education of Children of Low-Income Families.[100] Under section 205 of Title I,

> Payments under this title will be used for programs and projects (including the acquisition of equipment and where necessary the construction of school facilities) (A) which are designed to meet the special educational needs of educationally deprived children in school attendance areas having high concentrations of children from low-income families and (B) which are of sufficient size, scope, and quality to give reasonable promise of substantial progress toward meeting those ends, and nothing herein shall be deemed to preclude two or more educational agencies from entering into agreements, at their option, for carrying out jointly operated programs and projects under this title.[101]

Title I accounted for over 80 percent of the total funds authorized for the ESEA when it was passed by Congress. Perhaps not surprisingly, Title I received the most attention by school administrators at all levels, members of Congress, and those involved in federal fiscal management.[102]

A concise summary of the ESEA in terms of federalism is provided by Stephen Bailey and Edith Mosher:

> That the recent emergence of substantial Federal involvement in education has taken the form of an active partnership, rather than that of a passive and distant financial patron, is not without irony. For, as late as the early 1960s, most of the pressures for extensive Federal aid to education were couched in terms of general relief to local school budgets through unrestricted Federal grants for school construction and/or teachers' salaries, and in public schools only. When the first great breakthrough in Federal school aid occurred, as it did in the Elementary and Secondary Education Act of 1965, it involved a series of programmatic and innovative imperatives which plunged the Federal government smack into the middle of the total educational enterprise—public and private. ESEA was not a form of general relief to the local education agency . . . for operating and capital budgets. Its provisions were directive and categorical, yet far more flexible than those, say, in the Smith-Hughes Vocational Education Act or in the National Defense Education Act of 1958 . . . Title I of ESEA dictated the use of massive Federal funds for the general purpose of upgrading the education of children who were culturally and economically disadvantaged, but it left vast discretion of local education agency's in developing local programs to achieve this goal. Title II had no "poverty" formula, but it did focus upon a particular rather than a general need of schools—public and private: the improvement of school libraries, textbooks, and instructional materials; but even here the organizational nature of Title II was far broader than

similar materials provisions in the original version of NDEA. Title III funds were earmarked not for the general support of existing programs, but for innovative or supplementary educational centers and services approved by the U.S. Commissioner of Education. Once again, categorical aid was stressed, but it did provide enormous flexibility in scope and emphasis. Title IV grants for research and development and for regional educational laboratories were to be directly allocated from Washington. Under Title V, Federal funds were to be made available for strengthening of State education agencies according to criteria established in the act. In sum, ESEA was not just a Federal handout to ease State and local educational budgets. It mandated a series of programs and priorities which involved a massive shift in the locus of policy-making power in American education.[103]

But with the end of the Johnson era in 1969, the ESEA would remain the most substantive federal intervention in public K–12 education until the early twenty-first century. During the 2000 presidential campaign, the Republican nominee, George W. Bush, reiterated that he had two major policy objectives in mind if elected president. He advocated a significant tax cut, especially for more affluent Americans, at the federal level, and he championed his vision of education reform. He signed an initial tax cut passed by Congress into law during the summer of his first year in office. His views on reforming public education would later be enacted into law early in 2002 in the NCLB law.

The Second Major Federal Intervention in K–12 Public Education: The NCLB Act of 2001

On December 13, 2001, the NCLB Act passed in the U.S. House of Representatives by a vote of 381 to 41. Twelve representatives did not vote. It was a bipartisan vote in that 183 Republicans and 198 Democrats voted in favor of the bill. Thirty-three Republicans, six Democrats, and two Independents were in opposition to it.[104] Five days later, the Senate passed the measure by an 87–10 vote. Three senators did not vote. All senators present approved the measure except for Robert Bennett (R–UT), Mark Dayton (D–MN), Russ Feingold (D–WI), Charles Hagel (R–NE), Ernest (Fritz) Hollings (D–SC), Jim Jeffords (I–VT), Patrick Leahy (D–VT), Ben Nelson (D–NE), George Voinovich (R–OH), and Paul Wellstone (D–MN).[105] President George W. Bush signed the bill into law on January 8, 2002.[106] The signing ceremony was held at Hamilton High School in Hamilton, Ohio. The president was accompanied by, among others, Senator Ted Kennedy (D–MA) and Congressman John Boehner (R–OH).[107]

NCLB is a reauthorization of the ESEA. It is a very detailed piece of legislation; the final passage of NCLB is 669 pages in length.[108] The most significant components of NCLB include the following:

- Annual Testing: State education officials were required to begin testing students every year in grades 3 to 8 in reading and mathematics by the 2005–2006 school year. By 2007–2008, students had to be tested in science at least once in elementary, middle, and senior high school. The tests utilized would be created by the individual states; no national examination was created in order to implement NCLB. In addition, a sample of fourth and eighth graders in each state would participate in the National Assessment of Education Progress testing program in reading and mathematics every other year to provide a comparison between and among the states.

- Academic Progress: Under NCLB, state educators are required to ensure that all students are up to the "proficient" level on state examinations by the 2013–2014 school year. Individual schools are required to meet state "adequate yearly progress" targets toward achieving this goal (based on a formula included in the law) both for their student population as a whole and for certain demographic subgroups as well. If a Title I school fails to meet the target two years in a row, it would be provided with technical assistance, and its students would be offered a choice of other public schools to attend (including charter schools). Students in schools that failed to meet adequate yearly progress three years in a row were also offered supplemental educational services, including private tutoring. Continued school failure to meet adequate yearly progress would make it subject to corrective measures, including possible governance changes.

- Report Cards: Beginning with the 2002–2003 school year, state officials were required to furnish annual report cards on the performance of school districts. The information provided must include student achievement data broken down by subgroup. School districts officials, in turn, must provide similar report cards showing data at the school level.

- Teacher Qualifications: Beginning with the 2002–2003 school year, all new teachers hired with federal Title I money had to be "highly qualified." This generally meant that a teacher must be certified and demonstrably proficient in his or her subject matter. By the end of the 2005–2006 school year, every teacher in core content areas working in a public school must be "highly qualified" in each subject taught. By the end of the 2005–2006 school year, all school paraprofessionals hired with Title I money must have completed at least two years of college, obtained an associate's degree or higher, or passed an evaluation to demonstrate knowledge and teaching ability.

- Reading First: The NCLB act created a new competitive grant program titled Reading First. The intent of the program is to help state and district officials set up "scientific, research-based" reading programs for children in grades K–3. Priority would be given to high-poverty regions.
- Funding Changes: The Title I funding formula was changed, so NCLB was expected to better target resources to school districts with high concentrations of poor children. The law also purported to afford state and district officials with greater flexibility in how they spent their federal funds.[109]

While NCLB represents the second major federal intervention in K–12 public education in America's history, it is much more extensive and profound when compared to the ESEA. As Patrick McGuinn explained,

> The passage of No Child Left Behind in 2002 fundamentally changed the ends and means of federal education policy from those put forward in the original ESEA legislation and, in so doing, created a new policy regime. The old federal education policy regime, created in 1965, was based on a policy paradigm that saw the central purpose of school reform as promoting equity and access for disadvantaged students, a policymaking arrangement that focused on procedural mandates, and a political alignment in which Republicans opposed federal activism and liberals sought to maintain the federal focus on resources and poor and minority students. The old regime was governed by a largely congressional and interest group—dominated policymaking process made possible by the issue's relatively low salience with the public. Interest groups—the unions and education providers on the left and social, religious, and states' rights conservatives on the right—largely determined the positions of the Democratic and Republican parties on education. The policy paradigm at the heart of the NCLB regime is centered on the much broader goal of improving education for all students and seeks to do so by significantly reducing federal influence over process and inputs while replacing it with increased accountability for school performance. The adoption of tough new federal timetables and accountability measures in NCLB was seen as essential to force states to comply with the standards and testing reforms introduced in 1994. The new federal focus on accountability, meanwhile, was only possible because of important shifts in the political alignment and policymaking arrangement. The development of a more competitive national electoral environment and the rise of education to the top of the public agenda in the 1990s eventually led both parties to embrace a more proactive and reform-oriented federal role in improving schools. The convergence of the parties' positions on education was evident in the remarkable degree of bipartisan agreement and broad moderate

leadership that characterized the legislative discussions over NCLB, when Democrats and Republicans agreed on substantially increased federal spending, enhanced flexibility and public choice, and the framework of a national accountability system that would have been unthinkable just a few years before.[110]

Federal officials currently have an unprecedented level of involvement in the nation's public schools.[111] While the implementation and the reaction to NCLB has often been contentious and wrought with acrimony, determining the relative effectiveness of the law—and by what criteria—remains debatable.[112] Education researchers, scholars, and practitioners have a number of perspectives, however.

THE SERIOUS AND SOMBER POLICY IMPLICATIONS OF NCLB

Diane Ravitch was the assistant secretary of education from 1991 to 1993, when George H. W. Bush was president. She was later appointed to the National Assessment Governing Board by President Bill Clinton. She was an early advocate for NCLB and believed that the combination of enhanced accountability through testing and school choice would improve America's public schools. She changed her mind about the matter, however. In her own words,

> My support for NCLB remained strong until November 30, 2006. I can pinpoint the date exactly because that was the day I realized that NCLB was a failure. I went to a conference at the American Enterprise Institute in Washington, D.C.—a well-respected conservative think tank—to hear a dozen or so scholars present their analyses of NCLB's remedies. Organized by Frederick M. Hess and Chester E. Finn, Jr., the conference examined whether the major remedies prescribed by NCLB—especially choice and after-school tutoring—were effective. Was the "NCLB toolkit" working? Were the various sanctions prescribed by the law improving achievement? The various presentations that day demonstrated that state education departments were drowning in new bureaucratic requirements, procedures, and routines, and that none of the prescribed remedies was making a difference.[113]

To reiterate the theme of Chapter 2, ideas are of the utmost importance in politics. NCLB is based, in part, on a laissez-faire assumption that marketplace competition will force deficient schools and their officials to improve or cease to exist. The competition paradigm ignores a very important reality—poverty matters when it comes to education. This does not mean that children of indigent social class backgrounds cannot learn. But elected officials and policymakers cannot ignore the reality that poverty has always been an important factor in education. If we measure the relative effectiveness of a school by only one standardized test, as is the case with NCLB, then many schools may be set up to fail in spite of the fact that they may be improving on a number of other fronts that cannot be quantified in terms of measurement and cannot be filed in a database. In other words, NCLB has established a zero-sum game—either increase test scores, or run the risk of becoming a charter school or, worse, be closed altogether.

Charter schools are publicly funded elementary or secondary schools; they are nontraditional public schools whose officials are freed from some of the rules, regulations, and statutes that apply to other public schools. In return, charter school officials are held accountable for producing certain results, typically higher standardized test scores, that are set forth in the charter, or contract, for each charter school.[114] Charter schools can be managed by nonprofit groups or for-profit corporations. They can be managed by community groups at the local level or by a national organization.[115] This is one element of choice touted by conservatives as a way to improve public education. Conservatives typically advocate school voucher programs as well. School vouchers, also known as education vouchers, are literally certificates issued by the government that parents can utilize to send their children to alternative schools, including private and/or parochial schools.[116] Again, based on the theory of marketplace capitalism, there is an underlying assumption that institutions in the public sector are lacking when compared to their counterparts in the private arena. When forced to compete, the deficient schools will either improve or be shut down.

Ravitch has changed her mind with regard to testing and the issue of choice in education. She has done so both in a theoretical sense and in terms of empirical research in education. With regard to testing, she contends that

> our schools will not improve if we rely exclusively on tests as the means of deciding the fate of students, teachers, principals, and schools. When tests are the primary means of evaluation and accountability, everyone feels pressure to raise the scores, by hook or by crook. Some will cheat to get a reward or to avoid humiliation. Schools may manipulate who takes the test and who does not; district and state officials may fiddle with the scoring of the test. Districts and states may require intensive test preparation that mirrors the actual state tests and borders on

institutionalized cheating. Any test score gains that result solely from incentives are meaningless because gains that are purchased with cash are short-lived and have nothing to do with real education.[117]

As I argued recently, an essential starting point with regard to NCLB is federalism.[118] While Ravitch examines the many shortcomings of standardized testing, it is important to remember that NCLB architects determined that each state would utilize its own instrument to determine how many students in their state were proficient in the various subjects. But what do the numbers mean? What do we conclude if 70 percent of students pass a science test in Indiana as compared to 75 percent in Maine or 80 percent in Massachusetts? The only true answer is that we conclude absolutely nothing because the testing instrument varies state by state.

With regard to school choice and the theory that marketplace competition is necessary to reform public education, Ravitch provides the following observation:

> Our schools will not improve if we expect them to act like private, profit-seeking enterprises. Schools are not businesses; they are a public good. The goal of education is not to produce higher scores, but to educate children to become responsible people with well-developed minds and good character. Schools should not be expected to turn a profit in the form of value-added scores. The unrelenting focus on data that has become commonplace in recent years is distorting the nature and quality of education. There are many examples of healthy competition in schools, such as science fairs, essay contests, debates, chess tournaments, and athletic events. But the competition among schools to get higher scores is of a different nature; in the current climate, it is sure to cause teachers to spend more time preparing students for state tests, not on thoughtful writing, critical reading, scientific experiments, or historical study. Nor should we expect schools to vie with one another for students, as businesses vie for customers, advertising their wares and marketing their services. For schools to learn from one another, they must readily share information about their successes and failures, as medical professionals do, rather than act as rivals in a struggle for survival.[119]

The theoretical framework of NCLB is fundamentally flawed. Although the goal of NCLB is commendable and something that yields an overwhelming affirmation, the law has been a major setback to the cause of common schooling in the United States.[120] Many progressives have long maintained that national governmental officials should assist their state and local peers in the deliverance of education to their children.

The assumption, however, in this vision of federalism is that the assistance in question would actually be helpful to the nation's schoolchildren and to society as well. There is ample evidence to suggest that while NCLB has increased the federal presence in K–12 public education, the consequences of this intervention have not been positive. Thus, perhaps there is another nuance to the federalism debate. Instead of focusing the discourse simply on states' rights versus a stronger national government, one denominator must be established akin to a geometric given. Regardless of the identity of the officials involved and which level of government they happen to represent, the intervention(s) in question must be plausible. Issues and debates and federalism will always be secondary to bad public policies. It does not matter who creates an ineffective and perhaps harmful policy. In the case of children, they deserve better, and elected and appointed officials should be accountable to them accordingly.

4

Education and the Politics of Consumerism and Conservatism

Before discussing the evolution of the consumerist ideology in the United States, it is necessary to understand the basics of how children were educated before the 1890s in the United States. For more than 150 years, dating back to the late 1600s, the *New England Primer* served as the primary textbook for millions of colonists and early American citizens. It is estimated that between 6 million and 8 million copies were sold by 1830.[1] This early textbook reflected the norms of Puritan culture and propagated those norms into early American thought.[2] Besides the Bible, another prominent text for children was Noah Webster's *American Spelling Book*.[3] According to the noted biographer of Noah Webster, Harry Warfel, 20 million copies of the speller were sold by 1829 and 75 million by 1875.[4]

The Horace Mann obelisk at Antioch College. It was erected in 1883 to commemorate his original grave on the grounds of Antioch College in 1859. He was later reinterred to Providence, Rhode Island. (Image courtesy of Antiochiana, Antioch College.)

THE *McGUFFEY READERS* OF THE NINETEENTH AND EARLY TWENTIETH CENTURIES

Arguably the most prominent textbooks for American children in the nineteenth century were the *McGuffey Readers*. According to Richard Mosier, between 1836 and 1920, about 122 million copies were sold.[5] The *McGuffey Readers* were published by seven different companies.[6] It is important to note, however, that these books were revised many times over the years.[7] Nevertheless, the readers were a prelude to the consumer society that would ensue in American history.

William Holmes McGuffey was born in 1800 in Pennsylvania. His family moved near Youngstown, Ohio, when he was two years of age. Due to his family's emphasis on education, he graduated from Washington College in Pennsylvania in 1826. Embarking on a career in academia, he became a professor of languages at Miami University in Oxford, Ohio, and then became chair of the Department of Mental Philosophy and Philology. He resigned this position in 1836 to become the president of Cincinnati College; he left in 1839 to become president of Ohio University in Athens, where he remained until 1843, when he returned to Cincinnati as a professor at Woodward College. In 1845, Professor McGuffey took a position in the Department of Moral Philosophy at the University of Virginia, where he remained until his death in 1873.[8]

McGuffey wrote the primer and first, second, third, and fourth eclectic readers in his series. His brother, Alexander, actually wrote the fifth and sixth eclectic readers as well as the eclectic speller, even though they appear in print with William McGuffey's name.[9] Classic themes in the *McGuffey Readers* include honesty, goodness, kindness, promptness, respect, religious values, and piety. Harvey Minnich provided an assessment of the impact of the *McGuffey Readers* on those children who were educated in the common schools:

> It is acknowledged by the testimonies of men and women of every social level and of every occupation and profession whose early education came under the influence of the McGuffey Readers that the social teachings of these books were major controls throughout a lifetime. Historians and sociologists have acknowledged the great influence of these readers in shaping the character of the civilization of the Middle West. The long lists of men distinguished in politics, jurisprudence, invention, literature, industry, and public education who sprang from the common schools in which the McGuffey Readers were almost universally used

bear evidence of the influence of the lessons of these books. A complete list of persons born west of the Allegheny Mountains between 1840 and 1885 whose names occur in *Who's Who in America* may be considered alumni of the moral and social teachings of the McGuffey Readers. Taft, Harding, McKinley, Glenn Frank, Beveridge, Borah, Henry Ford, Edison, Ade, Darrow, Garland, Zona Gale, Herbert Quick, Lorado Taft, Mark Twain, Gunsaulus, Edgar Stillman Kelley, Gene Stratton Porter, Rutherford B. Hayes, Robert LaFollette, Lew Wallace, James Whitcomb Riley serve to represent the culture and citizenship of the McGuffey land.[10]

Henry Vail also believed that the *McGuffey Readers* were particularly influential in nineteenth-century America: "The teaching power of a schoolbook cannot be weighed in the grocer scales nor measured with a pint cup. In the field open to free and constant competition, the readers best suited to the wants of each community will in the end succeed. It was under such conditions that the McGuffey Readers won and held their place in the schools."[11] While a brief illustration of some of the themes covered in the books is illuminating, the reader must be advised that consuming the readers en masse will prove quite gratifying from a number of different perspectives.

In *McGuffey's Second Eclectic Reader,* one of the lessons was titled "A Good Old Man."[12] Here is the lesson provided by McGuffey:

1. There once lived an old man in a snug, little cottage. It had two rooms and only two windows. A small garden lay just behind it.
2. Old as the poor man was, he used to work in the fields. Often he would come home very tired and weak, with his hoe or spade on his shoulder.
3. And who do you think met him at the door? Mary and Jane, his two little grandchildren.
4. They were too young to work, except to weed in the garden, or bring water from the spring.
5. In winter, as they were too poor to buy much wood or coal, they had little fire; so they used to sit close together to keep warm. Mary would sit on one of the old man's knees, and Jane on the other.
6. Sometimes their grandfather would tell them a droll story. Sometimes he would teach them a hymn.
7. He would often talk to them of their father, who had gone to sea, or of their good, kind mother, who was in her grave. Every night he prayed God to bless them, and to bring back their father in safety.
8. The old man grew weaker every year; but the little girls were glad to work for him, who had been so good to them.
9. One cold, windy night, they heard a knock at the door. The little girls ran and opened it. Oh, joy to them! There stood their father.

10. He had been at sea a long time. He had saved some money, and had now come home to stay.
11. After this the old man did not have to work. His son worked for him, and his grandchildren took care of him. Many happy days they spent together.[13]

Obviously, McGuffey was highlighting and accentuating positive aspects of life for his young readers in this lesson. But *McGuffey's Readers* also included lessons of a less positive nature. One such lesson was titled "The Greedy Girl":[14]

1. Laura English is a greedy little girl. Indeed, she is quite a glutton. Do you know what a glutton is? A glutton is one who eats too much, because the food tastes well.
2. Laura's mother is always willing she should have as much to eat as is good for her; but sometimes, when her mother is not watching, she eats so much that it makes her sick.
3. I do not know why she is so silly. Her kitten never eats more than it needs. It leaves the nice bones on the plate, and lies down to sleep when it has eaten enough.
4. The bee is wiser than Laura. It flies all day among the flowers to gather honey, and might eat the whole time if it pleased. But it eats just enough, and carries all the rest to its hive.
5. The squirrel eats a few nuts or acorns, and frisks about as gayly as if he had dined at the king's table.
6. Did you ever see a squirrel with a nut in his paws? How bright and lovely he looks as he eats it!
7. If he lived in a house made of acorns, he would never need a doctor. He would not eat an acorn too much.
8. I do not love little girls who eat too much. Do you, my little readers?
9. I do not think they have such rosy cheeks, or such bright eyes, or such sweet, happy tempers as those who eat less.[15]

In a story undoubtedly targeted toward older, male students, McGuffey offered a classic tale of good versus evil titled "Courage and Cowardice":[16]

1. Robert and Henry were going home from school, when, on turning a corner, Robert cried out, "A fight! Let us go and see!"
2. "No," said Henry; "let us go quietly home and not meddle with this quarrel. We have nothing to do with it, and may get into mischief."
3. "You are a coward, and afraid to go," said Robert, and off he ran. Henry went straight home, and in the afternoon went to school, as usual.
4. But Robert had told all the boys that Henry was a coward, and they laughed at him a great deal.

5. Henry had learned, however, that true courage is shown most in bearing reproach when not deserved, and that he ought to be afraid of nothing but doing wrong.
6. A few days after, Robert was bathing with some schoolmates, and got out of his depth. He struggled, and screamed for help, but all in vain.
7. The boys who called Henry a coward, got out of the water as fast as they could, but they did not even try to help him.
8. Robert was fast sinking, when Henry threw off his clothes, and sprang into the water. He reached Robert just as he was sinking the last time.
9. By great effort, and with much danger to himself, he brought Robert to the shore, and thus saved his life.
10. Robert and his schoolmates were ashamed at having called Henry a coward. They owned that he had more courage than any of them.
11. Never be afraid to do good, but always fear to do evil.[17]

The *McGuffey Readers* are very significant in U.S. education history. Like anything else in history, they are contextual and reflective of nineteenth- and early twentieth-century America. Indeed, they highlight American values during that period and reflect the reality that common school advocates then fused religious teachings into their educational lessons. To Richard Mosier,

> It is clear that the morality and religion found in the McGuffey readers were those of the overwhelming majority of Americans in the nineteenth century, and that in exerting their influence in matters of religion and morality the McGuffey readers called many back to that stricter piety and sharper mentality known only to the older generations. In the cause of religious toleration, as we saw in the case of the Catholic question, the readers performed nobly, speaking with liberality on the subject of toleration and decency. With respect to matters of religious and racial tolerance, with respect to simply piety and healthy morals, the McGuffey readers were, and are, supreme. That this strong emphasis on religious conviction and moral enthusiasm ultimately played into the hands of conservatism and reaction in politics, and ultimately strengthened the influence of conservative arguments, was hardly the fault of the readers, but was rather inevitable in an age that found the pattern of ideas in the McGuffey readers so widely accepted in the system of values of nineteenth century America.[18]

One thing has not changed in U.S. history. It is difficult to understand a historical phenomenon, such as the *McGuffey Readers*, unless the context of the time period in question is carefully considered. The sales of the *McGuffey Readers* were most impressive; they were incredibly popular in American society because they were philosophically in sync with much or most of the population. In short, McGuffey's teachings resonated with the American people at that point in evolution in the American democracy.

CONSUMERISM DEFINED

Joel Spring has written a very informative book about the evolution of the consumer ideology in the United States.[19] In it, he describes his theory about consumerism in America:

> A premise of this book is that consumerism is the dominant ideology of the United States and the driving force of the global economy. Mass-consumer culture integrates consumerism into all aspects of life from birth to death, including, but not limited to, education, leisure time activities, the popular arts, the home, travel, and personal imagination. Mass-consumer culture captures the fantasy world of people with brand names and fashions that promise personal transformation, the vicarious thrill of imaging the glamorous lives of celebrities, the promise of escape from hard work through packaged travel and cruises to an envisioned paradise, and the idea that in America everyone has an equal opportunity to consume.[20]

He defines a consumer-citizen as a "person who accepts any political situation as long as there is an abundance of consumer goods."[21] To Spring, the consumer ideology is unique among the emerging ideologies in U.S. history.

Other ideologies place an emphasis on either social harmony or an abandonment of material concerns. This is not the case with the consumerist ideology. During the nineteenth century, the Protestant work ethic was dominant with its emphasis on saving, avoiding debt, and simple living. The goal of the modern consumer is to spend, maximize his or her credit, and consume as much as possible. Although the consumerist ideology emerged in the early twentieth century, it was a mixture of earlier ideas about equality of opportunity, the accumulation of wealth, and the value of work.[22] The basic ideas that form consumerism (work ethic, equality of opportunity, and savings) existed in the early nineteenth century. But these ideas took on a new meaning in the context of America in the early twentieth century. First, the meaning of the work ethic changed. Instead of being a value itself, hard work now provided a means to purchase goods that promised personal transformation.[23] Equality of opportunity no longer simply meant having an equal chance to get ahead in society. As of the early twentieth century, it entailed the equality of opportunity to consume.[24] Finally, the virtue of saving and delaying immediate gratification was present in nineteenth century America. In the early twentieth century, savings was used to justify consumer credit plans as forced savings. Consumer credit allows people to purchase goods immediately by providing a forced savings plan to pay the cost of the goods. Consumers must work diligently to pay off their debt, so the desire to purchase goods and the necessity of paying off consumer debt compels the consumer to work even harder.[25]

By way of summary, Spring contends that the basic ideas of the consumerist ideology include 12 tenets:

1. work is a virtue and it prevents people from engaging in a life of crime;
2. equality entails the equality of opportunity to pursue wealth and the ability to consume goods;
3. accumulation of material goods is evidence of personal success;
4. the rich are rich because of a strong work ethic and solid character whereas the poor are poor because they lack virtue;
5. the major financial goal of society is economic growth and the continued production of new goods;
6. consumers and producers should be united in efforts to maximize the production and consumption of goods;
7. people will want to work hard so that they can consume more material goods and experience more leisure;
8. differences in income levels is a social virtue because it motivates people to work harder;
9. advertising is good for society because it motivates people to work harder to consume products;
10. the consumer is irrational and can be manipulated in her or his choices through advertising;
11. the consumption of goods will transform an individual's life; and
12. consumer credit is forced savings allowing for the immediate consumption of products.[26]

Spring maintains that the common school became the symbol of equality of opportunity and therefore was the foundation of a mass-consumer society. The premise was simple: if one worked hard in school and worked hard after graduation, he or she would have a high income and a good life and be able to consume a lot of material goods.[27]

THE EVOLUTION OF THE CONSUMER IDEOLOGY

By the 1920s, Richard Wrightman Fox and T. J. Jackson Lears contend
that the consumer culture was well under way in the United States:

> Not only were middle-class Americans using credit to buy a vast array
> of goods in the 1920s; legions of publicists promoted, celebrated, or con-
> demned the centrality of consumption in Americans' lives beginning in
> the late nineteenth century. For some observers it meant fulfillment, for
> others enslavement. The most widely read critic of industrial capitalism
> in the 1890s, Edward Bellamy, saw in consumption the promise of deliv-
> erance from routinized toil and social anarchy. In *Looking Backward*
> (1888) he imagined twenty-first century Boston as a cooperative society
> of total leisure for all adults over 45; the masses passed their maturity in
> pursuit of "the good things of the world which they have helped to cre-
> ate." Thorstein Veblen had a less sanguine view of consumption. In his
> *Theory of the Leisure Class* (1899) he mocked "pecuniary emulation" and
> "conspicuous consumption" as socially functional but morally bank-
> rupt. After the turn of the century the "engineers"—for whom the
> "instinct of workmanship" was more precious than the possession of
> goods—gave him hope. But it was an engineer of genius, Henry Ford,
> who subverted his dream and created the cornerstone of the leisure
> society: the affordable automobile.[28]

From this perspective, Americans in the early twenty-first century
have continued a documented pattern that has existed for a century
in this country. That pattern prompts us to consume as much as possible and not question the values, ethics, and consequences of such
behavior.

The sociologists Robert and Helen Lynd captured the rise of a culture of self-conscious consumers in the United States in their famous
Middletown studies in 1929 and 1937.[29] Muncie, Indiana, was identified by the Lynds as a typical American city, and it became "Middletown" in their works.[30] About a quarter of a century ago, a content
analysis of Middletown literature identified almost 800 works on the
theme.[31] But the original Middletown studies were complicated, as
depicted by Fox:

> It is only by studying Lynd's life ... that we can make sense of the Mid-
> dletown volumes themselves. They were not just original, influential
> studies of the American consumer society, and key embodiments of
> the growing self-consciousness of consumer culture. They were also
> records of Lynd's own painful adjustment to the consumer world, and

documents of his stormy relationship with the elite Institute of Social and Religious Research, which funded the first volume. That book had such an enormous and immediate impact on its thousands of readers because it caught the subtle tensions and confusions of the early years of consumer society in America. The reason it caught them so flawlessly was that Robert Lynd had spent a decade sorting out those tensions and confusions in his own life. The two Middletown volumes, along with Lynd's third and final book, *Knowledge for What?*, map his progression from Christian minister to secular sociologist, from cultural analyst to political activist, from outsider to member of the professional elite, from critic of American consumer capitalism to critic of the irrational American consumer.[32]

Lynd and his wife provided an account of the pervasiveness of the consumer culture in America during the twentieth century in America. He very much detested the notion that the essence of living a good life entailed consuming material goods. He also vigorously opposed the invasion of the academic world by business values touting efficiency. His vision of a good life entailed a more moral existence with less emphasis on materialism, and many other Protestant Americans yearned for the same thing. He found himself in the vast minority, however, and would ultimately withdraw from the intellectual arena, quite dismayed with the changing nature of American society.[33]

Another historian, Charles McGovern, has documented the evolution of America to a consumer society between 1890 and 1945.[34] In a succinct manner, he describes the dramatic changes in American society:

Historians have come to understand the half century after 1880 as the time when the United States became a consumer society. Rapid demographic, economic, and institutional growth, along with technological, intellectual, and material changes, fueled the United States's transition to a complex bureaucratic state, an advanced industrial economy, and a modern consumer culture. Briefly, the most important factors in this history include a widespread, rationalized system of industrial production and labor controlled by managerial capital; new technologies and goods adapted to household uses; national media, including mass-circulation magazines, radio, film, sound recordings, electrical signs, and billboards; new institutions of national distribution; and new modes of thought about the self—all contributed to the emergence of mass consumption. By 1930, the American economic system had undergone a tremendous evolution, which made a staggering variety of goods available for purchase. Though much of the populace still lived

in small villages and towns and made a living from the land, the agrarian republic of local preindustrial economies had given way to an urban
nation of new values, experiences, and institutions. These all were
bound up intimately in a commercial system where anything—not only
food, clothing, and furniture but ideas, perceptions, and emotions themselves—could and did become a commodity. The United States became
a consumer society, its economy one of mass consumption, its culture
deeply influenced by commodities and spending.[35]

McGovern also presents the evolution of advertising in the United
States from 1880 to 1930. The collective impact of the advertisers on
American society is immeasurable in a quantitative sense but quite substantial from the perspective of historians and analysts in American
studies:

> Seemingly ubiquitous, advertising dominated both the structure and
> content of mass communications, assuming an unmistakable promi-
> nence in the built environment. Just as important, advertisers claimed
> for themselves the critical task of defining identity for Americans.
> Advertisements encouraged people to purchase a plethora of products
> to meet the material needs of their everyday lives. In conveying infor-
> mation about goods and ideal living, advertisers also provided images
> and prescriptions for the self. They encouraged consumers to under-
> stand themselves through their possessions and to fabricate identities
> in and through things. ... The late nineteenth-century experience of
> modernity in its many guises showed that the individual was not a
> fixed and stable character but a complex, changing entity shaped by
> the external world. Advertising encouraged consumers—now increas-
> ingly termed "consumers" by the national corporations that were sup-
> planting the face-to-face relationships of local commerce—literally to
> make themselves from their things. In this capacity, advertising shaped
> modern culture. This was achieved haltingly over many years and sel-
> dom with conscious purpose: after all, advertisers sold goods, not sym-
> bols. Yet they trafficked in images and ideals, and they educated
> consumers to interpret goods totemically as intimate, even animate,
> parts of their lives. As consumption helped define the self, advertisers
> taught Americans to view themselves as consumers.[36]

As an aggregate entity, the advertisers were enormously successful in
achieving the objective of transforming the American citizen and how
he or she views him- or herself. Very few question the morals of the consumerist ideology. Most Americans view those with numerous material
possessions as success stories (there is little thought or scrutiny of the
values inherent in the consumer society in which we live) and have done

so for more than 80 years with no apparent signs of reversing this course at all.

Tracing the development of advertising and examining past advertisements in history is most illuminating.[37] As Susan Strasser has documented, the marketing techniques used for products such as Crisco in the early twentieth century are universal in the early twenty-first century.[38] While few consumers are familiar with the production or distribution of the products they consume, most people are similar in one sense. Most Americans do not perceive that their consumption choices are matters of cultural and political importance. The American consumer, to a large extent, is not a critical or an analytical entity. Americans choose to avoid scrutinizing the implications of their own consumer choices. As a result, manufacturers, both in the past and in the present, have sought to promote brand loyalty to their customers. Through the use of marketing, manufacturers attempt to develop a relationship of sorts with Americans who choose to purchase their products.[39] The essence of advertising in the consumer era was depicted by Strasser about a quarter of a century ago:

> In advertisements, in the cultural attitudes they represent and stimulate, and in the habits of daily life, consumer products have embodied progress and promised convenient solutions to problems throughout the twentieth century. They have provided satisfactions and pastimes that have diverted people from the political arena. But there are no convenient solutions to the environmental challenge. These issues require new kinds of planning of matters that should not be left to private industrial firms to settle in their own interests, and new policies and strategies for everybody—consumers, factory managers, and governments around the world. Those new strategies must come, not from the sum of individual choices in the marketplace, but from a political process that addresses inherent conflicts and competing interests.[40]

Indeed, there are a number of concrete consequences of the consumerist ideology. We live in a throwaway generation that puts a significant strain on the natural world. Instead of purchasing products that can be expected to last a long time, we are encouraged to discard appliances, automobiles, and electronic equipment that could be in perfect working order but are considered outdated because the technology has been enhanced. Marketing reinforces this premise that we somehow deserve to have the best product available. Consider the impact of such decision making not only in a nation with about 315 million people but also in a world with an estimated population of more than 7 billion inhabitants.

Susan Matt's account of American historical consumerism also concludes that by 1930, the consumerist ideology had firmly entrenched itself in the United States. According to her,

> Bourgeois Americans of all ages had become accustomed to indulging their desires and acting on their envy. They had come to think of envy and discontent as emotions which indicated that they had aspirations, taste, and a desire for a higher standard of living. Rather than seeing envy as a sin and consumer activity as a threat to their moral integrity, Americans believed that they could better themselves through spending. They also believed that they could make themselves happier by making purchases. The way to gain true contentment was not to accept deprivations but to act on their envy and pursue the things they longed for. These new interpretations of envy, discontent, and contentment which consumers and merchants developed in the 1910s and 1920s continue to shape consumer behavior in our own time. Modern consumers accept not only the emotional codes that their grandparents and great-grandparents developed, but their larger social implications as well. They believe that all Americans, regardless of their location, age, or sex, have a right to purchase what they want.[41]

The paradigmatic shift in American history is quite profound. In nineteenth-century America, children were taught that envy is the enemy of contentment and must be conquered. By the early part of the twentieth century, middle-class Americans had embraced a new radical pedagogy:

> This transformation in envy's meaning and legitimacy was significant because it was part of an emerging emotional and behavioral style that supported the expansion of the consumer economy. America could sustain a full-fledged consumer economy only after men and women had overcome their religious reservations about materialism and had developed an emotional style that emphasized the value of pleasure, indulgence, and desire and downplayed the importance of restraint and delayed gratification. This emotional and behavioral model is widely evident today. Modern Americans take for granted that all can legitimately pursue their consumer desires, that they need not repress their envy, but can instead gain satisfaction by acting on it.[42]

While many educators and moralists attempted to restrain their envy and limit their level of economic activity in the marketplace, most Americans accepted the consumerist ideology in earnest. The pursuit of more material goods by American consumers was well under way.[43]

Juliet Schor has argued that while the effects of the consumerist ideology on American adults are well documented, advertisers have also sought to manipulate the consumption patterns of children:

> The architects of this culture—the companies that make, market, and advertise consumer products—have now set their sights on children. Although children have long participated in the consumer marketplace, until recently they were bit players, purchasers of cheap goods. They attracted little of the industry's talent and resources and were approached primarily through their mothers. That has changed. Kids and teens are now the epicenter of American consumer culture. They command the attention, creativity, and dollars of advertisers. Their tastes drive market trends. Their opinions shape brand strategies. Yet few adults recognize the magnitude of this shift and its consequences for the futures of our children and of our culture.[44]

Americans are working more on the job today than decades earlier.[45] They are doing so in order to be in the position not only to cover the costs of escalating basics, such as education and health care, but also to purchase more material goods, including vehicles and branded goods, as well as outlays for leisure, travel, and recreation. The problem for many American families is that they are spending more, saving less, and accumulating more debt.[46] This is reflective of government spending patterns at the national level as well in that, as of April 2013, the total national debt in the United States exceeded $16.7 trillion.[47]

THE COMMERCIALIZATION OF PUBLIC EDUCATION

Schor provides a sobering account of the impact of advertising on America's children:

> The typical American child is now immersed in the consumer marketplace to a degree that dwarfs all historical experience. At age one, she's watching *Teletubbies* and eating the food of its "promo partners" Burger King and McDonald's. Kids can recognize logos by eighteen months, and before reaching their second birthday, they're asking for products by brand name. By three or three and a half, experts say, children start to believe that brands communicate their personal qualities, for example, that they're cool, or strong, or smart. Even before starting school, the likelihood of having a television in their bedroom is 25 percent, and their viewing time is just over two hours a day. Upon arrival at the schoolhouse steps, the typical first grader can evoke 200 brands.

And he or she has already accumulated an unprecedented number of possessions, beginning with an average of seventy new toys a year. By age six or seven, girls are asking for the latest fashions, using nail polish, and singing pop music tunes. . . . Eight-year-old boys are enjoying Budweiser commercials (the consistent favorite ad for this age group), World Wrestling Entertainment, and graphically violent video games. . . . The average eight to thirteen year old is watching over three and a half hours of television a day. American children view an estimated 40,000 commercials annually. . . . As kids age, they turn to teen culture, which is saturated with violence, alcohol, drugs, and guns. Teen media depict a manipulated and gratuitous sexuality, based on unrealistic body images, constraining gender stereotypes, and, all too frequently, the degradation of women. The dominant teen culture is also rife with materialism and preaches that if you're not rich, you're a loser.[48]

Our children are absolutely inundated with commercialism. To what extent are children equipped to understand that they are being manipulated and the concomitant result is that advertising will affect their decision making for the rest of their lives? A prominent cultural studies scholar has provided a great deal of research on the subject.

Henry Giroux maintains that corporations have supplanted the public schools as the most important educational force in the United States.[49] The only manner in which to thwart this reality, to him, is to mobilize in a political sense:

Corporate power is pervasive and will not give up its resources willingly. Resistance to dominant corporate culture means developing pedagogical and political strategies that both educate and transform, that build alliances while recognizing different perspectives, and that foreground the struggle over democracy as the central issue. Any attempt to challenge media giants such as Disney demands linking cultural politics with policy battles. Changing consciousness must become part of practical politics designed to change legislation, to reorganize and distribute resources, and to redefine the relationship between pedagogy and social justice, between knowledge and power. Building alliances is especially important, and progressives need a new language for bringing together cultural workers that ordinarily have not worked well together. This suggests finding ways to organize educators at all levels of schooling in order to gain control over those pedagogical forces that shape our culture. And this means addressing the pedagogical force of those cultural industries that have supplanted the school as society's most important educational force.[50]

In another book, Giroux maintains that three myths in American society persist that all have the effect of limiting democracy and hurting the general welfare of its children: that the triumph of democracy is due largely to the triumph of the private marketplace, that children are unaffected by American politics, and that teaching and learning are no longer linked to improving the world.[51] In debunking these myths, Giroux concludes that if democracy is to remain a defining principle of public education and daily living for American citizens, then the people must collectively challenge the excessive power of corporations in America. Only an organized, systematic, and sustained effort can hope to curtail the economic, social, political, and cultural power that the corporate culture wields on American society in general but on children in particular.[52] There is a fundamental lesson that is highlighted by Giroux in both works. Substantive reform of any public policy does not typically occur with a singular intervention. There is no simple program that will address all the challenges that exist in any policy challenge. This is most certainly the case in any attempt to reform K–12 public education in America.

The deliberate targeting of children in advertising in the United States is an absolute disgrace. Collectively, America's children deserve better. It is akin to an indoctrination to a life of consumption, where the politics of avarice triumphs over the utilization of analysis and reasonable judgment. Another national travesty when it comes to children pertains to the poverty level for those under the age of 18. In 2013, the poverty rate for a family of four living in the 48 contiguous states was $23,550. By this measure, those households of this size with a total income over this amount were not considered to be living in poverty; those below it were classified as living in poverty.[53] The original measure of poverty was created by Mollie Orshansky of the Social Security Administration in 1963.[54] Many analysts for decades have contended that the poverty measure (and the rationale behind it) is flawed and that it undercounts the number of Americans who are truly living in poverty. In 2010, the official poverty rate was 15.1 percent, meaning that 46.2 million people were living in poverty under the federal definition. The poverty rate for children (those under 18) was 22 percent.[55] More than one-fifth of all children in America are living in poverty in the only nation that is generally regarded as a superpower, in both economic and military terms, in international politics.

I believe that it is incumbent on adults to provide a better future for our children. I do not think it to be extreme to make the contention that the adult population could provide a better future for the children of today by taking proactive measures, in both the public and the private sector, to reduce the ravages of poverty in America. The renowned Jonathan Kozol has offered some profound scholarship on this subject.[56] We know about the harmful effects of poverty, particularly on children, but the poverty rate for them is actually increasing. Additionally, there has to be a reasonable approach to advertising, one that protects children from being overtly exploited and manipulated while simultaneously upholding First Amendment protections for manufacturers. Surely, a balance can be achieved with the appropriate political will and determination.

Educator Alex Molnar provides a very accurate depiction of the consumerist ideology in contemporary America:

> The hallmark of America's advanced market economy is not universal well-being. It is universal advertising. ... In the United States, every available surface, from shopping carts to buses to computer Web pages to public schools, is now blanketed with commercials. Children are sold to advertisers from the time they are born, taught that possessions define their value, and blessed with lives filled with pseudo-events, pseudo-emotions, and pseudo-knowledge provided by the marketers. Yet we expect these children to grow up capable of making independent judgments and effectively participating in democratic civic life. The debate over public education reform cannot be understood by thinking only about schools. It is part of a much broader struggle: whether America will move in the direction of its democratic ideals or be further ensnared in the logic of the market. The outcome is by no means assured.[57]

Advertisers obviously wield a great deal of power in American society in general. The public schools are not exempt from this influence. In fact, corporate influence in public education has been a consistent mainstay in American history.

In 1929, the year the stock market crashed in the United States and the economy plunged into a depression mode, the National Education Association (NEA) published its *Report of the Committee on Propaganda in the Schools*. The author of the report, Edwin C. Broome, concluded that corporate-sponsored materials should be used in the public schools only if they were indispensable to the education of children. If such a standard were widely adopted, then most corporate-sponsored materials would be taken out of classrooms across the country.[58] On behalf of the committee members, Broome noted that

> propaganda, or the systematic direction of effort to gain support for an opinion, doctrine, or course of action, is not a new phenomenon. Systematic efforts to mold public opinion existed long before the press and other modern instruments of communication. The problem of the public schools in dealing with outside materials and influences can be seen in its proper perspective only when viewed as a phase of the whole propaganda movement. From the war came a sharpened appreciation of the effectiveness of propaganda. A tremendous organization fostered and supported by the government was created with the Committee on Public Information as a nucleus, and "carried the gospel of Americanism to every corner of the globe." Millions were similarly expended by foreign countries at home and abroad. According to one estimate England alone spent $150,000,000 for propaganda purposes in the United States during the war. Thousands of men had the opportunity of observing the success with which public opinion could be made and unmade, and of having a part in the process. It is not surprising, therefore, that the last decade has witnessed expansion of the propaganda movement. The ramifications of the great game of "putting it over" are sufficiently apparent. There are the advertising activities designed to sell or to create goodwill for some commercial product or concern. The newspapers, magazines, car cards, billboards, electric signs, theater programs, sky-writers, form letters, and wrappers of every commodity purchased are incessantly beseeching us to avoid this dire fate, to achieve this charming personal characteristic, or to make this noble contribution to the public welfare. All of these ends may be achieved only if we purchase some specific product.[59]

The advice that Broome offered was not heeded by policymakers and educators alike:

> In the years following the NEA report, corporate attempts to place propaganda in the schools accelerated. In the early and mid-1950s, two professional organizations took notice and issued reports describing how to best use what they blandly referred to as "free materials." By 1957, one researcher had found that 97 percent of the teachers he interviewed used sponsored materials. To his dismay, few of the teachers indicated that they used any ethical standard in deciding which materials to use, and virtually no teacher received any guidance on the matter from his or her school administrator. It was left to Sheila Harty to sound a clear and credible alarm in her 1979 report *Hucksters in the Classroom*. Harty found a shocking amount of self-serving corporate material was

being used in the nation's schools. She particularly focused on industry propaganda in four areas: nutrition, nuclear power, the environment, and economics. Since 1979, in the deregulatory, turn-a-quick-buck, what-business-says-goes, "public-private partnership" American political environment, this sort of corporate marketing in the schools has grown like mold spores in a warm petri dish.[60]

The involvement of corporations in public education has a long history, one that coincides with the evolution of the consumerist ideology. As Molnar noted,

Although you would never guess it from the corporate public relations handouts, corporate involvement in the schools is nothing new. The contours of public education in the United States have been, in large measure, shaped by a wave of business involvement in education policy and practice that began a century ago. Throughout the history of American public education, businesspeople have dominated virtually every aspect of the enterprise, from national and state policymaking bodies to local school boards to the boards of grant-making foundations.[61]

As a collective entity, for-profit industries have been very successful at promoting their products and values in the public schools. Many perceive that a "partnership" between the business community and the schools is both desirable and advantageous. But is this relationship truly beneficial to children? Why are many business officials interested in the schools? The honest answer is that good entrepreneurs know a good deal when they see it.

A prime example of the previously mentioned "partnership" is Pizza Hut's BOOK IT! program. The background and expansion of this program is quite intriguing:

Pizza Hut's BOOK IT! national reading incentive program began in 1984 with an enrollment of 200,000 elementary school students across the nation. By the 1998–1999 school year, 22 million children in 895,000 classrooms were enrolled. The program serves as a public relations project, as advertising gimmick, and indirectly sells extra pizzas to parents of student winners. As advertisers suggested in the early 20th century, it is important to implant brand names in children to establish adult preferences. Under the program, children who achieve their monthly reading goals are rewarded with a Personal Pan Pizza and a button from the manager of the local Pizza Hut restaurant. Achieving 6-month goals earns an All-Star Medallion at a local Pizza Hut restaurant. In 1998, the BOOK IT! BEGINNERS PROGRAM started for preschool and kindergarten students with a monthly Personal Pan Pizza award. In 1999, this beginners program was active in 20,000 kindergarten classrooms and day-care centers around the country. BOOK IT is a win-win program. Children, particularly preschoolers and kindergartners, are usually escorted by their parents to the local Pizza Hut restaurant. Do the parents simply sit and watch their child eat a Personal Pan Pizza or do they also buy the child a drink and pizzas and drinks for themselves? It is possible that the parents might spend more than the cost of the award. In fact, Pizza Hut might actually make money by giving the award while implanting their brand name in the child's mind. In addition, Pizza Hut gets free help for their advertising campaign from the local school system. Principals and teachers enroll the students in the program, and teachers set monthly goals, verify completion of reading assignments, and mark wall charts to monitor children's progress toward their Personal Pan Pizza.[62]

The "partnership" between business, in this case Pizza Hut, and the public schools is one sided. It is understandable why Pizza Hut officials want to be associated with reading. It is positive advertising for their restaurants, and it may be profitable as well. But why do school officials promote Pizza Hut in their curricula? As children are taught the importance of a healthy diet, officials are seemingly undermining this important message by rewarding children with a salty, high-fat meal that will probably be accompanied with a sugary soft drink. Perhaps a bit more analysis into this program would cause many educators and parents alike to rethink the plausibility of it for their children and other students as well.[63]

In 1932, an educator presented a plan for eliminating propaganda in the public schools.[64] Howard Parker determined that propaganda "is the effort of individuals or organizations to influence the habits, attitudes, or ideals of the pupils in certain desired ways. It ranges from the direct and aboveboard action of the man who prints his advertisement on blotters to be distributed free to the school children to the more subtle use of contests and biased statements in textbooks and supplementary reading material."[65] Parker concluded that there were eight different types of propaganda utilized in the public schools over 80 years ago. These included the free distribution of manufactured products; the distribution of various forms of supplementary teaching materials that emphasize attitudes that will lead to the purchase of certain commodities; the distribution of accessories bearing printed advertisements, such as pencils and erasers; the use of biased commentary in textbooks; the promotion of contests in such fields as spelling, essay writing, oratory, and poster making; the furnishing of external speakers; the promotion of the observance of special days and weeks; and the mass utilization of children for donating, collecting, or appearing in public functions.[66] To Parker, all of these efforts should be considered propaganda. Propaganda includes all activities that seek to mold and direct public opinion whether the resulting opinion is sound or unsound, just or unjust, honest or dishonest, or plausible or implausible.[67]

For each type of propaganda, Parker recommended proactive measures to combat the use of propaganda in the public schools. First, officials in firms desiring to distribute free samples should do so outside the school grounds. To him, the public school is sacred and should not be utilized to promote the advertising and consumption of material goods. Second, if members of an advisory group consider literature to have educational value, then literature presenting the opposite perspective needs to be given out simultaneously. Third, accessories for students bearing printed advertising cannot be defended and should never be distributed in the schools; representatives of the advertiser can promote their products outside of the school. Fourth, textbooks should be reviewed by an advisory group to determine whether any propaganda has been inserted. Books that include propaganda should not be disseminated to the students. Fifth, Parker believed that contests are the greatest source of annoyance to school administrators. If a contest is believed to have educational value by an advisory group, then it is legitimate. Otherwise, the contest in question should be sponsored by another organization in the community. Sixth, persons who are invited to speak to students in the public schools should be investigated before they interact with children. A member of an advisory group or a reliable judge outside the group should investigate the speaker and determine whether he or she can contribute to the educational program of the school. Seventh, propaganda for special days and weeks should be carefully scrutinized so that they do not compromise the integrity of the school and its mission. Finally, Parker maintained that the mass utilization of pupils for outside activities is the most pernicious form of propaganda and one of the most difficult with which to contend. Again, if advisory committee members determine that an activity does not meet the requirements of their schools to be impartial, then the school's children should not be involved in the promotion of a group that does not conform to the educational mission of the school.[68] This educator from several generations in the past had many substantive points about the use of propaganda in the public schools in America. Simply put, children should be protected from it, and it has no place in the common schools. The "partnership" that is commonly packaged as being mutually beneficial to business and education is heavily skewed in favor of business. Indeed, there is no true partnership but plenty of exploitation. Children should be shielded from this type of egregious behavior.

In the estimation of Molnar, commercialism in the public schools has taken on three different forms: selling to schools (vending), selling in schools (advertising and public relations), and selling of schools (privatization).[69] Selling to schools has been a longitudinal practice in the United States and dates back to at least the initial *McGuffey Readers*. Private vendors have produced such products as textbooks, pencils, pens, paper, cleaning supplies, and food since the common school evolved. Virtually everything used in the public schools is created by private companies.[70]

Selling in schools has been practiced for over a century.[71] This is precisely what prompted the appointment of an NEA committee in the late 1920s to study the problem in the first place.[72] The concerns articulated in the committee's report remain relevant today.[73] In fact, efforts to commercialize the nation's public schools are far more intense than when the committee's report was published in 1929.[74]

The selling of schools entails privatization. Public schools in the United States provide a number of opportunities for privatization of certain services. At a basic level, this might include hiring a private company to provide lunch and/or breakfast to students, the provision of janitorial services in a school district, and/or the transportation of students from home to school and back.[75] At a more fundamental level, it may involve publicly funded schools being operated by education management companies on a for-profit basis.[76] More discussion of this current trend in public education will ensue.

As Molnar reports, parent and citizen groups have formed with the purpose of opposing school commercialism. Some local school board officials have also taken action to reduce the amount of commercialism in the public schools. Some professional organizations, such as the NEA, have voluntary guidelines available in order to discern which corporate-sponsored materials, if any, have education merit. Some state legislators have chosen to make this issue a higher priority in their public policy agenda.[77] To date, however, these movements, while encouraging, are still very small and do not impact most children in the public schools.

Perhaps the most challenging aspect of the consumerist ideology is that the culture in America does not question the assumptions or values inherent in the movement. Although the harmful effects of consumerism have been identified and documented for decades, not much has been done to protect children from advertising and the use of propaganda. Molnar provides a very astute summary of the last 100 years on the subject:

> The last century has seen increasingly powerful efforts to transform the ideal of state run schools as democratizing civic institutions into the ideal of schools as a consumerist marketplace. The education marketplace is intended to provide inviting venues for advertising and public relations and to offer up schools themselves as commodities to be bought and sold. To succeed, efforts to create an education marketplace must necessarily seek to remove control of schools from the communities they serve. Thus, market-oriented measures to reform schools don't reflect popular will so much as they reflect the ideological supremacy of economic efficiency over all other values in elite political decision-making and the abandonment of democratic values in favor of a social order tied together by the values of the marketplace. Market values are concerned with buying and selling. They offer no guidance on matters of justice or fairness and cannot, therefore, represent the interests of all children. Turning children over to the market ensures that they will inevitably be treated as an expense to be reduced or a resource to be harvested. In the process some children and their families will necessarily be considered more valuable than others. For the market to produce winners, it requires that there be losers.[78]

The conservative laissez-faire ideology has real consequences that advocates routinely ignore when they tout the plausibility of marketplace competition. By permitting the commercialization of public education and deregulation in general, defenders of both laissez-faire capitalism and the consumerist ideology have allowed the exploitation of America's children en masse. To those who are critical of self-absorbed, materialistic children; to those who are saddened with children who have deficient self-esteem due, in part, to marketplace advertising; and to those who wonder why young people are not that interested in civic duty and public affairs in general, is it any wonder? Our society has failed children in a way that Horace Mann probably did not envision during the course of his lifetime. Consumerism has run amok in virtually all aspects of American life. The feigned reformer from the conservative political right is the very same person who supports policies that have undermined public education and would like to do so even further, mostly in the guise of marketplace competition. Children in this democracy should be shielded from those who do not care about their emotional and physical development and view them only as pawns to be exploited.

Consider Schor's research on advertising to those who are somewhat skeptical about the use of marketing and propaganda in our society:

> This commercialization of childhood is being driven by a number of factors. . . . But underlying them all is a marketing juggernaut characterized by growing reach, effectiveness, and audacity. One clue to the marketing mentality is industry language. It's a war out there. Those at whom ads are directed are "targets.". . . There's not much doubt about who's winning this war either. When Nickelodeon tells its advertisers that it "owns kids aged 2–12," the boast is closer to the mark than most of us realize.[79]

Our collective unwillingness to regulate advertisers, particularly in the public schools, has had a harmful effect on the development of children in this country. We need to focus on them first and not some rigid ideological premise that private businesses and their officials somehow have an unfettered constitutional right to peddle their products in the public schools without any restrictions or limitations.

A CENTURY-OLD ILLUSION

In the early twentieth century, the economist Simon Patten argued that the desire to buy the new products created due to technological advances would prompt people to work more diligently and reduce their leisure time. To some in America over 100 years ago, there was concern that the industrial revolution and mechanized agriculture would result in less work, more leisure time, and a heightened level of moral decay.[80] Patten made this declaration in a book he originally published in 1907:

> One summer day I took my note-book to a wooded hillside whence I could overlook a rich and beautiful valley. The well-tended farms, the strong stone houses, the busy men and animals moving peacefully over roads and fields, would inspire me, I was sure, with the opening theme of this book. As I seated myself under a chestnut tree a fellow-guest at the hotel came by, and glancing at my memoranda asked if I,

like himself, was writing a lecture. He too had come to the woods, he
said, to meditate and to be inspired by nature. But his thesis, enthusias-
tically unfolded, was the opposite to mine. It was a part of his faith as a
Second Adventist that the world is becoming more unhappy and more
wicked; and it is now so evil that the end of it approaches. On the face
of the earth are wars and in the air rumors of war. Disease, famine,
and disaster surround us; vice reigns, moral decay spreads, and only
the annihilation of mankind can satisfy divine justice and purify the
way for the practice of the long-deferred divine plan. To find inspiration
for this text my companion had also come to look upon the teeming
farm lands owned by clean and well-housed folk. Where I marked the
progress of humanity and thrilled with the hope that poverty will soon
be banished from the world as it has been from this happy valley, he
saw a threatening scene of worldliness where prosperity lulled spiritual
alarms to a dangerous moral peace. The general argument that degener-
ation follows a prolonged period of material success is familiar to the
reader, and I need not give the outline colored by the social and religious philosophy of his sect. Yet in spite of the fundamental differences
in our training it seemed strange to me that two men looking at the
same picture could agree wholly upon truths it painted and forthwith
interpret them as differently as we did. Looking down into this plentiful
valley, one fortified his belief that divine wrath must be invoked upon a
region carnal and depraved; while the other joyfully exclaimed, "Here
is the basis of a new civilization; here is evidence that economic forces
can sweep away poverty, banish misery, and by giving men work bring
forth right and enduring character within the race."[81]

Patten had a distinguished career in his field. His forecast about the
concept of abundance did not emerge as time evolved. As Daniel
Horowitz observed over 30 years ago with regard to *The New Basis of
Civilization,*

> Patten elaborated and clarified the shifts he had been struggling to make
> for more than twenty years: from the exclusion of the poor to their inclu-
> sion in an abundant society; from emphasis on individual character to
> concentration on the social causes of poverty; and from individual salva-
> tion by restraint to social salvation through public use of the economic
> surplus. The new environment of abundance, Patten asserted, at least
> made it possible to raise the masses to a place above necessity so that their
> heredity and character might be permanently improved. . . . Recognizing
> the brutal nature of labor under modern industrial conditions, Patten
> was one of the few social scientists of his generation to turn away from
> the world of work as the source of pleasure. He pointed instead to the
> realm of leisure and argued that public amusements—carnivals, picnics,

and ethnic festivals—would take the laborer's latent vitality and primitive instincts and use them as a fulcrum for uplift. Consequently, he could see an infusion of passions as an aid to higher aspirations, not as a cause of declension or a sign of weak character. That was as far as Patten could go in 1907 in rethinking the relation between desire and restraint. Once passions had uplifted the poor, he argued, the motive of abstinence would emerge, and the nation would advance into a period of restrained living. Citizens of an abundant society would eventually pursue goodness and culture, not indulgence and materialism. A complete day, which balanced good work and leisure, would subject impulses to control. Immigrants and poor, once raised above grinding necessity, would become productive citizens.[82]

His vision was not tangible in the sense that he did not comprehend the enormous power of the consumer ideology and the economic interests associated with it. As noted earlier, Americans for generations have been indoctrinated to accept the premise that hard work allows people to consume as much as they desire, even if the pursuit of the material goods causes financial and emotional consternation and general unhappiness as a result. The consumption cycle for many is never ending, and it is coupled with constant advertising to convince citizens to purchase and consume even more products. The result is that many in American society are consuming too much in terms of their disposable household incomes. The "goodness" that Patten referenced does not depict the reality of the consumption patterns of many in contemporary society. Indeed, many Americans are not saving much of their income and are spending more than they can afford precisely because they have succumbed to indulgence and the politics of materialism. It is difficult for many to practice civic virtue in our society if they are so inwardly focused as a result of such behavioral practices.

Spring offered the following description of the contemporary time period and the consumer ideology:

> The wedding of education, advertising, and the media resulted from efforts to redefine femininity and masculinity in the corporate age, reform the American family, control American youth, resolve conflicts between schools and media over cultural control, use media and schools as part of national defense in the Cold War, create efficiency in food production, and maintain the ideology of consumerism, which makes increased production dependent on increased consumption. Within this framework, increased consumption requires motivating

consumer desires through advertising, which becomes the driving force of the economy. Every space, including public spaces, becomes an advertising opportunity. The promise of increased levels of schooling is not greater happiness but increased levels of consumption. Equality of opportunity means equality of opportunity to consume. America's cuisine, advertising, and media are its most important contributions to world culture. Schools may prepare future citizens to think of education as a means to a high income, which will ensure high levels of consumption. Consumerism now dominates global educational policies as policymakers claim education will increase economic growth and equalize global spending on consumer items.[83]

This fundamental reconception of equality of opportunity is downright sobering. Instead of focusing on fairness, equality between and among diverse groups and society, and social justice, many are focused on economics while other important issues remain ignored in the public discourse as well as the public policymaking process. The politics of consumption truly dominates way too much of the political agenda today in tangible terms, much to the detriment of children in particular. One of the great ironies in the modern world is that technology has improved the quality of life for many, especially the more affluent in society. In a simultaneous and ironic manner, however, these advances may not have contributed to general progress in our overall humanity with respect to how we treat one another in the global community. In the early twenty-first century, there is still a great deal of violence, poverty, unfairness, and exploitation. Technological advancements will not make for a more humane world unless there is a collective desire to reshift values away from consumption and toward more meaningful matters.

There is no simple solution to the challenge inherent in the politics of consumption. I can say with a great deal of confidence that it will require more education and discourse in order to prompt more public attentiveness to the matter. One researcher noted that

> I sometimes feel guilty for being a privileged consumer, and sometimes I feel virtuous for making consumer decisions I believe to be socially and ecologically responsible. But I do not believe guilt and righteousness move us toward greater knowledge and more compassionate acts. Maybe the best we can do is to continue raising each other's awareness of the issues involved in making our choices. Unpacking the knapsack of consumer privilege may be a private and personal journey, but it is also one that really begins to develop once it is shared openly with

others, especially others who approach the issues from different experiential, cultural, and geographical contexts. We can give each other some ideas of where to go next without the righteousness that impedes the process of change.[84]

More public discussion and debate about the pedagogy of consumption in the contemporary time period would undoubtedly prompt more and more people to focus on the necessity of embracing the three Rs—reduce, recycle, and reuse.[85] An expansive and extended dialogue of this nature would undoubtedly result in tangible and positive changes that would be extremely beneficial in global terms.

Some would contend that the United States is a right-of-center country in ideological terms.[86] Inherent in this philosophy is a sacred belief. It has been long posited (see Chapter 2) that a lightly regulated marketplace is advantageous and will result in a better society where hard work, prudent choices, and freedom from government control and interference will pay off in terms of prosperity. A basic conservative premise is that less government regulation will result in more competition between companies, resulting in more choices, better quality, and lower prices for the American "consumer." If this is true, then why are so many products priced at basically the same level? Is competition driving down prices, or are many companies in a number of different industries peacefully coexisting because it is profitable to do so? If the conservative ethos was an accurate depiction of reality, why do many company officials spend so lavishly on advertising? If competition was driving down prices, then why are countless billions allocated for advertising? It would appear that the marketplace ideology does not factor in the truism, past and present, that company officials do not always make moral and ethical decisions in terms of their products, their workers, or citizens in general, and sometimes avarice trumps over everything else. Efficiency does not prevail for that matter, either, for waste does exist in both the private and the public sector.

If the laissez-faire philosophy was plausible, then why do marketers resort to using propaganda to manipulate citizens to purchase their products? What would the price of the products be without mass advertising? It seems highly likely that consumers are funding this type of propaganda through higher prices on goods. Ironically, less advertising may be more advantageous, at least for people who purchase the goods or services in question. If a product is excellent by various criteria, then why spend a lot of money to tell people how wonderful the product is when they may already know it?

While many pay homage to education, the laissez-faire philosophy undermines Mann's vision of common (public) schools for all children. Every time a parent ponders what is best for his or her child when it pertains to education without considering the community as a whole, Mann's common school vision is undermined and devalued. It is compromised precisely because we are conceptually viewing the world in a limited and isolated manner—what is best for my family only as opposed to a much broader set of issues, namely, what is best for the community at large. It may be that what is best for my family is also prudent for society in a general sense. Mann believed in common schools for all, resulting in a better society for all members. He did not envision the sacrificing of public education so that certain children could perhaps be the recipient of a substantive education while other children were not afforded the same opportunity. He rejected the notion that education was a zero-sum game where privileged students would be fine in education terms and the less affluent would be sacrificed to some extent. In other words, he understood education to be not a stratified commodity but rather one where all children had access to the same quality regardless of their economic, social, or political plight in this world.

Our decisions as individuals impact one another. The United States is not a nation of millions of isolated individuals; in fact, citizens are interconnected and interdependent on one another in ways that most of us do not fully comprehend. Citizen decisions about consumption, education, and a vast array of policy issues affect society members in a broad and profound manner. Thus, it is important, as Mann maintained over 150 years ago, to train citizens to be analytical and critical thinkers in this republic.

5

Education in the Early Twenty-First Century

Before analyzing some issues that currently dominate the K–12 education policy agenda, it is important to acknowledge and discuss an issue that has not received much attention by citizens in recent

The executive residence of Horace Mann, completed in 1856. It was later destroyed by fire in 1924. (Image courtesy of Antiochiana, Antioch College.)

decades. It is a compelling civil rights issue that was very much in the forefront of education policy debates in the 1950s, 1960s, and 1970s. I am referring to public school desegregation in the post *Brown* decision era (1954 to the present). Desegregating America's public schools was once a noteworthy objective in the quest to become a more fair, equitable, and moral society. Just because it has fallen off the political radar screen for many elected and appointed officials does not mean that it should continue to be ignored.

K–12 PUBLIC SCHOOL DESEGREGATION

The constitutional focus of public school desegregation is the equal protection clause of the Fourteenth Amendment: "No State shall . . . deny to any person within its jurisdiction the equal protection of the laws." The interpretation of this fundamental equality clause in the federal Constitution has evolved quite dramatically since the tragic case of *Plessy v. Ferguson* in 1896.[1]

Plessy v. Ferguson

In 1890, the Louisiana state legislators enacted a law that required separate railway cars for African Americans and Caucasians. Two years later, Homer Adolph Plessy, who was seven-eighths Caucasian and one-eighth African American, took a seat in the "whites only" car of a Louisiana train. The conductor asked Plessy to vacate the car, and he declined. He was subsequently removed, with the assistance of a police officer, and arrested. Having lost in the Louisiana court system, Plessy appealed to the U.S. Supreme Court.[2]

By a seven-to-one margin, Plessy lost his case again in the federal Supreme Court. Voting in the majority were Justices Henry Billings Brown, Stephen Field, Horace Gray, George Shiras, Howell Jackson, and Edward White and Chief Justice Melville Fuller. The lone dissenter was Justice John Marshall Harlan (Justice David Brewer

---

Portions of this chapter were adapted from Brian L. Fife, "The Supreme Court and School Desegregation since 1896," *Equity and Excellence in Education* 29, no. 2 (1996), with permission from Taylor & Francis.

did not participate in the case).[3] Justice Brown wrote the majority opinion, and the justices upheld the constitutionality of state-imposed racial segregation under the Fourteenth Amendment:

> The object of the amendment was undoubtedly to enforce the absolute equality of the two races before the law, but, in the nature of things, it could not have been intended to abolish distinctions based upon color, or to enforce social, as distinguished from political, equality, or a commingling of the two races upon terms unsatisfactory to either. Laws permitting, and even requiring, their separation, in places where they are liable to be brought into contact, do not necessarily imply the inferiority of either race to the other, and have been generally, if not universally, recognized as within the competency of the state legislatures in the exercise of their police power. The most common instance of this is connected with the establishment of separate schools for white and colored children, which have held to be a valid exercise of the legislative power even by courts of states where the political rights of the colored race have been longest and most earnestly enforced.[4]

The Court's majority based its decision on the "separate but equal" doctrine, though the phrase "separate but equal" does not exist in the opinion. Although this was a hoax at the time, the premise was that states did not violate the Fourteenth Amendment as long as the physical facilities provided for African Americans and Caucasians were equal.

Justice Brown's opinion has many cultural components to it and is obviously reflective of the historical time period in question. There is no reliance on sound constitutional convictions and principles. He determined that

> we consider the underlying fallacy of the plaintiff's argument to consist in the assumption that the enforced separation of the two races stamps the colored race with a badge of inferiority. If this be so, it is not by reason of anything found in the act, but solely because the colored race chooses to put that construction upon it. The argument necessarily assumes that if, as has been more than once the case, and is not unlikely to be so again, the colored race should become the dominant power in the state legislature, and should enact a law in precisely similar terms, it would thereby relegate the white race to an inferior position. We imagine that the white race, at least, would not acquiesce in this assumption. The argument also assumes that social prejudices may be overcome by legislation, and that equal rights cannot be secured to the negro except by an enforced commingling of the two races. We cannot

accept this proposition. If the two races are to meet upon terms of social equality, it must be the result of natural affinities, a mutual appreciation of each other's merits, and a voluntary consent of individuals. . . . Legislation is powerless to eradicate racial instincts, or to abolish distinctions based upon physical differences, and the attempt to do so can only result in accentuating the difficulties of the present situation. If the civil and political rights of both races be equal, one cannot be inferior to the other civilly or politically. If one race be inferior to the other socially, the constitution of the United States cannot put them upon the same plane.[5]

The seven justices in the majority did not utilize a standard of reasonableness in 1896. Instead of compelling states to treat all citizens in the same manner, the justices chose to sanction the practice of state-sponsored segregation in the *Plessy* case.

Justice Harlan's often-cited dissent would become the law of the land 58 years later, long after his death in 1911. He declared that

the white race deems itself to be the dominant race in this country. And so it is, in prestige, in achievements, in education, in wealth, and in power. So, I doubt not, it will continue to be for all time, if it remains true to its great heritage, and holds fast to the principles of constitutional liberty. But in view of the constitution, in the eye of the law, there is in this country no superior, dominant, ruling class of citizens. There is no caste here. Our constitution is color-blind, and neither knows nor tolerates classes among citizens. In respect to civil rights, all citizens are equal before the law. The humblest is the peer of the most powerful. The law regards man as man, and takes no account of his surroundings or of his color when his civil rights as guarantied by the supreme law of the land are involved. It is therefore to be regretted that this high tribunal, the final expositor of the fundamental law of the land, has reached the conclusion that it is competent for a state to regulate the enjoyment by citizens of their civil rights solely upon the basis of race. In my opinion, the judgment this day rendered will, in time, prove to be quite as pernicious as the decision made by this tribunal in the Dred Scott Case.[6]

Justice Harlan admonished his colleagues in a very poignant manner. In comparing *Plessy* to *Dred Scott*, he was clearly making the argument that the harm to society would be profound and substantial.[7] The interpretation of the Fourteenth Amendment by the seven justices in *Plessy* perpetuated the reality that first- and second-class citizenship existed in the United States. His interpretation and understanding of the Constitution would be vindicated about three generations later in *Brown v. Board of Education of Topeka, Kansas.*[8]

Brown v. Board of Education of Topeka, Kansas

The *Brown* case encompassed a consolidation of cases not only from Kansas but from Delaware, South Carolina, and Virginia as well.[9] All cases involved African American children who were denied admission to public schools attended by Caucasian children under state laws requiring or permitting racial segregation. Prior to *Brown* and consistent with the *Plessy* ruling, the justices had ruled that segregation was constitutional as long as tangible factors, such as buildings, curriculum, and the qualifications, salaries, and benefits of teachers, were either equal or being equalized. Yet the cases emanating from these four states would be viewed differently by the justices in 1954.

Chief Justice Fred Vinson died unexpectedly in 1953. President Dwight D. Eisenhower decided to nominate Earl Warren, the Republican governor of California, to replace him.[10]

Through his persuasive efforts, as well as his honed political skills, the new chief justice was able to secure a unanimous decision in the *Brown* decision.[11] The other justices serving at the time included Hugo Black, Stanley Reed, Felix Frankfurter, William Douglas, Robert Jackson, Harold Burton, Tom Clark, and Sherman Minton.[12] Chief Justice Warren emphasized the importance of public education in the United States:

> Today, education is perhaps the most important function of state and local governments. Compulsory school attendance laws and the great expenditures for education both demonstrate our recognition of the importance of education to our democratic society. It is required in the performance of our most basic public responsibilities, even service in the armed forces. It is the very foundation of good citizenship. Today it is a principal instrument in awakening the child to cultural values, in preparing him for later professional training, and in helping him to adjust normally to his environment. In these days, it is doubtful that any child may reasonably be expected to succeed in life if he is denied the opportunity of an education. Such an opportunity, where the state has undertaken to provide it, is a right which must be made available to all on equal terms.[13]

Chief Justice Warren proceeded to answer the critical question in the case as he perceived it: "Does segregation of children in public schools solely on the basis of race, even though the physical facilities and other 'tangible' factors may be equal, deprive the children of the minority group of equal educational opportunities?"[14] To the chief justice and his colleagues on the Court in 1954, the question was answered in a definitive manner in the affirmative. Chief Justice Warren declared, "We conclude that in the field of public education the doctrine of "separate but equal" has no place. Separate educational facilities are inherently unequal. Therefore, we hold that the plaintiffs and others similarly situated for whom the actions have been brought are, by reason of segregation complained of, deprived of the equal protection of the laws guaranteed by the Fourteenth Amendment."[15] Justice Harlan's dissent in 1896 was now the law of the land.

It is important to note that the justices invalidated de jure segregation (segregation by law or state action) but not de facto segregation (segregation by fact of where people live) in the *Brown* decision. A year later, in 1955, the justices provided implementation guidelines for desegregation in a case commonly referred to as *Brown II*.[16] Chief Justice Warren penned the majority opinion for a unanimous Court. Justice Jackson died in the fall of 1954 and was succeeded by John Marshall Harlan, the namesake of his grandfather and former justice.[17] Otherwise, the rest of the Court's personnel were intact from the previous year. The responsibility for overseeing public school desegregation efforts nationwide was delegated to federal district court judges:

> Full implementation of these constitutional principles may require solution of varied local school problems. School authorities have the primary responsibility for elucidating, assessing, and solving these problems; courts will have to consider whether the action of school authorities constitutes good faith implementation of the governing constitutional principles. Because of their proximity to local conditions and the possible need for further hearings, the courts which originally heard these cases can best perform this judicial appraisal. Accordingly, we believe it appropriate to remand the cases to those courts.[18]

According to Chief Justice Warren, school district officials should desegregate their schools "with all deliberate speed."[19] The lead attorney for the National Association for the Advancement of Colored People, Thurgood Marshall, pleaded with the justices to order local officials to desegregate swiftly and without delay. Ultimately, the justices feared that too much violence would ensue with an aggressive implementation strategy, and this is why they decided to create broad parameters, much to Marshall's chagrin.[20]

Major Supreme Court Rulings from 1954 to 1974

Thurgood Marshall's plea for rapid national desegregation was undoubtedly prudent and justified, for many school district officials largely ignored the *Brown* decree for years after the case was decided by the justices. Dual school systems were prevalent all across the country by the late 1960s. A series of Supreme Court cases, beginning in 1968, began the process of truly implementing the original *Brown* decree. The justices unanimously (Chief Justice Warren and Justices Black, Douglas, Harlan II, William Brennan, Potter Stewart, Byron White, Abe Fortas, and Thurgood Marshall) ended the use of freedom of choice plans as an exclusive desegregation remedy in *Green v. County School Board of New Kent County*.[21] New Kent County was a rural district in eastern Virginia. De facto segregation was not present because both Caucasians and African Americans resided throughout the county. The school district had only two schools (New Kent School on the east side of the county was a combined Caucasian elementary and senior high school, George W. Watkins School was a combined African American elementary and senior high school). Students could attend either school under the freedom-of-choice plan. After three years of operation, no Caucasian students participated in the plan. While 115 African American children enrolled in New Kent in 1967, 85 percent of African American children still remained in Watkins. Justice Brennan wrote for the Court's majority:

> All we decide today is that, in desegregating a dual system, a plan utilizing "freedom of choice" is not an end in itself. . . . Although the general experience under "freedom of choice" to date has been such as to indicate its ineffectiveness as a tool of desegregation, there may well be instances in which it can serve as an effective device. Where it offers real promise of aiding a desegregation program to effectuate conversion of a state-imposed dual system to a unitary, non-racial system there might be no objection to allowing such a device to prove itself in operation. On the other hand, if there are reasonably available other ways, such for illustration as zoning, promising speedier and more effective conversion to a unitary, nonracial school system, "freedom of choice" must be held unacceptable.[22]

It was clear in 1968 that Caucasian resistance to desegregation was still very substantial in the South in particular. Freedom of choice plans typically meant that most Caucasian parents did nothing to enhance racial balance in their schools, while a small percentage of African American parents transferred their children to predominantly Caucasian schools.

By the time that the *Swann v. Charlotte-Mecklenberg Board of Education* case was decided in 1971, Chief Justice Warren had retired, and his position was filled by President Richard Nixon with Warren Burger in 1969.[23] The *Swann* case dealt with the constitutionality of several controversial desegregation techniques, and the decision was unanimous (Chief Justice Burger and Justices Black, Douglas, Harlan II, Brennan, Stewart, White, Marshall, and Harry Blackmun). In his opinion, Chief Justice Burger admitted that the Supreme Court had not provided federal district court judges with comprehensive guidelines for school desegregation:

> This case and those argued with it arose in States having a long history of maintaining two sets of schools in a single school system deliberately operated to carry out a governmental policy to separate pupils in schools solely on the basis of race. That was what *Brown v. Board of Education* was all about. These cases present us with the problem of defining in more precise terms than heretofore the scope of the duty of school authorities and district courts in implementing *Brown I* and the mandate to eliminate dual systems and establish unitary systems at once. Meanwhile, district courts and courts of appeals have struggled in hundreds of cases with a multitude and variety of problems under this Court's general directive. Understandably, in an area of evolving remedies, those courts had to improvise and experiment without detailed or specific guidelines. This Court, in *Brown I*, appropriately dealt with the large constitutional principles; other federal courts had to grapple with the flinty, intractable realities of day-to-day implementation of those constitutional commands. Their efforts, of necessity, embraced a process of "trial and error," and our effort to formulate guidelines must take into account their experience.[24]

A federal district court judge approved a desegregation plan in 1965 based on geographic zoning with a free transfer option. After the *Green* decision in 1968, James Swann petitioned for further relief. Both parties agreed that school system officials failed to achieve unitary status. Two plans were submitted in order to achieve this objective, one by the school board and another by a court-appointed expert, Dr. John Finger.[25]

The district court judge endorsed the Finger plan, which required more desegregation than school board officials were willing to accept. The board plan would have closed seven schools and reassigned the students involved. Attendance zones were to be restructured to achieve greater levels of racial balance, but the existing grade structures were left intact. The board plan would have modified the free transfer plan into an optional majority to minority transfer system (students in a racial majority in one school could transfer to another school where they would be in the racial minority).[26]

Under the board plan, African Americans would be reassigned to 9 of the 10 high schools in the district, thereby producing an African American population of 17 to 36 percent in each. The tenth high school would have an African American population of 2 percent. The junior high schools would be rezoned so that all but one would range from 0 to 38 percent African American in attendance. One junior high school would still have an African American population of 90 percent. Attendance at the elementary schools, however, would still be based primarily on the neighborhood concept. Over half of the African American children at this level would remain in schools that were between 86 and 100 percent African American.

The Finger plan utilized the board zoning plan for high schools with one modification. Three hundred additional African American students would be transported to the nearly all-Caucasian Independence High School. This plan was also similar to the board plan pertaining to the junior high schools. Under the Finger plan, nine satellite zones would be created. Inner-city African American students would be assigned to nine outlying predominantly Caucasian junior high schools. As is commonly the case, the most controversy involved the elementary school students. Finger proposed the utilization of pairing and grouping techniques along with zoning, with the result that all elementary schools would have an African American proportion that would range from 9 to 38 percent. Pairing occurs when two schools, one predominantly African American and one predominantly Caucasian, are combined either by sending half the students in one school to the other for all grades or by sending all the children to one school for certain grades and then to the other school for the remaining grade levels.[27]

The Supreme Court justices accepted the Finger plan in the *Swann* case. In his opinion, Chief Justice Burger made four important rulings. Federal district court judges could decree as tools of desegregation the

following: reasonable bus transportation (busing), reasonable grouping of noncontiguous zones, the reasonable movement toward the
elimination of one-race schools, and the use of mathematical ratios of
African Americans and Caucasians in the schools as a starting point
toward racial desegregation.[28]

In 1973, the justices identified segregation in northern schools in
Keyes v. School District No. 1.[29] In 1969, the Denver school board members adopted three resolutions designed to desegregate the Park Hill
area in the northeastern section of the city. Following a school board
election, the resolutions were rescinded. A voluntary student transfer
program was implemented instead. Wilfred Keyes sought an injunction enjoining the board from rescinding the resolutions. A district
court judge determined that the school board members had been
guilty of an unconstitutional policy of deliberate racial segregation
with respect to the Park Hill area of the city. The board members were
ordered to implement the three resolutions. Yet segregation was
present in other sections of Denver as well, so Keyes petitioned the
court to desegregate all segregated schools in Denver. It was concluded at the district court level, however, that the rest of the school
district was not segregated by law or action; rather, a situation of de
facto segregation existed. No relief was provided for Keyes as a result.
It was acknowledged that the segregated core of schools in the city of
Denver was educationally inferior to other schools and that the school
board was required to provide "equal educational opportunity."[30]

On appeal, the judges on the Tenth Circuit Court of Appeals
affirmed the decree with regard to the Park Hill schools but reversed
the ruling with respect to the core city schools. On further appeal to
the Supreme Court, Justice Brennan wrote the majority opinion and
contended that actions taken by school board officials leading to de
facto segregation must be remedied in the same manner as that of de
jure segregation:

> We emphasize that the differentiating factor between *de jure* segregation
> and so-called *de facto* segregation to which we referred in *Swann* is pur-
> pose or intent to segregate. Where school authorities have been found to
> have practiced purposeful segregation in part of a school system, they
> may be expected to oppose system-wide desegregation, as did the
> respondents in this case, on the ground that their purposefully segregat-
> ive actions were isolated and individual events, thus leaving the plain-
> tiffs with the burden of proving otherwise. But at that point where
> an intentionally segregative policy is practiced in a meaningful or

significant segment of a school system, as in this case, the school authorities cannot be heard to argue that plaintiffs have proved only "isolated and individual" unlawfully segregative actions. In that circumstance, it is both fair and reasonable to require that the school authorities bear the burden of showing that their actions as to other segregated schools within the system were not also motivated by segregative intent.[31]

Keyes was a seven-to-one decision. Chief Justice Burger, along with Justices Douglas, Stewart, Marshall, Blackmun, and Lewis Powell, sided with the majority opinion. Justice William Rehnquist dissented, and Justice White did not participate. Justice Rehnquist determined that the unconstitutional segregation in the Park Hill area did not prove that the entire district was segregated in violation of the original *Brown* decision. *Keyes* is also significant because it extended the desegregation remedy to Latino Americans in addition to African Americans.[32] A year later, desegregation advocates in America would experience a devastating setback.

Milliken v. Bradley

The *Milliken* case was decided by a five-to-four vote.[33] A class-action suit was launched by Ronald and Richard Bradley on behalf of all minority students attending the Detroit public schools and the Detroit branch of the National Association for the Advancement of Colored People against Michigan Governor William Milliken, the State Board of Education, Detroit's superintendent and school board, and other state officials, alleging racial segregation in the Detroit public schools. A federal district court judge ruled in favor of the African American students. The school board members were ordered to formulate desegregation plans for the city school district; state officials were directed to devise plans for a metropolitan unitary system involving three counties. Eighty-five school districts were allowed to participate in the process by the district court judge, even though de jure segregation was not evident in these areas. A panel was appointed to devise a regional desegregation plan that included 53 of the 85 public suburban districts. The overseeing judge also ordered the Detroit public school system to purchase 295 school buses for transportation purposes. The district court's ruling was affirmed by the Sixth Circuit Court of Appeals but remanded the case for more extensive hearings involving suburban school officials. It also tentatively rescinded the purchase order for the additional buses.[34]

Chief Justice Burger penned the majority opinion in *Milliken* and was supported by Justices Stewart, Blackmun, Powell, and Rehnquist. The dissenters included Justices Douglas, Brennan, White, and Marshall. The Court's majority reversed the lower-court rulings. Chief Justice Burger contended that the lower-court judges erred in the assumption that the Detroit public schools could not be desegregated without including the suburban districts:

> The record before us, voluminous as it is, contains evidence of *de jure* segregated conditions only in the Detroit schools; indeed, that was the theory on which the litigation was initially based and on which the District Court took evidence. With no showing of significant violation by the 53 outlying school districts and no evidence of any inter-district violation or effect, the court went beyond the original theory of the case as framed by the pleadings and mandated a metropolitan area remedy. To approve the remedy ordered by the court would impose on the outlying districts, not shown to have committed any constitutional violation, a wholly impermissible remedy based on a standard not hinted at in *Brown I* and *II* or any holding of this Court.[35]

The *Milliken* decision remains a very significant precedent in American jurisprudence. In the mid-1970s, the justices limited the scope of public school desegregation to only those districts where de jure segregation was present. This means that school desegregation has remained an urban phenomenon and that suburban America has been largely excluded to this day. Poor families—and, disproportionately, non-Caucasian ones—have become increasingly isolated in central cities all across the country. Desegregation has become more challenging and cumbersome as a result.[36] Justice Marshall strongly rebuked his colleagues in the majority in his dissent:

> Desegregation is not and was never expected to be an easy task. Racial attitudes ingrained in our Nation's childhood and adolescence are not quickly thrown aside in its middle years. But just as the inconvenience of some cannot be allowed to stand in the way of the rights of others, so public opposition, no matter how strident, cannot be permitted to divert this Court from the enforcement of the constitutional principles at issue in this case. Today's holding, I fear, is more a reflection of a perceived public mood that we have gone far enough in enforcing the Constitution's guarantee of equal justice than it is the product of neutral principles of law. In the short run, it may seem to be the easier course to

allow our great metropolitan areas to be divided up each into two cities—one white, the other black—but it is a course, I predict, our people will ultimately regret.[37]

Justice Marshall was a competent soothsayer. *Milliken*—and the general unwillingness to revisit the matter of metropolitan desegregation by judges and politicians alike—has stymied progress toward more enhanced levels of racial balance in the public schools.[38] The impact of *Milliken* was well documented by Gary Orfield. He indicated, "When the Supreme Court, through *Milliken I*, slammed the door on the only possible desegregation strategy for cities with few whites, it shifted the attention of urban educators and civil rights lawyers away from desegregation and toward other approaches for helping minority children confined to segregated and inferior city schools."[39] Simply put, school desegregation has not been a policy issue at or near the top of the national political agenda since 1974.

The Prevailing Status Quo since the *Milliken* Era

The Supreme Court justices have issued some important rulings with regard to public school desegregation since 1974. I believe that it is accurate to depict all of them as eroding the promise of *Brown*. In *Board of Education of Oklahoma City v. Dowell* (1991), some rather deep cleavages on the issue of applying the Constitution to school desegregation were apparent. William Rehnquist was elevated to chief justice by President Reagan in 1986, and he wrote the majority opinion. He was joined by Justices White, Scalia, Sandra Day O'Connor, and Anthony Kennedy. Justices Marshall, Blackmun, and John Paul Stevens dissented. Justice David Souter did not participate.[40]

In 1961, several African American students and their parents brought suit against the board of education in Oklahoma City, alleging that the city's public schools were unlawfully segregated. In 1970, federal district court judges determined that previous efforts to desegregate were not successful and ordered mandatory student assignments for students in a number of schools in order to achieve a unitary status. In 1977, an "Order Terminating Case" was issued by a district court judge based on the conclusion that the desegregation plan implemented by a decree in 1972 had worked, substantial compliance had been witnessed, and a unitary school system had been achieved. Later, during the 1985–1986 academic year, the members of the school board adopted a new student assignment plan relying on neighborhood assignments and a voluntary transfer plan. Some African American students alleged that the school board members had not achieved unitary status and that the new plan would result in resegregation. At that time, the district court judges refused to reopen the case. The judges on the Tenth Circuit Court of Appeals reversed the decision on appeal, indicating that the 1977 order was binding to the parties in the case but that nothing in the order indicated that the 1972 injunction itself was terminated. The case was remanded back to the district court level. In 1987, a district court judge determined that the 1972 decree should be vacated and that the schools should be returned to local control. On appeal, the judges on the Tenth Circuit Court of Appeals again reversed the ruling and maintained that a desegregation decree generally remains in effect until school district officials can demonstrate a "grievous wrong" evoked by new and unforeseen conditions. The justices on the Supreme Court, however, reversed the judgment of the Tenth Circuit.[41]

Chief Justice Rehnquist determined that the oversight of school desegregation plans by federal judges was intended to be a temporary measure:

> A district court need not accept at face value the profession of a school board which has intentionally discriminated that it will cease to do so in the future. But in deciding whether to modify or dissolve a desegregation decree, a school board's compliance with previous court orders is obviously relevant. In this case, the original finding of *de jure* segregation was entered in 1961, the injunctive decree from which the Board seeks relief was entered in 1972, and the Board complied with the decree in good faith until 1985. Not only do the personnel of school boards change over time, but the same passage of time enables the District Court to observe the good faith of the school board in complying with the decree. The test espoused by the Court of Appeals would condemn a school district, once governed by a board which intentionally discriminated, to judicial tutelage for the indefinite future. Neither the principles governing the entry and dissolution of injunctive decrees nor the commands of the Equal Protection Clause of the Fourteenth Amendment require any such Draconian result.[42]

The five justices in the majority believed that the Tenth Circuit's test for dissolving a desegregation decree was too stringent under the equal protection clause. To the dissenters, those in the majority were guilty of creating a "milder standard" for judicial oversight of school desegregation plans.[43]

In 1992, the justices unanimously (Clarence Thomas did not participate) ruled in *Freeman v. Pitts* that federal district court judges
in ongoing school desegregation cases have the discretion to order
incremental withdrawal of supervision over school district authorities. Justice Kennedy wrote for Chief Justice Rehnquist and Justices
White, Blackmun, Stevens, O'Connor, Scalia, and Souter, "A district
court need not retain active control over every aspect of school
administration until a school district has demonstrated unitary status
in all facets of its system."[44] The DeKalb County (Georgia) School
System (DCSS) had been subject to the supervision and jurisdiction
of a federal district court judge since 1969, when it was ordered to
desegregate. In 1986, DCSS officials filed a motion for final dismissal.
Since the *Green* decision, district court judges have operated under
the guidelines that school districts need to achieve unitary status for
several years in six areas: student assignment, transportation, faculty,
staff, extracurricular activities, and facilities. A district court judge
ruled that DCSS officials had achieved unitary status in student
assignment and three other areas. As a result, the judge relinquis-
hed remedial control in these areas but maintained authority over
the school district for those aspects in which it was not in full
compliance.[45]

On appeal, the decision was reversed by the Court of Appeals for
the Eleventh Circuit. The appellate court judges ruled that district
court judges must retain full authority over a school system until it
achieves unitary status in six categories simultaneously for several
years (the *Green* standard). The Supreme Court's majority disagreed.
Justice Kennedy determined that

> to say, as did the Court of Appeals, that a school district must meet all
> six Green factors before the trial court can declare the system unitary
> and relinquish its control over school attendance zones, and to hold fur-
> ther that racial balancing by all necessary means is required in the
> interim, is simply to vindicate a legal phrase. The law is not so formalis-
> tic. A proper rule must be based on the necessity to find a feasible rem-
> edy that insures system-wide compliance with the court decree and that
> is directed to curing the effects of the specific violation.[46]

The more stringent criteria for desegregation established by *Green* are no
longer in effect. According to the justices for over 20 years, school desegregation can be achieved in an incremental manner. The justices ruling
in *Missouri v. Jenkins* three years later basically reaffirmed this stance.[47]

A divided Court restricted the ability of public school district officials to use race to determine which schools students can attend in *Parents Involved in Community Schools v. Seattle School District No. 1* in 2007.[48] Chief Justice John Roberts wrote the majority opinion and was joined by Justices Scalia, Kennedy, Thomas, and Samuel Alito. Justice Stephen Breyer wrote a dissent, and he was joined by Justices Stevens, Souter, and Ruth Bader Ginsburg.[49]

Seattle School District officials allowed students to apply to any senior high school in the district. As a result, some schools became oversubscribed when too many students identified them as their first choice; district officials utilized a tiebreaker system. The second most important tiebreaker was race in order to maintain racial balance. If the racial demographics of any school in the district deviated sufficiently enough from the overall student population (40 percent Caucasian and 60 percent non-Caucasian), the racial tiebreaker went into effect. At a particular school, either Caucasians or non-Caucasians could be favored for admission depending on which race would bring the racial balance closer to the overall racial mix of the district. A nonprofit group, Parents Involved in Community Schools, sued the district, maintaining that the racial tiebreaker violated the equal protection clause, the Civil Rights Act of 1964, and Washington state law. A district court judge dismissed the suit, upholding the tiebreaker. That decision was initially reversed by a panel of judges on the Ninth Circuit Court of Appeals.[50] The Ninth Circuit judges later granted rehearing en banc, and overruled the panel decision, affirming the district court judge's determination that Seattle's plan was narrowly tailored to serve a compelling government interest. The justices combined this case with a similar one from the Jefferson County (Kentucky) Public Schools.[51]

Chief Justice Roberts, along with four of his colleagues, utilized a strict scrutiny test and determined that Seattle's racial tiebreaker system was unconstitutional under the equal protection clause:

> What do the racial classifications do in these cases, if not determine admission to a public school on a racial basis? Before *Brown*, schoolchildren were told where they could and could not go to school based on the color of their skin. The school districts in these cases have not carried the heavy burden of demonstrating that we should allow this once again—even for very different reasons. For schools that never segregated on the basis of race, such as Seattle, or that have removed the vestiges of past segregation, such as Jefferson County, the way "to achieve a

system of determining admission to the public schools on a nonracial basis," *Brown II*, is to stop assigning students on a racial basis. The way to stop discrimination on the basis of race is to stop discriminating on the basis of race.[52]

The chief justice believed that officials in both school districts were well intended in their desire to maintain racial diversity in the public schools. These intentions, however, to him, were not sufficient enough to overcome the constitutional protections of individual rights.

Justice Breyer's dissent is quite unequivocal and, to many school desegregation advocates, rightfully so:

These cases consider the longstanding efforts of two local school boards to integrate their public schools. The school board plans before us resemble many others adopted in the last 50 years by primary and secondary schools throughout the Nation. All of those plans represent local efforts to bring about the kind of racially integrated education that *Brown v. Board of Education* (1954), long ago promised—efforts that this Court has repeatedly required, permitted, and encouraged local authorities to undertake. This Court has recognized that the public interests at stake in such cases are "compelling." We have approved of "narrowly tailored" plans that are no less race-conscious than the plans before us. And we have understood that the Constitution *permits* local communities to adopt desegregation plans even where it does not *require* them to do so. The plurality pays inadequate attention to this law, to past opinions' rationales, their language, and the contexts in which they arise. As a result, it reverses course and reaches the wrong conclusion. In doing so, it distorts precedent, it misapplies the relevant constitutional principles, it announces legal rules that will obstruct efforts by state and local governments to deal effectively with the growing resegregation of public schools, it threatens to substitute for present calm a disruptive round of race-related litigation, and it undermines *Brown's* promise of integrated primary and secondary education that local communities have sought to make a reality. This cannot be justified in the name of the Equal Protection Clause.[53]

The judicial retrenchment from the original *Brown* decision, if not completed by *Milliken* toward the end of the Nixon era, has been absolutely secured by this decision. It is safe to presume, at this juncture, that the only way that the justices of the Supreme Court will make school desegregation policy a prominent part of their agenda is for several of the existing justices to retire and have them replaced with jurists with a markedly different interpretation of the federal Constitution. Not much political activity in school desegregation has been witnessed in the other branches of government for that matter as well. Collectively, the members of Congress and presidents for more than 30 years have showed very little interest in the subject.

As Orfield has documented, public schools in America today are more segregated than they were in the late 1960s and early 1970s.[54] Jonathan Kozol refers to this reality as "the shame of the nation" in one of his books.[55] According to Orfield,

> Fifty-five years years after the *Brown* decision, blacks and Latinos in American schools are more segregated than they have been in more than four decades. The Supreme Court's 2007 decision in the Seattle and Louisville voluntary desegregation cases has not only taken away some important tools used by districts to combat this rising isolation, but this decision is also certain to intensify these trends. Segregation is fast spreading into large sectors of suburbia and there is little or no assistance for communities wishing to resist the pressures of resegregation and ghetto creation in order to build successfully integrated schools and neighborhoods. Desegregation plans that were successful for decades are being shut down by orders from conservative courts, federal civil rights officials have pressured communities to abandon their voluntary desegregation efforts, and magnet schools are losing their focus on desegregation.[56]

Indeed, Kozol is absolutely justified in his description of resegregation in America. Americans could have continued their progress toward the fulfillment of the hope and promise of *Brown*. Instead, the United States is regressing when it comes to desegregation and the pursuit of a truly integrated society. Civil rights leaders such as Martin Luther King Jr. and his supporters, Thurgood Marshall, and countless millions of other Americans who support fairness, equality, and justice have been truly let down by the opposition to desegregation apparent in the judiciary and the general indifference by other institutions of government as well as by society itself.

SCHOOL CHOICE IN THE CONTEMPORARY WORLD

In the ongoing era of the No Child Left Behind Act, there is a general assault on Horace Mann's common school ideology. Conservatives who espouse more school choice and marketplace competition continue to undermine the common school ideal. For the past few decades, conservatives have vigorously sought to advance two primary alternatives to traditional public schools: charter schools and voucher programs. Both approaches to K–12 education raise fundamental questions of fairness with serious implications in a democratic society.

The Politics of Charter Schools

Charter schools are nontraditional public schools. While they are publicly funded elementary or secondary schools, charter school officials are not bound by some of the rules, regulations, and laws that apply to traditional public schools in exchange for some other type of accountability mechanism. The details of the arrangement established by officials on behalf of the charter school and the authorizing body are delineated in the school's charter (see Chapter 3).[57] The premise of charter schools is that advocates believe that they will improve on traditional public schools in two ways: by developing and sharing innovative teaching practices and by promoting competition.[58] The charter school movement is a part of a national trend that emphasized more choice elements in public education in the 1990s that is still ongoing. Charter school legislation was initially created in Minnesota in 1991.[59] According to the Center for Education Reform, a charter school advocacy organization, there are more than 5,700 charter schools operating in the United States and serving about 2 million children as of December 2011.[60] Charter school legislation has been passed and implemented in 41 states and the District of Columbia; the nine states that do not have charter school laws are Alabama, Kentucky, Montana, Nebraska, North Dakota, South Dakota, Vermont, Washington, and West Virginia.[61] Since 1992, over 1,000 charter schools have closed, meaning that 15 percent of all charter schools created have closed for cause.[62]

Gary Miron believes that after 20 years of operation in the United States, as well as substantial growth in the number of charter schools since 1991, charter school advocates have strayed significantly from the original vision of the movement. Charter schools are not achieving the original goals established by early supporters. Based on his analysis of charter schools in several states, as well as a growing body of research on charter schools, he offers the following conclusions about charter schools:

- One of the original goals of charter schools entailed the involvement of more local citizens and groups in K–12 education. The involvement of people at the local level is shrinking in the charter school movement, and they have been replaced by outsiders, especially private education management organizations. Schools are run by officials in distant corporate headquarters.

- Another goal of the charter school movement is to increase opportunities for parental involvement in education. Parents who choose schools may be more engaged in the education of their children, presumably leading to higher student achievement and other positive outcomes. However, the evidence on parent satisfaction of charter schools is based on surveys of parents whose children remain in charter schools and does not include parents whose children have left the schools. More studies need to be conducted, but the increase in charter schools in the United States at least suggests that they are popular with many parents in the country.

- Charter schools are based on the premise that they create new opportunities for school choice with open access for all children. Advocates contend that choice will spur students, parents, and teachers to work harder to support the schools they have chosen. Research evidence, however, suggests that charter schools attract and enroll students by race, class, and ability. Increasingly, charter school leaders are using admissions or placement tests. Evidence to date indicates that only 25 percent of charter schools in operation have student demographic populations that are similar to local school districts in terms of ethnic composition and proportion of low income students. Demographics of students with disabilities and those classified as English language learners are even more imbalanced.

- The charter school concept is one that encourages innovation in curriculum and instruction. Research findings to date, however, do not support the contention that charter schools are more innovative than traditional public schools.

- Charter schools are supposed to enhance professional autonomy and opportunities for professional development of teachers. Some charter schools have clearly created and fostered professional opportunities for teachers. But charter schools have been continually plagued by a high level of teacher attrition, which does not suggest that many teachers find charter school employment to be rewarding and fulfilling.

- Charter schools are typically created based on the premise that students will learn more and increase their achievement on state standardized test scores. A growing body of empirical evidence, however, indicates that children in charter schools perform similar or even worse than children in demographically matched traditional public schools.

- In exchange for more autonomy over the academic curriculum, charter school officials are supposed to be held more accountable for student achievement than their counterparts in traditional public schools. Schools that fail to meet their performance objectives can have their charter revoked or not renewed; those that do not satisfy parents may lose students and ultimately go out of business. Yet closure rates are relatively low as indicated above, and most charter schools that fail do so because of financial mismanagement, not because of performance or market accountability.[63]

Charter schools have afforded more choice for parents in many states with regard to their children's education. The choice has come at a significant price, however. Charter schools have provided an easy route for the privatization of public education in that many state laws permit the conversion of private schools to public charter schools. In addition, there is growing reliance on private education management organizations in the operation of charter schools. Charter schools are more segregated than traditional public schools, and they are less likely to admit children with special needs or children whose native language is not English. Even if a reasonable measure of charter school effectiveness would be standardized testing performance, which is debatable, charter schools are strikingly similar to comparable traditional public schools in many areas across the country. One of the great challenges today with charter schools, not unlike the arena of electoral politics for that matter, is that many charter school advocacy group officials continually market their product regardless of the facts. As Miron noted, "Strong and effective lobbying and advocacy groups for charter schools quickly reinterpret research and shape the message to fit their needs rather than the long-term interests of the movement. They attack evidence that questions the performance of charter schools and offer anecdotal evidence, rarely substantiated by technical reports, in rebuttal. Such lobbying has undermined reasonable discourse and made improving charter schools more difficult."[64]

A comprehensive national study on charter school quality was conducted by investigators at Stanford University's Center for Research on Education Outcomes.[65] Center researchers conducted a longitudinal student-level analysis of more than 70 percent of all charter school students in the United States. The results are demonstrative of a wide variation in student performance. The evaluators determined that almost half (46 percent) of all charter school students have testing results that are no different than students from the local traditional public schools. While 17 percent of all charter school students receive superior education opportunities compared to their traditional public school peers, 37 percent of charter school students did significantly worse than their public school counterparts. States where charter school students demonstrated the most improvement are those with relatively few charter schools and arguably more effective oversight.[66] The Stanford researchers have debunked some assumptions, particularly on the part of political conservatives, that choice and competition will result in better student achievement. Less than one-fifth of charter school students in the nation have experienced a more qualitative education as a result of leaving the common school in favor of the market-driven entity known as a charter school.

The Politics of Vouchers

A school or education voucher certificate issued by a government can be utilized by recipient parents to apply toward tuition at a private school rather sending their child to an assigned traditional public school. To school choice advocates, voucher programs allow parents and their children more choice with regard to education and forces public schools to compete with private schools in order to enhance education quality (see Chapter 3). According to officials at the Center for Education Reform, there are 15 school voucher programs in eight states plus the District of Columbia and Douglas County, Colorado. During the 2011–2012 school year, more than 80,000 students participated in voucher programs, and almost $500 million was spent on voucher programs across the United States.[67]

The nation's most expansive voucher program exists in Indiana. On May 5, 2011, Indiana's Republican governor, Mitch Daniels, signed the School Scholarship Act (House Bill 1003) into law, creating a voucher program with the broadest eligibility of any other voucher program in the United States.[68] Families of four earning up to $62,000 are eligible for some level of scholarship. The program is being phased in over a three-year span of time: 7,500 scholarships awarded in 2011–2012 and 15,000 in 2012–2013, and then the program is uncapped beginning in 2013–2014.[69]

Over a decade ago, the justices of the Supreme Court were asked to determine the constitutionality of vouchers in a case from Cleveland, Ohio.[70] In March 1995, the legislators in the Ohio General Assembly enacted the Pilot Project Scholarship Program to provide a limited number of vouchers to allow parents of public school students in Cleveland the opportunity for their children to attend private schools, including those operated by religious organizations. The vouchers were made available for the first time in the 1996–1997 school year and allowed up to $2,250 per child to attend private schools. Once admitted, students could continue receiving vouchers through middle school, subject to continued state funding.[71]

Of the more than 3,700 students who participated in the Ohio scholarship program, 96 percent enrolled in religiously affiliated schools. In August 1999, a federal district court judge barred further implementation of the program. In December 2000, a divided panel of the Sixth Circuit Court of Appeals affirmed the judgment made at the district court level. The Ohio program was judged to have the effect of advancing religion in violation of the establishment clause of the First Amendment. Chief Justice Rehnquist wrote the majority opinion in the *Zelman* case, and he was joined by Justices O'Connor, Scalia, Kennedy, and Thomas.[72]

Chief Justice Rehnquist articulated his belief that Supreme Court precedents for 20 years had consistently drawn a distinction between government programs that provide aid directly to religious schools and programs and programs of true private choice, where government aid reaches religious schools only as a result of individual free choices. The three precedents that he utilized in *Zelman* were *Mueller v. Allen* (1983), *Witters v. Washington Department of Services for the Blind* (1986), and *Zobrest v. Catalina* (1993).[73] In *Mueller*, the justices upheld a Minnesota program that authorized tax deductions for educational expenses including private school tuition, even though 96 percent of beneficiaries were parents of children in religious schools.[74] In the *Witters* case, the justices upheld the use of a vocational scholarship program that provided tuition assistance to a student studying at a religious school to become a pastor.[75] Finally, the justices endorsed a federal program that allowed sign-language interpreters to assist hearing-impaired students enrolled in religious schools in *Zobrest*.[76] Chief Justice Rehnquist argued that

> *Mueller, Witters,* and *Zobrest* thus make clear that where a government aid program is neutral with respect to religion, and provides assistance directly to a broad class of citizens who, in turn, direct government aid to religious schools wholly as a result of their own genuine and independent private choice, the program is not readily subject to challenge under the Establishment Clause. A program that shares these features permits government aid to reach religious institutions only by way of the deliberate choices of numerous individual recipients. The incidental advancement of a religious mission, or the perceived endorsement of a religious mission, is reasonably attributable to the individual recipient,

not to the government, whose role ends with the disbursement of benefits.[77]

The chief justice concluded his majority opinion by declaring that

> in sum, the Ohio program is entirely neutral with respect to religion. It provides benefits directly to a wide spectrum of individuals, defined only by financial need and residence in a particular school district. It permits such individuals to exercise genuine choice among options public and private, secular and religious. The program is therefore a program of true private choice. In keeping with an unbroken line of decisions rejecting challenges to similar programs, we hold that the program does not offend the Establishment Clause.[78]

In his separate concurring opinion, Justice Thomas emphasized the importance of the doctrine of states' rights:

> While the Federal Government may "make no law respecting an establishment of religion," the States may pass laws that include or touch on religious matters so long as these laws do not impede free exercise rights or any other individual religious liberty interest. By considering the particular religious liberty right alleged to be invaded by a State, federal courts can strike a proper balance between the demands of the Fourteenth Amendment on the one hand and the federalism prerogatives of States on the other.[79]

To the dissenters, there is nothing in the Constitution that allows states to promote religious activity by utilizing citizens' tax money in the guise of promoting school choice for school-aged children.

Justice Stevens indicated that he dissented for three primary reasons. First, the reality that the Cleveland Metropolitan School District was in a crisis state that resulted in the creation of a voucher program was not relevant to the issue of the program's constitutionality. Second, the array of choices that were made available to students within the Cleveland public schools had no bearing on the question of whether the Ohio state legislature could subsidize the tuition for students to attend religious schools. Third, the voluntary nature of the program, again, was not germane to the issue of the constitutionality of the voucher program. By way of conclusion, Justice Stevens observed that

> for the reasons stated by Justice Souter and Justice Breyer, I am convinced that the Court's decision is profoundly misguided. Admittedly, in reaching that conclusion I have been influenced by my understanding of the impact of religious strife on the decisions of our forbears to

migrate to this continent, and on the decisions of neighbors in the Balkans, Northern Ireland, and the Middle East to mistrust one another. Whenever we remove a brick from the wall that was designed to separate religion and government, we increase the risk of religious strife and weaken the foundation of our democracy.[80]

Justice Souter's dissent was particularly pronounced in the *Zelman* case.

Justice Souter believed that the Court's majority had overturned the essential precedent in establishment clause cases, *Everson v. Board of Education of Ewing* (1947).[81] In *Everson*, the justices ruled that no taxes whatsoever could be used to support religious activities or institutions, no matter what form they could take. In that compelling case decided two years after the end of World War II, Justice Black wrote the majority opinion and declared that

the "establishment of religion" clause of the First Amendment means at least this: neither a state nor the Federal Government can set up a church. Neither can pass laws which aid one religion, aid all religions, or prefer one religion over another. Neither can force nor influence a person to go to or to remain away from church against his will or force him to profess a belief or disbelief in any religion. No person can be punished for entertaining or professing religious beliefs or disbeliefs, for church attendance or non-attendance. No tax in any amount, large or small, can be levied to support any religious activities or institutions, whatever they may be called, or whatever form they may adopt to teach or practice religion. Neither a state nor the Federal Government can, openly or secretly, participate in the affairs of any religious organizations or groups, and vice versa. In the words of Jefferson, the clause against establishment of religion by law was intended to erect "a wall of separation between church and State."[82]

Thomas Jefferson was highlighted by Justice Black. In October 1801, the new president received a letter from the Danbury Baptists concerning their religious liberty, and President Jefferson responded on January 1, 1802.[83] In his letter, this president, a man of deep religious conviction, contended that

believing with you that religion is a matter which lies solely between man & his god, that he owes account to none other for his faith or his worship, that the legitimate powers of government reach actions only and not opinions, I contemplate with sovereign reverence that act of the whole American people which declared that their legislature should "make no law respecting an establishment of religion, or prohibiting the free exercise therof;" thus building a wall of eternal separation between Church & State.[84]

In the history of the American republic, this letter and the beliefs communicated by President Jefferson have been scrutinized by many Americans for over 200 years.

Justice Souter posed a very important question in *Zelman*:

> How can a Court consistently leave *Everson* on the books and approve the Ohio vouchers? The answer is that it cannot. It is only by ignoring *Everson* that the majority can claim to rest on traditional law in its invocation of neutral aid provisions and private choice to sanction the Ohio law. It is, moreover, only by ignoring the meaning of neutrality and private choice themselves that the majority can even pretend to rest today's decision on those criteria.[85]

The Court's majority of five purported to rule in favor of vouchers while simultaneously declaring the *Everson* precedent to be still intact. As Justice Souter articulated, the five justices in the majority undoubtedly achieved their public policy objective by sanctioning vouchers to be constitutional under the establishment clause. *Everson*, however, has been overturned in real terms because the stipulations set forth by Justice Black regarding the separation of church and state are clearly no longer in effect.

Justice Souter reflected on the political and societal implications of the majority's decision in *Zelman*:

> If the divisiveness permitted by today's majority is to be avoided in the short term, it will be avoided only by action of the political branches at the state and national levels. Legislatures not driven to desperation by the problems of public education may be able to see the threat in vouchers negotiable in sectarian schools. Perhaps even cities with problems like Cleveland's will perceive the danger, now that they know a federal court will not save them from it. My own course as a judge on the Court cannot, however, simply be to hope that the political branches will save us from the consequences of the majority's decision. *Everson*'s statement is still the touchstone of sound law, even though the reality is that in the matter of educational aid the Establishment Clause has largely been read away. True, the majority has not approved vouchers for religious schools alone, or aid earmarked for religious instruction. But no scheme so clumsy will ever get before us, and in the cases that we may see, like these, the Establishment Clause is largely silenced. I do not have the option to leave it silent, and I hope that a future Court will

reconsider today's dramatic departure from basic Establishment Clause principle.[86]

This dissent, from the perspectives of many public school advocates and subscribers to the common school philosophy, may well be the substantive foundation for a reversal of the *Zelman* decision at some point in time. That time has not arrived yet, however.

Justice Breyer agreed with Justices Souter and Stevens but desired to emphasize the possible risk of publicly financed voucher systems on religiously based social conflict. To Justice Breyer,

> The Court, in effect, turns the clock back. It adopts, under the name of "neutrality," an interpretation of the Establishment Clause that this Court rejected more than half a century ago. In its view, the parental choice that offers each religious group a kind of equal opportunity to secure government funding overcomes the Establishment Clause concern for social concord. An earlier Court found that "equal opportunity" principle insufficient; it read the Clause as insisting upon greater separation of church and state, at least in respect to primary education. . . . In a society composed of many different religious creeds, I fear that this present departure from the Court's earlier understanding risks creating a form of religiously based conflict potentially harmful to the Nation's social fabric.[87]

Thus, it was the Rehnquist Court that sanctioned the use of vouchers in K–12 education. Although many states did not create voucher systems in the immediate aftermath of *Zelman*, states where Republicans have captured majority status in the state legislature along with securing the governor's mansion have begun creating vouchers in earnest. The passage of time will determine whether the prophecies of the dissenters becomes reality.

The Home-Schooling Movement

Home schooling, also known as home education or home-based learning, occurs when children are educated at home, typically by parents but sometimes by tutors. Home schooling is another form of school choice.[88] According to researchers at the U.S. Department of Education, the home-schooling movement in the United States has grown significantly in recent decades, from about 15,000 students in 1970 to more than 1.5 million students in 2007.[89]

Online Schools and Digital Learning

Another form of school choice is conducted through online schools. Online schools can be run publicly or privately and allow students to work with their curriculum and teachers over the Internet. Online learning can be utilized in combination with traditional classroom learning or can replace it altogether.[90] According to advocates at the International Association for K–12 Online Learning, 40 states have virtual schools, 30 states and the District of Columbia have statewide full-time online schools, and over 1.8 million students were enrolled in distance-education courses in K–12 school districts in 2009–2010, most of which were online courses.[91]

REVISITING THE SCHOOL CHOICE DEBATE

Advocates of school choice focus on the ability of parents to choose the appropriate school for their children based on the marketplace assumption of competition. Competition will force deficient schools to improve or shut down. There are other important issues, however, that should be debated much more vigorously than is presently the case. In the case of charter schools, there is a paramount issue of fairness. Is it fair to absolve charter school officials of conforming to certain regulations that are binding to traditional public schools? Since both schools are publicly funded, then why should one entity, the charter school, be put in a more advantageous position than the traditional public school? It is difficult to contend that absolving those in charter schools of some regulations is justified because the officials in the charter schools are held to a higher standard when less than one-fifth of charter school students in the country outperform their peers in traditional public schools. While I do not support the premise that we can measure a child's knowledge base with a single test, this is, in fact, the standard typically espoused by charter school officials in creating the charter in the first place. When charter schools are launched, in part, it is typically because their backers contend that standardized test scores will go up by some percentage at a given point in time. By that criterion, many charter schools are clearly failing by their own definition of failure.

With regard to vouchers, no matter what the justices of the Supreme Court may have ruled in 2002, public funds are being utilized to subsidize religious schools. This absolutely runs counter to the wall of separation delineated by Thomas Jefferson in that famous letter to the Danbury Baptists while he was serving as the third president of the United States. The justices in the majority focused on choice in the Cleveland case and determined that the Ohio program provided choice for parents. Parents could send their children to different public schools, or the taxpayers' funds could be used to help pay the tuition bill at a private school, including those with a primary religious mission. But the issue is not choice per se; that controversy was all about the proper interpretation of the establishment clause. Instead of relying on sound precedent and jurisprudence, the conservative justices in the majority focused on public policy outcomes. Vouchers have been pursued in education policy by conservatives in a vigilant manner, particularly since the 1980s, largely through the efforts of Milton Friedman and his supporters. A political opportunity to sanction vouchers came through the Cleveland voucher case, and the conservatives on the Supreme Court seized the opportunity and declared that vouchers were constitutional as long as parents could choose between other public schools and private schools simultaneously. The fact that 96 percent of all parents at the time in Cleveland selected parochial schools was not important to the justices in the majority at the time.

Home schooling is another growing movement in the choice debate. Parents want to keep their children safe, whether they attend public schools or not. This can be accepted as a universal given. Those who choose to provide home education for their children feel as though they are keeping their children safe from outside elements in society. Yet part of education, according to Mann, entails bringing children together from diverse backgrounds so that they can ultimately learn to peacefully coexist, work together, and be tolerant of different social class, racial, ethnic, religious, and preference backgrounds. This is part of the essence of the great American experiment in self-governance—that children from different backgrounds will learn from one another and learn that they have much in common even though they come from different backgrounds. This aspect of civic education is commonly (and perhaps conveniently) ignored by choice advocates.

Online education is another element of choice that purports to reform K–12 education. There is no doubt that children should learn to be competent when it comes to using technology to enhance their education. However, a very important aspect of education is ignored with an undue emphasis on digital learning. What is the value of bringing children together, in a classroom setting, in terms of their overall educational experience? This is almost impossible to measure in a quantitative sense but has worked rather well for many generations. Children learn to interact with one another, they experience the reality that learning is not a passive phenomenon by definition, and they experience what it is like to make a commitment to something that is worthwhile not only for them as individuals but also for the betterment of society as an aggregate entity. Many American children watch way too much television and spend a great deal of time playing with video games. Do we somehow want our children to be even more passive, collectively, than they already are by having them "attend" virtual schools that do not permit them to be together in a physical sense? While this may give parents more choice, what will become of American society if we choose to isolate ourselves even more than is presently the case? How will our children get along? How will they engage in civil discourse when their peers do not share their same worldview or political viewpoints?

The focus on choice misses an important point about the role of education in a constitutional republic. The democratic ethos envisioned by Mann and many of his contemporaries was something that needed to be learned, cultivated, and nurtured through the common school experience. Common schools, funded by all citizens through taxation, was part of the very foundation of democracy in America. Public schools are instrumental to the viability of democracy in this country; instead of undermining them in the guise of choice, a better approach to reforming education in America would be to reform the public schools rather than setting them up to fail in the era of the No Child Left Behind Act with "accountability" standards and dubious assumptions about marketplace economics that do not apply to public sector entities. All children in this country, no matter what their current family situation may be, deserve the opportunity to truly succeed in a country with the oldest republican government on earth.

6

Citizenship in a Republican Form of Government in the Twenty-First Century

Too often in the American republic, some underestimate an important reality in democratic political systems. The people are the ultimate sovereigns in a democracy, and the authority of governing officials stems directly from the consent of the citizenry. Thus, to game theorists, one important player in the game of American national government is the public. Before assessing the role of the citizen in K–12 education, it is important to highlight the existence of systems theory in political science. There are many key political actors in the American democracy. While many recognize the plausibility of studying the three traditional institutions of government (Congress, the presidency, and the Supreme Court), the diligent student of

Photograph of Horace Mann taken before his years at Antioch College (1853–1859). (Image courtesy of Antiochiana, Antioch College.)

American politics would not want to ignore the roles played by a number of other actors in national politics. Among these actors include public administrators, political party leaders, journalists in the mass media, and the people of the United States.

THE OMNIPRESENT REALITY OF SYSTEMS THEORY

The importance of theory in the social sciences was articulated by David Easton in 1953:

> All mature scientific knowledge is theoretical. Obviously this does not mean that facts are immaterial. At the present highly empirical stage in the development of the social sciences, there is little need to insist that scientific knowledge must be well-grounded in facts. What does need emphasis, however, is that in and of themselves facts do not enable us to explain or understand an event. Facts must be ordered in some way so that we can see their connections. The higher the level of generality in ordering such facts and clarifying their relations, the broader will be the range of explanation and understanding. A set of generalizations that orders all the kinds of facts we call political would obviously be more useful for purposes of understanding political activity than a single generalization that related only two such facts. It is for this reason ... that the search for reliable knowledge about empirical political phenomena requires ultimately the construction of systematic theory, the name for the highest order of generalization.[1]

The essence of politics is ideas. The only manner in which to gain a better understanding of the complex web of American politics is through the power of thinking and analysis.

Easton contended that systems theory is a plausible approach to gaining more substantive knowledge about political events. It was about 60 years ago when he declared that

> we must recognize, as I have intimated, that ultimately all social life is interdependent and, as a result, that it is artificial to isolate any set of social relations from the whole for special attention. But this artificiality is imposed upon political scientists by the need for simplification of their data. Since everything is related to everything else, the task of pursuing the determinants of any given relation would be so vast and ramifying that it would defy any tools of investigation available either to the social or physical sciences. Instead, political science is compelled to abstract from the whole social system some variables which seem to cohere more closely than others, much as price, supply, demand, and

choice among wants do in economics, and to look upon them as a sub-system which can be profitably examined, temporarily, apart from the whole social system. The analytic or mental tool for this purpose is the theoretical system (systematic theory). It consists, first, of a set of concepts corresponding to the important political variables and, second, of statements about the relations among these concepts. Systematic theory corresponds at the level of thought to the concrete empirical political system of daily life.[2]

Embodied in systems theory is the notion that the political world is a complicated entity. Although many may prefer simplistic explanations in terms of understanding how public policies are crafted, simplicity is illusory in nature. Public policymaking can be truly understood only in the context of factoring in the many contributions, or inputs, by multiple players in a dynamic, fluid, and evolutionary system.

In a later work, Easton provided a cogent description of systems theory in the political arena:

> Once we begin to speak of political life as a system of activity, certain consequences follow for the way in which we can undertake to analyze the working of a system. The very idea of a system suggests that we can separate political life from the rest of social activity, at least for analytical purposes, and examine it as though for the moment it were a self-contained entity surrounded by, but clearly distinguishable from, the environment or setting in which it operates. In much the same way, astronomers consider the solar system a complex of events isolated for certain purposes from the rest of the universe. Furthermore, if we hold the system of political actions as a unit before our mind's eye, as it were, we can see that what keeps the system going are inputs of various kinds. These inputs are converted by the processes of the system into outputs and these, in turn, have consequences both for the system and for the environment in which the system exists.[3]

While understanding K–12 public education through systems theory is obviously a worthwhile and important endeavor, I seek only, at this juncture, to ascertain and even speculate as to how citizens in this republic can maximize their own inputs into what government officials choose to do or not to do in terms of policymaking.[4]

THE ROLE OF THE CITIZEN IN A REPUBLIC

Some time ago, during the Great Depression, Charles Merriam edited a series of books titled *Studies in the Making of Citizens*. The sixth volume was titled *Civic Education in the United States.*[5] The reader in the early twenty-first century may find it interesting that perspectives about technological changes 75 years ago are strikingly similar to the prevailing contemporary sentiment:

> Looking to the future of America, there is no single feature of our social life more important than the type of civic training the oncoming generation receives. This will condition and determine the range and type of the decisions made by people and by government, the nature of the economic, the social, the political order. This has been true of every generation, but the tempo of the present era, the importance and number of the decisions to be made, the speed with which adjustments must be carried through, the universality and elaborateness of education—these have never been surpassed or equalled in any period of history; and they impose an exceptional burden upon the present. We now come into times when incompetence in government and people might be written large in the ghastly tragedy possible only in a highly organized technical civilization.[6]

What has changed since 1934 with regard to popular perceptions about the spread of technology in a given time period? In comparable terms, there is no measurable difference between the 1930s and the present generation. Technology was rapidly evolving in both time periods, and this trend will likely continue, as it has been a consistent aspect of American history since the republic officially started in 1789.

Merriam and his colleagues believed that it was of the utmost importance that the political education of citizens include coverage of the emergent problems and challenges in the political world. To them, during the Depression years, there were a number of significant challenges to address. But two dominant trends were highlighted because of their prominence during the New Deal era:

1. The relation of technological development to social life in general and political life in particular
2. The rise of new forms of organizations thrusting up through the older types, especially in the economic world[7]

The scholars who were studying civic education in America were clearly interested in learning more about the effects of scientific developments on American national government. How would technological changes in communication and transportation affect the relationship between citizens and their government? How would the rise of new forms of political power, such as the modern corporation, affect

American politics.[8] The saliency and relevancy of such questions are still well documented today.

Although civic education can render a vigorous debate in terms of what is taught and what is not, the importance of imparting civic education on to children has been a theoretical assumption for many decades. It is a distinctly democratic value worthy of continued reconsideration. As Merriam put it so eloquently,

> In the sale of commodities in the commercial world, it is well understood that wants and possibilities of satisfying wants must be developed before goods can be set in motion; and the skillful advertiser addresses himself to this problem before he has gone far along the way. The American consumer of government would unquestionably demand more excellence in government if he realized the practical possibilities under present conditions. The city manager governments, for example, often afford striking illustrations of what is feasible as things now are; and there are many other types of cases of cities, states, and governments all along the line where advancement has actually been made, advances not generally realized as possible today. In the field of police administration phenomenal progress has been actually made in cities like Berkeley, Milwaukee, Cincinnati, and this may be illustrated by chapter and verse. If dirty secrets may be cleaned, or if hold-ups may be prevented, or rural services improved; or if the unit costs of government may be reduced, these situations may well be made the subject of civic instruction, along with the darker side of the chamber of horrors often exhibited as if typical and unavoidable under given conditions.[9]

A more knowledgeable and civic-oriented citizenry would not tolerate corruption or political ineptness and incompetence. It is possible that more Americans would find reason to believe, based on their own astute observations, that elected officials and public administrators could, in fact, successfully address some of today's challenges through policy intervention. The current state of citizen cynicism with regard to politics and public affairs is well documented and has been for years.[10] A little more idealism, because trust in public officials has been renewed, is desperately needed at the present time. It should be noted, however, that what was observed in the 1930s by Merriam may still be widely applicable today:

> The deadliest foe of governmental advance anywhere is cynicism, which ignorantly classes all government and governors as black, without any gray or white. The strongest supporter of government is the

discriminating citizen who understands what might be achieved under existing conditions, practically, and avoids the yes or no answer which is so common, especially among those who are educated and intelligent, but not politically. I am constantly dismayed by the dogmatic ignorance with which many presumably well educated citizens pass judgment on governmental personalities and processes, on which they might readily enlighten themselves.[11]

Rampant cynicism will not reform public education. On the contrary, it will ultimately contribute to its demise. This trend, reversible in nature, can be quantified. The continued expansion of voucher programs, charter schools, Internet-based classrooms, and home schooling is prima facie evidence of the common school ideal under siege by the conservative right in the United States. Citizens who today believe in the plausibility and perhaps even sanctity of Horace Mann's nineteenth-century vision need to defend the public school ethos and philosophy and actively engage in the political and electoral processes. Those seeking to undermine public education are generally well funded, well organized, and committed to their particular causes. Subscribers to the Mann philosophy will have to be willing to thwart their opponents in the political arena.

POLITICAL PARTICIPATION IN A REPUBLIC

In the years following Thomas Jefferson's tenure as president, he articulated a vision for the optimum form of republicanism in the United States:

> After leaving the presidency and returning to Monticello, Thomas Jefferson focused considerable attention on the implementation of a local form of government called ward republics. Jefferson saw the creation of a system of small republics—wards—as the full realization of republicanism and the only way to protect self-government. These wards, as Jefferson envisioned them, were to be small enough so that citizens could participate *directly* in deciding public issues of importance to the community, but large enough to carry on the functions of local government. . . . Jefferson's theory of ward republics is based on his fundamental belief that the strength of the Republic lay in the capacity of its citizens to participate in the public realm and his dedication to the notion that citizens must decide their own fate. Although the concept of wards came later in Jefferson's life, after he had returned to Monticello from his service as president, the idea was a predictable

outcome of his circumstances and experiences. The concept of smaller units in the newly formed democracy was an evolution of Jefferson's earlier thinking, not a departure from it. His early interest in the Greeks, his continuing opposition to the finality of the Constitution, his confidence that citizens must have a role in government, and his commitment to the rural, agrarian way of life forged the ideas that undergird his ward theory.[12]

Jefferson presented his vision of ward republics in a letter to Joseph Cabell dated February 2, 1816.[13] As history would have it, Jefferson would live another decade. Both he and President John Adams passed away on the same day, July 4, 1826, exactly 50 years after the Declaration of Independence was announced. In his own words, President Jefferson explained,

> No, my friend, the way to have good and safe government, is not to trust it all to one, but to divide it among the many, distributing to every one exactly the functions he is competent to. Let the national government be entrusted with the defence of the nation, and its foreign and federal relations; the State governments with the civil rights, laws, police, and administration of what concerns the State generally; the counties with the local concerns of the counties, and each ward direct the interests within itself. It is by dividing and subdividing these republics from the great national one down through all its subordinations, until it ends in the administration of every man's farm by himself; by placing every one what his own eye may superintend, that all will be for the best. What has destroyed liberty and the rights of man in every government which has ever existed under the sun? The generalizing and concentrating all cares and power into one body, no matter whether the autocrats of Russia or France, or of the aristocrats of a Venetian senate. And I do believe that if the Almighty has not decreed that man shall never be free, (and it is a blasphemy to believe it,) that the secret will be found in the making himself the depository of the powers respecting himself, so far as he is competent to them, and delegating only what is beyond his competence by a synthetical process, to higher and higher orders of functionaries, so as to trust fewer and fewer powers in proportion as the trustees become more and more oligarchical. The elementary republics of the wards, the county republics, the State republics, and the republic of the Union, would form a gradation of authorities, standing each on the basis of law, holding every one its delegated share of powers, and constituting truly a system of fundamental balances and checks for the government. Where every man is a sharer in the direction of his ward-republic, or of some of the higher ones, and feels that he is a participator in the government of affairs,

not merely at an election one day in the year, but every day; when there shall not be a man in the State who will not be a member of some one of its councils, great or small, he will let the heart be torn out of his body sooner than his power be wrested from him by a Caesar or a Bonaparte.[14]

Jefferson envisioned proactive citizens who were willing to hold their leaders accountable to them. To him, a republican form of government required civic-oriented citizens who were willing to preserve their liberties by actively participating in democratic governance. Another important figure in American history, Benjamin Franklin, shared this vision of republicanism at the end of the Philadelphia Convention in 1787.

On the last day of the convention (September 17, 1787), Franklin rose to give a speech, but due to his challenged health, he asked his Pennsylvania colleague, James Wilson, to read his speech.[15] The legendary American then delineated his steadfast support for republicanism:

> I confess that there are several parts of this constitution which I do not at present approve, but I am not sure I shall never approve them: For having lived long, I have experienced many instances of being obliged by better information or fuller consideration, to change opinions even on important subjects, which I once thought right, but found to be otherwise. It is therefore that the older I grow, the more apt I am to doubt my own judgment, and to pay more respect to the judgment of others. . . . Thus I consent, Sir, to this Constitution because I expect no better, and because I am not sure, that it is not the best.[16]

The American experiment in democracy, according to the great inventor and more, was best continued in the guise of a federal republic since the confederacy established by the Articles of Confederation and Perpetual Union failed miserably.

It would not be until 1906 when the notes of James McHenry, one of the delegates to the Philadelphia Convention from Maryland, were published. They were first published in *The American Historical Review*.[17] According to McHenry's notes, "A lady asked Dr. Franklin Well Doctor what have we got a republic or a monarchy. A republic replied the Doctor if you can keep it."[18] An account of McHenry's notes is provided by the historian Philip Dray:

> A small crowd had gathered outside the State House door on the rumor that the Convention had completed its work. As the delegates emerged, Elizabeth Willing Powel, a prominent local intellectual and wife of Samuel Powel, the mayor of Philadelphia, caught a glimpse of

Franklin's unmistakable profile. "Doctor, what have we got," she asked, "a republic or a monarchy?" Franklin, finally free to speak of the Convention's achievement, called out, "A republic, if you can keep it."[19]

Although McHenry's story may be fictitious, undoubtedly the American people in the summer of 1787 were very curious about what the framers were doing in Philadelphia over the course of several months.[20] McHenry's anecdote was also included in Max Farrand's account of the Philadelphia Convention in 1911.[21]

Improving public education in the United States is a longitudinal objective; the pursuit of a more effective education system for America's children will never cease by definition, for efforts to enhance the human condition are an integral reality since our species evolved over 160,000 years ago.[22] Our own collective efforts to be better citizens in a republican form of government must also persist, for Americans need to play a more substantive role in politics and public affairs than is presently the case.

Citizen Knowledge of Politics and History in Contemporary America

In spite of the advent of the Internet in particular, citizen knowledge of politics and history is still quite low. According to Michael Delli Carpini, "Over 50 years of survey research on Americans' knowledge of politics leads to several consistent conclusions. The most powerful and influential of these conclusions is that the 'average' citizen is woefully uninformed about political institutions and processes, substantive policies and socioeconomic conditions, and important political actors such as elected officials and political parties."[23] Not much has changed since the 1960s in terms of Americans' knowledge about politics and public affairs. Many Americans know very little because politics is not a high priority to them. Some of the polling results are discouraging and perhaps even downright embarrassing. For example, in a 2012 poll taken by officials from the Pew Research Center for the People and the Press regarding what the people know about the two major political parties, 85 percent of Americans knew Ronald Reagan's party affiliation (Republican), 84 percent knew that Bill Clinton is a Democrat, 78 percent correctly responded that John Kennedy was a Democrat, 61 percent knew that former Speaker of the House Nancy Pelosi is a Democrat, 58 percent identified Franklin

Roosevelt's party affiliation (Democratic), and 55 percent knew that Abraham Lincoln and the current Speaker of the House, John Boehner, subscribed to the Republican Party.[24] Presidential scholars continually rank Abraham Lincoln as the best president in U.S. history, and Franklin Roosevelt is typically ranked as the second- or third-best president.[25] Yet barely half of the adults polled could properly identify the party affiliations of these iconic political figures. The Speaker of the House is the second most powerful elected political position in the country behind the president. In spite of this reality, almost half of the adult population cannot identify Speaker Boehner's political party.[26]

In a Gallup Poll taken in 2003 measuring Americans' knowledge of history, the results, once again, were unimpressive.[27] While 92 percent of Americans knew that George Washington was the first president, 33 percent did not know that Abraham Lincoln delivered the Gettysburg Address, 43 percent did not know the third branch of the national government (judiciary), 41 percent did not know that there are two U.S. senators allocated for each state, 66 percent did not know that the words "We hold these truths to be self-evident, that all men are created equal" emanated from the Declaration of Independence, 67 percent did not know that Martin Luther King Jr. wrote the "Letter from the Birmingham Jail," 53 percent of adults did not know that the first 10 amendments to the federal Constitution are called the Bill of Rights, 31 percent of Americans could not identify Dick Cheney as the vice president when the poll was taken, and 83 percent could not identify William Rehnquist as the chief justice of the Supreme Court.[28] Obviously, these results are disheartening to those who believe that citizens must be more engaged in the American representative democracy. While interpretations of such results may vary, it would be difficult to counter the premise that there is ample room for improvement when it comes to Americans' knowledge of politics and history.

Survey after survey results depict Americans as vastly ignorant when it comes to politics and public affairs. My task here is not to restate something that is already well known. The more important question is, how can the status quo be enhanced? Obviously, as an aggregate entity, Americans can be more proactive when it comes to political knowledge. A passive population is not likely to experience fundamental change when it comes to public policy. Culturally, much can be done to change the negative perception that many people have about politics. A passé attitude about citizenship in a republic needs to change, and rhetoric alone is insufficient to facilitate necessary reforms. Would it be unreasonable for all students at the senior high school level to take one full year of American national government at the high school level? Citizenship is a lifetime phenomenon. In the state of Indiana, for example, 40 credits are required to complete a high school diploma. One credit of U.S. government is required for students receiving a Core 40 general high school diploma, a Core 40 diploma with academic hours, or a Core 40 diploma with technical honors, though in the latter two options students must earn a minimum of an additional seven credits beyond the Core 40. Regardless of diploma type, however, one credit out of the Core 40 accounts for 2.5 percent of the student's curriculum and is weighted the same as health and wellness and less than physical education (two credits are required).[29] Health and physical education are important subjects to cover in high school, as Horace Mann contended in the nineteenth century. But American children need to know more about their own government as well so that they can be equipped to perform their roles in the American republic.

More emphasis on civic education is not only reasonable across all states but also absolutely essential. Competence is clearly needed in English/language arts, mathematics, science, and social studies, among other subjects, at the high school level, but what about competence in citizenship? How this objective can be achieved across the 50 states and the District of Columbia is a practical matter. Given the evolution of American K–12 public education, many would view this proposal as a states' rights issue. At some point, however, we need to stop debating extraneous political matters and highlight the substantive reality. American adults know little about politics. Is this an acceptable situation? For those who value more democratic participation and governance, something tangible must be attempted in the education sector. What happens after graduation from high school is another matter. The steadfast hope is that politics becomes more important to more citizens. The product of this evolution could be manifested in many positive ways, such as more political awareness and knowledge, higher voter turnout, and higher levels of other means of political participation. American children must be better equipped to handle their duties and responsibilities as citizens of this republic. The time to act is way past due.

Before advancing further in this discussion, it is important to consider Delli Carpini's summary of political knowledge in the United States:

> The portrait of the American citizen presented thus far is generally consistent with the call for a more realistic set of expectations regarding the informational requisites of civic life. This picture becomes more complicated, and to my mind, problematic when one looks at the variance in knowledge across citizens, however. Too often "the citizenry" is described in monolithic terms. The evidence suggests, however, that there are dramatic differences in how informed Americans are. For example, as noted above, a 50-question "quiz" of political knowledge given to a national sample of American adults produced an average score of almost 50% correct. But the most informed 30% of the sample averaged better than 7-in-10 correct answers, while the least informed 30% could only answer 1 in 4 questions correctly. In short, there is no *single* portrait of the American citizen: a substantial percentage is very informed, an equally large percentage is very poorly informed, and the plurality of citizens fall somewhere in between.[30]

Not all adults in America are ignorant or indifferent to the current state of political affairs. Indeed, some Americans are very much engaged in politics and have a high level of interest and knowledge in political, social, and economic issues. It would be misleading and erroneous to view Americans as a monolithic entity, for there is ample diversity between and among citizens.

Civic knowledge is central to democratic citizenship. Nothing positive is likely to ensue from ignorance, misperceptions, stereotypes, and indifference. In providing a summary of major research findings on civic knowledge, William Galston offers seven fundamental reasons why enhanced civic knowledge would be beneficial to American society:

1. Civic knowledge helps citizens understand their interests as individuals and as members of groups. The more knowledge we have, the better we can understand the impact of public policies on our interests and the more effectively we can promote our interests in the political process.
2. Civic knowledge increases the consistency of views across issues and across time.
3. Unless citizens possess a basic level of civic knowledge—especially concerning political institutions and processes—it is difficult for them to understand political events or to integrate new information into an existing framework.

4. General civic knowledge can alter our views on specific public issues. For example, the more knowledge citizens have about civic matters, the less likely they are to fear new immigrants and their impact on our country.
5. The more knowledge citizens have of civic affairs, the less likely they are to experience a generalized mistrust of, or alienation from, public life. Ignorance is the father of fear, and knowledge is the mother of trust.
6. Civic knowledge promotes support for democratic values. For example, the more knowledge citizens have of political principles and institutions, the more likely they are to support core democratic principles, starting with tolerance.
7. Civic knowledge promotes political participation. All other things being equal, the more knowledge citizens have, the more likely they are to participate in public matters.[31]

A more enlightened and knowledgeable citizenry would be better equipped to comprehend and contend with the inherent perplexities of democratic life in a republican form of government.

Voter Turnout in Federal Elections

The traditional measure of voter turnout in the United States and elsewhere is basically a simple fraction. It is the percentage of the voting-age population that actually voted in a given election. Since 1972, the voting-age population has been all Americans 18 years of age and older. Prior to the 1972 elections, the voting-age population encompassed all Americans 21 years of age and older. Thus, voter turnout equals the total number of voters divided by the total voting-age population.[32] This measure allows analysts to compare not only voter turnout in the American states but also voter turnout in the United States in relation to other democracies.

Federal elections are held in the United States every two years due to the fact that U.S. House members have two-year terms under the Constitution. Senators have six-year terms, but one-third of the Senate seats are contested every two years. Since the president has a four-year term, there are two different types of federal elections in America: presidential elections (every four years) and midterm elections (two years after a presidential election). Voter turnout is always higher in a presidential election year.

There were 21 presidential elections from 1932 to 2012. During this time period, turnout in four elections in the 1960s and 1950s (1960,

1952, 1964, and 1968) exceeded 60 percent, with the highest turnout recorded in 1960 (62.8 percent) in the contest between John Kennedy and Richard Nixon. When 18-, 19-, and 20-year-olds were included in the voting-age population in 1972, turnout declined by over 5 percent. It has never reached the 60 percent threshold since the Twenty-Sixth Amendment was added to the federal Constitution.[33]

The average voter turnout in presidential elections between 1932 and 2012 is 55.6 percent. With the inclusion of more youthful voters since 1972, turnout has been higher than the average during this time period only once, and that was 2008 presidential contest between Barack Obama and John McCain. Voter turnout in 2008 (56.8 percent) was the highest since 1968, though not as high as many analysts were projecting right before the election. Voter turnout dipped below 50 percent only once since 1932, and this occurred in 1996, when Bill Clinton defeated Bob Dole.[34]

Since 1934, the first midterm election during Franklin Roosevelt's presidency, there have been a total of 20 midterm (nonpresidential) elections. The average voter turnout during these midterm elections in the modern era is 38.2 percent. Voter turnout was highest during this time period in 1962 and 1966 (45.4 percent) and lowest in 1942 (32.5 percent). Turnout in seven midterm elections since the days of Franklin Roosevelt exceeded 40 percent (1934, 1950, 1954, 1958, 1962, 1966, and 1970). Otherwise, turnout in U.S. midterm elections has been in the thirtieth percentile. It has never been over the 40 percent threshold since ratification of the Twenty-Sixth Amendment.[35]

When voter turnout in the United States is compared to other industrialized democracies, it is clear that voter turnout in America is low when compared with similar nations. Officials at the International Institute for Democracy and Electoral Assistance (International IDEA), an intergovernmental organization headquartered in Stockholm, Sweden, provide voter turnout statistics for national presidential and parliamentary elections since 1945. The 2008 presidential election was compared with the most recent applicable election (parliamentary or presidential) in 20 other nations.[36] America ranked twentieth out of the 21 nations in the universe. Whereas about 55 percent of the voting-age population currently exercises the franchise in U.S. presidential elections, the average turnout of the other 20 nations in the most recent analogous national election was 71.1 percent.[37] The only nation that had a lower voter turnout than

America was Switzerland (39.8 percent); the Swiss have had a low rate of voter turnout at the polls since the 1970s.[38]

Slightly more than half of the voting-age population in the United States bothers to vote in recent presidential elections. Meanwhile, citizens in many other industrialized democracies regularly vote in their national, mostly parliamentary elections, at a level in the seventieth and eightieth percentiles.[39] While there are some reasonable explanations for comparatively low voter turnout in the United States (e.g., Americans fundamentally have only two viable political parties and winner-take-all elections in the lower house of the legislature [House of Representatives] in lieu of proportional representation), clearly there is ample room for reform when it comes to citizen participation in America with regard to voting. The untapped political influence of the millions of people who do not vote regularly is significant. Voting is perhaps the most obvious form of political participation. Citizens in the world's oldest democracy should undoubtedly ponder the state of public affairs in the United States if more citizens held policymakers accountable at the ballot box.

Interest Group Participation in the Early Twenty-First Century

James Madison, as well as the other framers of the U.S. Constitution, understood that in a republican form of government, organized interest groups through their officials would continually attempt to exert political influence on the process of public policymaking. He defined the term interest group, or what he called a "faction," in *The Federalist* No. 10: "By a faction, I understand a number of citizens, whether amounting to a majority or a minority of the whole, who are united and actuated by some common impulse of passion, or of interest, adversed to the rights of other citizens, or to the permanent and aggregate interests of the community."[40] In making a case for ratification of the Constitution after the Philadelphia Convention ended, Madison argued that the remedy for interest groups lies not in trying to eliminate them but to control for their harmful effects in a pluralist democracy. He declared,

> There are two methods of curing the mischiefs of faction: the one, by removing its causes; the other, by controlling its effects. There are again two methods of removing the causes of factions: the one, by destroying

the liberty which is essential to its existence; the other, by giving to every citizen the same opinions, the same passions, and the same interests. It could never be more truly said than of the first remedy, that it was worse than the disease. Liberty is to faction what air is to fire, an aliment without which it instantly expires. But it could not be less folly to abolish liberty, which is essential to political life, because it nourishes faction, than it would be to wish the annihilation of air, which is essential to animal life, because it imparts to fire its destructive agency. The second expedient is as impracticable as the first would be unwise. As long as the reason of man continues fallible, and he is at liberty to exercise it, different opinions will be formed. As long as the connection subsists between his reason and his self-love, his opinions and his passions will have a reciprocal influence to each other; and the former will be objects to which the latter will attach themselves. The diversity in the faculties of men, from which the rights of property originate, is not less an insuperable obstacle to a uniformity of interests. The protection of these faculties is the first object of government. From the protection of different and unequal faculties of acquiring property, the possession of different degrees and kinds of property immediately results; and from the influence of these on the sentiments and views of the respective proprietors, ensues a division of the society into different interests and parties.[41]

According to the great Constitution builder, the best thing to do in a pluralist society is to encourage the proliferation of diverse interest groups of different sizes, motives, and levels of political influence so that no one group dominates public policymaking.

There is an important historical context to consider when it comes to citizen involvement with interest group activity in the United States. In the early nineteenth century, the French aristocrat Alexis de Tocqueville came to the United States in 1831 when he was only 25 years old. He traveled with Gustave de Beaumont, and their official purpose was to study the U.S. prison system and report back to France. The unofficial purpose of their trip, however, was far more important. They simply wanted to observe democracy in America and proceeded to do so during a 271-day stay in the United States that included a visit to 18 of 24 states in the union and a meeting with the current president at that time, Andrew Jackson, as well as his immediate predecessor, John Quincy Adams. The Frenchmen spent most of their time in Boston, New York, and Philadelphia but traveled extensively in the United States and even spent some time in Canada as well.[42] After returning to France, de Tocqueville's account of his experience took eight years to write. He published volume 1 of *Democracy in America* in 1835, and volume 2 was subsequently published in 1840.[43] From his aristocratic experience in France, he was surprised with how much equality pervaded American life. In France, social class mattered greatly; to de Tocqueville, social class did not seem to be so important, and people expected to be treated the same. At this time in history, however, the focus of equality in America was primarily on white males, as full citizenship rights belonged only to this group. Women were legally controlled by their husbands. African Americans were considered the property of their slave owners. Native Americans were viewed as alien people in their own ancestral lands.[44]

One of the more intriguing discoveries made by the French aristocrat on his trip to America is his observation that a large number of Americans were involved in public affairs. He was particularly impressed with New England town meetings, where citizens directly determined local policy issues.[45] One of the most significant revelations made by de Tocqueville is the frequency with which Americans joined together in various organizations that he called "associations." In volume 1 of *Democracy in America*, he reported that

it is not impossible to conceive the immense freedom that Americans enjoy; one can get an idea of their extreme equality as well; but what one cannot comprehend without having already been witness to it is the political activity that reigns in the United States. Scarcely have you descended on the soil of America when you find yourself in the midst of a sort of tumult; a confused clamor is raised on all sides; a thousand voices come to your ear at the same time, each of them expressing some social needs. Around you everything moves: here, the people of one neighborhood have gathered to learn if a church ought to be built; there, they are working on the choice of a representative; farther on, the deputies of a district are going to town in all haste in order to decide about some local improvements; in another place, the farmers of a village abandon their furrows to go discuss the plan of a road or a school. Citizens assemble with the sole goal of declaring that they disapprove of the course of government, whereas others gather to proclaim that the men in place are the fathers of their country. Here are others still who, regarding drunkenness as the principal source of the evils of the state, come solemnly to pledge themselves to give an example of temperance. The great political movement that constantly agitates American legislatures, the only one that is perceived from the outside, is only one episode and a sort of prolongation of the universal movement that begins in the lowest ranks of the people and afterwards spreads gradually to all classes of citizens. One cannot work more laboriously at being happy.[46]

Today, we call these nineteenth-century associations "interest groups." The extensive interest group participation by Americans documented in the 1830s is still omnipresent today in American society.

There are about 14,000 organized interest groups in Washington, D.C., at the present time.[47] Interest group activity is still very apparent and extensive, at least from a comparative perspective.[48] Yet it is important to understand E. E. Schattschneider's seminal criticism of pluralism that he published over 60 years ago. The diversity that exists in American society is not evenly represented in interest group politics:

> The class bias of associational activity gives meaning to the limited scope of the pressure system, because *scope and bias are aspects of the same tendency.* The data raise a serious question about the validity of the proposition that special-interest groups are a universal form of political organization reflecting *all* interests. As a matter of fact, to suppose that everyone participates in pressure-group activity and that all interests get themselves organized in the pressure system is to destroy the meaning of this form of politics. The pressure system makes sense only as the political instrument of a segment of the community. It gets results by being selective and biased; *if everybody got into the act the unique advantages of this form of organization would be destroyed, for it is possible that if all interests could be mobilized the result would be a stalemate.* Special-interest organizations are most easily formed when they deal with small numbers of individuals who are acutely aware of their exclusive interests. To describe the conditions of pressure-group organization in this way is, however, to say that it is primarily a business phenomenon. Aside from a few very large organizations (the churches, organized labor, farm organizations, and veterans' organizations) the residue is a small segment of the population. *Pressure politics is essentially the politics of small groups.* The vice of the groupist theory is that it conceals the most significant aspects of the system. The flaw in the pluralist heaven is that the heavenly chorus sings with a strong upper-class accent. Probably about 90 percent of the people cannot get into the pressure system. The notion that the pressure system is automatically representative of the whole community is a myth fostered by the universalizing tendency of modern group theories. *Pressure politics is a selective process* ill designed to serve diffuse interests. The system is skewed, loaded, and unbalanced in favor of a fraction of a minority.[49]

About 20 years later, Theodore Lowi also presented a scathing critique of the role of interest groups in American politics.[50] Both political scientists did not concur with theories of pluralism espoused by Robert Dahl, who contended that interest group competition provided a crucial link between the people and public policies made by government officials.[51] Perhaps there is a reality when it comes to both voting and interest group participation in the United States. More citizen participation in both venues would enhance the opportunity to witness more diversity in the policymaking process at the national level. In other words, millions of Americans, with the potential for a substantial amount of political influence, choose not to participate in politics, and if Schattschneider and Lowi are correct, it is to their detriment because the rich and powerful make their presence and influence felt in a continual manner and undoubtedly reap the rewards for doing so. In short, a passive citizenry can expect more of the same when it comes to politics and public policy. Thus, if people are satisfied with the status quo, then they should be content with their reticence, for change is unwelcome to them. If, however, people do not endorse the current state of American politics, only diligence and activity can thwart the current state of affairs and start the process of political, social, and economic reform in the world's oldest republic.

Minimizing the Importance of Money in Federal Elections

The cost of financing federal political campaigns has escalated dramatically in the past few decades.[52] There is no indication that this trend will change at any point in the foreseeable future given the structural rules governing campaign finance in the United States and their current interpretation by a majority of the justices serving on the Supreme Court. A brief history of the evolution of campaign finance law may prove to be facilitative in terms of understanding why this country does not have publicly financed campaigns like many other democratic countries.[53]

President Theodore Roosevelt is commonly credited with formally launching a substantive public debate about campaign finance reform in 1905. In his fifth State of the Union Address to Congress, he surmised that

> in political campaigns in a country as large and populous as ours it is inevitable that there should be much expense of an entirely legitimate kind. This, of course, means that many contributions, and some of them of large size, must be made, and, as a matter of fact, in any big political

contest such contributions are always made to both sides. It is entirely proper both to give and receive them, unless there is an improper motive connected with either gift or reception. If they are extorted by any kind of pressure or promise, express or implied, direct or indirect, in the way of favor or immunity, then the giving or receiving becomes not only improper but criminal. It will undoubtedly be difficult, as a matter of practical detail, to shape an act which shall guard with reasonable certainty against such misconduct; but if it is possible to secure by law the full and verified publication in detail of all sums contributed to and expended by the candidates or committees of any political parties, the result cannot but be wholesome. All contributions by corporations to any political committee or for any political purpose should be forbidden by law; directors should not be permitted to use stockholders' money for such purposes; and moreover, a prohibition of this kind would be, as far as it went, an effective method of stopping the evils aimed at in corrupt practices acts. Not only should both the National and the several State Legislatures forbid any officer of a corporation from using the money of the corporation in or about any election, but they should also forbid such use of money in connection with any legislation save by the employment of counsel in public manner for distinctly legal services.[54]

In 1905, President Roosevelt articulated his vision that campaign contributions had to be regulated by Congress in order to protect the greater public good. Two years later, he endorsed publicly financed federal campaigns in his seventh State of the Union Address:

Under our form of government voting is not merely a right but a duty, and, moreover, a fundamental and necessary duty if a man is to be a good citizen. It is well to provide that corporations shall not contribute to Presidential or National campaigns, and furthermore to provide for the publication of both contributions and expenditures. There is, however, always danger in laws of this kind, which from their very nature are difficult of enforcement; the danger being lest they be obeyed only by the honest, and disobeyed by the unscrupulous, so as to act only as a penalty upon honest men. Moreover, no such law would hamper an unscrupulous man of unlimited means from buying his own way into office. There is a very radical measure which would, I believe, work a substantial improvement in our system of conducting a campaign, although I am well aware that it will take some time for people so to familiarize themselves with such a proposal as to be willing to consider its adoption. The need for collecting large campaign funds would vanish if Congress provided an appropriation for the proper and legitimate expenses of each of the great national parties, an appropriation ample enough to meet the necessity for thorough organization and machinery, which requires a large expenditure of money. Then the stipulation should be made that no party receiving campaign funds from the Treasury should accept more than a fixed amount from any individual subscriber or donor; and the necessary publicity for receipts and expenditures could without difficulty be provided.[55]

Ironically, Roosevelt would later be the first president to publicly espouse the concept of national health insurance for all citizens. He did so in the 1912 presidential campaign when he sought the presidency as the nominee for the Progressive Party.[56] Thus, Roosevelt has the distinction of touting two public policies that have not come to fruition in spite of a century of debate on the dual issues involved.

The presidential election of 1904 provided the context for President Roosevelt's endorsement of campaign finance reform. The Democratic nominee, Judge Alton Parker, alleged that corporations were providing the incumbent Republican president with campaign gifts in order to purchase influence within the administration. Roosevelt denied the charges, but it became publicly known that officials from several major companies made substantial contributions to the Republican Party. Congress responded, in part, to Roosevelt's proposals by passing the Tillman Act in 1907. This law prohibited any contributions by corporations and businesses to political parties and election committees. This is the first law to specifically address campaign funding at the federal level, but it was easily circumvented. Many businesses and corporations adopted the practice of giving their employees large bonuses with the understanding that the bonus would, in turn, be given to a candidate endorsed by the company in question.[57]

A few years later, right before the 1910 midterm elections, the Republican majority in Congress passed the Federal Corrupt Practices Act, commonly called the Publicity Act of 1910, which required nothing more than postelection reports of the receipts and expenditures of national party committees or committees operating in two or more states. The bill initially applied only to the U.S. House of Representatives, as members were directly elected by the people and the Seventeenth Amendment providing for popular election of U.S. senators had not been ratified yet. The law did not require disclosure prior to an election. Amendments to the act in 1911 improved disclosure and established the first spending limits for federal campaigns. Disclosure was extended so that primaries and conventions would also be included, and the amendments required preelection and postelection disclosure of receipts. The law limited House expenditures to a total of $5,000 and Senate expenditures to $10,000 or the amount established by state law (whichever was less).[58]

The spending limits were controversial and became the subject of judicial scrutiny. In 1918, Truman Newberry, a Michigan Republican candidate for the U.S. Senate, defeated Henry Ford in a hotly contested primary. His campaign expenditures greatly exceeded the state spending limits at the time. Consequently, he was found guilty of violating the amendments to the Publicity Act in Michigan state courts. He appealed his conviction to the Supreme Court and prevailed.[59] In 1921, a majority of the Supreme Court's justices determined that Congress's authority to regulate federal elections did not extend to party primary and nomination activities. The spending limits were therefore stuck down.[60] The favorable ruling ended Newberry's difficulties in criminal court; however, his tenure in the Senate proved to be quite brief. Senator Newberry's expenditures were investigated by his colleagues, and on January 12, 1922, the Senate "severely condemned" Newberry's activities and found his expenditures to be "harmful to the honor and dignity of the Senate."[61] He was not expelled from the chamber, however. But mounting public pressure against him prompted him to resign his seat on November 18, 1922.[62]

Twenty years later, the justices reviewed the precedent established in *Newberry v. U.S.* (1921) and overturned it in *United States v. Classic* (1941).[63] Whereas the justices determined that Congress did not have the authority under Article I, Section 4, of the Constitution to regulate primary elections in *Newberry*, the justices in 1941, through Harlan Fiske Stone, had a different interpretation of congressional power:

> For we think that the authority of Congress, given by Section 4, includes the authority to regulate primary elections when, as in this case, they are a step in the exercise by the people of their choice of representatives in Congress. ... In *Newberry v. United States*, four Justices of this Court were of opinion that the term "elections" in Section 4 of Article I did not embrace a primary election, since that procedure was unknown to the framers. A fifth Justice, who with them pronounced the judgment of the Court, was of opinion that a primary, held under a law enacted before the adoption of the Seventeenth Amendment, for the nomination of candidates for Senator, was not an election within the meaning of Section 4 of Article I of the Constitution, presumably because the choice of the primary imposed no legal restrictions on the election of Senators by the state legislatures to which their election had been committed by

Article I, Section 3. The remaining four Justices were of the opinion that a primary election for the choice of candidates for Senator or Representative were elections subject to regulation by Congress within the meaning of Section 4 of Article I.[64]

About a half a year before the United States formally entered World War II, the justices maintained that Congress had the authority under Article I of the Constitution to regulate primaries wherever state law made them part of the election process and wherever they effectively determined the outcome of the general election.[65]

For almost 30 years following the end of World War II, members of Congress did not address the issue of campaign finance reform. By the late 1960s, however, many members of Congress became increasingly concerned about the spiraling costs of federal campaigns. Democrats, in particular, became attentive to the rising costs of campaigns as Republicans continually outpaced them in terms of fund-raising. In the 1968 presidential election, Republican Richard Nixon narrowly defeated his Democratic rival, Hubert Humphrey, even though he raised more than twice as much money as Vice President Humphrey. With this renewed interest in the topic of campaign finance reform, members of Congress passed the Federal Election Campaign Act (FECA) of 1971.[66]

FECA was signed into law by President Richard Nixon on February 7, 1972, and went into effect 60 days later. Under this legislation, members of Congress attempted to establish detailed spending limits for all federal campaigns and impose strict public disclosure procedures on federal candidates and political committees.[67]

The major provisions of FECA included the limitation of personal contributions, the establishment of specific ceilings for media expenditures, and the requirement of full public disclosure of campaign receipts and disbursements. The act limited personal contributions by candidates and their immediate families to a combined total of $50,000 for presidential and vice-presidential candidates, $35,000 for Senate candidates, and $25,000 for House candidates.[68] With regard to media expenditures, candidates for federal office were limited in any election to $50,000 or $0.10 times the voting-age population of the jurisdiction covered by the election, whichever was greater.[69] In the area of disclosure, the law required every candidate or political action committee (PAC) active in a federal campaign to file quarterly reports of receipts and expenditures. These reports had to list any contribution or expenditure of $100 or more and include the name, address, occupation, and principal place of business of the donor or recipient. During election years, any contribution of $5,000 or more had to be reported with 48 hours of its receipt, and all reports had to be made available to the public within 48 hours of receipt. A short time later, in the aftermath of Watergate and reports of widespread financial abuse in the Nixon reelection campaign of 1972, legislators in Congress revised FECA by passing a series of amendments to the law in 1974.[70]

The amendments changed the original law substantially. In order to eliminate the potential corruptive influence of large donors, the 1974 amendments established strict limits on individual donors. An individual could contribute no more than $1,000 per candidate per election. Individuals could not exceed $25,000 in annual aggregate contributions to all federal candidates. Political action committees were limited to $5,000 per candidate per election but had no aggregate limits. Independent expenditures made on behalf of a candidate were limited to $1,000 a year, and cash donations in excess of $100 were prohibited.[71]

Complicated spending ceilings were created through the amendments as well for House, Senate, and presidential candidates.[72] In addition, the Federal Election Commission (FEC) was established and charged with the mission of administering and enforcing federal campaign finance regulations. The law stipulated that the FEC would be bipartisan and consist of six members. Finally, the bill mandated for the first time the creation of a public financing system for presidential election campaigns financed from the tax checkoff receipts deposited in the Presidential Election Campaign Fund. If candidates agreed to eschew private donations, they could receive the full amount authorized by the law for the general election ($20 million). Minor-party candidates could receive a fraction of this amount. To qualify, a candidate was required to raise at least $5,000 in contributions of $250 or less in at least 20 states. Almost immediately, and perhaps quite predictably, key provisions of the law were challenged as unconstitutional.[73]

The constitutional challenge was embodied in a case called *Buckley v. Valeo* (1976).[74] The key point of contention had to do with the interpretation of First Amendment protections of freedom of speech and association. Did the contribution limits placed on individuals violate the First Amendment? The decision in *Buckley* is complicated, but the justices made two substantive conclusions through a per curiam opinion.

First, the restrictions placed on individual contributions to political campaigns did not violate the First Amendment:

> It is unnecessary to look beyond the Act's primary purpose—to limit the actuality and appearance of corruption resulting from large individual financial contributions—in order to find a constitutionally sufficient justification for the $1,000 contribution limitation. Under a system of private financing of elections, a candidate lacking immense personal or family wealth must depend on financial contributions from others to provide the resources necessary to conduct a successful campaign. The increasing importance of the communications media and sophisticated mass-mailing and polling operations to effective campaigning make the raising of large sums of money an ever more essential ingredient of an effective candidacy. To the extent that large contributions are given to secure a political *quid pro quo* from current and potential office holders, the integrity of our system of representative democracy is undermined. Although the scope of such pernicious practices can never be reliably ascertained, the deeply disturbing examples surfacing after the 1972 election demonstrate that the problem is not an illusory one.[75]

Second, the justices ruled that the congressional restriction of independent expenditures in campaigns, the limitations on expenditures by candidates from their own personal resources, and the limitation on total campaign expenditures violated the First Amendment. To a majority of justices in 1976, the previously mentioned practices did not necessarily enhance the potential for corruption in the same vein as individual contributions to candidates, and therefore restricting them did not serve a government interest compelling enough to warrant a curtailment on free speech and association:

> In sum, the provisions of the Act that impose a $1,000 limitation on contributions to a single candidate, a $5,000 limitation on contributions by a political action committee to a single candidate, and a $25,000 limitation on total contributions by an individual during any calendar year, are constitutionally valid. These limitations, along with the disclosure provisions, constitute the Act's primary weapons against the reality or appearance of improper influence stemming from the dependence of candidates on large campaign contributions. The contribution ceilings thus serve the basic governmental interest in safeguarding the integrity of the electoral process without directly impinging upon the rights of individual citizens and candidates to engage in political debate and discussion. By contrast, the First Amendment requires the invalidation of the Act's independent expenditure ceiling, its limitation on a candidate's expenditures from his own personal funds, and its ceilings on

over-all campaign expenditures. These provisions place substantial and direct restrictions on the ability of candidates, citizens, and associations to engage in protected political expression, restrictions that the First Amendment cannot tolerate.[76]

There were also a few other rulings promulgated by the justices in this decision. Under the 1974 amendments, the original members of the FEC were appointed by the president, the speaker of the House, and the president pro tempore of the Senate (each appointed two members). This was deemed a violation of separation of powers, as four of the commissioners were appointed by Congress but exercised executive authority. This appointment mechanism needed to be changed by Congress. The justices also upheld the FECA provision that authorized measures to promote public financing of presidential campaigns, such as the income tax checkoff. Later in the same year, members of Congress passed new amendments to FECA that required all six members of the FEC to be appointed by the president and confirmed by the Senate.[77]

Amendments to FECA were added in 1979 to increase the threshold amount for reportable contributions or expenditures from $100 to $200 and increased the threshold for disclosing independent expenditures from $100 to $250. These changes substantially reduced the amount of information that candidates and committees had to file with the FEC.[78] But another fundamentally important change in the law was made presumably to enhance the role of political parties in elections and to encourage higher levels of citizen participation in the electoral process. The revised law exempted certain types of party-related activity from spending limits, including grassroots volunteer activities and voter registration and turnout drives. Political committees could also spend unlimited amounts on materials related to grassroots or volunteer activities provided that the funds in question were not drawn from contributions designated for a specific candidate.[79] Thereafter, these exemptions, or loopholes, were generally referred to as "soft money." The 1979 amendments to FECA would be the last major campaign finance reforms of the twentieth century in the United States.

Advocates of campaign finance reform in the 1990s and 2000s argued that unprecedented activities during the 1996 presidential campaign rendered FECA relatively meaningless and necessitated new changes in federal law. Specifically, the increase in soft-money contributions to both major political parties demonstrated that changes in the law were essential, or the prominence of money in federal political campaigns would get only worse. The primary sponsors of legislation in the Senate were John McCain (R–AZ) and Russell Feingold (D–WI). In the late 1990s, the two senators received majority support for their bill but were defeated by a filibuster in the Senate conducted by Mitch McConnell (R–KY). In 2000, soft-money fundraising by both major parties increased dramatically; a surge in issue advocacy advertising also ensued. As a result of the election, more supporters of campaign finance reform were elected, and the scandal involving the Enron Corporation facilitated the passage of the Bipartisan Campaign Reform Act (BCRA) of 2002. President George W. Bush signed the bill into law on March 27, 2002. Almost immediately, the bill's constitutionality was challenged in federal court.[80]

Soft money in federal elections was banned by the BCRA. The law also banned nonpartisan "issue ads" funded by soft money from corporations and labor unions. Ads referring to candidates for federal elections without expressly advocating their election or defeat were banned 30 days prior to a primary election and 60 days prior to a general election. The limits of hard-money contributions by individuals were raised and indexed for inflation. The law went into effect on November 6, 2002, one day after the midterm election. The individual contribution limit was raised from $1,000 to $2,000 per candidate per election.[81] Because the limits were indexed for inflation, the individual contribution limits for 2011–2012 were as follows:

- $2,500 per candidate per election
- $5,000 to a political action committee per year
- $10,000 per year combined limit for state, district, and local party committees
- $30,800 per year to a national party committee
- $117,000 overall biennial limit ($46,200 to all candidates and $70,800 to all PACs and parties)[82]

The constitutionality of the BCRA was decided the following year after its passage in *McConnell v. Federal Election Commission*.[83] Two central questions were addressed by the justices. First, did the ban on soft-money contributions in the BCRA exceed the authority of Congress to regulate elections under Article I, Section, 4 and/or violate freedom of speech under the First Amendment? Second, do regulations of the source, content, or timing of political advertising under the BCRA violate freedom of speech under the First Amendment? To a considerable extent, the justices answered both questions in the negative in a five-to-four decision written by Justices Sandra Day O'Connor and John Paul Stevens.[84] Justices O'Connor and Stevens concluded,

> Many years ago we observed that "[t]o say that Congress is without power to pass appropriate legislation to safeguard ... an election from the improper use of money to influence the result is to deny to the nation in a vital particular the power of self-protection." We abide by that conviction in considering Congress' most recent effort to confine the ill effects of aggregated wealth on our political system. We are under no illusion that BCRA will be the last congressional statement on the matter. Money, like water, will always find an outlet. What problems will arise, and how Congress will respond, are concerns for another day. In the main we uphold BCRA's two principal, complementary features: the control of soft money and the regulation of electioneering communications.[85]

Five years later, another controversy involving the BCRA would occur as a result of the 2008 presidential campaign. This time, the justices would interpret the BCRA and the Constitution quite differently in *Citizens United v. Federal Election Commission*.[86]

Legal analyst Jeffrey Toobin presented an apt historical overview of *Citizens United* in 2012:

> In one sense, the story of the Citizens United case goes back more than a hundred years. It begins in the Gilded Age, when the Supreme Court barred most attempts by the government to ameliorate the harsh effects of market forces. In that era, the Court said, for the first time, that corporations, like people, have constitutional rights. The Progressive Era, which followed, saw the development of activist government and the first major efforts to limit the impact of money in politics. Since then, the sides in the continuing battle have remained more or less the same: progressives (or liberals) vs. conservatives, Democrats vs. Republicans, regulators vs. libertarians. One side has favored government rules to limit the influence of the moneyed in political campaigns; the other has supported a freer market, allowing individuals and corporations to contribute as they see fit. Citizens United marked another round in this contest.[87]

What appeared to be a narrow issue concerning the BCRA turned out to be a landmark ruling that will affect the nature of federal campaigns for the foreseeable future.[88]

The BCRA prohibited corporations from running television commercials for or against presidential candidates for 30 days before primaries. During the 2008 Democratic presidential primaries, officials operating Citizens United, a nonprofit organization, wished to broadcast a documentary titled *Hillary: The Movie* within the 30-day time period but was not allowed to do so by regulators at the FEC in conjunction with the BCRA, which forbade "electioneering communication" during this time period before a primary. The documentary was critical of Hillary Clinton, one of the Democratic candidates for president. Attorneys for Citizens United maintained that the BCRA applied only to commercials and not to 90-minute documentaries and sought a judgment from the Supreme Court accordingly. Chief Justice John Roberts, in particular, used the case as a political opportunity to do much more than the litigants requested.[89] In a five-to-four decision written by Justice Anthony Kennedy, the majority of the Court's members determined that corporations and unions have the same free speech rights as individuals under the First Amendment. The Court's majority found no compelling governmental interest for prohibiting corporations and unions from using their general treasury funds to make election-related independent expenditures. The justices determined that the restrictions in the BCRA amount to censorship and were consequently prohibited by the First Amendment's guarantee of free speech. Justice Kennedy concluded that

> modern day movies, television comedies, or skits on Youtube.com might portray public officials or public policies in unflattering ways. Yet if a covered transmission during the blackout period creates the background for candidate endorsement or opposition, a felony occurs solely because the corporation, other than an exempt media corporation, has made the "purchase, payment, distribution, loan, advance, deposit, or gift of money or anything of value" in order to engage in political speech. Speech would be suppressed in the realm where its necessity is most evident: in the public dialogue preceding a real election. Governments are often hostile to speech, but under our law and our tradition it seems stranger than fiction for our Government to make this political speech a crime. Yet this is the statute's purpose and design.[90]

As a result of *Citizens United*, any outside group can use corporate money to make a direct case for or against a particular candidate or cause. Groups can engage in such activities right up until Election

Day as well. In addition, one of the consequences of this case is that so-called super PACs have proliferated in American politics since 2010. Super PACs are a special type of PAC. Officials representing super PACs may not make contributions to candidates or political parties, but they are allowed to engage in unlimited political spending independent of campaigns and parties. Unlike the traditional PACs, super PACs can raise unlimited funds from individuals, corporations, unions, and other groups. According to the Court's majority, these activities are protected by freedom of speech.

In dissent, Justice John Paul Stevens offered a fundamentally different point of view and a differential understanding of history than Justice Kennedy:

> In the context of election to public office, the distinction between corporate and human speakers is significant. Although they make enormous contributions to our society, corporations are actually not members of it. They cannot vote or run for office. Because they may be managed and controlled by nonresidents, their interests may conflict in fundamental respects with the interests of eligible voters. The financial resources, legal structure, and instrumental orientation of corporations raise legitimate concerns about their role in the electoral process. Our lawmakers have a compelling constitutional basis, if not also a democratic duty, to take measures designed to guard against the potentially deleterious effects of corporate spending in local and national races. The majority's approach to corporate electioneering marks a dramatic break from our past. Congress has placed special limitations on campaign spending by corporations ever since the passage of the Tillman Act in 1907.[91]

Justice Stevens admonished his colleagues in the majority with his concluding statement. He opined that

> in a democratic society, the longstanding consensus on the need to limit corporate campaign spending should outweigh the wooden application of judge-made rules. The majority's rejection of this principle "elevate[s] corporations to a level of deference which has not been seen at least since the days when substantive due process was regularly used to invalidate regulatory legislation thought to unfairly impinge upon established economic interests." At bottom, the Court's opinion is thus a rejection of the common sense of the American people, who have recognized a need to prevent corporations from undermining self-government since the founding, and who have fought against the distinctive corrupting potential of corporate electioneering since the days

of Theodore Roosevelt. It is a strange time to repudiate that common sense. While American democracy is imperfect, few outside the majority of this Court would have thought its flaws included a dearth of corporate money in politics.[92]

In 2012, the justices reaffirmed *Citizens United* in a case stemming from the state of Montana.[93] In doing so, the justices overturned a 1912 Montana law that barred corporate contributions to political parties and candidates. [94]

THE MORE PROACTIVE CITIZEN IN THE AMERICAN REPUBLIC

Almost 200 years ago, Horace Mann largely spearheaded the common school movement in the United States and believed that every child should be ensured a basic education funded by local taxes. He believed that public, secular education was central to good citizenship, democratic governance, and a prosperous society. His theory and vision are still universally applicable today. With regard to citizenship in a federal republic, systems theory is predicated on a fundamental premise that it takes a multivariate approach to understanding public policy initiatives in the United States. While the public education system across the 50 states and the District of Columbia is in need of reform, the American people, collectively, can improve their efforts and performance as citizens as well.

It is through education that citizens will become more enlightened in terms of their civic responsibilities in a republican form of government. A more vigorous curricular focus on civic education at the state level would help to fully operationalize the Mann vision of the nineteenth century. In addition, however, citizens must take a reformist approach to their own inputs into the democratic process. Collectively, we must enhance our own interest and knowledge about politics and public affairs. If Americans want a more effective government, then we have to hold policymakers accountable to a much greater extent than is presently the case. It is difficult to maximize accountability in the guise of vast ignorance about the state of public affairs. The key to policy reform in the United States was well understood by Mann a long time ago. While Americans will continue to pursue a more perfect union, clearly, the way to achieve such a lofty and worthwhile goal is through education.

Reticence will not reform the status quo. A more proactive citizenry would vote at higher rates and participate en masse in interest group politics. The more affluent and more highly educated in this society are well represented in politics and adept at holding decision makers accountable. The same adage can apply to the underrepresented in American society as well. State officials could do what some of their peers have already done in other states in order to encourage their citizens to vote. In 1973, Election Day registration (EDR) was established in Maine, allowing citizens to register and then vote on Election Day. Officials in Minnesota and Wisconsin passed similar laws later that decade. In the 1980s and 1990s, EDR was adopted in Idaho, Iowa, Montana, New Hampshire, and Wyoming. North Carolina's version of EDR went into effect in 2007. Thus, nine states currently have some form of EDR, and average turnout rates are typically 10 to 12 percent higher in EDR states than the national average.[95] State officials could also avoid or repeal existing laws that discourage citizens from voting in elections. Yet certain reforms are needed in society and are absolutely critical if citizens are to reach their potential in this republic. Arguably, the most prominent reform needed in American politics has to do with money. President Theodore Roosevelt promoted the idea of public financing of federal campaigns over 100 years ago. Critics of reform adhere to the argument that Congress is limited in its ability to regulate elections due to freedom of speech. This is a convenient argument, however, for it perpetuates the status quo and allows moneyed interests to continue dominating the American political landscape. Where does it say in the Constitution that corporations, like individuals, have the freedom to dominate who gets elected and who does not simply because they have a lot of financial resources? *Citizens United* is a dangerous precedent that needs to be reversed. We need not wait until there are key personnel changes on the Supreme Court, however. The American people have the ultimate authority to demand changes in campaign finance since this is a representative democracy. Members of Congress will be pay attention if citizens require them to do so.

Education: A Public Good Worth Defending

According to educator William Hayes, Horace Mann's vision of the public schools is still relevant today.[1] While he posited that Mann would have taken exception to the school choice movement, the current curriculums being offered, and high-stakes testing, Hayes offered the following conclusion about the founder of the common school:

Photograph of Horace Mann taken before his years at Antioch College (1853–1859). (Image courtesy of Antiochiana, Antioch College.)

> Much of what has happened with public schools since his death would be pleasing to Horace Mann. The fact that we now have free tax-supported schools in every community and that they enroll at least 90 percent of the school-age children would be a source of great pride to him and to his fellow pioneers in the public school movement. He would be surprised and gratified by the fact that public education is now in place for secondary students as well as those in the elementary grades. In addition, he would undoubtedly be thrilled by the

fact that there are compulsory attendance laws in every state. Given the condition of school buildings during his lifetime, Horace Mann could not help but be impressed by the buildings that now house many of our finest public schools. The education programs currently preparing teachers in our private and public colleges go far beyond the meager instruction available in the normal schools established by Horace Mann. He would be pleased with the present requirements for teacher certification and would applaud the states and districts that have ongoing professional growth programs for their teachers. In regard to the curriculum being taught in our public schools, Mann would be supportive of the current requirements in language arts, mathematics, science, physical education, health, and music. There is little question that he would approve as well of the partnership that has developed between local and state governments in financing and managing the schools. It is doubtful that after his service in Congress, Horace Mann would have quarreled with the fact that the federal government has also become a partner in supporting public education. The centralization of smaller districts into larger districts is a trend that is also in keeping with his own programs in Massachusetts. Considering all this, Horace Mann could not help but be impressed by the way his vision of free, tax-supported schools has prospered.[2]

Mann believed that education is inherently a public good and should be delivered to all students in secular, public schools funded by the taxpayers of all communities in America. A public good, by definition, is an entity that provides a service for all children on an equal basis regardless of race, creed, social class, and a host of other factors. Vouchers to promote parochial education, at taxpayers' expense, runs counter to what he was trying to accomplish with the creation of common schools. In addition, school choice advocates have yet to demonstrate that their approach to education will ever solve segregation problems in the United States or the academic achievement gap between Caucasian and Asian American students on one hand and African American, Latino American, and Native American children on the other.[3]

THE NEED FOR A FEARLESS ADVOCATE OF PUBLIC EDUCATION

Mann was an unapologetic advocate for public schools. In the contemporary world, such a visible spokesperson for public education has been noticeably absent and sorely needed. One might think that the

U.S. secretary of education in today's world would have a similar platform to promote public schools as Mann did in the nineteenth century. The federal Department of Education (DOE) was created in 1979 when President Jimmy Carter signed the Department of Education Organization Act into law.[4] But the creation of a federal department of education was an idea that had existed for decades. Between 1908 and 1975, there were more than 130 bills introduced in Congress to accomplish this objective, but two important events occurred to facilitate the bill's passage. First, Abraham Ribicoff was initially elected to the U.S. Senate in 1962 and ultimately served in that body for 18 years. Senator Ribicoff (D–CT) was the former secretary of health, education, and welfare, and began work on the founding of the DOE in the 1960s. Second, officials at the National Education Association (NEA) grew increasingly more interested in a federal presence in K–12 education. In 1975, the union's leaders endorsed Jimmy Carter for president, marking the first time in the organization's history that the NEA endorsed a presidential candidate. The NEA's support was helpful in President Carter's electoral victory in 1976.[5]

Since the DOE was created, the appointed secretaries have never been staunch advocates for public education in the philosophical mold of Mann. The DOE's first secretary was Shirley Hufstedler, an appointee of President Carter. In her career, she has had more extensive achievements in the judicial and legal sectors than in education.[6] With Ronald Reagan's victory in 1980, she was succeed by Terrel Bell, William Bennett, and Lauro Cavazos, respectively. Secretary Bell was initially appointed by President Reagan to abolish the DOE, a political stance still favored by many conservatives today but subsequently promoted the publication of *A Nation at Risk*, which has been utilized by many conservatives since 1983 to undermine public education.[7] Secretary Bennett is a prominent social conservative who is known more for advocating Christian fundamentalism within the Republican Party than for crusading on behalf of the nation's public schools.[8] In 1988, President Reagan was accused of political pandering by critics when he appointed Lauro Cavazos, a Democrat and the first Latino American cabinet secretary, to be the head of the DOE. Some suggested that the Republicans were seeking to ingratiate themselves with Latino voters in advance of the 1988 presidential election.[9] Secretary Cavazos continued being secretary of the DOE under President George H. W. Bush until late 1990, when he resigned amid a policy difference with the Bush administration concerning scholarships designated solely for minority students.[10] President Bush appointed Lamar Alexander to replace him. Alexander supports charter schools and vouchers.[11] The Democrats regained the presidency after 12 years with the election of Bill Clinton in 1992. His education secretary, Richard Riley, supported charter schools but was vehemently opposed to vouchers, not unlike President Clinton himself.[12]

George W. Bush appointed two education secretaries during his eight-year tenure: Rod Paige and Margaret Spellings. Both were strong school choice advocates in terms of their support for charter schools and vouchers.[13] President Obama selected Arne Duncan as his education secretary in 2009. Not unlike President Clinton, President Obama selected an individual that strongly supported charter schools but opposed school vouchers in Secretary Duncan.[14] If reforming public education is the primary objective, however, we need a president who has a strong commitment to Mann's vision of public education and who is willing to appoint an education secretary who embraces the Mann philosophy and has the political acumen, fortitude, and courage to pursue the cause of reforming the public schools in America without setting them up to fail in the first place.

REVISITING THE INDIVIDUALIST CREED IN THE UNITED STATES

In advance of assessing the public nature of education, it is important to ponder a very important cultural reality in the United States. In America, throughout its history, citizens have always celebrated individualism through literature, movies, and television. In the political arena, public policy debates have typically been portrayed in highly individualistic terms, and many Americans tend to assess public policy issues in terms of their perceived impact on them as individuals, that is, how will the proposed policy changes affect citizens at the individual level as opposed to embracing more of a communitarian perspective and assessing public policy issues in terms of how they may affect the greater community, first and foremost.[15] As Hudson has noted, individualism is part of the American creed:

> People in most other nations understand their national attachment in terms of a common historical experience, usually common ethnicity, and often common religious belief. As a nation of immigrants, the United States contains a diversity of people with different histories,

ethnic backgrounds, and religions. What has held the nation together is a widely held commitment to the ideals symbolized in the founding events of the nation—the American Revolution and constitutional ratification—and the principles found in the documents connected to those events. ... What are these ideals—the American creed—that define American identity? For the most part, they are the ideals of classical liberalism: limited government, the rule of law, liberty, political equality, and individualism. ... Whereas John Locke may have understood liberal ideals to be relevant to the political goals of English gentleman property holders, the American revolutionaries applied them—especially political liberty, equality, and individualism—to all citizens, as is evident in the Declaration of Independence. The American Revolution produced a democratized version of classical liberalism that became the American creed.[16]

Indeed, rugged individualism (or radical individualism, as Hudson calls it) has deep roots in American history. Alexis de Tocqueville utilized the term "individualism" when he came to America in the 1830s.[17] The European elite defined individualism in the following manner:

Individualism is a reflective and peaceable sentiment that disposes each citizen to isolate himself from the mass of those like him and to withdraw to one side with his family and his friends, so that after having thus created a little society for his own use, he willingly abandons society at large to itself. Selfishness is born of a blind instinct; individualism proceeds from an erroneous judgment rather than a depraved sentiment. It has its source in the defects of the mind as much as in the vices of the heart.[18]

While Americans had a very positive view of individualism, de Tocqueville had some serious concerns about this aspect of American society.

De Tocqueville may have appreciated the value of individualism in his time, but he had a different view of individualism and democracy than most Americans. He felt that individualism could be taken too far and actually undermine democracy. From his perspective, "Selfishness withers the seed of all the virtues; individualism at first dries up only the source of public virtues; but in the long term it attacks and destroys all the others and will finally be absorbed by selfishness. Selfishness is a vice as old as the world. It scarcely belongs more to one form of society than to another."[19] To him, individualism taken to an extreme could denigrate into egoism. Hudson believes that a society of egoists is one that does not put the greater common good ahead of individual self-interest.[20] To the Frenchman in the early nineteenth century, egoism taken to an extreme will reduce civic virtue. Citizens become too inward in their analytical framework and thus succeed in isolating themselves from one another when they undoubtedly have more in common than they realize.

Hudson maintains that Americans in the 1830s had not yet succumbed to radical individualism when de Tocqueville visited the country.[21] To de Tocqueville, his experience in America led him to conclude that Americans were committed to civic participation and therefore had developed "habits of the heart" that would result in a successful participatory democracy. He believed that Americans had achieved a relative balance between individualism and civic virtue.[22] Hudson believes that American society has degenerated into the egoistic pride and selfishness that de Tocqueville wrote about in the nineteenth century.

Hudson contends that almost 30 years ago, sociologist Robert Bellah and his colleagues documented the growing reality that radical individualism had pervaded America with the publication of *Habits of the Heart*.[23] In their study of several hundred middle-class Americans regarding their beliefs about politics, religion, morality, family, and community, the researchers discovered that most Americans defined every aspect of their life in highly individualistic terms.[24] Bellah et al. provided the following appraisal of individualism in America in the 1980s:

> We spoke of the belief of Madison and the other founders that our form of government was dependent on the existence of virtue among the people. It was such virtue that they expected to resolve the tension between private interest and the public good. Without civic virtue, they thought, the republic would decline into factional chaos and probably end in authoritarian rule. Half a century later, this idea was reiterated in Tocqueville's argument about the importance of the mores—the "habits of the heart"—of Americans. Even at the end of the nineteenth century, when Establishment and Populist visions were the chief antagonists in the continuing argument about the shape of our society, Madisonian ideas were still presupposed. The tension between private interest and the public good is never completely resolved in any society. But in a free republic, it is the task of the citizen, whether ruler or ruled, to cultivate civic virtue in order to mitigate the tension and render it manageable. As the twentieth century has progressed, that understanding, so important through most of our history, has begun to slip from

our grasp. As we unthinkingly use the oxymoron "private citizen," the very meaning of citizenship escapes us. And with Ronald Reagan's assertion that "we the people" are a "special interest group," our concern for the economy being the only thing that holds us together, we have reached a kind of end of the line. The citizen has been swallowed up in "economic man." Yet this kind of economic liberalism is not ultimately liberating, for, as became quite clear with the final two visions of the public good described, when economics is the main model for our common life, we are more and more tempted to put ourselves in the hands of the manager and the expert. If society is shattered into as many special interests as there are individuals, then, as Tocqueville foresaw, there is only the schoolmaster state left to take care of us and keep us from one another's throats.[25]

To these researchers, it is the realm of ideas and political imagination that will determine whether a society meets its challenges. It is through political vision that citizens, together, can collaborate and work toward facilitating change wherever needed in society. In order to succeed at effectuating change, however, Americans must stop defining themselves as individuals and instead revert back to becoming citizens again. We must embrace civic virtue and put the needs of society ahead of our own self-interest. According to Bellah et al. and Hudson, a resurgence of civic virtue in America is not likely to occur.[26]

The ethos of individualism runs counter to the communitarian sentiment echoed by John F. Kennedy when he was inaugurated as president on January 20, 1961: "And so, my fellow Americans: ask not what your country can do for you—ask what you can do for your country."[27] Hudson espouses a communitarian approach to public policy in the same philosophical tradition as the nation's 35th president:

> Bringing about a better balance between community and the individual in the United States requires a more communitarian approach to politics. Such an approach challenges the libertarian view that individuals are completely autonomous authors of their own existence; instead, it regards people as products of the many communities—from their families and neighborhoods to the national community—in which they live. Unlike the libertarians, who recognize only freedom from community-imposed constraints, communitarians understand that human freedom and dignity require the support of a network of social institutions. A communitarian approach would seek to nurture and protect such institutions, rather than letting them decay as libertarians have. Instead

of a libertarian preoccupation with rights, communitarianism emphasizes the need to balance rights with responsibilities, if rights are to be
preserved.[28]

Collectively, Americans must understand that there are implications
that coincide with our public policy choices. For example, if taxes on
personal income are cut, which generally meets with a good deal of
popular approval, how does this policy affect other things in society,
such as education, health care, protection of the environment, assistance for the indigent, and so forth? The political and social reality in
America is that we are mutually interdependent on one another,
whether we choose to accept the premise or not. This was the fundamental philosophical premise embraced by Mann, and it still has utility in the twenty-first century.

Education historians Wayne Urban and Jennings Wagoner provided the following synopsis of Mann and the common school
movement:

> In spite of obvious disagreements and conflicts, Americans in
> northeastern and midwestern sections of the country rallied around
> the concept of "the common school" for several decades after the Civil
> War. Democrats and Whigs, workingmen and capitalists, and country
> folk and urban dwellers joined forces in sufficient numbers to create
> what many considered to be *the* indispensable institution of American
> democracy. Leaders of the movement, exemplified by Horace Mann of
> Massachusetts, generated enthusiasm for the idea of the common
> school by appealing to a variety of motives, not all of which were consis-
> tent or compatible. Essentially a movement that reflected the values of
> republicanism, Protestantism, and capitalism, the common school
> revival held out the promise that the educational frontier was as open
> and promising as the land itself. The common school movement
> unleashed a set of ideas and a series of trends that are still in motion.
> Schools should be free, not based on fees. They should be open to all,
> not just a few. They should foster morality and ethics but avoid sectar-
> ian entanglements. Teachers should be prepared for their calling and
> temperamentally suited to deal with children from different walks of
> life. Schools should foster the public good as well as prepare individuals
> for success in life.[29]

Remarkably, and in spite of policies embraced by the political right,
the common school ideology has persevered through many generations in American history. Perhaps there are some substantive explanations for this veritable truism in American education.

WHAT IS A PUBLIC GOOD?

The definition of a public, collective, or common good was provided by Mancur Olson in 1965 in his seminal book *The Logic of Collective Action*.[30] In his view, Olson determined that

> the reason the state cannot survive on voluntary dues or payments, but must rely on taxation, is that the most fundamental services a nation-state provides are, in one important respect, like the higher price in a competitive market: they must be available to everyone if they are available to anyone. The basic and most elementary goods or services provided by the government, like defense and police protection, and the system of law and order generally, are such that they go to everyone or practically everyone in the nation. It would obviously not be feasible, if indeed it were possible, to deny the protection provided by the military services, the police, and the courts to those who did not voluntarily pay their share of the costs of government, and taxation is accordingly necessary. The common or collective benefits provided by governments are usually called "public goods" by economists, and the concept of public goods is one of the oldest and most important ideas in the study of public finance. A common, collective, or public good is here defined as any good such that, if any person X_i in a group $X_1, \ldots, X_i, \ldots, X_n$ consumes it, it cannot feasibly be withheld from the others in that group. In other words, those who do not purchase or pay for any of the public or collective good cannot be excluded or kept from sharing in the consumption of the good, as they can where noncollective goods are concerned.[31]

So what are examples of public goods beyond those mentioned by Olson (military security/national defense, police protection, and the criminal justice system)? This list is not meant to be exhaustive by any means, but infrastructure should be included because the provision of roads, bridges, streetlights, street signs, lighthouses, and the like not only provide citizens with transportation but also create the conditions to help make economic prosperity possible. The postal system is a public good. It permits all citizens to communicate with one another and is an additional means of achieving economic growth. Fire protection, similar to police protection, is a way to provide security and protection to the public. It is my personal belief that access to health care is also a public good in that all citizens should have equal and unfettered access to medical assistance. What makes Mann and his contemporaries who believed in the common school philosophy so special in U.S. history is that they understood the fundamental premise that K–12 education is a public good as well.[32]

Education as a Public Good

Mann, as spiritual as he may have been, believed that the government should not be in the business of promoting any specific religious denomination in its activities. Although his advocacy of the teaching of Christian principles in public schools has been nullified by constitutional law today, some of his commentary concerning the role of government when it comes to religion is still highly relevant today. To some of his contemporary critics of public education, Mann offered a prophesy of his own:

> It is known, too, that our noble system of free schools for the whole people is strenuously opposed by a few persons in our own State, and by no inconsiderable numbers in some of the other states of this Union; and that a rival system of "parochial" or "sectarian schools" is now urged upon the public by a numerous, a powerful, and a well-organized body of men. It has pleased the advocates of this rival system, in various public addresses, in reports, and through periodicals devoted to their cause, to denounce our system as irreligious and anti-Christian. They do not trouble themselves to describe what our system is, but adopt a more summary way to forestall public opinion against it by using general epithets of reproach, and signals of alarm.[33]

Opponents to traditional public schools have also reverted to using a public perception, shared by some, that public schools are deficient in a general sense when compared to alternative schools. By trying to build up their niche (charter schools, parochial schools, online learning, or home schooling), many do so by utilizing negative commentary when it comes to public education. The assumption is typically based on a conservative belief that the private entity can outperform the government bureaucracy in the vast majority of all cases.

This educator and theologian made an important distinction with regard to government and religious activity, one not unlike that made by Thomas Jefferson years earlier. His substantive premise is important to consider with regard to education vouchers today, no matter what the justices may have determined about school choice more than a decade ago:

> All the schemes ever devised by governments to secure the prevalence and permanence of religion among the people, however variant in form

they may have been, are substantially resolvable into two systems. One of these systems holds the regulation and control of the religious belief of the people to be one of the functions of government, like the command of the army or the navy, or the establishment of courts, or the collection of revenues. According to the other system, religious belief is a matter of individual and parental concern; and, while the government furnishes all practicable facilities for the independent formation of that belief, it exercises no authority to prescribe, or coercion to enforce it. The former is the system, which, with very few exceptions, has prevailed throughout Christendom for fifteen hundred years. Our own government is almost a solitary example among the nations of the earth, where freedom of opinion, and the inviolability of conscience, have been even theoretically recognized by the law.[34]

Is the promotion of religion an appropriate government activity? Mann believed that it is not, precisely because he defined religion in terms of individual rights. To him, religious worship is a private matter for adults—and the parents of children—to determine free of government constraints. Thus, government officials should not have the authority to promote any specific religious denominations with the use of public tax revenue.

Mann did advocate the teaching of nonsectarian religion in the public schools. As indicated earlier, this nineteenth-century nuance has mostly vanished from contemporary education due to the prevailing judicial interpretation of the separation between church and state today. In a book published in 1929, Raymond Culver captured the essence of Mann's accomplishments with regard to religion and education in Massachusetts public schools:

> By such sectarian jealousies the teaching of non-sectarian religion was hindered in the days of Horace Mann. He saved the public schools from the destruction that would have followed had the agents of reaction had their way. He was not able to arrest the tide of secularization that has robbed our schools of religion. The secularized school of today is the result of such jealousy on the part of the Roman Catholics, Protestants, and Jews, and the price we are paying in juvenile delinquency and adult crime is high.[35]

Culver was a Baptist educator who obviously lamented the absence of religion in secular education. In addition, however, he seemingly highlighted the wisdom of the early founders of the new republic regarding the debate between church and state. In rejecting a state-endorsed denomination as the official religion of the United States,

James Madison and others understood that such practices only enhanced conflict and strife between and among religious groups. Instead, they wisely decided to let the people worship as they please, free of government intervention. This is part of the reason why the contemporary debate about school vouchers is intriguing from a historical perspective. In many parts of the country, diverting taxpayers' money to support Protestant and Catholic schools will probably not render a great deal of controversy. Yet in the aftermath of the September 11, 2001. terrorist attacks, will citizens in the United States have similar views for less popular faiths? Since this is unlikely to be the case, the full implications of vouchers, outside of the choice analytical framework, have undoubtedly not been aired and debated sufficiently.

Another important distinction is made between the operation of private and public schools by the education philosopher. In a summary of public education in the commonwealth of Massachusetts, Mann declared that

> such, then, in a religious point of view, is the Massachusetts system of common schools. Reverently it recognizes and affirms the sovereign rights of the Creator, sedulously and sacredly it guards the religious rights of the creature; while it seeks to remove all hindrances, and to supply all furtherances, to a filial and paternal communion between man and his Maker. In a social and political sense, it is a *free* school-system. It knows no distinction of rich and poor, of bond and free, or between those, who, in the imperfect light of this world, are seeking, through different avenues, to reach the gate of heaven. Without money and without price, it throws open its doors, and spreads the table of its bounty, for all the children of the State. Like the sun, it shines not only upon the good, but upon the evil, that they may become good; and, like the rain, its blessings descend not only upon the just, but upon the unjust, that their injustice may depart from them, and be known no more.[36]

We know that there is an important operational difference between private and traditional public schools. As Mann indicated, public schools are open to all children, assuming, of course, reasonable behavior toward others. Private school officials, however, are not bound by the same maxim. They are free to select some children but not admit others into their schools. The standard of accountability is quite different when comparing the public and private sectors.

On July 4, 1842, Horace Mann delivered a lengthy oration before the authorities of the city of Boston.[37] In his closing statement, he issued a challenge to his contemporaries that I believe is still relevant today in the era of the No Child Left Behind Act and accountability:

> Remember, then, the child whose voice first lisps, to-day, before that voice shall whisper sedition in secret, or thunder treason at the head of an armed band. Remember the child whose hand, to-day, first lifts its tiny bauble, before that hand shall scatter fire-brands, arrows and death. Remember those sportive groups of youth in whose halcyon bosoms there sleeps an ocean, as yet scarcely ruffled by the passions, which soon shall heave it as with the tempest's strength. Remember, that whatever station in life you may fill, these mortals,—these immortals, are your care. Devote, expend, consecrate yourselves to the holy work of their improvement. Pour out light and truth, as God pours sunshine and rain. No longer seek knowledge as the luxury of a few, but dispense it amongst all as the bread of life. Learn only how the ignorant may learn; how the innocent may be preserved; the vicious reclaimed. Call down the astronomer from the skies; call up the geologist from his subterranean explorations; summon, if need be, the mightiest intellects from the Council Chamber of the nation; enter cloistered halls, where the scholiast muses over superfluous annotations; dissolve conclave and synod, where subtle polemics are vainly discussing their barren dogmas;—collect whatever of talent, or erudition, or eloquence, or authority, the broad land can supply, *and go forth*, AND TEACH THIS PEOPLE. For, in the name of the living God, it must be proclaimed, that licentiousness shall be the liberty; and violence and chicanery shall be the law; and superstition and craft shall be the religion; and the self-destructive indulgence of all sensual and unhallowed passions shall be the only happiness of that people who neglect the education of their children.[38]

Clearly, Mann embraced the notion that, even though there were religious schools in the nineteenth century that continue to exist to this day, education is a public good and should be provided to all children in an even manner, regardless of their plight, social condition, social status, or economic condition. To him, the essence of a republican form of government is an educated citizenry, one where children from diverse backgrounds come together, learn to get along, and receive a quality education because it is an essential tool in a upwardly mobile democracy. Not much has changed in this sense since 1859, when Mann died. His challenge to Antioch students in his final baccalaureate address to them was stark and quite definitive:

So, in the infinitely nobler battle in which you are engaged against error and wrong, if ever repulsed or stricken down, may you always be solaced and cheered by the exulting cry of triumph over some abuse in Church or State, some vice or folly in society, some false opinion or cruelty or guilt which you have overcome! And I beseech you to treasure up in your hearts these my parting words: *Be ashamed to die until you have won some victory for humanity.*[39]

Mann's victory for humanity could be measured in a number of different ways, starting most importantly with the creation of the common school. To advocates of privatizing education through choice and marketplace competition, I can only wonder whether they are honestly trying to reform education or whether they are really pursuing the privatization of a commodity that is public by its very nature. If this is the case, is reform the true focus of their quest, or are they trying to fundamentally change the nature of secular education in the United States? An open and transparent debate should ensue in American society regarding public education. The children of the country deserve such honesty considering the substantive and historic stakes at issue.

According to the education consultant Nancy Kober, the public nature of education has played a vital role in the evolution of the American democracy but is increasingly under attack by those who attempt to shift the debate about education away from its public, collective nature and to an individualistic viewpoint:

From the early days of the nation, public education has played a vital role in American democratic society. In addition to preparing young people for productive work and fulfilling lives, public education has also been expected to accomplish certain collective missions aimed at promoting the common good. These include, among others, preparing youth to become responsible citizens, forging a common culture from a nation of immigrants, and reducing inequalities in American society. In recent years, however, some of these public-spirited missions of education have been neglected and are in danger of being abandoned. Most current efforts to reform public education have focused on increasing students' academic achievement—without a doubt, a central purpose of schooling. But the reasons given for why it's important to improve achievement often stress individual or private economic benefits (such as preparing youth for good jobs in a global economy), rather than public benefits (such as preparing youth for active citizenship in a democratic society). An emphasis on the individual goals of education is especially obvious in proposals to give families vouchers toward private school tuition—proposals that treat education as a private consumer good.[40]

Analytical frameworks in politics are of considerable importance. If conservatives prevail at encouraging people to individualize education policy, then Mann's common school vision, where education is a collective good, will be reversed after almost 200 years. This democratic tradition is worth keeping and perpetuating over time. Some (though certainly not all) features of the old (nineteenth-century) school have significant intrinsic value and should be preserved and maintained by this generation instead of cast aside without fully appreciating their contributions to the democratic way of life in America.

Kober delineates six public missions of American public schools: to provide universal access to free education, to guarantee equal opportunities for all children, to unify a diverse population, to prepare people for citizenship in a democratic society, to prepare people to become economically self-sufficient, and to improve social conditions.[41] In the arena of public opinion, Americans endorse these six missions.[42] Yet it is important to note that public schools serve a variety of other purposes as well in society. Many of these purposes do not lend themselves to exact quantitative measurement and are undoubtedly not appreciated as much as they should be accordingly. As Kober put it, "Education enriches individuals' lives by developing their capacities to think critically, appreciate culture, and maintain a sense of curiosity about the world. Education exposes children to new ways of thinking. Perhaps most importantly, a good elementary and secondary education can spur young people to go on to higher education and pursue learning all their lives."[43] How does one measure the extent to which children in the public schools are taught to think for themselves and the extent to which their education has enhanced their lives and the lives of the community in which they live?

Accountability in the public sector is an important part of democracy. Public school officials must be accountable to the citizens of this country. But citizens must be accountable for their children's education as well. Citizens must be willing to pursue reforms that will help improve education quality without compromising the public nature of education. Clearly, there is room for reform in public education. K–12 education in the United States is not perfect, but it can and must be enhanced without setting up some schools to fail and others to succeed. Collectively, we must embrace reforms that will help all schoolchildren, teachers, administrators, and support staff to live up to the standards that we establish as being exemplary in the early twenty-first century.[44]

Carl Kaestle offered a similar assertion the same year that *A Nation at Risk* was published:

> Some readers have suggested that my interpretation supports the position of present-day critics who advocate more public aid to nonpublic schools and who maintain that the public schools' failure to teach cognitive skills effectively while grappling with ideals of equality and diversity justifies a rejection of the idea of a common-school system. For what it is worth, that is not my own view. I believe that we need a unified, tax-supported common-school system. I believe that the public school systems of our states and localities need to be more common in some respects, that is, more equal and more integrated. But they also need to be much more diverse in other respects—more open to different teaching and learning styles, different cultural content, different parental preferences, and different community needs. Like most people, I agree with some aspects of cosmopolitan school reform and central control while I disagree with others. My personal inclination is to support cosmopolitan solutions on constitutional issues like separation of church and state, equal rights, and free expression, which require staunch central protection whatever the views of local majorities. I am more skeptical and selective about supporting the standardization of curriculum, program organization, or learning style, which is often argued on grounds of efficiency, upgrading standards, or the superior abilities of central decision makers. The apportioning of authority among federal, state, and local levels is a delicate matter, one which will continue to be debated in the decades ahead. But that is good. Centralization should not be mindless drift or merely a matter of who is more powerful. We need not be trapped by history, nor by the language of modernization and efficiency. We must be imaginative about the control of schools.[45]

The need for common schools still exists as does the need to reform them. What is different about the modern era is that many officials, elected and unelected, seek to undermine the whole common school philosophy because they do not support it and have a different agenda in mind when it comes to K–12 education. More by way of substance concerning education reform will ensue in chapter 8. Suffice it to say at this juncture, however, that maintaining a commitment to public education and the continuance of it as a public good for all children is one of the most important political battles in the early part of the twenty-first century.

Public Education in the American Democracy

There is little conflict in America on one highly important manner. Even though democracy can be very inefficient and wrought with conflict and controversy, Americans overwhelmingly support the democratic way of life. This reality actually unites many people with very divergent views; liberals, conservatives, Democrats, Republicans, Libertarians, and Socialists all agree on this issue. As the eminent education and history professor David Tyack has argued, "Democracy is about making wise collective choices. Democracy in education and education in democracy are not quaint legacies from a distant and happier time. They have never been more essential to wise self-rule than they are today."[46] Tyack highlights the crucial role that public education plays in the American way of life:

> Although Adlai Stevenson believed that public education was "the most American thing about America," many people do not share that view today. Some citizens speak of "government schools" as if they were alien invaders of their communities instead of long-standing neighborhood institutions. At the turn of the twentieth-first century, people talk about the cash value of schooling or the latest innovation but rarely speak about the powerful ideas that link public schooling to our political past and future. Daily, new get-smart-quick schemes to re-form the schools pop up. Pupils should address teachers as "ma'am" and "sir." School-children should wear uniforms. School districts can raise money by giving Coca-Cola exclusive rights to tout and sell its sodas on campus. Students should fill in the proper bubbles on their standardized tests with no. 2 pencils, and if they don't, they should repeat the grade. Social promotion is out; nonsocial nonpromotion is in. For more than a century public schools have been robust institutions, able to survive war, depressions, massive demographic changes, and even reformers. Amidst these trials, people retained a strong sense that education was part of the answer to problems, not the problem itself. But in recent decades, as schools have been drawn into the vortex of many social and political conflicts, and as an ideology of privatization has rapidly spread, doubts have arisen. Has public education failed the nation? Or, perhaps, has the nation failed education? The political and moral purposes that gave resonance to public education in earlier times have become muted, and constituencies that once supported

common schools have become splintered and confused about where to invest their educational loyalties. I am a partisan for the public schools—albeit a *critical* one. . . . I do not argue that public schools do a better—or worse—job than private schools in educating citizens (in any case we never have enough good schools, public or private, for the students who need them). But I believe that public schools represent a special kind of civic space that deserves to be supported by citizens whether they have children or not. The United States would be much impoverished if the public school system went to ruin. And one way to begin that impoverishment is to privatize the *purposes* of education.[47]

Education does occupy the very kind of civic space that Tyack discusses precisely because it is a public good by definition. By encouraging citizens to look inward, those in the individualistic camp are seeking to manipulate the policy outcomes they desire so that their fellow Americans will ignore their own history, tear down the common school, and replace it with a dangerous alternative that will disrupt democracy as we know it and devalue the importance of diversity in the modern era. Be aware of the alleged education reformer who endorses this type of approach to education policy. Any person can presume to improve a given scenario; an assessment of the ideas, political motivations, and values may prove illuminating and transparent, however.

Patience is an important virtue to consider in democratic nations. Patience in education is clearly needed at this time. While we must hold students, teachers, and administrators to high standards, it is important to heed historian Patricia Albjerg Graham's sage counsel:

What we do know is this: in the past schools have achieved the objectives set for them, but it has taken a long time. I am hopeful that we will have the same success with the goals of achievement and accountability. Yet in the case of universal academic achievement, schools cannot accomplish this alone. Their efforts must be supported by the culture in which the students, particularly adolescents, live and which recognizes that the prime business of youth is to get educated.[48]

In tracing the evolution of the public schools in U.S. history, Graham contends that a plethora of challenges have existed in the cause of educating America's children. In the twentieth and twenty-first centuries, she identifies four discernible eras in public education: assimilation (1900–1920), adjustment (1920–1954), access (1954–1983), and achievement (1983 to the present).[49] In the first three time periods, she concludes that each primary goal was partially achieved.[50]

However, the goals were never achieved as quickly as proponents desired.[51] In the case of the ongoing era of achievement and accountability, we should not expect dramatic academic changes in a short period of time unless more systemic change in American society is forthcoming, particularly since wealth is so stratified in the United States:

> Despite the slogan of "academic achievement for all," the reality has been that the current metric of school reform, test scores, has become one that directly helps those who have many advantages already and whose schools need relatively little reform. For those without such benefits, much school reform is necessary, but, in a society increasingly stratified by wealth, it has not been easy to make the changes either in schooling or in the community that would facilitate such increased academic learning. Nonetheless, the effort to undertake such changes in opportunities for academic learning is deeply laudable, and in various forms we have been working on this effort at democratizing access to learning for some time.[52]

Dramatic reform in public policy is typically a longitudinal matter in most cases. The common schools have been around for a long time. They are worth keeping and improving even if the measurable progress, at least in a quantitative sense, takes longer than we might have planned or prejudged.

Why Education Should Not Be Privatized

According to privatization advocates Clive Belfield and Henry Levin, "Privatization is the transfer of activities, assets, and responsibilities from government/public institutions and organizations to private individuals and agencies."[53] Milton Friedman argued that public education in America should be privatized en masse almost 20 years ago:

> Our elementary and secondary educational system needs to be radically restructured. Such a reconstruction can be achieved only by privatizing a major segment of the educational system—i.e., by enabling a private, for-profit industry to develop that will provide a wide variety of learning opportunities and offer effective competition to public schools. The most feasible way to bring about such a transfer from government to private enterprise is to enact in each state a voucher system that enables parents to choose freely the schools their children attend. The voucher must be universal, available to all parents, and large enough to cover

the costs of a high-quality education. No conditions should be attached to vouchers that interfere with the freedom of private enterprises to experiment, to explore, and to innovate.[54]

The laissez-faire premise articulated by Friedman is that the competition for students between and among school districts, both public and private, will result in improved education systems, especially when it pertains to public schools.[55] Either test scores are improved in the perceived deficient public school, or it may be closed altogether or taken over by a private management company. In short, either the competition, it is believed by political conservatives, will result in enhanced educational achievement, or there will be consequences to bear for the underperforming public school in question.

There are debatable assumptions made in this marketplace analysis of education that have already been discussed. Yet there are important implications to consider when attempting to apply the privatization paradigm to something as vital as the education of America's school-children. Public goods are provided for all on an equal basis by government entities because of one of the key tenets of democracy—accountability. The governmental entity is accountable to citizens, as they are collectively funding the enterprise to begin with and all children, regardless of background, have a right to a quality education. Public officials cannot deny an education to a child, even if the child in question has a number of academic, emotional, physical, and psychological challenges with which to contend. Only illicit behavior on the part of a child can result in expulsion from a public school system. Accountability standards warrant that the due process rights of parents and their children be afforded if this drastic measure is implemented.

The accountability standards are different for private and parochial schools. Officials do not have to admit students who may be struggling academically, nor do they have to offer admission to students who may have some of the challenges noted above. Should taxpayer funds be utilized by entities that cannot be held accountable in the same manner as public schools? This is a fundamental question with very serious societal implications.

Alex Molnar and David Garcia provide a capsule summary of the privatization movement in the realm of education in America:

The merits of a marketplace model for public education have been among the most prominent themes in education policy discussions over the last two decades. Advocates of market approaches to education reform contend that creating a market in educational services will foster competition among providers and thus spur delivery of better services at the same or lower cost than providing them through traditional public schools. Whether this is the case is debatable. It is clear, however, that the policy preferences of the past 25 years have increasingly leaned toward privatization. These preferences have been expressed in repeated efforts to promote educational vouchers and by the advocacy of "strong" state charter school laws. Most recently, the reauthorization of the Elementary and Secondary Education Act, popularly known as the "No Child Left Behind" Act (NCLB), has accelerated the three decade-long trend toward private, for-profit activities in public education.[56]

Clearly, conservatives are on the offensive when it comes to education policy in the United States. Defenders of public education have not thwarted the advances made in the charter school, voucher, virtual, and home-schooling movements.

Molnar and Garcia explain that privatizing activity today falls into two broad categories: the provision of supplemental educational services and the overall management or operation of schools.[57] To them, the NCLB law has had some serious implications on education policy in the United States:

> At the federal level, the No Child Left Behind legislation favors the expansion of privatizing approaches to education through district to charter school conversions of schools labeled failing and by creating a market for supplemental education services. NCLB requires schools, in return for federal education aid, to conduct standardized testing annually in grades 3 through 8. Schools that fail to demonstrate Adequate Yearly Progress (AYP) face a series of "corrective actions" that escalate in severity if a school continues to under-perform according to NCLB standards. Sanctions for a school that has failed to achieve AYP after five consecutive years include privatizing options such as reopening as a charter school and contracting with an outside organization to manage the school.[58]

Yet the emphasis created by those who drafted NCLB is on for-profit education activity. This law forbids public school officials themselves from providing federally funded tutoring if the school has failed to achieve AYP for two consecutive years.[59] Public school officials must contract with outside providers for tutoring. As Molnar and Garcia have noted, this requirement has effectively created a federally subsidized market for private tutoring firms.[60] It is no wonder that operators at many learning centers across the country have experienced a tremendous growth in business and profits over the past several years.[61]

Proponents of education privatization claim that market-oriented policies provide greater accountability to parents. With traditional public schools, parents readily know the identity of the officials responsible for their child's education, including teachers, principals, superintendents, boards of trustees, and other support staff personnel. In other words, there is transparency when it comes to the accountability issue. The same transparency does not exist in the case of for-profit schools.[62] The governance structures of for-profit companies are often not known to the public because they are intentionally obscured. Many researchers identify for-profit companies that operate public schools as education management organizations, somewhat analogous to the health maintenance organizations in the health care sector.[63] Sometimes, for-profit company officials establish nonprofit entities that appear to be fronts for the for-profit firm. This is precisely why ascertaining governance structures of for-profit companies can be very cumbersome and challenging.[64]

One important—and harmful—legacy of NCLB from a common school perspective is very much deeply intertwined with the privatization debate. According to Molnar and Garcia,

> Over the last two and a half decades privatization advocates have in policy discussions succeeded in combining the idea of educational reform through standards and outcomes with the idea of an educational marketplace. As a result education reform policy has shifted the focus of public school improvement away from the public schools themselves and toward an external market in educational services. Thus, the standards and accountability provisions of No Child Left Behind require all states to measure school academic performance using standardized tests and report school performance on a standardized report card for the expressed purpose of informing parents about possible school choices. Indeed, the very notion of keeping score according to a standardized criterion, which in many cases teachers themselves help create through assisting in the development of academic standards and assessments, creates the impression among policy makers and the general public that the "bottom line" in public education is not only measurable but that standardized test scores are the measure.[65]

Privatization enthusiasts are dominating the debate over education reform in the United States. The inherent assumption—and it is not very subtle at all—is that public education will reform only by replicating policies in the business sector. In other words, privatization advocates are communicating a powerful message to citizens across the country: public education cannot reform itself but must rely on private business and the competitive marketplace to do so. What happens after a generation or two passes with this fundamental philosophy intact? Many Americans are likely to accept the underlying assumptions in this paradigm without questioning their legitimacy, accuracy, and credibility.

The marketplace philosophy has been expressed in a number of works by a leading contemporary education scholar, Paul E. Peterson. In *Choice and Competition in American Education*, Peterson contends that

> school reform has long been on the nation's agenda. Earlier strategies tried out new curricular ideas, new management techniques, or the commitment of additional financial resources. But, recently, two more sweeping reforms—one holding schools accountable for specific educational outcomes, the other introducing choice and competition—have been placed on the table. The first involves setting state standards and measuring student performance by means of standardized tests. . . . The other option, choice and competition, is less well known, though some believe it to be the more promising reform strategy. It takes American business and industry as the appropriate model for schools to follow. In the private economy, consumers make choices, businesses make profits when they satisfy consumers more than their competitors do, and new inventions constantly drive the economy to ever-higher levels of productivity. Choice and competition: it's the American way—most of the time.[66]

While the latter point is certainly reflective of a capitalist economy, choice and competition may be suitable for general consumer choices. The choice-and-competition analytical framework is of dubious value, however, when pondering the future of public education in America. Outsourcing the delivery of public goods threatens the American democracy and will not result in reforming education in particular but will ultimately destroy it.

Allowing private companies to operate and manage public schools, as in the case of charter schools in most states and the use of education vouchers in some states, amounts to a form of outsourcing that poses a number of fundamental challenges in a democratic republic. Some contend that there are three different forms of privatization:

> "Privatization" is an umbrella term covering several distinct types of transactions. Broadly speaking, it means the shift of some or all of the responsibility for a function from government to the private sector. The term has most commonly been applied to the divestiture, by sale or long-term lease, of a state-owned enterprise to private investors. But another major form of privatization is the granting of a long-term franchise or concession under which the private sector finances, builds, and operates a major infrastructure project. A third type of privatization involves government selecting a private entity to deliver a public service that had previously been produced in-house by public employees. This form of privatization is increasingly called outsourcing.[67]

The type of outsourcing that is being allowed across the country in a number of public school systems represents a practice that Horace Mann would not have endorsed based on the common school ideology. Perhaps even more important, however, outsourcing of education and other public goods undermines the American democracy and its sovereignty as a nation.

Law school professor Paul Verkuil believes that the practice of using private contractors to perform essential functions in the military and civilian sectors of the government ought to be avoided in a democracy. Outsourcing, on principle, is not appropriate for vital public services for a nonnegotiable, fundamental reason:

> The government exercises sovereign powers. When those powers are delegated to outsiders, the capacity to govern is undermined. A government appointment creates a public servant who, whether through the oath, the security clearance, the desire to achieve public goals, or the psychic income of service, is different from those in the private sector. The office itself is honored. This is why many in our democratic system live in a dual reality, decrying the president, whether it be Bush or Clinton, Reagan or Roosevelt, but respecting the presidency, the office of George Washington, the first among the heroes of our Republic. Those offices that fall under the president deserve similar respect. Anyone who has served in government, from a buck private to a cabinet official, knows this feeling. And they also know that the public and private sectors have different boundaries. Outsourcing tests these boundaries. By doing so, it pushes government to justify delegations of public power in private hands.[68]

Public officials should not be in the practice of delegating and abrogating their responsibilities to provide major public services to private companies. Private officials are not bound by the same standards as their counterparts in the public sector. Public officials are supposed to be focused on the promotion of the greater public good as the penultimate objective; private officials do not operate in the same manner.

It turns out that the values embodied in the privatization movement have been in existence for some time. According to Louis Gawthrop, "For well over the past 100 years, public administrators have been admonished to adopt the techniques, to reflect the attitudes, and to embrace the philosophy of their private-sector counterparts. The drive for civil service reform that began in the wake of the Civil War was simply the running salvo of a much more extensive and intensive campaign designed to shape the managerial operations of government in the image of the private sector."[69] An important article by a famous American in history may be part of the reason why this philosophy is still so pervasive today.

In 1887, political science professor Woodrow Wilson published a journal article titled "The Study of Administration."[70] Wilson provided the following definition of public administration: "Administration is the most obvious part of government; it is government in action; it is the executive, the operative, the most visible side of government, and is of course as old as government itself. It is government in action, and one might very naturally expect to find that government in action had arrested the attention and provoked the scrutiny of writers of politics very early in the history of systematic thought."[71] His argument about administration was clearly reflective of his time, and his basic paradigm has had a substantial impact on public administration ever since.[72]

In describing the subdiscipline of public administration in the late nineteenth century, Wilson maintained that

> the field of public administration is a field of business. It is removed from the hurry and strife of politics; it at most points stands apart even from the debatable ground of constitutional study. It is a part of political life only as the methods of the counting-house are a part of the life of society; only as machinery is part of the manufactured product. But it is, at the same time, raised very far above the dull level of mere technical detail by the fact that through its greater principles it is directly connected with the lasting maxims of political wisdom, the permanent truths of political progress.[73]

Gawthrop astutely notes that the acceptance of the private sector emphasis on efficiency in the public arena traces back to the time period following the Civil War. This special attention on efficiency in public administration may actually be gaining in influence at the present time; it is certainly not declining by any reasonable perspective:

> Indeed, if the present mood in the United States is any gauge, there appears to be a strong current running in favor of an increased reliance on the *private* sector for the implementation of public policy. This attitude seems to reflect an enticing conviction that the private sector, governed as it is by clearly focused managerial strategies dictated by an entrepreneurial spirit is more reliable than a commitment by the public sector's career bureaucracy to the spirit of democracy. The "bottom-line" argument inherent in this assumption is that the pragmatic, "no-nonsense" rubrics of private-sector management are certain to yield greater efficiency, effectiveness, and accountability than are obtained from the kaleidoscopic attitudes and values reflected in the public-sector bureaucracy.[74]

One of the most recent substantive efforts to reform public administration in America at the federal level occurred in the early years of the Clinton administration. This effort culminated in the publication of the *Report of the National Performance Review,* which was an effort directed by Vice President Al Gore.[75]

The primary focus of the report, commonly called the Gore Report, is the promotion of the idea that public managers should behave like private sector entrepreneurs. The value of efficiency supersedes all others, especially the promotion of equity and fairness. As noted by Gawthrop, the word "customer" appears in the Gore Report 214 times as compared to the utilization of the term "citizen," which only appears 18 times.[76] Gawthrop aptly concluded, "The ethos of public service, so essential for the spirit of democracy to flourish, can be realized only if directed by a moral imperative bound to the common good."[77] The moral imperative at issue in education policy is the defense and the promotion of Mann's common school ideal.

Jane Grant has noted that privatization efforts on the part of conservatives have become even more extreme in recent years. A classic example of this behavior occurred during the presidency of George W. Bush with regard to the war in Iraq:

> The other strand of contemporary conservatism that departs from both the civic and procedural republican ethos is the radical insistence on

the privatization of public services, even those that have traditionally been associated with government. A civic republic is concerned with what is needed to make a good society; that position is compatible with the contemporary expansion of rights, particularly social rights that inform our obligations to others in our own society. At the same time, a procedural republic, seeking to support both freedom and equality, is appropriately focused on policies that insure that citizens have sufficient security to be able to fully realize those goals. The one arena where even conservatives have agreed that the role of the federal government is crucial, that of defending the nation, has now been the focus of increased privatization initiatives, under the administration of George W. Bush. By July 2007, there were more privately contracted personnel serving in the Iraq war than members of the nation's Armed Services.[78]

I concur with this scholar in her categorization of this type of behavior by President Bush as "radical." It is radical because privatization undermines democracy, and anything, including the utilization of the ideology of laissez-faire capitalism in order to advance one's political agenda, that threatens the sovereignty of the country must yield to the greater common good. While there are procedures to hold public officials, including military personnel, accountable, the same fundamental principle does not exist in the private sector.

Verkuil concluded his study of outsourcing by issuing a very meaningful and needed plea to contemporary citizens:

> The People's Constitution has spoken. As faithful agents, the branches must reply. The use of contractors to displace functions normally performed by government officials who exercise significant authority can be a danger to the Republic; it should be curtailed in the future. Given its embedded nature and the fuzzy lines inherent and competitive functions, this cannot be done overnight. But what we require now, as Ted Sorensen asked for at a different but no less perilous time, are watchmen in the night: People who can help secure and preserve our values in an era of unprecedented delegations of power to the private sector.[79]

The delivery of public services should not be delegated to entrepreneurs in the private sector. Government officials have a responsibility to the citizens in this republic to provide quality services at a reasonable cost. This is what public servants are supposed to do, as their primary job is to promote the greater public good in a constitutional republic. The early founders of the American republic understood this fundamental reality.[80] The framers of the federal Constitution demonstrated their astute understanding of the role of a public servant in a democracy in the preamble of the document that they created: "We the people of the United States, in order to form a more perfect union, establish justice, insure domestic tranquility, provide for the common defense, promote the general welfare, and secure the blessings of liberty to ourselves and our posterity, do ordain and establish the Constitution of the United States of America."

The schoolchildren of America are dependent on adults to provide them with a quality educational experience during their K–12 years. Mann and the advocates of common schools believed that public sector employees were in the best and proper position to deliver public education to America's children. Not only would the children receive an education that would help them develop as individuals and as contributing citizens in a republican form of government, they would learn to embrace a common culture and basically learn how to peacefully coexist as fellow citizens in a democracy. The privatization paradigm runs counter to this vision of education. All adults in the country need to take responsibility for the education of children in the United States. It is a civic duty that will, in fact, make for a more perfect union in which school officials are held accountable for their actions. The reform of education starts by the utilization of a public sector model where accountability is transparent and where public officials are not permitted to delegate their duties to private sector employees. In spite of a perception by some that privatization is advisable and will enhance education reform efforts, it should be rejected as a policy option precisely because it is undemocratic by definition.

8

Blueprint for Progressive Reform

Reform is necessary in any human endeavor. We are fallible by definition, so there is no question that K–12 public education in America is in need of reform. As core groups responsible for the delivery of public education, teachers and administrators have a central mission to provide a quality education for all students. Improvements in the status quo can and should be expected. That process is never ending. However, I believe that reforming public education should come in the context of the preservation of Horace Mann's common school ideal. I am reminded of the words of Senator Ted Kennedy at the 1980 Democratic National Convention, when he conceded the Democratic nomination for president to the incumbent president, Jimmy Carter. At a time when Senator Kennedy undoubtedly realized that he would never be president like his brother John (or possibly even Robert as well, though we will never know if he could have prevailed in the 1968 presidential

The Horace Mann statue at Antioch College. It was erected in 1936 on the site of the Mann farm and today is part of the Glen Helen Nature Preserve. (Image courtesy of Antiochiana, Antioch College.)

election due to his assassination), he quoted some passages in *Ulysses*, a poem by Alfred Lord Tennyson:[1]

> I am a part of all that I have met;
> Though much is taken, much abides; and though
> We are not now that strength which in the old days
> Moved earth and heaven; that which we are, we are,
> One equal-temper of heroic hearts,
> Made weak by time and fate, but strong in will
> To strive, to seek, to find, and not to yield.[2]

Senator Kennedy concluded his speech by saying that his campaign for the presidency was over. However, the causes that he espoused during his campaign did not end with his unsuccessful bid for the presidency. In perhaps his most eloquent speech in a long political career, he declared that "for all those whose cares have been our concern, the work goes on, the cause endures, the hope still lives, and the dream shall never die."[3] The cause and the hope of common schools for all children are still worth pursuing after many years. It is a cause that has not runs its course, notwithstanding political opposition from the political right.

There are no simple solutions to the cause of reforming K–12 public education in America. While some contend that school choice, standardized testing, and the weakening of state teacher unions will result in more effective schools, a more candid assessment of the status quo suggests that improving public education in America will take a longitudinal commitment on the part of citizens and will require fundamental and systemic changes in society. Such a prognosis is typically not what most people wish to hear. The following will serve as a blueprint for substantive education reform in the United States, understanding that gimmickry and false promises have no place in any discussion involving the lives and future of children in America. The reform ideas are not rank ordered in terms of importance, although the first premise is clearly the most important by definition.

REFORM PREMISE A: MAINTAIN HORACE MANN'S COMMON SCHOOL IDEAL

It is of crucial importance in the United States to maintain education as a public good. Horace Mann's common school ideal needs to be preserved so that all children can be provided a quality education first and foremost but that other constitutional and moral imperatives can be addressed simultaneously as well. We must never return to the days where public sector officials intentionally segregate schools by policy and by action. Segregation and Jim Crow laws must never be revisited in the land of equal opportunity for all. But the American experiment has other fundamentally important features, one of which is to bring citizens from diverse backgrounds together and teach them the art of citizenship and that they are members of a civil society where conflict and differences of opinion are expected to be addressed in a peaceful and nonviolent manner.

In closing his biography on Mann, Jonathan Messerli offered the following synopsis of the great educator's life as he died at Antioch College:

> On August 4, a student climbed up into the room beneath the bell tower at the college and slowly and rhythmically pulled on the rope. The mourners fell into step as the tolling of the bell set a solemn cadence for the procession of students and friends who accompanied Mann's body from the manse to a temporary burial place on the campus. At the gravesite, Reverend Eli Fay struggled again for the words of a brief eulogy and prayer, and students sang a hymn, and the coffin was lowered into the ground. High above, the dark clouds which had formed in the west that morning were now finally bringing relief to the dry earth, the large raindrops all the more noticeable as they fell on top of the coffin resting on the bottom of the pit. Others would carry on at Antioch. It was now time for Horace Mann to storm heaven. In Boston, Samuel Gridley Howe was too grief-stricken to write to Mary immediately, but he soon called together Josiah Quincy, Ezra Gannett, Gideon Thayer, Samuel Downer, and a few others. Having failed once to make good on his threat to pull down the statue of Daniel Webster in front of the State House, Howe, and his friends now vowed that there would be a statue of Mann there of equal prominence. In Europe, [Charles] Sumner was completing a convalescent tour of the continent in preparation for his return home to join others in a massive effort to destroy the evil of slavery. And the following month, across the country countless number of children, more than ever before, would be hurrying on to their classrooms, fulfilling in part Mann's vision of an entire nation going to school.[4]

Mann thought that eight years of formal schooling would be sufficient for full participation in society during his lifetime.[5] Today, of course, many people argue that at least a bachelor's degree is needed to achieve this objective. But Mann's dream is still a work in progress in America today. A careful and thoughtful reformulation of the Mann vision would be prudent in the contemporary world. An abdication of the Mann vision would have a deleterious impact on general society.

In an anthology in defense of public education in America, Nel Noddings argues that individuals belonging to the religious right have sought to advance their own values and priorities by denigrating public education:

> A general case against the public schools—their bureaucratic sluggishness, monopolistic power, and lack of responsiveness—has been made by a great variety of critics. The more specialized case brought by the religious right against the public schools is usually expressed in two phases. In the first, schools are criticized from a religious perspective; in the second, a recommendation is made for public funding of religious schools. It may be that the criticisms raised in phase one could be answered in a way that would make the recommendation of phase two unnecessary. That should be the first line of response. If no reasonable and caring reconciliation can be reached, defenders of public schooling should still resist the separation called for in phase two.[6]

Given the fundamental premise that education is a public good by definition, the author provides sage counsel. Furthermore, citizens should be aware of the terminology utilized by opponents of public education:

> [Richard A.] Baer and other critics of public schools ("government" schools) want "to get the state out of the business of operating schools." As part of their campaign, they refer to public schools as *government* schools. This change in language is deeply disturbing, first, because the designation "public" applied to schools has long been a term of some approbation in contrast to anything associated with government and government control. Even more disturbing, however, is the implication that the schools no longer serve a recognizable public and that, therefore, citizens need no longer concern themselves with education as a public good. Even if it is true that the schools are in a period of unparalleled struggle to serve many publics, the continued search for a solid public must remain a high priority.[7]

Opponents of public education perceive themselves to be waging a moral crusade against big, onerous, and oppressive government. In order to build their own empire, opponents to the Mann vision feel compelled to attack the notion that public sector entities can create programs and policies that truly serve the greater public good. This trend in contemporary politics is dangerous in the extreme precisely because it attempts to individualize a public good. Citizens, over time, may reject the Mann premise that we are all responsible for the education of all children because all of us in society, even adults with no children, benefit from an educated citizenry. Opponents to public education maintain that competition will enhance the public schools because they are deficient by definition. Yet it is important to consider some fundamental realities in American politics. To those with a free market philosophy, vouchers are viewed as a way to privatize public education. In so doing, it would open up more than $600 billion and remove education from the realm of democratic control. To libertarians, vouchers would dismantle the biggest and most important public institution in America and would therefore, in their minds, promote the cause of individual freedom.[8] But imagine the societal implications of a mass privatization of education. Educational quality standards, issues of accessibility, separation of church and state legal mandates, student safety, environmental safeguards, and a plethora of other issues would be left to private companies.[9] America would be in danger of becoming a theocracy among many other possibilities.

REFORM PREMISE B: MAINTAIN AND EXPAND CIVIC EDUCATION IN THE PUBLIC SCHOOLS

In this present era of expanding libertarianism, many have chosen to ignore a crucial function of public schools. Mann believed the schools should provide a diverse array of children with knowledge necessary to be contributing citizens in a republican form of government. The eminent pioneering psychologist and educator and the first president of Clark University, G. Stanley Hall, understood this premise and provided an eloquent statement over a century ago on the matter:

> The school is the training ship for the ship of state and is freighted, like it, with all our hopes and fears, and on the fate of one we hang no less breathlessly than on the other. It is chartered by the people and plies between the river of childhood and the open sea of adult life. It should not be idly moored in shallow waters in some sheltered nook, but hoist anchor, spread sail, and boldly venture out where the tide and current buffet each other. It should teach not mere ship discipline, but the art and craft of sailing, and this it cannot do without braving at least some of the slighter dangers of navigation in open seas. If the timorous

counsels of safeness constitute our only wisdom, then every topic on which there are vital differences of opinion must be tabooed, and the school dies. To change the trope once more, the life of the country is the very placenta of the school, and if the umbilicus that joins it to the embryo citizen is cut, abortion follows. Thus, civics in the above large sense must be the new religion of the secular schools. The old religion gave but the motive that created and for centuries dominated education through all its grades. We need not say, and do not believe, that this old motivation has spent its force, but to-day it has little or no influence upon public education and its absence has left the system more or less motiveless and soulless. In the new civics, however, we have the best substitute, a philanthropic social religion. In honoring and serving men as the race long did God, and in living for and in the present as we long did for a future life, we seem to be at the dawn of a new dispensation, imminent rather than transcendent, and perhaps already hardly less full of premise and potency than was the old.[10]

Civic education is of vital importance to American society as suggested by Hall. In this No Child Left Behind era in which we live, I challenge the skilled empirical researcher to devise a reliable indicator that measures the extent to which civic education may impact American society. While it would be very nice to know this information, it would obviously be extremely difficult and cumbersome to create a singular measure for a complicated phenomenon. I have made the argument earlier in this book that more emphasis should be placed on this aspect of public education, particularly at the senior high school level. The last thing we need is to ignore this component of public education. While it may be convenient for some with an alternative agenda, to those of us who embrace the Mann common school ideal and appreciate and recognize the important role that public schoolteachers provide in terms of educating children to be citizens in a democratic republic, this aspect of the common school must remain intact for future generations of Americans. Goals are important, for if we want a society of self-interested, inwardlooking individuals, then why not eliminate the civic education role of public education? If we embrace the vision articulated by Mann in the nineteenth century, then perhaps it would be wise to focus on espousing communitarian goals so that the needs of the citizenry as a whole are addressed instead of trying to embrace the politics of radical individualism and the libertarian philosophy.

REFORM PREMISE C: REPEAL NCLB IN ITS ENTIRETY AND DEEMPHASIZE HIGH-STAKES STANDARDIZED TESTING

As of this writing, the fate of NCLB is unknown. It is assumed by many analysts that at some point following the 2012 elections, Congress and the president will have to come to some consensus about NCLB. But the future of this legislation is a political question that will be brokered by leaders in the two traditional branches of government. President Barack Obama pledged to pursue the repeal of NCLB in his 2008 presidential campaign; as of late 2012, 33 states and the District of Columbia have been granted waivers by the U.S. Department of Education from some of the requirements of NCLB.[11] Clearly, President Obama is attempting to permit more flexibility to state educators when it pertains to enhancing the academic achievement of their students. If state officials are collectively successful at enhancing the educational experience of their students, then NCLB may actually represent a bipartisan opportunity to end an unpopular law and, it is hoped, renew a substantive debate about how public education can be reformed without being unnecessarily shortsighted and punitive in nature.

The undue emphasis on high-stakes testing in the NCLB law should be changed as well. Holding educators accountable as professionals is plausible and essential to the cause of education reform. Mann's common school vision embraced the notion that trained professionals would bear the responsibility of imparting knowledge to America's children. The NCLB methodology is not the way to enhance public education, however. Our institutions of government must be preserved and remain intact for future generations. While Americans do not always approve of the job performance of the members of Congress, there has not been a movement to amend the Constitution and abolish Congress. We should expect the same to be true with regard to public education. Providing a more effective education for K–12 children should always be a top policy objective; privatizing the schools and losing democratic accountability, however, is not a reasonable option in pursuit of this goal. It is incumbent on researchers and practitioners to create multiple measures of academic performance and attempt to hold educators accountable to them. Citizens must always understand, however, that not everything worthwhile in education policy is necessarily measurable in a quantitative sense.

It is also important to reflect on the history of standardized testing to remind ourselves of the reality that politics and education are most often deeply intertwined. Ironically, Mann was one of the leading advocates for achievement testing in the nineteenth century.[12] However, many historians believe that his advocacy was a reflection of the context of his time. First, under Secretary Mann's leadership, the commonwealth of Massachusetts moved from subjective oral examinations given by teachers to more standardized and objective written instruments.[13] This was done primarily to make test taking more efficient in that it made it easier to assess a growing student population. Besides desiring children in a one-room rural schoolhouse to have the same quality education as their counterparts in large cities, he also had a political motivation as well: "But Mann had other reasons for introducing standardized testing. He had been engaged in an ideological battle with the Boston headmasters, who perceived him as a 'radical.' This disagreement reflected a wider schism in the Nation between reformers like Mann who believed in stimulating student interest in learning through greater emphasis on the 'real world,' and hard-liners who believed in discipline, rote recitation, and adherence to texts."[14] To Mann, testing was a way to ensure quality education for all children. He did not support standardized testing because he wanted to thwart his own common school vision and replace secular schools with religious schools.

Gail Sunderman offers three tangible common sense reform ideas with regard to NCLB:

> First, more needs to be done to develop an accountability system that is fair, yields information that informs and advances student learning goals, and contributes to improving instruction. There are some concrete steps that can make NCLB accountability better by altering some of its provisions. The unrealistic goal of 100 percent proficiency should be replaced with a goal that is still ambitious, but also realistic and obtainable. Adopting multiple measures of student progress that reflect improvement across a range of performance indicators will help to reduce incentives to ignore some groups of students or push them out in order to boost test scores. These should include such factors as attendance, course passage, and graduation and grade retention rates. . . . Second, there needs to be greater investment in capacity building in the nation's lowest-performing schools and districts. The high expectations written into NCLB must be paired with adequate support and investment in school reform if low-performing schools and districts

are to improve. This includes requiring schools to use resources more productively, but also federal investment in programmatic and systemic reforms and recognition that schools need help. . . . Finally, we need to re-examine the premises underlying this reform strategy. Research presented in this book suggests that the lofty goals of NCLB—to improve student achievement and narrow the achievement gap—are not being accomplished, and careful analysis concludes that schools will not reach the 100 percent proficiency goals by 2014. For educational systems to move in directions that will ensure high levels of learning for all students, we need to engage in a serious reassessment of whether an external, test-driven accountability policy will ultimately lead us in that direction.[15]

Part of the reason that state officials have sought and secured waivers from some of the NCLB requirements is precisely because Sunderman was correct in her assertion when she made it. Most states are not even close to the 100 percent proficiency mandate in mathematics and reading. Good intentions are often endemic in the legislative process; however, when good intentions are accompanied by punitive measures that actually hinder the education experience of children, a change in course is required.

REFORM PREMISE D: REDUCE POVERTY IN AMERICA

Poverty figures in this country of vast wealth are absolutely shameful (refer back to chapter 4). Gross domestic product (GDP) is often used as a measure of a nation state's overall wealth. It is the monetary value of all goods and services produced in a nation in a given year. It includes all public and private consumption, government outlays, investments, and exports minus imports. According to the World Bank, 15 nations had a GDP in excess of $1 trillion in 2011. The United States was ranked first with a GDP of $15.1 trillion, followed by China ($7.3 trillion), Japan ($5.9 trillion), Germany ($3.6 trillion), France ($2.8 trillion), Brazil ($2.5 trillion), the United Kingdom ($2.4 trillion), Italy ($2.2 trillion), the Russian Federation ($1.9 trillion), India ($1.8 trillion), Canada ($1.7 trillion), Spain ($1.5 trillion), Australia ($1.4 trillion), Mexico ($1.2 trillion), and the Republic of Korea ($1.1 trillion).[16] The United States is clearly the dominant economic nation-state in the global arena.

According to the researchers at the United Nations Children's Fund (UNICEF), the United States has one of the highest rates of children who are living in relative poverty in the world's richest countries.[17]

In fact, the United States ranked 34th among the 35 most affluent nations in terms of children living in relative poverty.[18] Iceland had the lowest percentage of children living in relative poverty (4.7 percent) in this comparison of affluent countries in the world. Romania had the highest percentage (25.5 percent). According to UNICEF researchers, 23.1 percent of America's children are currently living in relative poverty.[19] When almost one-fourth of all children in the richest nation on earth are living in poverty, we literally have millions of children who are ill equipped to start a new day of school with the same energy, attention span, resources, and support system in place than that of their peers. Somehow, in a collective manner, policymakers and citizens alike have to find ways to combat the ravages of poverty in American society. The problem has endured too long. While the existence of poverty has plagued human populations since modern humans evolved on this planet, researchers have been particularly aware of the effect of poverty on school children, especially on children of color, at least since the publication of the Moynihan Report in 1965.[20]

Daniel Patrick Moynihan was a sociologist who wrote a report about African Americans living in poverty when he was the assistant secretary of labor in the Johnson administration. He would later serve as a U.S. senator (D–NY) from 1977 to 2001. In 1965, Moynihan maintained that without access to employment and the economic means to support their families, African American men would become alienated from their social roles as husbands and fathers. He warned that if this trend continued, rates of divorce, out-of-wedlock births, and abandonment would escalate in the African American community.[21] This report was influential in the construction of President Johnson's War on Poverty social programs in the 1960s. A major criticism of the report came from civil rights advocates and liberals who believed that the report stereotyped African American people and culture and was therefore racist by definition.

Almost 50 years after the report was issued, it is clear that scholars may view Moynihan's findings differently than some analysts did in the 1960s and 1970s in particular. In 2009, an entire issue of the *Annals of the American Academy of Political and Social Science* was dedicated to revisiting the Moynihan Report.[22] Douglas Massey and Robert Sampson edited the special issue, and some contend that Moynihan's ideas and beliefs about poverty were utilized in crafting the Personal Responsibility and Work Opportunity Reconciliation Act of 1996.[23]

Dennis Orthner believes that the key to reducing poverty in America is through education in the public schools:

> Our public education system is the foundation upon which our nation's opportunity structure is built. Just as in building a house, the bigger and stronger the foundation, the more can be built on top of it. A house with a larger and stronger foundation provides a base for more rooms, people, and activities. Likewise, a person with a stronger educational foundation has more room for other educational and career options, and the potential skill base upon which to consider evolving opportunities in the future. If the educational foundation is small and weak, however, then it is very difficult to build on top of it a robust and diverse opportunity structure. America's universities and community colleges try to help young adults compensate for weak educational foundations, but it is very difficult for most students to compensate for early school failures or having a weak knowledge base.[24]

Indeed, a substantive and effective K–12 education system is absolutely essential in order to reduce the ill effects of poverty in the United States. He envisions schools with a shared learning culture in which parents, teachers, and administrators regularly examine different options for improving all aspects of the school that contributes to the student learning process. The creation of a true learning culture, to him, necessitates that students and adults alike benefit from engaging in the learning process.[25] Clearly, the ethos of NCLB does not create a learning environment. Instead, a culture of teaching to the test pervades, and this situation will not be resolved in a positive manner until excellent public schools emerge all across the country, not only in affluent suburbs but in urban and rural America as well.

A holistic framework of analysis must be utilized to combat poverty. The noted author David Shipley has expressed his vision for the reduction of poverty in this country:

> If schools, probation departments, job-training centers, medical clinics, and other institutions were broadened into gateways through which needy families could pass into multiple services for their multiple problems, a great deal of good could be done. Here and there, this happens in fragmented forms, mostly in private, nonprofit agencies. But the approach needs to be widespread. Then, teachers could do more than gripe among themselves about kids not learning, trainers could do more than instruct in hard skills, and doctors could do more then dispense medication vainly against the onslaught of disease-producing poverty. Would this cost money? Yes, but some of the expense would ultimately

be saved. The more we invest in children, the less we will have to invest later in prisons. The more we invest in health insurance and preventive care, the more productive our workforce will be. The lower the dropout rate from high school, the lower the associated costs in later life, and these savings can be substantial.[26]

Citizens could save some money by embracing the "gateway" approach to poverty. It is also important to note that addressing poverty, in fact, is not all about efficiency and money. Many Americans have a great deal of compassion toward their fellow citizens and also have a strong sense of civic virtue and simply believe that an aggressive poverty policy is just the right thing to do, especially on behalf of children currently living in poverty.

Members of Congress passed the Patient Protection and Affordable Care Act in 2010, and President Obama signed it into law.[27] I would include universal health coverage (UHC) as an additional reform premise but am operating on the assumption that with implementation of the law in 2014, the United States will join the other countries of the world in having UHC. By the way, UHC has been achieved in a given country if more than 90 percent of the population has health insurance.[28] Once the law is implemented, it is projected that about 96 percent of the American population will have health insurance. In the summer of 2012, a divided Supreme Court upheld the constitutionality of the health care law.[29]

REFORM PREMISE E: CITIZENS MUST BECOME MORE ENGAGED IN THE ELECTORAL PROCESS

As noted in chapter 6 and in a recent book on electoral reform, there is much that Americans can do to enhance democratic accountability in the electoral and political processes, including fully exercising their right to vote.[30] Many American adults are disengaged and do not participate in democratic elections. Before focusing on citizens as individuals, it is important to note that there are many reforms that state legislators across the country could enact to promote more citizen participation in politics.[31] First, the state legislators in 49 states and the District of Columbia could replicate the model used in North Dakota, where all citizens become eligible to vote when they reach their eighteenth birthday. The state law requires state officials, not the individual citizens, to make sure that legal adults are registered to vote. In other words, the burden of proof for voter registration in North Dakota is on the state government, not on the individual citizen.[32] The potential electorate in America would expand dramatically if all state residents were eligible to vote when they became 18 years of age. Another option to ensure that more citizens are at least eligible to vote is if laws were passed in all state legislatures that established Election Day registration. Although this approach to electoral reform would still be reliant on citizens voluntarily registering to vote, it would at the very least allow citizens to vote on Election Day if they so desired.[33]

As many advocates of democracy contend, voting is a preeminent right in a democracy. Since the equal protection clause of the Fourteenth Amendment stipulates that all Americans are intrinsically the same, state election laws should facilitate as much participation as possible. Since Election Day in November is fairly institutionalized at this juncture in U.S. history, it should remain intact. However, early voting, which can manifest itself in many ways, should be afforded to all citizens on an equal basis. Our political leaders should do as much as possible to ensure that as many American adults vote in elections as possible, regardless of one's economic, political, or social condition.[34]

There continues to be considerable disparity between and among the states when it comes to voting. Should convicted felons be permitted to vote? In Virginia and Kentucky, citizens are permanently disenfranchised if convicted of a felony.[35] In Maine and Vermont, convicted felons can vote while they are serving their prison terms.[36] The other 46 states and the District of Columbia are somewhere between these two extreme ends of the continuum. A more uniform public policy would be advantageous, as there are currently over 5 million Americans who cannot vote due to a criminal conviction, and 13 percent of African American men have lost the right to vote, a rate that is seven times the national average.[37]

State legislators and governors are also responsible for stringent voter identification laws, even though fraud is commonly not cited as a reason to justify such legislation. Such laws, particularly in the absence of documented fraudulent voting, are designed to thwart certain Americans from voting: recent immigrants, the indigent, the elderly, and racial minorities in general. No legislator is going to boldly declare that he or she is seeking to disenfranchise certain people from voting because people who may fit the previously mentioned type of demographics probably would not vote for them. But that is the impact, and in spite of what the Supreme Court justices have determined with regard to photo identification requirements, which put the onus back on the individual, there is a disparate impact, and public policy is not supposed to discriminate against certain classes of people, especially when the issue involves voting in the world's oldest democracy.[38]

Lawmakers at the federal level need to pass legislation establishing publicly financed campaigns for federal offices, including the presidency, the U.S. Senate, and the U.S. House of Representatives. Federal officials have done little to regulate the influence of powerful interest groups in elections, especially when compared to many European democracies. Reformers have advocated enacting this change for generations, and our elected officials in Congress have not responded. Legislation is needed in order to balance individual and collective interests in society. Some claim that the First Amendment freedom of speech and expression permits them to spend as much as they please to advocate for specific candidates and political causes. However, if the interests of the rich and powerful are overrepresented in the public arena to the detriment of the less affluent and politically connected, then members of Congress have a responsibility to ensure that the rich and powerful do not effectively drown out other ideas through the use of vast sums of money, particularly on television advertising. Publicly financed campaigns might also have the effect of making House and Senate races more competitive so that the incumbent does not almost always prevail over the challenger.[39]

Systemic change is necessary in order to reform public education as well as other policy issues. This is why I have offered a number of ideas, not original to be sure, in order to improve the status quo in terms of governance. But citizens are an essential part of the equation as well. Electing candidates who support public education and oppose efforts to undermine the traditional public schools will preserve Mann's vision for future generations. One way to do this is for citizens to mobilize. We have federal elections every two years in the United States. All 435 seats in the House of Representatives are contested every two years and one-third of Senate seats. The presidency is contested every four years. Almost half the electorate does not bother to vote in a presidential election, the most important election in the United States. In a literal sense, there are tens of millions of Americans who have opted not to participate. Just think of the potential clout of a group of citizens this large in scope. In midterm elections, over 60 percent of the electorate does not participate. For those Americans who are concerned with the direction of the nation as a whole, a repudiation of the status quo is necessary to promote the cause of reform. Those who do not vote are essentially allowing those who do exercise the franchise and prevail in winner-take-all elections to control public policymaking. I cannot help but think that more citizen input would promote more diversity in public policymaking and would largely prevent decision makers from pursuing drastic and unreasonable policies that citizens do not endorse. It seems to me that no one can sustain the premise that a healthy, robust, and vibrant democracy exists when almost half the adults in society do not even bother to vote in the most important election in the republic.

There are a number of considerations for those citizens who may lack confidence in their political knowledge base. Political parties are still an important cue in American politics. Generally, mainstream Democrats favor more regulation of the domestic economy in order to promote social equality and fairness, which are top objectives for contemporary Democrats. Today's Republican adherents favor less regulation of the domestic economy in order to promote more individual freedom and devolution of centralized authority away from Washington, D.C., and to the states. When it comes to privacy issues, however, both parties are a contradiction in terms. Democrats, particularly liberals, believe that government should not regulate privacy matters, whereas Republicans, especially conservatives, tend to favor government restrictions on privacy rights, including the abortion and gay marriage debates.

Citizens have to collectively understand and embrace the reality that elected officials affect their lives in a profound manner. Candidates and campaign officials exploit our own indifference—and ignorance—about politics and public affairs in order to manipulate how we vote if we fall in either the registered or the likely-voter category. Very little attention is paid to the interests of the citizen who is not registered to vote and to the nonvoter in general. There is definitely an opportunity cost associated with keeping up with current events. Social class still matters to be certain, as more affluent citizens have more abundant resources to assist them in maintaining their base of political knowledge. Not all adults have personal computers and Internet access in their home environment. However, a more constant and earnest emphasis on politics would behoove Americans considerably. In short, our ignorance about politics makes it difficult to hold elected officials accountable. We must make it a point to follow politics more closely and do more homework as citizens of a republican form of government. It is our job, and we can perform it more effectively.

I have one final point to make with regard to voting. I have focused on the nonvoter to a considerable extent. Those who regularly engage in voting need to be proactive when it comes to educating themselves about the great issues of the day as well. We should always know the causes and policies we are promoting when we vote for specific candidates. The fact that we may like specific candidates and that they seem personable is fine, but it is much more important to know their substantive views on the issues. It is really important for many of us to deemphasize style to a certain extent and start accentuating substance to a greater degree. There is far too much focus on intangible matters, such as charisma and oratory skills, and not enough on candidates' views on the issues, their philosophy of government, and their overall worldview. In short, citizens need to understand the implications of electing certain candidates to public office. This is part of the essence of democratic governance.

REFORM PREMISE F: EMBRACE THE COMMUNITARIAN PHILOSOPHY

Political scientist William Hudson contends that American politics must be substantially reformed in order to make our political system more democratic and responsive to the will of the people.[40] Too many Americans, in his estimation, view politics and public affairs in an isolated, individualistic manner. He suggests that American officials and citizens need to embrace a communitarian philosophy in public policy analysis:

> Bringing about a better balance between community and the individual in the United States requires a more communitarian approach to politics. Such an approach challenges the libertarian view that individuals are completely autonomous authors of their own existence; instead, it regards people as products of the many communities—from their families and neighborhoods to the national community—in which they live. Unlike the libertarians, who recognize only freedom from community-imposed constraints, communitarians understand that human freedom and dignity require the support of a network of social institutions. A communitarian approach would seek to nurture and protect such

institutions, rather than letting them decay as libertarians have. Instead of a libertarian preoccupation with rights, communitarianism emphasizes the need to balance rights with responsibilities, if rights are to be preserved.[41]

Amitai Etzioni, considered by many analysts and academicians as the guru of the communitarian movement,[42] defines communitarianism as

> a social philosophy that maintains that society should articulate what is good—that such articulations are both needed and legitimate. Communitarianism is often contrasted with classical liberalism, a philosophical position that holds each individual should formulate the good on his or her own. Communitarians examine the ways shared conceptions of the good (values) are formed, transmitted, justified, and enforced. Hence their interest in communities (and moral dialogues within them), historically transmitted values and mores, and the societal units that transmit and enforce values such [as] the family, schools, and voluntary associations (social clubs, churches, and so forth), which are all parts of communities.[43]

To communitarians, American society should not be viewed as a nation of millions of isolated individuals but rather as a pluralist nation where citizens are interconnected through shared common values and social institutions.

Hudson believes that a communitarian sentiment pervaded American society during the Progressive Era. To him, it is possible to recapture a general ethos where citizens prioritized the greater public good above individual self-interest:

> Encouraging a more communitarian political culture requires building a communitarian movement, and in recent years a number of Americans have begun to do that. Communitarians, including the movement's leader, sociologist Amitai Etzioni, seek to renew communities and the sense of individual civic obligation in ways that enhance democracy. . . . Since the issuance of their platform in 1991, communitarians have received much attention and have begun to have an impact on both public policy and national politics. They were a force in the Clinton administration, advocating passage of community-support legislation such as the Family and Medical Leave Act and the Americorps national service program. Etzioni hopes that the communitarian movement will have a reforming impact—moderating excessive individualism and promoting community-regarding policies—equivalent to the widespread policy results of the Progressive movement.[44]

Mann was articulating communitarian values when he espoused public schools for all children in the nineteenth century. He was asking Americans to temper their individualistic impulses and to contribute financially to a cause that he believed would benefit the greater public good. To those who did not have school-aged children or who chose to enroll them in parochial schools, Mann contended that an educated populace, where all children had an equal opportunity to succeed and pursue their dreams, would lead to a more prosperous economy, a better community with less crime, and a society where children were taught shared values and would be educated about their duties and obligations as citizens in the American republic. The communitarian values expressed by Mann are still of paramount importance today.

REFORM PREMISE G: REVISIT FEDERAL BUDGETARY PRIORITIES

Historically, K–12 and higher education have been top budgetary priorities at the state level. This continues to be the case today. The financing of education at all levels typically consumes more than 50 percent of the general fund appropriations at the state level.[45] At the federal level, however, even though the U.S. Department of Education has an annual budget of almost $70 billion, this represents about 2 percent of all federal spending in a $3.8 trillion budget.[46] A much greater portion of the budget is allocated to entitlement programs, including Social Security, Medicare, and Medicaid. National defense accounts for almost 20 percent of the total budget. Interest on the national debt is a much higher expenditure than other policy issues, including education, energy, the environment, and scientific research.[47]

Not only does the United States have the largest economy in the world, but decision makers in Washington, D.C., spend vastly more on national defense than any other country on earth. Officials at the Stockholm International Peace Research Institute (SIPRI) have been compiling data on defense spending for a number of years.[48] In 2011, the United States allocated $711 billion for military spending. The rest of the nations in the top 15 in the world include the People's Republic of China ($143 billion), Russia ($71.9 billion), the United Kingdom ($62.7 billion), France ($62.5 billion), Japan ($59.3 billion), Saudi Arabia ($48.5 billion), India ($46.8 billion), Germany ($46.7 billion), Brazil ($35.4 billion), Italy ($34.5 billion), South Korea ($30.8 billion), Australia ($26.7 billion), Canada ($24.7 billion), and Turkey

($17.9 billion).[49] In other words, military spending for the 14 countries on this list combined equals the American financial commitment to defense in 2011. Decision makers in both major political parties at the federal level have accepted the premise that the United States will be the only superpower in the world in terms of the armed forces.

One of the most fundamental duties of the national government is to keep citizens safe. Regardless of politics and ideology, Americans want their government to promote national security. In a world of finite resources, however, there is a limit in terms of how much money can be allocated to national defense on an annual basis. Unfortunately, there is no guarantee that spending any amount of money will ensure the safety of all citizens from foreign and domestic terrorists. There is no magic number in this enterprise. But the security of a nation-state is truly a multifacted entity. A country with an inordinate amount of poverty and significant gaps on multiple measures between the rich and poor is not destined to be a secure country into the future. Officials must protect the citizens and keep them secure and at the same time implement policies that will promote economic prosperity today and well into the future.

The Mann vision of a prosperous economy was fundamentally based on a simple premise, namely, that he path to a prosperous economy is through an educated citizenry. Federal officials could be doing more to assist state and local officials when it comes to funding education at the K–12 level. During the recession of the past several years, many state officials have cut funding for education. The plausibility of such an action can be debated, even during difficult economic times. But all across the country, there are a number of financial challenges confronting public school officials, particularly in urban America. Schools are in need of repair. Some should be torn down and replaced, but there are insufficient funds to address the needs in question, especially during an economic downturn.

Federal budgeters (the 535 voting members of Congress and the president) are in a position to help state and local officials promote the cause of education reform in the United States. In his State of the Union Address in 1999, President Bill Clinton recommended two noteworthy policies: the hiring of 100,000 new teachers to reduce class sizes across the country, especially in grades K–3, and the building or modernizing of 5,000 public schools.[50] Members of Congress have not incorporated these ideas into legislation. While the numbers can be debated (100,000 new teachers and building or repairing 5,000 schools), the ideas are both substantive and intuitive and federal funds would be utilized to accomplish the objectives in question. The costs could come by way of subsidy, partial subsidy, low-interest loans, or perhaps even no-interest loans. If we are serious about enhancing education standards in the traditional public schools, more teachers are needed. Ideally, class sizes in all grades should be lowered simultaneously. If the costs become too burdensome, however, President Clinton had prioritized the lower grades for good reason. These early years in education are crucial for development, particularly when it comes to reading. I am not recommending a federal takeover of K–12 education. I believe that federal officials can play a facilitative role in public education in that they can help their colleagues at the state and local levels accomplish Mann's vision of public education. This kind of federal involvement in K–12 education would certainly be more substantive and helpful than such measures as NCLB.

I must make one additional point here. Culturally, we have done little to attract talented, bright, high-achieving young people to the teaching profession in recent years. Too many of the current perceived woes in society are blamed on public school teachers. Many public schoolteachers have been portrayed as self-interested, lacking in work ethic, uncaring, perpetual defenders of "tenure," mediocre in their capabilities, and puppets of teacher unions. We must always hold public sector employees accountable. This is the essence of democracy. But the politicization of public education, particularly from the far right in recent decades, has had a deleterious impact on education in general and on children in particular. This negativity needs to stop, and instead we need to collaborate in order to promote the cause of reforming public education.

REFORM PREMISE H: RETHINKING THE STATUS QUO WITH REGARD TO THE SCHOOL YEAR AND THE SCHOOL DAY

We do not have a federal law in the United States that stipulates the length of the academic calendar in the states. Historically and even today, this issue has been perceived by many as a states' rights matter. According to officials at the Center for Education Policy at the University of Southern Maine, there have been numerous proposals across the states to extend the school year.[51] One proposal was touted by the former Democratic governor of Ohio, Ted Strickland, in 2009. He sought to increase the school year from 180 to 200 days by increasing the school year by two days for a decade.[52] The average number of school days across the states in a given academic year today is 180, whereas the world's average is 200 days of instruction.[53]

Extending the school year in America has been touted by advocates since the publication of *A Nation at Risk* in the 1980s. In recent years, President Obama has reiterated his belief in increasing the school year across the country, though he has not specified an exact amount, undoubtedly due, in part, to the differential laws across the states.[54] But some school officials in public schools across the country are already extending their school year in order to increase learning time for their students.[55]

Yet the idea of increasing the school year has been debated at least since 1894, when the commissioner of education, William T. Harris, presented his annual report on the state of K–12 public education.[56] Harris declared that

> a liberal estimate would give 950 hours as the actual time devoted to school work in a year under the present conditions, while 1,320 hours would be a moderate statement of the annual school term as it was at the beginning of the school system. The boy of to-day therefore must attend school 11.1 years in order to receive as much instruction, quantitatively, as the boy of fifty years ago received in 8 years; and the plain arithmetical conclusion is that if the elementary and high-school course could be completed in the time now required for the elementary course alone. This may not be true to its full extent, but that it approaches the truth can not be denied. In the countries of Continental Europe the sessions and terms have not been subjected to the steady reduction that our schools have suffered; it is scarcely necessary to look further than this for the explanation for the greater amount of work accomplished in a given number of years in the German and French than in the American Schools.[57]

The very same type of criticism of the length of the school year in the United States was echoed in 1994 by the members of the National Education Commission on Time and Learning.[58] Thus, why not follow through with Harris's suggestion from the nineteenth century and extend the school year? I recommend that states increase their school year by 10 days, and this policy could be phased in over a five-year span of time. This would raise the overall average of the states to 190 school days in an academic year. Many assumptions are inherent in this recommendation. The extra days would be utilized for quality instruction and for no other purpose. When the plan is fully implemented, all schools and school systems could review the extent to which extending the school year made a difference in the quality of education of the children involved. As is commonly the case with policy implementation, adjustments can be made as needed.

Obviously, such a plan would be expensive. Also inherent in my plan is that teachers would be compensated for the additional work. Many generations in the annals of American history have reiterated the same thing—teachers do not receive an adequate wage when compared to many other professions in society. I believe that the fulfillment of this recommendation not only would enhance the quality of education and the academic achievement of children but also would have the extra benefit of raising teacher salaries in order to address the extension of the academic calendar. This is simply the right thing to do for those dedicated to an honorable profession. If policymakers are serious about improving public education, then investing additional resources, wisely and prudently, will be necessary. This approach to reforming public education is truly within the spirit of the common schools as articulated by Mann.

It is also important to note that the extension of the school year coincides with my earlier point about high-stakes testing under NCLB. Extending the school year should not place additional testing burdens on children. This policy is all about enhancing the quality of education, and undoubtedly the best judges as to how to achieve this noteworthy objective are the teachers themselves. Let them instruct, impart knowledge, and engage students without focusing on standardized testing during the additional days, and all parties are destined to flourish as a result.

On a pragmatic note, extending the school year by effectively two weeks would still leave summer vacation intact all across the country. Many students who go to school for 180 days currently have 10 weeks off during the summer. If the year were extended by 10 days, then students would still have eight weeks off during the summer. This would permit them to still participate in other activities, enjoy being a child while still having a lengthy summer vacation, and permit older students to work during the summer.

The length of the school day is frequently debated as well. According to a researcher at the Education Commission of the States, the average minimum number of instructional minutes in a high school day (grades 9–12) across the 50 states is 314 minutes (5.2 hours), 302 minutes (5.0 hours) for elementary students (grades 1–5), and 310 minutes (5.2 hours) for middle school students (grades 6–8).[59] If the paramount goal is to increase quality instruction for students, then extending the school year would not require the extension of the school day itself. It may be prudent, however, for education officials to revisit the issue of how the school day is allocated. For example, senior high school students in some states start their day around 7:30 a.m. and complete it around 2:30 p.m. Many high school students today have jobs after school and are continuing to experience growth spurts so that additional sleep is required. Perhaps it would be wise for high school students to start their days a little later, and it may make more sense to have elementary schoolchildren, who typically start later in the day, start earlier, as many young children rise from their slumber earlier than their teenage counterparts. Such schema entails multiple factors, including local factors, work routines, and transportation schedules. Revisiting this issue may result in additional positive change. Starting the school day later in general, particularly in the northern states, would help to limit the amount of school delays in the case of inclement weather so that children would be missing less time in school. Local officials must always use their best judgment, however, in the case of canceling school for the day due to severe weather conditions or other emergencies. The safety of the children is always paramount.

REFORM PREMISE I: MINIMIZE THE INFLUENCE OF BUSINESS IN PUBLIC EDUCATION

It has been the general perception, ever since the nineteenth century, that some sort of partnership between business entrepreneurs and educators is prudent. Members of the business community have every right to offer their feedback, expertise, and knowledge when it comes to educating children. Those involved in business are citizen stakeholders just like many other groups in society. However, the amount of influence that has been wielded by business advocates has been substantial when compared to many other vested interests.

Often, members of the business community are focused heavily on job skills. They seek a trained and skilled workforce. At times, this has entailed the advocacy of a significant amount of vocational training. But the nature of global economics is changing, as is technology. For the very sake of the children themselves, the most important aspect of education is to help children develop their own analytical and writing skills. Students need to be taught to think for themselves in a critical manner. We must not allow children to be exploited by some who would put their own economic self-interest ahead of what may be best for the child. Since education is essential to the future of all children and for society in general, the children's needs must be prioritized ahead of other groups which may be well intended but may not be focusing on the longitudinal needs of young people in an increasingly competitive, interconnected global economy.

REFORM PREMISE J: STUDENTS, PARENTS, AND CAREGIVERS ARE PART OF THE SOLUTION

Inherent in this analytical framework of reforming public education is an emphasis on systemic measures that can be taken in order to improve the quality of education in the United States. The final recommendation I offer is focused on the students, their parents, and their caregivers. Students must collectively take their education seriously and work as diligently as possible. Behavior at school must be exemplary. All children have a right to a quality education, but too many teachers have to contend with unnecessary behavioral problems inside and outside the classroom. This reality needs to fundamentally change now both for the sake of all children, most of whom follow the rules in a reasonable manner, and for society. Disruptive students who will not alter their behavior will have to be expelled in a manner consistent with due process and fairness.

Many parents and caregivers do an excellent job at making sure their children are destined to succeed in school by being involved with their day-to-day academic work and extracurricular activities. Although this is always a challenge in light of the other duties and responsibilities of the adult world, millions of parents and caregivers should do nothing more than continue their current efforts because they are impressive in nature. To those adults who may not fit this description, it is not too late to reverse course. Children who may be struggling in school, suffering from hunger and health issues, and otherwise experiencing neglect need to know that the adults in their lives will always make it a priority to address their needs to the maximum extent possible. Some parents and caregivers need more assistance, and this is why I recommended more attentiveness to the omnipresent challenge of poverty in the United States. Some adults are embroiled in their own internal issues and are overwhelmed with the vicissitudes of day-to-day life. To those who may fall in this category, seek assistance without delay, from private community groups as well as government programs that may be available. All parents and caregivers have a legacy, and that legacy is focused on our children. Our measure of relative success will always be the extent to which we did all that we could in order to enhance the well-being and education of our children.

A CONCLUDING COMMENT

The educator Joy Elmer Morgan, once an editor of the *Journal of the National Education Association*, offered the following analysis of Mann on the centennial of his becoming the first secretary of education in Massachusetts:

> In 1837 when Horace Mann came to the secretaryship of the Massachusetts newly-created Board of Education, a financial panic dominated the nation. Fear, greed, and confusion were everywhere. Unemployment, misery, and distress prevailed. Schools were poor, teachers unprepared and underpaid. The well-to-do were sending their sons and daughters to private schools. They felt little or no concern for the public schools which they thought only good enough for paupers. In such a time people needed especially to place a higher value upon themselves—to attach more importance to the homely virtues and to thinking as a way of life. In 1837 the time had come for an educational revival. Horace Mann—himself up from the soil—came forward to express the needs of the people in a language so clear that his writings are an important part of the national culture.[60]

Economic times have been difficult for many in this country for the past several years, not unlike in 1837 for Mann and his contemporaries. Yet the great education reformer found a way to put education at the forefront of the political agenda during his time on earth. It was not an easy task. But it was not an impossible task, either. This is our mission in the early twenty-first century. It is time for another educational revival and a renewed commitment to public education and to the vision so eloquently articulated by Mann. In a book focused on

Mann's life at Antioch College, Morgan offered this message to the future teachers of the United States:

> Into your keeping is given a sacred trust—the American School. The free common school is the house of the people; the temple of democracy; the bulwark of self-government. To establish this house Horace Mann lived and labored triumphantly, even as Washington labored to establish the Republic, and Lincoln to preserve it. It is fitting that the Future Teachers of America movement should have grown out of the Horace Mann Centennial for you are the keepers of his great purpose, his noble ideals, his unconquerable spirit. May you ever study his inspiring life and follow in his steps.[61]

Using history as a guide and the common school vision of Mann, public education can and must be saved for future generations. Adults today owe it to today's and tomorrow's children to preserve, protect, and improve their educational experience so that they can do the same when history calls on them to do so.

Notes

Chapter 1

1. C. Ford Worthington et al., eds., *Journals of the Continental Congress, 1774–1789*, vol. 26 (Washington, DC: Government Printing Office, 1928), 109–21.

2. Worthington et al., eds., *Journals of the Continental Congress, 1774–1789*, vol. 26, 273–79.

3. Worthington et al., eds., *Journals of the Continental Congress, 1774–1789*, vol. 28 (Washington, DC: Government Printing Office, 1933), 375–86.

4. Worthington et al., eds., *Journals of the Continental Congress, 1774–1789*, vol. 28, 375–78.

5. The Avalon Project: Documents in Law, History and Diplomacy, "Northwest Ordinance: July 13, 1787," http://avalon.law.yale.edu/18th _century/nworder.asp (accessed March 25, 2011); Worthington et al., eds., *Journals of Continental Congress, 1774–1789*, vol. 32 (Washington, DC: Government Printing Office, 1936), 334–43.

6. Max Farrand, ed., *The Records of the Federal Convention of 1787*, 3 vols. (New Haven, CT: Yale University Press, 1911).

7. The Avalon Project: Documents in Law, History and Diplomacy, "Northwest Ordinance: July 13, 1787."

8. The Avalon Project: Documents in Law, History and Diplomacy, "Northwest Ordinance: July 13, 1787."

9. L. H. Butterfield, *Letters of Benjamin Rush, Volume I: 1761–1792* (Princeton, NJ: Princeton University Press, 1951), 412–13.

10. Jodi Campbell, "Benjamin Rush and Women's Education: A Revolutionary's Disappointment, A Nation's Achievement," *John and Mary's Journal*

13 (2000), http://chronicles.dickinson.edu/johnandmary/JMJVolume13/campbell.hm (accessed March 9, 2011).

11. Andrew A. Lipscomb and Albert E. Bergh, eds., *The Writings of Thomas Jefferson*, vol. 12 (Washington, DC: Thomas Jefferson Memorial Association, 1903), xviii.

12. Lipscomb and Bergh, *The Writings of Thomas Jefferson*, vol. 14, 383–84.

13. Frederick Rudolph, ed., *Essays on Education in the Early Republic* (Cambridge, MA: Harvard University Press, 1965).

14. Rudolph, *Essays on Education in the Early Republic*, 3–8.

15. Rudolph, *Essays on Education in the Early Republic*, 6.

16. Rudolph, *Essays on Education in the Early Republic*, 43–77.

17. Rudolph, *Essays on Education in the Early Republic*, 43.

18. Rudolph, *Essays on Education in the Early Republic*, 79–145.

19. Rudolph, *Essays on Education in the Early Republic*, 135–36.

20. Rudolph, *Essays on Education in the Early Republic*, 147–65.

21. Rudolph, *Essays on Education in the Early Republic*, 164–65.

22. Rudolph, *Essays on Education in the Early Republic*, 167–223.

23. Rudolph, *Essays on Education in the Early Republic*, 221.

24. Rudolph, *Essays on Education in the Early Republic*, 225–70.

25. Rudolph, *Essays on Education in the Early Republic*, 225.

26. Rudolph, *Essays on Education in the Early Republic*, 228–29.

27. Rudolph, *Essays on Education in the Early Republic*, 271–372.

28. Rudolph, *Essays on Education in the Early Republic*, 274.

29. Rudolph, *Essays on Education in the Early Republic*, 294.

30. Oliver Wendell Holmes, "The Path of the Law," *Harvard Law Review* 10, no. 8 (1897): 477–78.

31. Holmes gave his address at the dedication of the Isaac Rich Hall at Boston University School of Law on January 8, 1897.

32. For example, see Brian L. Fife, *Reforming the Electoral Process in America: Toward More Democracy in the 21st Century* (Santa Barbara, CA: ABC-CLIO, 2010).

33. Holmes, "The Path of the Law," 469.

34. Joel Spring, *The American School: A Global Context from the Puritans to the Obama Era*, 8th ed. (New York: McGraw-Hill, 2011), 72–73.

35. *Dartmouth College v. Woodward*, 17 U.S. 518 (1819). The case was decided on February 2, 1819.

36. *McCulloch v. Maryland*, 17 U.S. 316 (1819). The case was decided on March 6, 1819.

37. *Dartmouth College v. Woodward* (1819).

38. Leon B. Richardson, *History of Dartmouth College*, vol. 1 (Hanover, NH: Dartmouth College Publications, 1932), 336; Frederick Rudolph, *The American College and University: A History* (New York: Vintage Books, 1962), 209.

39. Richardson, *History of Dartmouth* College, 335; Rudolph, *The American College and University: A History*, 209–10.

40. Rudolph, *The American College and University*, 210.

41. Richardson, *History of Dartmouth College*, 89.

42. Richardson, *History of Dartmouth College*, 335–46.

43. Spring, *The American School*, 79.

44. Robert B. Downs, *Horace Mann: Champion of Public Schools* (New York: Twayne, 1974), preface.

45. Downs, *Horace Mann*, preface.

46. Downs, *Horace Mann*, chronology.

47. Horace Mann, *Life and Works of Horace Mann*, 5 vols. (Boston: Lee and Shepard, 1891).

48. Mann, *Life and Works of Horace Mann*, vol. 1, 64.

49. Mann, *Life and Works of Horace Mann*, vol. 1, 64.

50. Lawrence A. Cremin, ed., *The Republic and the School: Horace Mann on the Education of Free Men* (New York: Teachers College Press, 1957), 3.

51. Mann, *Life and Works of Horace Mann*, vol. 1, 67; Cremin, *The Republic and the School*, 3.

52. The first meeting of the Massachusetts Board of Education was on June 29, 1837. Under the state law that created the board, a written report had to be submitted to the legislature on or before the second Wednesday in January on an annual basis. Mann, *Life and Works of Horace Mann*, vol. 2, 371.

53. Mann, *Life and Works of Horace Mann*, vol. 2, 389.

54. Mann, *Life and Works of Horace Mann*, vol. 2, 389–90.

55. U.S. Department of Education, National Center for Education Statistics, *The Condition of Education 2011*, http://nces.ed.gov/pubs2011/2011033 .pdf (accessed June 7, 2011).

56. Mann, *Life and Works of Horace Mann*, vol. 2, 390.

57. William J. Bushaw and Shane J. Lopez, "A Time for Change: The 42nd Annual Phi Delta Kappa/Gallup Poll of the Public's Attitudes toward the Public Schools," *Phi Delta Kappan* 92, no. 1 (2010): 9–26.

58. Mann, *Life and Works of Horace Mann*, vol. 2, 395.

59. Mann, *Life and Works of Horace Mann*, vol. 2, 408–9.

60. Mann, *Life and Works of Horace Mann*, vol. 2, 410.

61. Mann, *Life and Works of Horace Mann*, vol. 2, 419–20.

62. Cremin, *The Republic and the School*, 34.

63. Mann, *Life and Works of Horace Mann*, vol. 2, 510.

64. Mann, *Life and Works of Horace Mann*, vol. 2, 511.

65. Mann, *Life and Works of Horace Mann*, vol. 2, 511.

66. Mann, *Life and Works of Horace Mann*, vol. 2, 513.

67. Mann, *Life and Works of Horace Mann*, vol. 2, 516.

68. Mann, *Life and Works of Horace Mann*, vol. 3, 10–11.

69. HAPLR Index, "Hennen's American Public Library Ratings," http://
www.haplr-index.com/haplr100.htm (accessed June 26, 2011). The states
and libraries included in the 2010 survey are Ohio (Cuyahoga County Public
Library, Columbus Metropolitan Library, Cincinnati and Hamilton County
Public Library, Stark County District Library, Dayton Metro Library, Medina
County District Library, Wayne County Public Library, Greene County Public
Library, Washington-Centerville Public Library, Worthington Public Library,
Euclid Public Library, Willoughby-Eastlake Public Library, Westerville Public
Library, Lakewood Public Library, Porter Public Library, Upper Arlington
Public Library, Ella M. Everhard Public Library, North Canton Public Library,
Shaker Heights Public Library, Massillon Public Library, Twinsburg
Public Library, Orrville Public Library, Wickliffe Public Library, Madison Pub-
lic Library, Way Public Library, Avon Lake Public Library, Columbiana Public
Library, Bristol Public Library, Grandview Heights Public Library, Crestline
Public Library, Kinsman Free Public Library, Canal Fulton Public Library,
Wright Memorial Public Library, New Carlisle Public Library, Burton Public
Library, Grand Valley Public Library, Centerburg Public Library, Rock Creek
Public Library, and Wagnalls Memorial Library); Oregon (Multnomah
County Library); Colorado (Denver Public Library, Douglas County Libraries,
and Silverton Public Library); Utah (Salt Lake County Library System, Salt
Lake City Public Library, and Mount Pleasant Public Library); Washington
(King County Library System); Minnesota (Hennepin County Library, Ram-
sey County Library, Edgerton Runals Memorial Library, Grand Marais Public
Library, and Browns Valley Public Library); Maryland (Baltimore County
Public Library and Howard County Library); Indiana (Indianapolis-Marion
County Public Library, Allen County Public Library, Monroe County Public
Library, Evansville-Vanderburgh Public Library, Carmel Clay Public Library,
and Bell Memorial Public Library); California (Santa Clara County
Library and Santa Clara City Library); Missouri (Saint Charles City-County
Library District); Virginia (Central Rappahannock Regional Library and
Loudon County Public Library); Wisconsin (Madison Public Library, Middle-
ton Public Library, and Belleville Public Library); Illinois (Naperville Public
Library, Champaign Public Library, Elmhurst Public Library, St. Charles Pub-
lic Library District, Algonquin Area Public Library District, and Elk Grove
Public Library District); Michigan (Ann Arbor District Library and West
Bloomfield Township Public Library,); Massachusetts (Newton Free Library,
West Tisbury Free Public Library, Meekins Public Library, and Chilmark Free
Public Library); Kansas (Hays Public Library, Seneca Free Library, and Hardt-
ner Public Library); Pennsylvania (Peters Township Public Library); Connect-
icut (Darien Public Library); West Virginia (Bridgeport Public Library); Iowa
(James Kennedy Public Library); Nebraska (Central City Public Library, John
A. Stahl Library, Neligh Public Library, and Brunswick Public Library);
Alabama (Orange Beach Public Library and Flomaton Public Library); Texas

(Yoakum County/Cecil Bickley Library); New York (Sodus Free Library, New Woodstock Free Library, and Earlville Free Library); South Dakota (Beresford Public Library); and Alaska (Pelican Public Library and Eagle Public Library).

70. The American Presidency Project, "Election of 1840," http://www .presidency.ucsb.edu/showelection.php?year=1840 (accessed June 28, 2011). Martin Van Buren (Democrat), the eighth president of the United States, was seeking a second term. He was defeated by William Henry Harrison (Whig), who received almost 53 percent of the popular vote and 234 out of 294 electoral votes.

71. Mann, *Life and Works of Horace Mann*, vol. 3, 58.

72. Mann, *Life and Works of Horace Mann*, vol. 3, 61.

73. Mann, *Life and Works of Horace Mann*, vol. 3, 63–64.

74. Mann, *Life and Works of Horace Mann*, vol. 3, 67.

75. Mann, *Life and Works of Horace Mann*, vol. 3, 67.

76. Mann, *Life and Works of Horace Mann*, vol. 3, 68–69.

77. Cremin, *The Republic and the School*, 53.

78. Mann, *Life and Works of Horace Mann*, vol. 3, 96–97.

79. Mann, *Life and Works of Horace Mann*, vol. 3, 140.

80. Mann, *Life and Works of Horace Mann*, vol. 3, 138.

81. Centers for Disease Control and Prevention, "Data and Statistics: Obesity Rates among All Children in the United States," http://www.cdc .gov/obesity/childhood/data.html (accessed August 14, 2011).

82. Cremin, *The Republic and the School*, 54.

83. Mann, *Life and Works of Horace Mann*, vol. 3, 239.

84. Cremin, *The Republic and the School*, 54.

85. Mann, *Life and Works of Horace Mann*, vol. 3, 356.

86. Mann, *Life and Works of Horace Mann*, vol. 3, 357.

87. Cremin, *The Republic and the School*, 54.

88. By way of illustration, see Justice Joseph Bradley's concurring opinion in *Bradwell v. Illinois*, 83 U.S. 130 (1873).

89. Mann, *Life and Works of Horace Mann*, vol. 3, 427.

90. Mann, *Life and Works of Horace Mann*, vol. 4, 36–38.

91. National Conference of State Legislatures, "Compulsory Education," http://www.ncsl.org/IssuesResearch/Education/CompulsoryEducation Overview/tabid/12943/Default.aspx (accessed August 21, 2011).

92. Mann, *Life and Works of Horace Mann*, vol. 4, 114–15.

93. Mann, *Life and Works of Horace Mann*, vol. 4, 115–16.

94. Mann, *Life and Works of Horace Mann*, vol. 4, 184.

95. U.S. Equal Employment Opportunity Commission, "The Equal Pay Act of 1963," http://www.eeoc.gov/laws/statutes/epa.cfm (accessed August 22, 2011). The Equal Pay Act requires that men and women be paid the same for equal work. The jobs do not need to be identical, but they must

be substantially equal. Job content determines whether jobs are substantially equal and not job titles.

96. Cremin, *The Republic and the School*, 79.

97. Mann, *Life and Works of Horace Mann*, vol. 4, 228.

98. Mann, *Life and Works of Horace Mann*, vol. 4, 246–47.

99. Mann, *Life and Works of Horace Mann*, vol. 4, 251–52.

100. For more information about the Philadelphia Convention of 1787, see Edward J. Larson and Michael P. Winship, *The Constitutional Convention: A Narrative History from the Notes of James Madison* (New York: Modern Library, 2005); Christopher Collier and James Lincoln Collier, *Decision in Philadelphia: The Constitutional Convention of 1787* (New York: Ballantine, 2007); and David O. Stewart, *The Summer of 1787: The Men Who Invented the Constitution* (New York: Simon & Schuster, 2007).

101. Mann, *Life and Works of Horace Mann*, vol. 4, 270–71.

102. Warren E. Burger, " 'A Republic, If You Can Keep It': A Bicentennial Commentary," *Presidential Studies Quarterly* 18, no. 3 (1988): 473.

103. Burger, " 'A Republic, If You Can Keep It,' " 473; Joseph R. Biden, "The Constitution, the Senate, and the Court," *Wake Forest Law Review* 24 (1989): 951. More discussion of this historical occurrence is available in chapter 6.

104. Mann, *Life and Works of Horace Mann*, vol. 4, 283–84.

105. Mann, *Life and Works of Horace Mann*, vol. 4, 287–88.

106. Mann, *Life and Works of Horace Mann*, vol. 4, 312–13.

107. National Commission on Excellence in Education, *A Nation at Risk: The Imperative for Educational Reform* (Washington, DC: Government Printing Office, 1983).

Chapter 2

1. Adam Smith, *The Wealth of Nations*, 2 vols. (New York: E. P. Dutton, 1910).

2. Smith, *The Wealth of Nations*, vol. 1, 15.

3. Wendell Glick, ed., *The Writings of Henry D. Thoreau: Reform Papers* (Princeton, NJ: Princeton University Press, 1973), 63.

4. Thomas Jefferson's Monticello, "Research and Collections," http://www.monticello.org/site/research-and-collections (accessed September 21, 2011).

5. Cornell University Library, "The United States Democratic Review," http://ebooks.library.cornell.edu/u/usde/index.html (accessed September 21, 2011).

6. Thomas C. Taylor, *The Fundamentals of Austrian Economics* (London: Adam Smith Institute, 1981).

7. See, in particular, John Maynard Keynes, *The General Theory of Employment, Interest, and Money* (New York: Harcourt, Brace & World, 1935).

8. Library of Economics and Liberty, "Friedrich August Hayek (1899–1992)," http://www.econlib.org/library/Enc/bios/Hayek.html (accessed September 8, 2011); Library of Economics and Liberty, "John Maynard Keynes (1883–1946)," http://www.econlib.org/library/Enc/bios/Keynes.html (accessed September 8, 2011).

9. Friedrich A. Hayek, *The Road to Serfdom* (Chicago: University of Chicago Press, 1944), 10–11.

10. Hayek, *The Road to Serfdom*, 101–2.

11. Hayek, *The Road to Serfdom*, 240.

12. Hayek and Gunnar Myrdal were awarded the Nobel Prize for economic sciences in 1974. See Nobel Prizes, "All Nobel Prizes," http://www.nobelprize.org/nobel_prizes/lists/all (accessed September 28, 2011); Friedrich Hayek, *The Constitution of Liberty* (Chicago: University of Chicago Press, 1960).

13. Ronald Reagan served as U.S. president from 1981 to 1989, and Margaret Thatcher was the prime minister of the United Kingdom from 1979 to 1990.

14. Hayek, *The Constitution of Liberty*, 1–2.

15. Hayek, *The Constitution of Liberty*, 223.

16. Stanford Encyclopedia of Philosophy, "Leo Strauss," http://plato.stanford.edu/entries/strauss-leo. Strauss was born the same year as Friedrich Hayek (1899). He died in 1973.

17. J. G. York, "Neoconservatism and Leo Strauss: The Place of a Liberal Education," *Critical Studies in Education* 49, no. 1 (2008): 67–68.

18. Leo Strauss, *On Tyranny* (New York: Free Press of Glencoe, 1963), 22–23.

19. Leo Strauss, "What Is Political Philosophy?," *Journal of Politics* 19, no. 3 (1957): 343–68.

20. Nasser Behnegar, *Leo Strauss, Max Weber, and the Scientific Study of Politics* (Chicago: University of Chicago Press, 2003), 1–6; Nicholas Capaldi, "The Ethical Foundations of Free Market Societies," *Journal of Private Enterprise* 20, no. 1 (2004): 30–54.

21. Strauss, *On Tyranny*, 189.

22. Behnegar, *Leo Strauss, Max Weber, and the Scientific Study of Politics*, 2.

23. Shadia B. Drury, *Leo Strauss and the American Right* (New York: St. Martin's Press, 1997), 2.

24. Drury, *Leo Strauss and the American Right*, 3.

25. Drury, *Leo Strauss and the American Right*, 178.

26. Brian L. Fife and G. M. Miller, *Political Culture and Voting Systems in the United States: An Examination of the 2000 Presidential Election* (Westport, CT: Praeger, 2002).

27. George F. Will, *Statecraft as Soulcraft: What Government Does* (New York: Simon & Schuster, 1983), 94–95.

28. Willmoore Kendall, *The Conservative Affirmation* (Chicago: Henry Regnery, 1963), 203.

29. John A. Murley and John E. Alvis, eds., *Willmoore Kendall: Maverick of American Conservatives* (Lanham, MD: Lexington Books, 2002).

30. U.S. Congress, "Biographical Directory of the United States Congress, 1774–Present: Barry Morris Goldwater," http://bioguide.congress.gov (accessed January 9, 2012).

31. In the 1964 presidential election, the Democratic ticket of Lyndon Johnson (Texas) and Hubert Humphrey (Minnesota) received more than 61 percent of the popular vote over the Republican ticket of Barry Goldwater (Arizona) and William E. Miller (New York). The Democratic ticket prevailed in 44 states and the District of Columbia and won 486 electoral votes; the Republican ticket carried only six states (South Carolina, Georgia, Alabama, Mississippi, Louisiana, and Arizona) for a total of 52 electoral votes. See Dave Leip's Atlas of U.S. Presidential Elections, "1964 Presidential General Election Results," http://uselectionatlas.org/RESULTS (accessed January 9, 2012).

32. Barry Goldwater, *The Conscience of a Conservative* (New York: Hillman Books, 1960), 14.

33. Goldwater, *The Conscience of a Conservative*, 25–26.

34. Hubert H. Humphrey was a Democrat and was vice president of the United States from 1965 to 1969, a U.S. senator from 1949 to 1964 and 1971 to 1978, and mayor of Minneapolis from 1945 to 1948. He was the Democratic nominee for president in 1968, but he lost the election to Republican Richard M. Nixon. See U.S. Congress, "Biographical Directory of the United States Congress, 1774–Present: Hubert Horatio Humphrey, Jr.," http://bioguide.congress.gov (accessed January 9, 2012).

35. American Rhetoric, "Hubert Humphrey: Democratic National Convention Address, July 14, 1948," http://www.americanrhetoric.com/speeches/huberthumphey1948dnc.html (accessed January 9, 2012).

36. Jennifer L. Hochschild, *The New American Dilemma: Liberal Democracy and School Desegregation* (New Haven, CT: Yale University Press, 1984).

37. Max Farrand, ed., *The Records of the Federal Convention of 1787*, 3 vols. (New Haven, CT: Yale University Press, 1991).

38. *Brown v. Board of Education of Topeka, Kansas* 347 U.S. 483 (1954).

39. Goldwater, *The Conscience of a Conservative*, 38.

40. An illustration of this point can be extracted by reading Chief Justice John Marshall's opinion in *McCulloch v. Maryland* (1819).

41. Goldwater, *The Conscience of a Conservative*, 37.

42. Antonin Scalia, *A Matter of Interpretation: Federal Courts and the Law* (Princeton, NJ: Princeton University Press, 1997).

43. Scalia, *A Matter of Interpretation*, 37.

44. Scalia, *A Matter of Interpretation*, 46–47.

45. Stephen Breyer, *Active Liberty: Interpreting Our Democratic Constitution* (New York: Alfred A. Knopf, 2005).

46. Breyer, *Active Liberty*, 117.

47. For a comprehensive account of the ratification debates in the states, see Pauline Maier, *Ratification: The People Debate the Constitution, 1787–1788* (New York: Simon & Schuster, 2010).

48. Breyer, *Active Liberty*, 101.

49. Brian L. Fife, *Reforming the Electoral Process in America: Toward More Democracy in the 21st Century* (Santa Barbara, CA: ABC-CLIO, 2010), 121.

50. Friedman Foundation for Educational Choice, "Milton Friedman's Bio," http://www.edchoice.org/The-Friedmans/Milton-Friedman-s-Bio .aspx (accessed January 16, 2012).

51. Nobel Prizes, "All Nobel Prizes," http://www.nobelprize.org/nobel _prizes/lists/all (accessed September 28, 2011).

52. Nobel Prizes, "All Nobel Prizes"; Paul Krugman, "Who Was Milton Friedman?," *New York Review of Books*, February 15, 2007, http://www .nybooks.com/articles/archives/2007/feb/15/who-was-Milton-Friedman (accessed January 16, 2012).

53. Krugman, "Who Was Milton Friedman?"

54. Milton Friedman, *Capitalism and Freedom* (Chicago: University of Chicago Press, 1962), 2–3.

55. Milton Friedman, *Essays in Positive Economics* (Chicago: University of Chicago Press, 1953).

56. Milton Friedman and Rose Friedman, *Free to Choose: A Personal Statement* (New York: Harcourt Brace Jovanovich, 1980), 309–10.

57. Michael McGerr, *A Fierce Discontent: The Rise and Fall of the Progressive Movement in America, 1870–1920* (New York: Free Press, 2003).

58. Ron Chernow, *Titan: The Life of John D. Rockefeller, Sr.* (New York: Random House, 1998); David Nasaw, *Andrew Carnegie* (New York: Penguin, 2006); Steven Watts, *The People's Tycoon: Henry Ford and the American Century* (New York: Alfred A. Knopf, 2005); T. J. Stiles, *The First Tycoon: The Epic Life of Cornelius Vanderbilt* (New York: Alfred A. Knopf, 2009).

59. Chernow, *Titan*.

60. Dave Leip's Atlas of U.S. Presidential Elections, "1980 Presidential General Election Results," http://uselectionatlas.org/RESULTS (accessed January 24, 2012).

61. Dave Leip's Atlas of U.S. Presidential Elections, "1984 Presidential General Election Results," http://uselectionatlas.org/RESULTS (accessed January 24, 2012).

62. William E. Hudson, *The Libertarian Illusion: Ideology, Public Policy, and the Assault on the Common Good* (Washington, DC: CQ Press, 2008).

63. Hudson, *The Libertarian Illusion*, 23.

64. Hudson, *The Libertarian Illusion*, 3.

65. Thomas W. Evans, *The Education of Ronald Reagan: The General Electric Years and the Untold Story of His Conversion to Conservatism* (New York: Columbia University Press, 2006).

66. Evans, *The Education of Ronald Reagan*, 37–80.

67. Evans, *The Education of Ronald Reagan*, 37–56.

68. Evans, *The Education of Ronald Reagan: The General Electric Years and the Untold Story of His Conversion to Conservatism*, 238-49.

69. Evans, *The Education of Ronald Reagan*, 239–40.

70. Evans, *The Education of Ronald Reagan*, 238.

71. Evans, *The Education of Ronald Reagan*, 239.

72. Robert M. Collins, *Transforming America: Politics and Culture in the Reagan Years* (New York: Columbia University Press, 2007), 59.

73. Collins, *Transforming America*, 59–91.

74. Collins, *Transforming America*, 63–64.

75. Collins, *Transforming America*, 89.

76. American Rhetoric, "Ronald Reagan: Farewell Address to the Nation, January 11, 1989," http://www.americanrhetoric.com/speeches/ronald reaganfarewelladdress.html (accessed February 6, 2012).

77. David Farber, *The Rise and Fall of Modern Conservatism: A Short History* (Princeton, NJ: Princeton University Press, 2010), 207–8.

78. Dave Leip's Atlas of U.S. Presidential Elections, "1988 Presidential General Election Results," http://uselectionatlas.org/RESULTS (accessed February 6, 2012).

79. One elector in West Virginia cast her presidential vote for Lloyd Bentsen, who was the vice-presidential running mate of Michael Dukakis.

80. Dave Leip's Atlas of U.S. Presidential Elections, "1992 Presidential General Election Results," http://uselectionatlas.org/RESULTS (accessed February 6, 2012).

81. Dave Leip's Atlas of U.S. Presidential Elections, "1996 Presidential General Election Results," http://uselectionatlas.org/RESULTS (accessed February 6, 2012).

82. Dave Leip's Atlas of U.S. Presidential Elections, "2000 Presidential General Election Results," http://uselectionatlas.org/RESULTS (accessed February 6, 2012). A simple majority of the Electoral College vote is needed to win the presidency in the United States (270 of 538 electoral votes).

83. Dave Leip's Atlas of U.S. Presidential Elections, "2004 Presidential General Election Results," http://uselectionatlas.org/RESULTS (accessed February 6, 2012). In Minnesota, an elector pledged to support John Kerry for president but instead voted for John Edwards, his vice-presidential running mate.

84. Farber, *The Rise and Fall of Modern Conservatism*, 212.

85. *Bush v. Gore*, 531 U.S. 98 (2000).

86. Gallup Poll, "Presidential Approval Ratings—Gallup Historical Statistics and Trends," http://www.gallup.com/poll/116677/presidential -approval-ratings-gallup-historical-statistics-trends.aspx (accessed February 7, 2012).

87. Tim Conlan and John Dinan, "Federalism, the Bush Administration, and the Transformation of American Conservatism," *Publius: The Journal of Federalism* 37, no. 3 (2007): 297–98.

88. Conlan and Dinan, "Federalism, the Bush Administration, and the Transformation of American Conservatism," 298.

89. Adam Wolfson, "Conservatives and Neoconservatives," *The Public Interest* 154 (2004): 34.

90. George W. Bush, *A Charge to Keep* (New York: William Morrow, 1999), 235–36.

91. Bush, *A Charge to Keep*, 132–39.

92. Esther Kaplan, *With God on Their Side: How Christian Fundamentalists Trampled Science, Policy, and Democracy in George W. Bush's White House* (New York: New Press, 2004).

93. Charles Tiefer, *Veering Right: How the Bush Administration Subverts the Law for Conservative Causes* (Berkeley: University of California Press, 2004).

94. Paul Waldman, *Fraud: The Strategy behind the Bush Lies and Why the Media Didn't Tell You* (Naperville, IL: Sourcebooks, 2004), 280–81.

95. By way of example, see Julian E. Zelizer, ed., *The Presidency of George W. Bush: A First Historical Assessment* (Princeton, NJ: Princeton University Press, 2010); Eric Alterman and Mark Green, *The Book on Bush: How George W. (Mis)leads America* (New York: Viking, 2004); and Corey Robin, *The Reactionary Mind: Conservatism from Edmund Burke to Sarah Palin* (New York: Oxford University Press, 2011).

96. John W. Dean, *Worse Than Watergate: The Secret Presidency of George W. Bush* (New York: Little, Brown, 2004).

97. John W. Dean, *Conservatives without Conscience* (New York: Viking, 2006), 171–72. His book is dedicated to the memory of Senator Barry Goldwater, "a conservative with conscience."

98. Dean, *Conservatives without Conscience*.

99. Bruce Bartlett, *Impostor: How George W. Bush Bankrupted America and Betrayed the Reagan Legacy* (New York: Doubleday, 2006).

100. Bartlett, *Impostor*, 1–2.

101. Richard A. Viguerie, *Conservatives Betrayed: How George W. Bush and Other Big Government Republicans Hijacked the Conservative Cause* (Los Angeles: Bonus Books, 2006).

102. Viguerie, *Conservatives Betrayed*, 219–24.

103. Viguerie, *Conservatives Betrayed*, 21–25.

Chapter 3

1. For a historical summary of the creation of the federal republic in the United States, see Max Farrand, *The Fathers of the Constitution: A Chronicle of the Establishment of the Union* (New Haven, CT: Yale University Press, 1921).

2. Robert A. Goldwin, ed., *A Nation of States: Essays on the American Federal System* (Chicago: Rand McNally, 1963), preface.

3. *McCulloch v. Maryland* (1819).

4. Chief Justice John Marshall was appointed by President John Adams and took his judicial oath on February 4, 1801. He served as chief justice until his death on July 6, 1835. No chief justice has served longer than him in U.S. history.

5. *McCulloch v. Maryland* (1819).

6. *McCulloch v. Maryland* (1819).

7. Raoul Berger, *Federalism: The Founders' Design* (Norman: University of Oklahoma Press, 1987), 3.

8. Frederick D. Drake and Lynn R. Nelson, eds., *States' Rights and American Federalism: A Documentary History* (Westport, CT: Greenwood Press, 1999).

9. Saul K. Padover, ed., *The Forging of American Federalism: Selected Writings of James Madison* (New York: Harper & Row, 1965).

10. Padover, *The Forging of American Federalism*, 184.

11. Jacob E. Cooke, ed., *The Federalist* (Middletown, CT: Wesleyan University Press, 1961).

12. Gregory E. Maggs, "A Concise Guide to the Federalist Papers as a Source of the Original Meaning of the United States Constitution," *Boston University Law Review* 87 (2007): 807.

13. Maggs, "A Concise Guide to the Federalist Papers as a Source of the Original Meaning of the United States Constitution," 811.

14. Maggs, "A Concise Guide to the Federalist Papers as a Source of the Original Meaning of the United States Constitution," 811.

15. Maggs, "A Concise Guide to the Federalist Papers as a Source of the Original Meaning of the United States Constitution," 809.

16. Cooke, *The Federalist*.

17. The Avalon Project: Documents in Law, History, and Diplomacy, "The Federalist Papers: No. 46, January 29, 1788," http://avalon.yale.law.edu/18th_century/fed46.asp (accessed February 21, 2012).

18. Duane Lockard, *American Federalism* (St. Louis, MO: McGraw-Hill, 1969), 11.

19. Edward J. Larson, *A Magnificent Catastrophe: The Tumultuous Election of 1800, America's First Presidential Campaign* (New York: Free Press, 2007).

20. The Avalon Project: Documents in Law, History and Diplomacy, "Washington's Farewell Address, 1796," http://avalon.yale.edu/18th_century/washing.asp (accessed February 23, 2012).

21. Chief Justice Roger Taney was appointed by President Andrew Jackson and took his judicial oath on March 28, 1836. He served as chief justice until his death on October 12, 1864.

22. *License Cases*, 46 U.S. 504 (1847).

23. *License Cases* (1847).

24. *Dred Scott v. Sandford*, 60 U.S. 393 (1857).

25. *Marbury v. Madison*, 5 U.S. 137 (1803).

26. The Federalist Party did not last long in American history. For an overview of its demise, see Shaw Livermore Jr., *The Twilight of Federalism: The Disintegration of the Federalist Party, 1815–1830* (Princeton, NJ: Princeton University Press, 1962).

27. Richard H. Leach, *American Federalism* (New York: Norton, 1970), 13.

28. South Caroliniana Library, Books Division, *Exposition and Protest, Reported by the Special Committee of the House of Representatives, on the Tariff; Read and Ordered to be Printed, Dec. 19th, 1828* (Columbia, SC: D. W. Sims, 1829), http://www.teachingushistory.org/lessons/expositionandprotest1828.htm (accessed February 24, 2012).

29. The Avalon Project: Documents in Law, History and Diplomacy, "Alien Act: An Act Respecting Alien Enemies: July 6, 1798," http://avalon.law.yale.edu/18th_century.alien.asp (accessed February 24, 2012); The Avalon Project: Documents in Law, History and Diplomacy, "Sedition Act: An Act in Addition to the Act, Entitled 'An Act for the Punishment of Certain Crimes against the United States: July 14, 1798,'" http://avalon.law.yale.edu/18th_century/sedact.asp (accessed February 24, 2012).

30. The Avalon Project: Documents in Law, History and Diplomacy, "Virginia Resolution—Alien and Sedition Acts: December 24, 1798," http://avalon.law.yale.edu/18th_century/virres.asp (accessed February 24, 2012).

31. The Avalon Project: Documents in Law, History and Diplomacy, "Kentucky Resolution—Alien and Sedition Acts: December 3, 1799," http://avalon.law.yale.edu/18th_century/kenres.asp (accessed February 24, 2012).

32. Daniel J. Elazar, *The American Partnership: Intergovernmental Co-Operation in the Nineteenth-Century United States* (Chicago: University of Chicago Press, 1962), 11; Samuel H. Beer, "Federalism, Nationalism, and Democracy in America," *American Political Science Review* 72, no. 1 (1978): 9.

33. Edward S. Corwin, *The Twilight of the Supreme Court: A History of Our Constitutional Theory* (New Haven, CT: Yale University Press, 1934), 47–48.

34. Elazar, *The American Partnership*, 14.

35. Michael McGerr, *A Fierce Discontent: The Rise and Fall of the Progressive Movement in America, 1870–1920* (New York: Free Press, 2003).

36. Edward S. Corwin, "The Passing of Dual Federalism," *Virginia Law Review* 36 (1950): 1–24.

37. Corwin, "The Passing of Dual Federalism," 1–2.

38. Morton Grodzins, "The Federal System," in U.S. President's Commission on National Goals, *Goals for Americans* (New York: Prentice Hall, 1960), 265.

39. Morton Grodzins, "Centralization and Decentralization in the American Federal System," in Goldwin, *A Nation of States*, 1–23.

40. An alternative hypothesis is presented by Elazar, *The American Partnership*, 305. Elazar noted that "even during the nineteenth century, when the ethos of the times called forth a theory of dualism that was based on a functional demarcation between governments, the actual exigencies of the operation of the federal system demanded co-operation. Consequently, federal-state co-operation was developed in a wide variety of cases. Though it was usually opposed on the theoretical level, it persevered in practice in many forms and under different guises. Its procedures were refined through trial and error and, often subtly, through the arrangements of dedicated public servants at a time when formally accepted doctrines were occasionally applied to prevent its open recognition. Officially recognized or not, a system of intergovernmental co-operation was evolved to serve the dual purpose of maintaining the federal balance while providing needed governmental services. Where co-operation did not develop but should have, both the system and the programs in question suffered." In his book, he maintains that the framers of the Constitution planned for the development of cooperative federalism in terms of their collective vision of federalism in the American republic.

41. The reader may want to examine the following scholarly works on federalism: Nelson A. Rockefeller, *The Future of Federalism* (Cambridge, MA: Harvard University Press, 1962); William H. Riker, *Federalism: Origin, Operation, Significance* (Boston: Little, Brown, 1964); Daniel J. Elazar, ed., *The Politics of American Federalism* (Lexington, MA: D. C. Heath, 1969); Michael D. Reagan, *The New Federalism* (New York: Oxford University Press, 1972); Martha Derthick, *Between State and Nation: Regional Organizations of the United States* (Washington, DC: Brookings Institution, 1974); David B. Walker, *Toward a Functioning Federalism* (Cambridge, MA: Winthrop Publishers, 1981); Carl Lowe, ed., *Reaganomics: The New Federalism* (New York: H. W. Wilson, 1984); Samuel H. Beer, *To Make a Nation: The Rediscovery of American Federalism* (Cambridge, MA: The Belknap Press of Harvard University Press, 1993); and Timothy Conlan, *From New Federalism to Devolution: Twenty-Five Years of Intergovernmental Reform* (Washington, DC: Brookings Institution Press, 1998).

42. Rockefeller, *The Future of Federalism*, 27–28. Nelson Rockefeller (Republican) was governor of New York from 1959 to 1973 and vice president of the United States from 1974 to 1977.

43. Lyndon B. Johnson (Democrat) was president of the United States from 1963 to 1969.

44. Walker, *Toward a Functioning Federalism*, 102; Rockefeller, *The Future of Federalism*, 8–10.

45. Walker, *Toward a Functioning Federalism*, 175.

46. Richard M. Nixon (Republican) was president of the United States from 1969 to 1974.

47. Walker, *Toward a Functioning Federalism*, 104–5.

48. Walker, *Toward a Functioning Federalism*, 105.

49. Conlan, *From New Federalism to Devolution*, 93.

50. Gerald Ford (Republican) and Jimmy Carter (Democrat) were presidents of the United States from 1974 to 1977 and 1977 to 1981, respectively.

51. Conlan, *From New Federalism to Devolution*, 167–68.

52. Those following Ronald Reagan in the White House include George H. W. Bush (Republican), 1989–1993; Bill Clinton (Democrat), 1993–2001; George W. Bush (Republican), 2001–2009; and Barack Obama (Democrat), 2009 to the present.

53. Walker, *Toward a Functioning Federalism*, 101.

54. Dave Leip's Atlas of U.S. Presidential Elections, "1836 Presidential General Election Results," http://uselectionatlas.org/RESULTS (accessed March 5, 2012).

55. Dave Leip's Atlas of U.S. Presidential Elections, "1840 Presidential General Election Results," http://uselectionatlas.org/RESULTS (accessed March 5, 2012).

56. Dave Leip's Atlas of U.S. Presidential Elections, "1844 Presidential General Election Results," http://uselectionatlas.org/RESULTS (accessed March 5, 2012).

57. Dave Leip's Atlas of U.S. Presidential Elections, "1848 Presidential General Election Results," http://uselectionatlas.org/RESULTS (accessed March 5, 2012).

58. Dave Leip's Atlas of U.S. Presidential Elections, "1852 Presidential General Election Results," http://uselectionatlas.org/RESULTS (accessed March 5, 2012).

59. Dave Leip's Atlas of U.S. Presidential Elections, "1856 Presidential General Election Results," http://uselectionatlas.org/RESULTS (accessed March 5, 2012). Millard Fillmore, the Whig nominee, was a former president. He became president when Zachary Taylor died in 1850. By 1856, the Whig Party was known officially as the Whig-American Party.

60. One of the last known vestiges of the Whig's national campaign literature was in the 1856 presidential election. An intriguing juxtaposition between the Whig Party and its rivals is available in Whig Party Campaign Literature, "The Great Fraud upon the Public Credulity in the Organization of the Republican Party upon the Ruins of the 'Whig Party': An Address to the Old-Line Whigs of the Union" (Washington, DC: Printed at the Union Office, 1856).

61. The Whig Party platforms are available for 1844, 1848, 1852, and 1856. See American Presidency Project, "Whig Party Platform of 1844," http://www.presidency.ucsb.edu/ws/?pid=25852 (accessed March 5, 2012); American Presidency Project, "Whig Party Platform of 1848," http://www.presidency.ucsb.edu/ws/?pid=25855 (accessed March 5, 2012); American Presidency Project, "Whig Party Platform of 1852," http://www.presidency.ucsb.edu/ws/?pid=25856 (accessed March 5, 2012); and American Presidency Project, "Whig Party Platform of 1856," http://www.presidency.ucsb.edu/ws/?pid=258567 (accessed March 5, 2012).

62. Michael F. Holt, *The Rise and Fall of the American Whig Party: Jacksonian Politics and the Onset of the Civil War* (New York: Oxford University Press, 1999).

63. Mark Groen, "The Whig Party and the Rise of Common Schools, 1837–1854," *American Educational History Journal* 35, no. 2 (2008): 251.

64. Carl F. Kaestle, *Pillars of the Republic: Common Schools and American Society, 1780–1860* (New York: Hill and Wang, 1983).

65. Groen, "The Whig Party and the Rise of Common Schools, 1837–1854," 253.

66. Groen, "The Whig Party and the Rise of Common Schools, 1837–1854," 254.

67. Groen, "The Whig Party and the Rise of Common Schools, 1837–1854," 257.

68. Holt, *The Rise and Fall of the American Whig Party,* 582.

69. George Allen Hubbell, *Horace Mann: Educator, Patriot and Reformer: A Study in Leadership* (Philadelphia: Wm. F. Fell, 1910), 167–68.

70. Hubbell, *Horace Mann,* 168.

71. Groen, "The Whig Party and the Rise of Common Schools, 1837–1854," 259.

72. Joy Elmer Morgan, *Horace Mann: His Ideas and Ideals* (Washington, DC: National Home Library Foundation, 1936), 3.

73. U.S. Department of Education, "Overview: The Federal Role in Education," http://www2.ed.gov/about/overview/fed/role.html?src=ln (accessed March 7, 2012).

74. U.S. Department of Education, "No Child Left Behind: 10 Facts about K–12 Education Funding," http://www2.ed.gov/about/overview/fed/10facts/10facts.pdf (accessed March 7, 2012).

75. Center on Education Policy, "A Brief History of the Federal Role in Education: Why It Began and Why It's Still Needed" (Washington, DC: Center on Education Policy, 1999), ERIC Document ED 438335; Brian L. Fife, "Federalism, Education, and Citizenship in an Era of Democratic Deliberation," in *The Hope for Audacity: From Cynicism to Hope in Educational Leadership and Policy,* ed. Stella C. Batagiannis, Barry Kanpol, and Anna V. Wilson (New York: Peter Lang, 2012), 115–39.

76. Center on Education Policy, "A Brief History of the Federal Role in Education"; Fife, "Federalism, Education, and Citizenship in an Era of Democratic Deliberation," 126.

77. Center on Education Policy, "A Brief History of the Federal Role in Education"; Fife, "Federalism, Education, and Citizenship in an Era of Democratic Deliberation," 126.

78. National Commission on Excellence in Education, *A Nation at Risk: The Imperative for Educational Reform* (Washington, DC: Government Printing Office, 1983).

79. Public Law 103-227 (March 31, 1994), "Goals 2000: Educate America Act," http://www2.ed.gov/legislation/GOALS2000/TheAct/index.html (accessed March 8, 2012).

80. Public Law 107-110 (January 8, 2002), "No Child Left Behind Act of 2001," http://www2.ed.gov/policy/elsec/leg/esea02/107-110.pdf (accessed March 8, 2012); Fife, "Federalism, Education, and Citizenship in an Era of Democratic Deliberation," 126.

81. *Brown v. Board of Education of Topeka, Kansas* (1954).

82. Public Law 89-10 (April 11, 1965), "Elementary and Secondary Education Act of 1965," http://www.eric.ed.gov/PDFS/ED017539.pdf (accessed March 8, 2012).

83. Center on Education Policy, "A Brief History of the Federal Role in Education"; Fife, "Federalism, Education, and Citizenship in an Era of Democratic Deliberation," 126–27.

84. U.S. National Archives and Records Administration, "Morrill Act—Public Law 37-108, July 2, 1862," http://www.ourdocuments.gov/doc.php?doc=33 (accessed March 9, 2012).

85. Center on Education Policy, "A Brief History of the Federal Role in Education"; Fife, "Federalism, Education, and Citizenship in an Era of Democratic Deliberation," 127.

86. Center on Education Policy, "A Brief History of the Federal Role in Education"; Fife, "Federalism, Education, and Citizenship in an Era of Democratic Deliberation," 127.

87. U.S. National Archives and Records Administration, "Servicemen's Readjustment Act—Public Law 78-346, June 22, 1944," http://www.ourdocuments.gov/doc.php?doc=76 (accessed March 9, 2012).

88. Public Law 89-329 (November 8, 1965), "Higher Education Act of 1965," http://ftp.resource.org/gao.gov/89-329/00004C57.pdf (accessed March 9, 2012); Fife, "Federalism, Education, and Citizenship in an Era of Democratic Deliberation," 128.

89. Public Law 110-315 (August 14, 2008), "Higher Education Opportunity Act," http://www2.ed.gov/policy/highered/leg/hea08/index.html (accessed March 9, 2012); Fife, "Federalism, Education, and Citizenship in an Era of Democratic Deliberation," 128.

90. Public Law 85-864 (September 2, 1958), "National Defense Education Act of 1958," http://www.constitution.org/uslaw/sal/072_statutes_at_large .pdf (accessed March 9, 2012); Fife, "Federalism, Education, and Citizenship in an Era of Democratic Deliberation," 128.

91. U.S. Department of Education, "Overview"; Fife, "Federalism, Education, and Citizenship in an Era of Democratic Deliberation," 128.

92. Center on Education Policy, "A Brief History of the Federal Role in Education"; Fife, "Federalism, Education, and Citizenship in an Era of Democratic Deliberation," 128.

93. U.S. National Archives and Records Administration, "Remarks in Johnson City, Texas, upon Signing the Elementary and Secondary Education Bill, April 11, 1965," http://www.lbjlib.utexas.edu/johnson/archives.hom/ speeches.hom/650411.asp (accessed March 12, 2012).

94. U.S. National Archives and Records Administration, "Remarks in Johnson City, Texas, Upon Signing the Elementary and Secondary Education Bill, April 11, 1965."

95. Julia Hanna, "The Elementary and Secondary Education Act: 40 Years Later," Harvard University, Graduate School of Education, 2005, http://www .gse.harvard.edu/news_events/features/2005/08/esea0819.html (accessed March 9, 2012).

96. Leslie Standerfer, "Before NCLB: The History of ESEA," *Principal Leadership* 6, no. 8 (2006): 26.

97. Eugene Eidenberg and Roy D. Morey, *An Act of Congress: The Legislative Process and the Making of Education Policy* (New York: Norton, 1969), 172.

98. Julie Roy Jeffrey, *Education for Children of the Poor: A Study of the Origins and Implementation of the Elementary and Secondary Education Act of 1965* (Columbus: Ohio State University Press, 1978), 3.

99. Public Law 89-10 (April 11, 1965), "Elementary and Secondary Education Act of 1965."

100. Jeffrey, *Education for Children of the Poor*, 76.

101. Public Law 89-10 (April 11, 1965), "Elementary and Secondary Education Act of 1965."

102. Stephen K. Bailey and Edith K. Mosher, *ESEA: The Office of Education Administers a Law* (Syracuse, NY: Syracuse University Press, 1968), 49.

103. Bailey and Mosher, *ESEA*, 3.

104. U.S. House of Representatives, "U.S. House of Representatives Roll Call Vote 107th Congress—1st Session, Vote 497 (December 13, 2001)," http://clerk.house.gov/evs/2001/roll497.xml (accessed March 13, 2012).

105. U.S. Senate, "U.S. Senate Roll Call Vote 107th Congress—1st Session, Vote 371 (December 18, 2001)," http://www.senate.gov/legislative/LIS/ roll_call_lists/roll_call_vote_cfm.cfm?congress=107&session=1&vote=00371 (accessed March 13, 2012)

106. Public Law 107-110 (January 8, 2002), "No Child Left Behind Act of 2001," http://www2.ed.gov/policy/elsec/leg/esea02/107-110.pdf (accessed March 8, 2012).

107. C-SPAN Video Library, "Education Bill Signing Ceremony, January 8, 2002," http://www.c-spanvideo.org/program/168090-1 (accessed March 14, 2012).

108. Public Law 107-110 (January 8, 2002), "No Child Left Behind Act of 2001."

109. *Education Week*, "No Child Left Behind, September 19, 2011," http:// www.edweek.org/ew/issues/no-child-left-behind/ (accessed March 14, 2012); Patrick J. McGuinn, *No Child Left Behind and the Transformation of Federal Education Policy, 1965–2005* (Lawrence: University Press of Kansas, 2006), 180–81.

110. McGuinn, *No Child Left Behind and the Transformation of Federal Education Policy, 1965–2005*, 193–94.

111. McGuinn, *No Child Left Behind and the Transformation of Federal Education Policy, 1965–2005*, 195.

112. McGuinn, *No Child Left Behind and the Transformation of Federal Education Policy, 1965–2005*, 195.

113. Diane Ravitch, *The Death and Life of the Great American School System: How Testing and Choice Are Undermining Education* (New York: Basic Books, 2010), 99.

114. National Education Association, "Charter Schools," http://www.nea .org/home/16332.htm (accessed March 15, 2012).

115. Ravitch, *The Death and Life of the Great American School System*, 122.

116. *Education Week*, "Vouchers, August 11, 2011," http://www.edweek .org/ew/issues/vouchers (accessed March 15, 2012); National Conference of State Legislatures, "Education Program: Publicly Funded School Voucher Programs," http://www.ncsl.org/issues-research/educ/school-choice -vouchers.aspx (accessed March 15, 2012); National Education Association, "Charter Schools."

117. Ravitch, *The Death and Life of the Great American School System*, 226–27.

118. Fife, "Federalism, Education, and Citizenship in an Era of Democratic Deliberation," 136.

119. Ravitch, *The Death and Life of the Great American School System*, 227–28.

120. The reader may want to examine the following scholarly works on NCLB: Deborah Meier et al., eds., *Many Children Left Behind: How the No Child Left Behind Act Is Damaging Our Children and Our Schools* (Boston: Beacon Press, 2004); Maris A. Vinovskis, *From a Nation at Risk to No Child Left Behind: National Education Goals and the Creation of Federal Education Policy* (New York: Teachers College Press, 2009); Frederick M. Hess and Chester E. Finn Jr., eds., *Leaving No Child Behind? Options for Kids in Failing Schools* (New York: Palgrave Macmillan, 2004); Paul Manna, *School's In: Federalism and the National*

Education Agenda (Washington, DC: Georgetown University Press, 2006); and Christina Fisanick, ed., *At Issue: Has No Child Left Behind Been Good for Education?* (Detroit: Greenhaven Press, 2008).

Chapter 4

1. Westminster Assembly, *The New-England Primer; Much Improved. Containing, A Variety of Easy Lessons, for Attaining the True Reading of* English (Philadelphia: T. Dobson, at the Stone House, No. 41, S. Second Street, 1797); Samuel J. Smith, "New England Primer," in *Encyclopedia of Educational Reform and Dissent*, vol. 2, ed. Thomas C. Hunt, James C. Carper, Thomas J. Lasley, and C. Daniel Raisch (Thousand Oaks, CA: Sage, 2010), 661–62.

2. Smith, "New England Primer," 661.

3. Noah Webster, *American Spelling Book; Containing, the Rudiments of the English Language for the Use of Schools in the United States* (Hartford, CT: Hudson & Goodwin, 1809).

4. Harry Warfel, *Noah Webster: Schoolmaster to America* (New York: Macmillan, 1936), 71–75; Joel Spring, *Educating the Consumer-Citizen: A History of the Marriage of Schools, Advertising, and Media* (Mahwah, NJ: Lawrence Erlbaum Associates, 2003), 9.

5. Richard D. Mosier, *Making the American Mind: Social and Moral Ideas in the McGuffey Readers* (New York: King's Crown Press, 1947), 168. According to the president of the American Book Company, Louis Dilman, the sales of the *McGuffey Readers* were as follows: 1836–1850, 7 million copies; 1850–1870, 40 million copies; 1870–1890, 60 million copies; and 1890–1920, 15 million copies.

6. Harvey C. Minnich, *William Holmes McGuffey and His Readers* (New York: American Book Company, 1936), 40. According to Professor Minnich, the seven publishing houses of the *McGuffey Readers* were as follows: Truman and Smith (1834–1843); W. B. Smith (1843–1852); W. B. Smith & Company (1852–1863); Sargent, Wilson & Hinkle (1863–1868); Wilson, Hinkle & Company (1868–1877); Van Antwerp, Bragg & Company (1877–1890); and American Book Company (1890–1920).

7. For a comprehensive account of the *McGuffey Readers* and their subsequent revisions, see Miami University Libraries, "About the William Holmes McGuffey Collection," http://doyle.lib.muohio.edu/cdm4/about .php?CISOROOT=%2Fmcguffey (accessed March 20, 2012), and Indiana State University Library, "Floyd Family Collection: *McGuffey Readers and Spellers* (Arranged by Brother & Date)," http://library.indstate.edu/about/ units/rbsc/floyd/mcguffey.html (accessed March 20, 2012).

8. Ohio History Central, "William H. McGuffey," http://www .ohiohistorycentral.org/entry.php?rec=263 (accessed March 23, 2012); Henry

H. Vail, *A History of the McGuffey Readers* (Cleveland: Burrows Brothers Co., 1911).

9. Indiana State University Library, "Floyd Family Collection: *McGuffey Readers and Spellers* (Arranged by Brother & Date)." The complete series of readers is as follows: William H. McGuffey, *McGuffey's First Eclectic Reader*, rev. ed. (Cincinnati: Van Antwerp, Bragg & Co., 1879); William H. McGuffey, *McGuffey's Second Eclectic Reader*, rev. ed. (Cincinnati: Van Antwerp, Bragg & Co., 1879); William H. McGuffey, *McGuffey's Third Eclectic Reader*, rev. ed. (Cincinnati: Van Antwerp, Bragg & Co., 1879); William H. McGuffey, *McGuffey's Fourth Eclectic Reader*, rev. ed. (Cincinnati: Van Antwerp, Bragg & Co., 1879); William H. McGuffey, *McGuffey's Fifth Eclectic Reader*, rev. ed. (Cincinnati: Van Antwerp, Bragg & Co., 1879); and William H. McGuffey, *McGuffey's Sixth Eclectic Reader* (Cincinnati: Van Antwerp, Bragg & Co., 1879).

10. Minnich, *William Holmes McGuffey and His Readers*, 88.

11. Vail, *A History of the McGuffey Readers*, 72.

12. McGuffey, *McGuffey's Second Eclectic Reader*, 121.

13. McGuffey, *McGuffey's Second Eclectic Reader*, 121–23.

14. McGuffey, *McGuffey's Second Eclectic Reader*, 124.

15. McGuffey, *McGuffey's Second Eclectic Reader*, 124–26.

16. McGuffey, *McGuffey's Third Eclectic Reader*, 76.

17. McGuffey, *McGuffey's Third Eclectic Reader*, 76–78.

18. Mosier, *Making the American Mind*, 98.

19. Spring, *Educating the Consumer-Citizen*.

20. Spring, *Educating the Consumer-Citizen*, 1–2.

21. Spring, *Educating the Consumer-Citizen*, 4.

22. Spring, *Educating the Consumer-Citizen*, 4–5.

23. Spring, *Educating the Consumer-Citizen*, 5.

24. Spring, *Educating the Consumer-Citizen*, 5.

25. Spring, *Educating the Consumer-Citizen*, 5.

26. Spring, *Educating the Consumer-Citizen*, 5–6.

27. Spring, *Educating the Consumer-Citizen*, 10.

28. Richard Wrightman Fox and T. J. Jackson Lears, *The Culture of Consumption: Critical Essays in American History, 1880–1980* (New York: Pantheon, 1983), ix.

29. Robert S. Lynd and Helen M. Lynd, *Middletown: A Study in Contemporary American Culture* (New York: Harcourt Brace and Company, 1929); Robert S. Lynd and Helen M. Lynd, *Middletown in Transition: A Study in Cultural Conflicts* (New York: Harcourt Brace and Company, 1937).

30. See Ball State University, "Center for Middletown Studies," http://cms.bsu.edu/Academics/CentersandInstitutes/Middletown.aspx (accessed March 12, 2012).

31. David Tambo, Dwight Hoover, and John D. Hewitt, *Middletown: An Annotated Bibliography* (New York: Garland, 1988).

32. Richard Wrightman Fox, "Epitaph for Middletown: Robert S. Lynd and the Analyses of Consumer Culture," in Fox and Lears, *The Culture of Consumption*, 105.

33. Fox, "Epitaph for Middletown," 140–41.

34. Charles F. McGovern, *Sold American: Consumption and Citizenship, 1890–1945* (Chapel Hill: University of North Carolina Press, 2006).

35. McGovern, *Sold American*, 9–10.

36. McGovern, *Sold American*, 23–24.

37. The reader can extract a broad overview of advertising in the late nineteenth and twentieth centuries by consulting the following: Susan Strasser, *Satisfaction Guaranteed: The Making of the American Mass* Market (Washington, DC: Smithsonian Books, 1989); Ellen Gruber Garvey, *The Adman in the Parlor: Magazines and the Gendering of Consumer Culture, 1880s to 1910s* (New York: Oxford University Press, 1996); Juliann Sivulka, *Stronger Than Dirt: A Cultural History of Advertising Personal Hygiene in America, 1875 to 1940* (Amherst, NY: Humanity Books, 2001); Lisa Jacobson, *Raising Consumers: Children and the American Mass Market in the Early Twentieth Century* (New York: Columbia University Press, 2004); Juliann Sivulka, *Soap, Sex, and Cigarettes: A Cultural History of American Advertising*, 2nd ed. (Boston: Wadsworth, Cengage Learning, 2012); and Sheila Harty, *Hucksters in the Classroom: A Review of Industry Propaganda in Schools* (Washington, DC: Center for Study of Responsive Law, 1979).

38. Strasser, *Satisfaction Guaranteed*, 286–91.

39. Strasser, *Satisfaction Guaranteed*, 286.

40. Strasser, *Satisfaction Guaranteed*, 291.

41. Susan J. Matt, *Keeping Up with the Joneses: Envy in American Consumer Society, 1890–1930* (Philadelphia: University of Pennsylvania Press, 2003), 182–83.

42. Matt, *Keeping Up with the Joneses*, 2–3.

43. Matt, *Keeping Up with the Joneses*, 9–10.

44. Juliet B. Schor, *Born to Buy: The Commercialized Child and the New Consumer Culture* (New York: Scribner, 2004), 9.

45. Juliet B. Schor, *The Overworked American: The Unexpected Decline of Leisure* (New York: Basic Books, 1993).

46. Juliet B. Schor, *The Overspent American: Upscaling, Downshifting, and the New Consumer* (New York: Harper Perennial, 1999).

47. U.S. Department of Treasury, Bureau of the Public Debt, "The Debt to the Penny and Who Holds It," http://www.treasurydirect.gov/NP/BPDLogin?application=np (accessed April 2, 2013).

48. Schor, *Born to Buy*, 19–20.

49. Henry A. Giroux, *The Mouse That Roared: Disney and the End of Innocence* (Lanham, MD: Rowman & Littlefield, 1999), 168–69.

50. Giroux, *The Mouse That Roared*, 168–69.

51. Henry A. Giroux, *Stealing Innocence: Corporate Culture's War on Children* (New York: Palgrave, 2000), 1–3.

52. Giroux, *Stealing Innocence*, 101. By the way, the commercialization of schools is not just an American phenomenon. See, for example, Gary Wilkinson, "McSchools for McWorld? Mediating Global Pressures with a McDonaldizing Education Policy Response," *Cambridge Journal of Education* 36, no. 1 (2006): 81–98.

53. U.S. Department of Health and Human Services, "2013 HHS Poverty Guidelines," http://aspe.hhs.gov/poverty/13poverty.cfm (accessed April 2, 2013).

54. Gordon M. Fisher, "The Development and History of the U.S. Poverty Thresholds—A Brief Overview," http://aspe.hhs.gov/poverty/papers/hptgssiv.htm (accessed April 12, 2012).

55. U.S. Census Bureau, "Highlights," http://www.census.gov/hhes/www/poverty/about/overview/index.html (accessed April 12, 2012).

56. Jonathan Kozol, *Savage Inequalities: Children in America's Schools* (New York: Crown, 1991).

57. Alex Molnar, *Giving Kids the Business: The Commercialization of America's Schools* (Boulder, CO: Westview Press, 1996), 184.

58. Edwin C. Broome, *Report of the Committee on Propaganda in the Schools* (Washington, DC: National Education Association, 1929); Molnar, *Giving Kids the Business*, 39; Howard L. Parker, "A Plan for Sifting Propaganda in the Schools," *Elementary School Journal* 33, no. 4 (1932): 277–82.

59. Broome, *Report of the Committee on Propaganda in the Schools*, 3.

60. Molnar, *Giving Kids the Business*, 39.

61. Molnar, *Giving Kids the Business*, 1–2.

62. Spring, *Educating the Consumer-Citizen*, 204–5.

63. Molnar, *Giving Kids the Business*, 44–45.

64. Parker, "A Plan for Sifting Propaganda in the Schools."

65. Parker, "A Plan for Sifting Propaganda in the Schools," 277.

66. Parker, "A Plan for Sifting Propaganda in the Schools," 277.

67. Parker, "A Plan for Sifting Propaganda in the Schools," 277.

68. Parker, "A Plan for Sifting Propaganda in the Schools," 280–82.

69. Alex Molnar, "The Commercial Transformation of Public Education," *Journal of Education Policy* 21, no. 5 (2006): 621.

70. Molnar, "The Commercial Transformation of Public Education," 622.

71. Molnar, "The Commercial Transformation of Public Education," 622.

72. Broome, *Report of the Committee on Propaganda in the Schools*.

73. Molnar, "The Commercial Transformation of Public Education," 622; Molnar, *Giving Kids the Business*.

74. Molnar, "The Commercial Transformation of Public Education," 622.

75. Molnar, "The Commercial Transformation of Public Education," 625.

76. Molnar, "The Commercial Transformation of Public Education," 625.

77. Molnar, "The Commercial Transformation of Public Education," 631–32.

78. Molnar, "The Commercial Transformation of Public Education," 635.

79. Schor, *Born to Buy*, 20.

80. Joel Spring, "Schooling for Consumption," in *Critical Pedagogies of Consumption: Living and Learning in the Shadow of the "Shopocalypse,"* ed. Jennifer A. Sandlin and Peter McLaren (New York: Routledge, 2010), 69.

81. Simon N. Patten, *The New Basis of Civilization*, ed. Daniel M. Fox (Cambridge, MA: The Belknap Press of Harvard University Press, 1968), 3–4.

82. Daniel Horowitz, "Consumption and Its Discontents: Simon N. Patten, Thorstein Veblen, and George Gunton," *Journal of American History* 67, no. 2 (1980): 303–4.

83. Spring, "Schooling for Consumption," 80.

84. David A. Greenwood, "Chocolate, Place, and a Pedagogy of Consumer Privilege," in Sandlin and McLaren, *Critical Pedagogies of Consumption*, 199.

85. Michael Hoechsmann, "Rootlessness, Reenchantment, and Educating Desire: A Brief History of the Pedagogy of Consumption," in Sandlin and McLaren, *Critical Pedagogies of Consumption*, 34.

86. John Micklethwait and Adrian Woolridge, *The Right Nation: Conservative Power in America* (New York: Penguin, 2004).

Chapter 5

1. *Plessy v. Ferguson*, 163 U.S. 537 (1896); Brian L. Fife, "The Supreme Court and School Desegregation since 1896," 46.

2. *Plessy v. Ferguson* (1896).

3. *Plessy v. Ferguson* (1896).

4. *Plessy v. Ferguson* (1896).

5. *Plessy v. Ferguson* (1896).

6. *Plessy v. Ferguson* (1896).

7. *Dred Scott v. Sandford* (1857).

8. Brian L. Fife, *School Desegregation in the Twenty-First Century: The Focus Must Change* (Lewiston, NY: Edwin Mellen Press, 1997), 2–3; Fife, "The Supreme Court and School Desegregation since 1896," 46.

9. The other cases were *Briggs v. Elliott* (South Carolina), *Davis v. County School Board of Prince Edward County, Virginia* (Virginia), and *Gebhart v. Belton* (Delaware).

10. Richard Kluger, *Simple Justice: The History of Brown v. Board of Education and Black America's Struggle for Equality* (New York: Vintage Books, 2004), 660–702.

11. Kluger, *Simple Justice*, 696–702.

12. *Brown v. Board of Education of Topeka, Kansas* (1954).

13. *Brown v. Board of Education of Topeka, Kansas* (1954).

14. *Brown v. Board of Education of Topeka, Kansas* (1954).

15. *Brown v. Board of Education of Topeka, Kansas* (1954).

16. *Brown v. Board of Education of Topeka, Kansas* 349 U.S. 294 (1955).

17. John Marshall Harlan (1833–1911) served on the Supreme Court from 1877 to 1911. His grandson John Marshall Harlan II (1899–1971) served on the Supreme Court from 1955 to 1971.

18. *Brown v. Board of Education of Topeka, Kansas* (1955).

19. *Brown v. Board of Education of Topeka, Kansas* (1955).

20. Kluger, *Simple Justice*, 703–50.

21. *Green v. County School Board of New Kent County,* 391 U.S. 430 (1968).

22. *Green v. County School Board of New Kent County* (1968).

23. *Swann v. Charlotte-Mecklenberg Board of Education,* 402 U.S. 1 (1971).

24. *Swann v. Charlotte-Mecklenberg Board of Education* (1971).

25. *Swann v. Charlotte-Mecklenberg Board of Education* (1971).

26. *Swann v. Charlotte-Mecklenberg Board of Education* (1971).

27. *Swann v. Charlotte-Mecklenberg Board of Education* (1971).

28. *Swann v. Charlotte-Mecklenberg Board of Education* (1971).

29. *Keyes v. School District No. 1,* 413 U.S. 189 (1973).

30. *Keyes v. School District No. 1* (1973).

31. *Keyes v. School District No. 1* (1973).

32. *Keyes v. School District No. 1* (1973).

33. *Milliken v. Bradley,* 418 U.S. 717 (1974).

34. *Milliken v. Bradley* (1974); Joyce A. Baugh, *The Detroit School Busing Case: Milliken v. Bradley and the Controversy over Desegregation* (Lawrence: University Press of Kansas, 2011); Samantha Meinke, "*Milliken v. Bradley*: The Northern Battle for Desegregation," *Michigan Bar Journal,* September 2011, 20–22.

35. *Milliken v. Bradley* (1974).

36. Fife, *School Desegregation in the Twenty-First Century,* 14–16; Fife, "The Supreme Court and School Desegregation since 1896," 51.

37. *Milliken v. Bradley* (1974).

38. Gary Orfield, Susan E. Eaton, and the Harvard Project on School Desegregation, *Dismantling Desegregation: The Quiet Reversal of Brown v. Board of Education* (New York: New Press, 1996).

39. Orfield et al., *Dismantling Desegregation,* 12.

40. *Board of Education of Oklahoma City v. Dowell,* 498 U.S. 237 (1991).

41. *Board of Education of Oklahoma City v. Dowell* (1991).

42. *Board of Education of Oklahoma City v. Dowell* (1991).

43. *Board of Education of Oklahoma City v. Dowell* (1991).

44. *Freeman v. Pitts,* 503 U.S. 467 (1992).

45. *Freeman v. Pitts* (1992).

46. *Freeman v. Pitts* (1992).

47. *Missouri v. Jenkins*, 515 U.S. 70 (1995). The outcome of the case was a split decision. Chief Justice Rehnquist wrote the majority opinion, and he was joined by Justices O'Connor, Scalia, Kennedy, and Thomas. Justice Souter wrote the dissent, and he was joined by Justices Stevens, Ruth Bader Ginsburg, and Breyer.

48. *Parents Involved in Community Schools v. Seattle School District No. 1*, 551 U.S. 701 (2007).

49. *Parents Involved in Community Schools v. Seattle School District No. 1* (2007).

50. *Parents Involved in Community Schools v. Seattle School District No. 1* (2007).

51. *Parents Involved in Community Schools v. Seattle School District No. 1* (2007).

52. *Parents Involved in Community Schools v. Seattle School District No. 1* (2007).

53. *Parents Involved in Community Schools v. Seattle School District No. 1* (2007).

54. Gary Orfield, *Reviving the Goal of an Integrated Society: A 21st Century Challenge* (Los Angeles: Civil Rights Project/Proyecto Derechos Civiles at UCLA, 2009); Gary Orfield, Mark D. Bachmeier, David R. James, and Tamela Eide, "Deepening Segregation in American Public Schools," *Southern Changes* 19, no. 2 (1997): 11–18.

55. Jonathan Kozol, *The Shame of the Nation: The Restoration of Apartheid Schooling in America* (New York: Crown, 2005).

56. Orfield, *Reviving the Goal of an Integrated Society*, 3.

57. National Education Association, "Charter Schools," http://www.nea.org/home/16332.htm (accessed March 15, 2012); Brian L. Fife, "The Anatomy and Ideology of a Charter," ERIC Document ED501289 (2008).

58. Gary Miron, "Time to Stop and Rethink Charter Schools," http://edworkforce.house.gov/UploadedFiles/06.01.11_miron.pdf (accessed May 17, 2012); testimony prepared for a June 1, 2011, hearing of the U.S. House Committee on Education and the Workforce.

59. Fife, "The Anatomy and Ideology of a Charter."

60. Center for Education Reform, "Choice and Charter Schools: Facts," http://www.edreform.com/issues/choice-charter-schools/facts (accessed May 15, 2012).

61. Center for Education Reform, "Choice and Charter Schools: Just the FAQS," http://www.edreform.com/2012/03/15/just-the-faqs-charter-schools (accessed May 15, 2012).

62. Center for Education Reform, "Choice and Charter Schools: Facts."

63. Miron, "Time to Stop and Rethink Charter Schools."

64. Miron, "Time to Stop and Rethink Charter Schools."

65. Center for Research on Education Outcomes, Stanford University, "Multiple Choice: Charter School Performance in 16 States," http://credo.stanford.edu (accessed May 20, 2012).

66. Center for Research on Education Outcomes, Stanford University, "Multiple Choice," 1–2.

67. Center for Education Reform, "School Choice Programs across the Nation," http://www.edreform.com/in-the-states/explore-choice-programs (accessed May 15, 2012).

68. Friedman Foundation for Educational Choice, "Indiana Gov. Mitch Daniels Signs Historic Voucher Bill into Law," http://edchoice.org/ Newsroom/News/Indiana-Gov—Mitch-Daniels-Signs-Historic-Voucher -Bill-into-Law.aspx (accessed May 22, 2012).

69. School Choice Indiana, "Indiana Choice Scholarship Program," http:// www.schoolchoiceindiana.com/wp-content/uploads/2011/05/Program Summaries5.11.pdf (accessed May 22, 2012).

70. *Zelman v. Simmons-Harris*, 536 U.S. 639 (2002).

71. *Zelman v. Simmons-Harris* (2002) and Brian L. Fife, "The U.S. Supreme Court and the Politics of Vouchers," *International Journal of Educational Reform* 13, no. 1 (2004): 74.

72. *Zelman v. Simmons-Harris* (2002).

73. *Mueller v. Allen*, 463 U.S. 388 (1983); *Witters v. Washington Department of Services for the Blind*, 474 U.S. 481 (1986); *Zobrest v. Catalina*, 509 U.S. 1 (1993).

74. *Mueller v. Allen* (1983).

75. *Witters v. Washington Department of Services for the Blind* (1986).

76. *Zobrest v. Catalina* (1993).

77. *Zelman v. Simmons-Harris* (2002).

78. *Zelman v. Simmons-Harris* (2002).

79. *Zelman v. Simmons-Harris* (2002).

80. *Zelman v. Simmons-Harris* (2002).

81. *Everson v. Board of Education of Ewing*, 330 U.S. 1 (1947).

82. *Everson v. Board of Education of Ewing* (1947).

83. Library of Congress, "Jefferson's Letter to the Danbury Baptists," January 1, 1802, http://www.loc.gov/loc/lcib/9806/danpost.html (accessed May 23, 2012).

84. Library of Congress, "Jefferson's Letter to the Danbury Baptists."

85. *Zelman v. Simmons-Harris* (2002).

86. *Zelman v. Simmons-Harris* (2002).

87. *Zelman v. Simmons-Harris* (2002).

88. Friedman Foundation for Educational Choice, "Types of School Choice," http://www.edchoice.org/School-Choice/Types-of-School-Choice .aspx (accessed May 24, 2012).

89. U.S. Department of Education, National Center for Education Statistics, "Fast Facts: Homeschooling," http://nces.ed.gov/fastfacts/display.asp ?id=91 (accessed May 24, 2012); Friedman Foundation for Educational Choice, "Types of School Choice."

90. Friedman Foundation for Educational Choice, "Types of School Choice."

91. International Association for K–12 Online Learning, "Fast Facts about Online Learning," http://www.inacol.org (accessed May 24, 2012).

Chapter 6

1. David Easton, *The Political System: An Inquiry into the State of Political Science* (New York: Alfred A. Knopf, 1953), 4.

2. Easton, *The Political System*, 97–98.

3. David Easton, "An Approach to the Analysis of Political Systems," *World Politics* 9, no. 3 (1957): 384.

4. The reader may benefit by scrutinizing a subsequent book on systems theory by Easton. See David Easton, *A Framework for Political Analysis* (Englewood Cliffs, NJ: Prentice Hall, 1965).

5. Charles Merriam, *Civic Education in the United States* (New York: Charles Scribner's Sons, 1934), vii.

6. Merriam, *Civic Education in the United States*, xix.

7. Merriam, *Civic Education in the United States*, 114.

8. Merriam, *Civic Education in the United States*, 114–15.

9. Merriam, *Civic Education in the United States*, 164.

10. Gallup Poll, "Americans Express Historic Negativity toward U.S. Government," http://www.gallup.com/poll/149678/Americans-Express-Historic-Negativity-Toward-Government.aspx (accessed June 25, 2012). A record-high 81 percent of Americans indicated that they were dissatisfied with the way the country is being governed.

11. Merriam, *Civic Education in the United States*, 169.

12. Suzanne W. Morse, "Ward Republics: The Wisest Invention for Self-Government," in *Thomas Jefferson and the Education of a Citizen*, ed. James Gilreath (Hanover, NH: University Press of New England, 1999), 264–65.

13. Andrew A. Lipscomb and Albert E. Bergh, eds., *The Writings of Thomas Jefferson*, 20 vols. (Washington, DC: Thomas Jefferson Memorial Association, 1901), vol. 14, 417–23.

14. Lipscomb and Bergh, *The Writings of Thomas Jefferson*, vol. 14, 421–22.

15. Max Farrand, ed., *The Records of the Federal Convention of 1787*, 3 vols. (New Haven, CT: Yale University Press, 1911), vol. 2, 641–50.

16. Farrand, *The Records of the Federal Convention of 1787*, vol. 2, 641–42.

17. American Historical Association, "Papers of Dr. James McHenry on the Federal Convention of 1787," *American Historical Review* 11, no. 3 (1906): 595–624.

18. American Historical Association, "Papers of Dr. James McHenry on the Federal Convention of 1787," 618.

19. Philip Dray, *Stealing God's Thunder: Benjamin Franklin's Lightning Rod and the Invention of America* (New York: Random House, 2005), 197.

20. Library of Congress, "Creating the United States: Monarchy or a Republic?," http://www.myloc.gov/Exhibitions/creatingtheus/Constitution/Ratification/ExhibitObjects/MonarchyorRepublic.aspx (accessed July 4, 2012).

21. Farrand, *The Records of the Federal Convention of 1787*, vol. 3, 85.

22. Tanya M. Smith, Paul Tafforeau, Donald J. Reid, Rainer Grün, Stephen Eggins, Mohamed Boutakiout, and Jean-Jacques Hublin, "Earliest Evidence of Modern Human Life History in North African Early *Homo Sapiens*," *Proceedings of the National Academy of Sciences* 104, no. 15 (2007): 6128–33.

23. Michael X. Delli Carpini, "An Overview of the State of Citizens' Knowledge about Politics," Annenberg School for Communication Departmental Papers, University of Pennsylvania, http://repository.upenn.edu/asc_papers/53 (accessed July 9, 2012).

24. Pew Research Center for the People and the Press, "What the Public Knows about the Political Parties," http://www.people-press.org/2012/04/11/what-the-public-knows-about-the-political-parties/?src=iq-quiz (accessed July 9, 2012).

25. C-SPAN, "C-SPAN 2009 Historians Presidential Leadership Survey," http://legacy.c-span.org/PresidentialSurvey/presidential-leadership-survey.aspx (accessed July 10, 2012).

26. Pew Research Center for the People and the Press, "What the Public Knows about the Political Parties."

27. Gallup Poll, "How Many Americans Know U.S. History? Part I," http://www.gallup.com/poll/9526/how-many-americans-know-us-history-part.aspx (accessed July 10, 2012).

28. Gallup Poll, "How Many Americans Know U.S. History? Part I."

29. Indiana Department of Education, "Indiana's Diploma Requirements," http://www.doe.in.gov/achievement/curriculum/indianas-diploma-requirements (accessed July 11, 2012).

30. Delli Carpini, "An Overview of the State of Citizens' Knowledge about Politics," 33.

31. William A. Galston, "Political Knowledge, Political Engagement, and Civic Education," *Annual Review of Political Science* 4, no. 1 (2001): 223–24.

32. Brian L. Fife, *Reforming the Electoral Process in America: Toward More Democracy in the 21st Century* (Santa Barbara, CA: ABC-CLIO, 2010), 53; Walter Dean Burnham, "Those High Nineteenth-Century American Voting Turnouts: Fact or Fiction?," *Journal of Interdisciplinary History* 16, no. 4 (1986): 616.

33. Fife, *Reforming the Electoral Process in America*, 58–59.

34. Fife, *Reforming the Electoral Process in America*, 59–60.

35. Fife, *Reforming the Electoral Process in America*, 62–63.

36. The countries selected include Australia, Austria, Canada, Denmark, Finland, France, Germany, Greece, Iceland, Ireland, Israel, Italy, Japan, the Netherlands, New Zealand, Norway, Spain, Sweden, Switzerland, and the United Kingdom. See International Institute for Democracy and Electoral Assistance, "Voter Turnout," http://www.idea.int/vt (accessed July 12, 2012).

37. International Institute for Democracy and Electoral Assistance, "Voter Turnout," http://www.idea.int/vt (accessed July 12, 2012).

38. International Institute for Democracy and Electoral Assistance, "Voter Turnout."

39. In this sample of 20 nations, all countries except for France had parliamentary elections. The voter turnout statistic for France (71.2 percent) is from the 2012 presidential election.

40. The Avalon Project: Documents in Law, History and Diplomacy, "The Federalist Papers: No. 10," http://avalon.law.yale.edu/18th_century/fed10 .asp (accessed July 30, 2012).

41. The Avalon Project: Documents in Law, History and Diplomacy, "The Federalist Papers: No. 10."

42. C-SPAN, "The Alexis de Tocqueville Tour: Exploring Democracy in America, May 9, 1997–February 20, 1998," http://www.tocqueville.org (accessed July 29, 2012). Among the places that Alexis de Tocqueville and Gustave de Beaumont visited during their time in America and Canada (May 9, 1831–February 20, 1832) included the following: Connecticut (Hartford and Wethersfield); Massachusetts (Boston and Stockbridge); New York (Albany, Auburn, Batavia, Buffalo, Canadaigua, Fort Brewerton, New York City, Ossining, Peekskill, Syracuse, Utica, Whitehall, and Yonkers); Pennsylvania (Erie, Philadelphia, and Pittsburgh); Rhode Island (Newport); Quebec (Beaufort, La Prairie, Montreal, Quebec, and St. Jean); Alabama (Mobile); Washington, DC: Georgia (Augusta, Fort Mitchell, Knoxville, Macon, and Milledgeville); Louisiana (New Orleans); Maryland (Baltimore); North Carolina (Fayetteville); South Carolina (Columbia); Tennessee (Memphis, Nashville, and Sandy Bridge); Virginia (Norfolk); Kentucky (Louisville and Westport); Michigan (Detroit, Mackinac, Pontiac, Saginaw, and Saulte Ste. Marie); Ohio (Cincinnati and Cleveland); West Virginia (Wheeling); and Wisconsin (Green Bay).

43. Alexis de Tocqueville, *Democracy in America* (Chicago: University of Chicago Press, 2000).

44. Tocqueville, *Democracy in America*.

45. Tocqueville, *Democracy in America*, 58–75.

46. Tocqueville, *Democracy in America*, 232.

47. Kay L. Schlozman, "Who Sings in the Heavenly Chorus? The Shape of the Organized Interest System," in *The Oxford Handbook of American Political Parties and Interest Groups*, ed. L. Sandy Maisel and Jeffrey M. Berry (New York: Oxford University Press, 2010).

48. Schlozman, "Who Sings in the Heavenly Chorus?"

49. E. E. Schattschneider, *The Semi-Sovereign People: A Realist's View of Democracy in America* (Hinsdale, IL: Dryden Press, 1960), 34–35.

50. Theodore J. Lowi, *The End of Liberalism: Ideology, Policy, and the Crisis of Public Authority* (New York: Norton, 1969).

51. Robert A. Dahl, *Who Governs? Democracy and Power in an American City* (New Haven, CT: Yale University Press, 1961).

52. Fife, *Reforming the Electoral Process in America*, 87–89 (presidential elections) and 89–93 (House and Senate elections).

53. Library of Congress, "Campaign Finance: Comparative Summary," http://www.loc.gov/law/help/campaign-finance/comparative-summary .php (accessed August 4, 2012).

54. The American Presidency Project, "Theodore Roosevelt: Fifth Annual Message, December 5, 1905," http://www.presidency.ucsb.edu/ws/index .php?pid=29546 (accessed August 4, 2012).

55. The American Presidency Project, "Theodore Roosevelt: Seventh Annual Message, December 3, 1907," http://www.presidency.ucsb.edu/ws/ index.php?pid=29548 (accessed August 4, 2012).

56. Progressive National Committee, "A Contract with the People: Platform of the Progressive Party Adopted at Its First National Convention, Chicago, August 7th, 1912" (New York: Progressive National Committee, 1912).

57. Fife, *Reforming the Electoral Process in America*, 95; Anthony Corrado, Thomas E. Mann, Daniel R. Ortiz, and Trevor Potter, *The New Campaign Finance Sourcebook* (Washington, DC: Brookings Institution Press, 2005), 10–14.

58. Corrado et al., *The New Campaign Finance Sourcebook*, 14.

59. Fife, *Reforming the Electoral Process in America*, 95–96; Corrado et al., *The New Campaign Finance Sourcebook*, 14.

60. *Newberry v. United States*, 256 U.S. 232 (1921).

61. U.S. Senate, "The Expulsion Case of Truman H. Newberry of Michigan (1922)," http://www.senate.gov/artandhistory/history/common/expulsion _cases/102TrumanNewberry_expulsion.htm (accessed August 6, 2012).

62. U.S. Senate, "The Expulsion Case of Truman H. Newberry of Michigan (1922)."

63. *United States v. Classic*, 313 U.S. 299 (1941).

64. *United States v. Classic* (1941). The case was decided on May 26, 1941. Later that year, Harlan Fiske Stone would be elevated to chief justice by President Franklin Roosevelt.

65. Fife, *Reforming the Electoral Process in America*, 97–98; Corrado et al., *The New Campaign Finance Sourcebook*, 14.

66. Fife, *Reforming the Electoral Process in America*, 98–99.

67. Corrado et al., *The New Campaign Finance Sourcebook*, 20–21; Fife, *Reforming the Electoral Process in America*, 99.

68. Corrado et al., *The New Campaign Finance Sourcebook*, 21; Fife, *Reforming the Electoral Process in America*, 99.

69. Corrado et al., *The New Campaign Finance Sourcebook*, 21; Fife, *Reforming the Electoral Process in America*, 99.

70. Corrado et al., *The New Campaign Finance Sourcebook*, 21; Fife, *Reforming the Electoral Process in America*, 99.

71. Corrado et al., *The New Campaign Finance Sourcebook*, 22–27; Fife, *Reforming the Electoral Process in America*, 99–100.

72. Corrado et al., *The New Campaign Finance Sourcebook*, 22–27; Fife, *Reforming the Electoral Process in America*, 99–101.

73. Fife, *Reforming the Electoral Process in America*, 99–101.

74. *Buckley v. Valeo*, 424 U.S. 1 (1976).

75. *Buckley v. Valeo* (1976).

76. *Buckley v. Valeo* (1976).

77. *Buckley v. Valeo* was decided on January 30, 1976.

78. Corrado et al., *The New Campaign Finance Sourcebook*, 29; Fife, *Reforming the Electoral Process in America*, 103.

79. Corrado et al., *The New Campaign Finance Sourcebook*, 29–30; Fife, *Reforming the Electoral Process in America*, 103.

80. Corrado et al., *The New Campaign Finance Sourcebook*, 36–38; Fife, *Reforming the Electoral Process in America*, 103–5.

81. Fife, *Reforming the Electoral Process in America*, 104–5.

82. Federal Election Commission, "Contribution Limits for 2011–2012," http://www.fec.gov/info/contriblimits1112.pdf (accessed August 6, 2012).

83. *McConnell v. Federal Election Commission*, 540 U.S. 93 (2003).

84. Fife, *Reforming the Electoral Process in America*, 105–6.

85. *McConnell v. Federal Election Commission* (2003).

86. *Citizens United v. Federal Election Commission*, 558 U.S. 50 (2010).

87. Jeffrey Toobin, "Money Unlimited: How Chief Justice Roberts Orchestrated the Citizens United Decision," http://www.newyorker.com/reporting/2012/05/21/120521fa_fact_toobin (accessed August 7, 2012).

88. Jeffrey Toobin, "Money Unlimited."

89. Jeffrey Toobin, "Money Unlimited."

90. *Citizens United v. Federal Election Commission* (2010).

91. *Citizens United v. Federal Election Commission* (2010).

92. *Citizens United v. Federal Election Commission* (2010).

93. *American Tradition Partnership, Inc. v. Bullock*, 567 U.S. ___ (2012).

94. *American Tradition Partnership, Inc. v. Bullock* (2012).

95. Project Vote, "Election Day Registration," http://projectvote.org/election-day-reg.html (accessed July 1, 2012).

Chapter 7

1. William Hayes, *Horace Mann's Vision of the Public Schools: Is It Still Relevant?* (Lanham, MD: Rowman & Littlefield Education, 2006).

2. Hayes, *Horace Mann's Vision of the Public Schools*, 162–63.

3. Hayes, *Horace Mann's Vision of the Public Schools*, 164.

4. Public Law 96-88 (October 17, 1979), "Department of Education Organization Act of 1979," http://history.hih.gov/research/downloads/PL96-88.pdf (accessed August 19, 2012).

5. Center for Child and Family Policy, Duke University, "A Brief History of the United States Department of Education: 1979–2002," http://www .childandfamilypolicy.duke.edu/pdfs/pubpres/BriefHistoryofUS_DOE.pdf (accessed August 19, 2012).

6. Morrison and Foerster, LLP, "Attorney Biography: Shirley M. Hufstedler," http://www.mofo.com/shirley-hufstedler/ (accessed August 17, 2012); Federal Judicial Center, "Biographical Directory of Federal Judges: Shirley Ann Mount Hufstedler," http://www.fjc.gov/servlet/nGetInfo ?jid=1111 (accessed August 17, 2012).

7. *New York Times*, "Terrel H. Bell, 74, Education Chief in Reagan Years," http://www.nytimes.com/1996/06/24/us/terrel-h-bell-74-education-chief -in-reagan-years.html (accessed August 17, 2012).

8. Claremont Institute for the Study of Statesmanship and Political Philosophy, "William J. Bennett," http://www.claremont.org/scholars/id.37/ scholar.asp (accessed August 17, 2012).

9. *New York Times*, "Washington Talk/Working Profile: Lauro F. Cavazos; In Search of a National Commitment to Education," http://www.nytimes .com/1988/10/20/us/washington-talk-working-profile-lauro-f-cavazos -search-national-commitment.html?pagewanted=print&src=pm (accessed August 19, 2012).

10. *New York Times*, "Cavazos Quits as Education Chief amid Pressure from White House," http://www.nytimes.com/1990/12/13/us/cavazos -quits-as-education-chief-amid-pressure-from-white-house.html?page wanted=all&src=pm (accessed August 19, 2012).

11. OnTheIssues.org, "Lamar Alexander on Education," http://www .ontheissues.org/celeb/Lamar_Alexander_Education.htm (accessed August 19, 2012).

12. Dollars & Sense: Real World Economics, "Charter Schools Expand: Will They Encourage Public School Reform?," http://www.dollarsandsense .org/archives/1998/0398rofes.html (accessed August 19, 2012); "Catholic Official Attacks Education Secretary Over School Vouchers," *Church and State* 50 (1997): 16–17.

13. *New York Times*, "Education Secretary Defends Charter Schools," http://www.nytimes.com/2004/08/18/education/18charter.html?pagewanted =print (accessed August 19, 2012); *Houston Chronicle*, "Paige Pushes School Voucher Program," http://www.chron.com/news/houston-texas/article/ Paige-pushes-school-voucher-program-1795047.php (accessed August 19, 2012); "Secretary Spellings Wants More Vouchers," *Human Events: The National Conservative Weekly* 63 (2007): 1, 6; redefinED: The New Definition of Public Education, "Margaret Spellings: Status Quo Benefits If Feds Don't Push Ed Reform, School Choice," http://www.redefinedonline.org/2012/08/spellings -status-quo-benefits-if-feds-dont-push-ed-reform-more-school-choice (accessed August 19, 2012).

14. ABC News, "Duncan Promotes Charter School Debate," http://abcnews.go.com/Politics/story?id=7977326&page=1 (accessed August 20, 2012); *Education Week*, "Duncan: Administration's Position Hasn't Changed on D.C. Vouchers," http://blogs.edweek.org/edweek/campaign-k-12/2012/06/duncan_administrations_positio.html (accessed August 20, 2012).

15. William E. Hudson, *American Democracy in Peril: Eight Challenges to America's Future* (Washington, DC: CQ Press, 2013), 105–7.

16. Hudson, *American Democracy in Peril*, 107–8.

17. Hudson, *American Democracy in Peril*, 108.

18. Alexis de Tocqueville, *Democracy in America* (Chicago: University of Chicago Press, 2000), 482.

19. Tocqueville, *Democracy in America*, 483.

20. Hudson, *American Democracy in Peril*, 110.

21. Hudson, *American Democracy in Peril*, 110.

22. Hudson, *American Democracy in Peril*, 110.

23. Robert N. Bellah, Richard Madsen, William M. Sullivan, Ann Swidler, and Steven M. Tipton, *Habits of the Heart: Individualism and Commitment in American Life* (Berkeley: University of California Press, 1985).

24. Bellah et al., *Habits of the Heart*.

25. Bellah et al., *Habits of the Heart*, 270–71.

26. Bellah et al., *Habits of the Heart*; Hudson, *American Democracy in Peril*.

27. The American Presidency Project, "John F. Kennedy: Inaugural Address, January 20, 1961," http://www.presidency.ucsb.edu/ws/index.php?pid=8032 (accessed August 22, 2012). Many believe that President Kennedy's adviser, Theodore Sorensen, may have authored this famous passage. See *New York Times*, "Theodore C. Sorensen, 82, Kennedy Counselor, Dies," http://www.nytimes.com/2010/11/01/us/01sorensen.html?_r=1&pagewanted=all (accessed August 22, 2012).

28. Hudson, *American Democracy in Peril*, 133.

29. Wayne J. Urban and Jennings L. Wagoner Jr., *American Education: A History*, 2nd ed. (Boston: McGraw-Hill, 2000), 118.

30. Mancur Olson, *The Logic of Collective Action: Public Goods and the Theory of Groups* (Cambridge, MA: Harvard University Press, 1965).

31. Olson, *The Logic of Collective Action*, 13–15.

32. There are varying conceptions of examples of public goods. A useful guide can be found in Angela Kallhoff, *Why Democracy Needs Public Goods* (Lanham, MD: Rowman & Littlefield, 2011). Kallhoff contends that there are seven different types of public goods: inner and outer security, infrastructure, education and science, environmental goods, public space, cultural goods, and institutions of care.

33. Horace Mann, *The Life and Works of Horace Mann*, 5 vols. (Boston: Lee and Shepard, 1891), vol. 4, 298.

34. Mann, *Life and Works of Horace Mann*, vol. 4, 299.

35. Raymond B. Culver, *Horace Mann and Religion in the Massachusetts Public Schools* (New Haven, CT: Yale University Press, 1929), 238.

36. Mann, *Life and Works of Horace Mann*, vol. 4, 336.

37. Mann, *Life and Works of Horace Mann*, vol. 4, 341–403.

38. Mann, *Life and Works of Horace Mann*, vol. 4, 403.

39. Mann, *Life and Works of Horace Mann*, vol. 5, 524.

40. Center on Education Policy, "Why We Still Need Public Schools: Public Education for the Common Good," http://www.cep-dc.org/publications/index.cfm?selectedYear=2007 (accessed August 27, 2012), 1.

41. Center on Education Policy, "Why We Still Need Public Schools: Public Education for the Common Good," 7–13.

42. Center on Education Policy, "Why We Still Need Public Schools: Public Education for the Common Good," 13.

43. Center on Education Policy, "Why We Still Need Public Schools: Public Education for the Common Good," 13.

44. Center on Education Policy, "Why We Still Need Public Schools: Public Education for the Common Good," 15–16.

45. Carl F. Kaestle, *Pillars of the Republic: Common Schools and American Society, 1780–1860* (New York: Hill and Wang, 1983), 223–24.

46. David Tyack, *Seeking Common Ground: Public Schools in a Diverse Society* (Cambridge, MA: Harvard University Press, 2003), 185.

47. Tyack, *Seeking Common Ground*, 181–82.

48. Patricia Albjerg Graham, *Schooling America: How the Public Schools Meet the Nation's Changing Needs* (New York: Oxford University Press, 2005), 252.

49. Graham, *Schooling America*.

50. Graham, *Schooling America*, 2.

51. Graham, *Schooling America*, 2.

52. Graham, *Schooling America*, 252.

53. United Nations Educational, Scientific and Cultural Organization, International Institute for Educational Planning, "Education Privatization: Causes, Consequences and Planning Implications," http://unesdoc.unesco.org/images/0013/001330/133075e.pdf (accessed September 6, 2012).

54. Cato Institute: Briefing Papers, "Public Schools: Make Them Private" (Briefing Paper No. 23), http://www.cato.org/pubs/briefs/bp-023.html (accessed September 6, 2012).

55. Cato Institute: Briefing Papers, "Public Schools"; Caroline Hoxby, "Do Vouchers and Charters Push Public Schools to Improve?," in *Choice and Competition in American Education*, ed. Paul E. Peterson (Lanham, MD: Rowman & Littlefield, 2006), 194–205.

56. Alex Molnar and David R. Garcia, "The Expanding Role of Privatization in Education: Implications for Teacher Education and Development," *Teacher Education Quarterly* 34, no. 2 (2007): 11.

57. Molnar and Garcia, "The Expanding Role of Privatization in Education," 12.

58. Molnar and Garcia, "The Expanding Role of Privatization in Education," 12.

59. Molnar and Garcia, "The Expanding Role of Privatization in Education," 15.

60. Molnar and Garcia, "The Expanding Role of Privatization in Education," 15.

61. Molnar and Garcia, "The Expanding Role of Privatization in Education," 14–16.

62. Molnar and Garcia, "The Expanding Role of Privatization in Education," 18–20.

63. Molnar and Garcia, "The Expanding Role of Privatization in Education," 12.

64. Molnar and Garcia, "The Expanding Role of Privatization in Education," 19.

65. Molnar and Garcia, "The Expanding Role of Privatization in Education," 20.

66. Paul E. Peterson, "The Use of Market Incentives in Education," in Peterson, *Choice and Competition in American Education*, 3.

67. Library of Economics and Liberty, "Privatization," http://www.econlib.org/library/Enc/Privatization.html (accessed September 10, 2012).

68. Paul R. Verkuil, *Outsourcing Sovereignty: Why Privatization of Government Functions Threatens Democracy and What Can Be Done about It* (New York: Cambridge University Press, 2007), 1.

69. Louis C. Gawthrop, *Public Service and Democracy: Ethical Imperatives for the 21st Century* (New York: Chatham House, 1998), 126.

70. Woodrow Wilson, "The Study of Administration," *Political Science Quarterly* 2, no. 2 (1887): 197–222. Wilson later became the twenty-eighth president of the United States and served from 1913 to 1921.

71. Wilson, "The Study of Administration," 198.

72. Gawthrop, *Public Service and Democracy*, 126–27.

73. Wilson, "The Study of Administration," 209–10.

74. Gawthrop, *Public Service and Democracy*, 125.

75. Al Gore, *Creating a Government That Works Better and Costs Less: Report of the National Performance Review* (Washington, DC: Government Printing Office, 1993).

76. Gawthrop, *Public Service and Democracy*, 18.

77. Gawthrop, *Public Service and Democracy*, xiii.

78. Jane A. Grant, *The New American Social Compact: Rights and Responsibilities in the Twenty-First Century* (Lanham, MD: Lexington Books, 2008), 146.

79. Verkuil, *Outsourcing Sovereignty*, 196. Ted Sorensen was describing the effect of the Watergate scandal on the U.S. presidency, and he urged vigilance

over the executive branch accordingly. See Theodore C. Sorensen, *Watchmen in the Night: Presidential Accountability after Watergate* (Cambridge, MA: MIT Press, 1975).

80. Gawthrop, *Public Service and Democracy*, 1–3.

Chapter 8

1. Famous Poetry Online, "Ulysses—A Poem by Alfred Lord Tennyson," http://www.poetry-online.org/tennyson_ulysses.htm (accessed June 22, 2012).

2. Famous Poetry Online, "Ulysses."

3. American Rhetoric, "Ted Kennedy: 1980 Democratic National Convention Address," http://www.americanrhetoric.com/speeches/tedkennedy1980dnc.htm (accessed June 6, 2012).

4. Jonathan Messerli, *Horace Mann: A Biography* (New York: Alfred A. Knopf, 1972), 588–89.

5. Robert V. Bullough, *The Forgotten Dream of American Public Education* (Ames: Iowa State University Press, 1988), 4.

6. Nel Noddings, "Education as a Public Good," in *Not for Sale: In Defense of Public Goods*, ed. Anatole Anton, Milton Fisk, and Nancy Holmstrom (Boulder, CO: Westview Press, 2000), 284–85.

7. Noddings, "Education as a Public Good," 289.

8. Bob Peterson and Barbara Miner, "The Color of 'Choice,' " in Anton et al., *Not for Sale*, 295.

9. Peterson and Miner, "The Color of 'Choice,' " 295–96.

10. G. Stanley Hall, *Educational Problems*, vol. 2 (New York: D. Appleton and Company, 1911), 681–82.

11. U.S. Department of Education, "ESEA Flexibility," http://www.ed.gov/esea/flexibility (accessed October 9, 2012); U.S. Department of Education, "ESEA Flexibility Requests and Related Documents," http://www.ed.gov/esea/flexibility/requests (accessed October 9, 2012). The 33 states include Arkansas, Arizona, Colorado, Connecticut, Delaware, Florida, Georgia, Indiana, Kansas, Kentucky, Louisiana, Maryland, Massachusetts, Michigan, Minnesota, Mississippi, Missouri, Nevada, New Jersey, New Mexico, New York, North Carolina, Ohio, Oklahoma, Oregon, Rhode Island, South Carolina, South Dakota, Tennessee, Utah, Virginia, Washington, and Wisconsin.

12. Mark J. Garrison, *A Measure of Failure: The Political Origins of Standardized Testing* (Albany: State University of New York Press, 2009), 59–72; U.S. Congress, Office of Technology Assessment, *Testing in American Schools: Asking the Right Questions* (Washington, DC: Government Printing Office, 1992), 106–12.

13. U.S. Congress, Office of Technology Assessment, *Testing in American Schools*, 107.

14. U.S. Congress, Office of Technology Assessment, *Testing in American Schools*, 108.

15. Gail L. Sunderman, ed., *Holding NCLB Accountable: Achieving Accountability, Equity, and School Reform* (Thousand Oaks, CA: Corwin Press, 2008), 224–25.

16. World Bank, "Gross Domestic Product 2011," http://databank .worldbank.org/databank/download/GDP.pdf (accessed October 11, 2012).

17. United Nations Children's Fund, *Measuring Child Poverty: New League Tables of Child Poverty in the World's Richest Countries*, http://www.unicef.org .uk/Documents/Publications/RC10-measuring-child-poverty.pdf (accessed October 12, 2012).

18. The UNICEF analysis of relative child poverty included the following 35 nations: Australia, Austria, Belgium, Bulgaria, Canada, Cyprus, Czech Republic, Denmark, Estonia, Finland, France, Germany, Greece, Hungary, Iceland, Ireland, Italy, Japan, Latvia, Lithuania, Luxembourg, Malta, the Netherlands, New Zealand, Norway, Poland, Portugal, Romania, Slovakia, Slovenia, Spain, Sweden, Switzerland, the United Kingdom, and the United States.

19. United Nations Children's Fund, *Measuring Child Poverty*.

20. U.S. Department of Labor, Office of Policy Planning and Research, "The Negro Family: The Case for National Action," http://www.dol.gov/ oasam/programs/history/webid-meynihan.htm (accessed October 12, 2012).

21. U.S. Department of Labor, Office of Policy Planning and Research, "The Negro Family."

22. Contributors to this special issue included Douglas Massey and Robert Sampson; James Q. Wilson; William Julius Wilson; Harry Holzer; Devah Pager and Diana Karafin; Frank Furstenberg; Sara McLanahan; Linda Burton and M. Belinda Tucker; Kathryn Edin, Laura Tach, and Ronald Mincy; Andrew Cherlin, Bianca Frogner, David Ribar, and Robert Moffitt; Frank Bean, Cynthia Feliciano, Jennifer Lee, and Jennifer Van Hook; Bruce Western and Christopher Wildeman; Lawrence Bobo and Camille Charles; and Ron Haskins.

23. Public Law 104-193, "Personal Responsibility and Work Opportunity Reconciliation Act of 1996," http://www.gpo.gov/fdsys/pkg/PLAW -104publ193/html/PLAW-104publ193.htm (accessed October 14, 2012).

24. Dennis K. Orthner, "Public Schools: Building Capacity for Hope and Opportunity," in *Ending Poverty in America: How to Restore the American Dream*, ed. John Edwards, Marion Crain, and Arne L. Kalleberg (New York: New Press, 2007), 219.

25. Orthner, "Public Schools," 227–28.

26. David K. Shipler, "Connecting the Dots," in Edwards et al., *Ending Poverty in America*, 20–21.

27. Public Law 111-148, "Patient Protection and Affordable Care Act," http://www.gpo/fdsys/pkg/PLAW-111publ148/pdf/PLAW-111publ148 .pdf (accessed October 18, 2012).

28. David Stuckler, Andrea B. Feigl, Sanjay Basu, and Martin McKee, "The Political Economy of Universal Health Coverage," http://www.pacifichealth summit.org/downloads/UHC/the%20political%20economy%20of%20uhc .PDF (accessed October 17, 2012).

29. *National Federation of Independent Business v. Sebelius*, 567 U.S. ___ (2012).

30. Brian L. Fife, *Reforming the Electoral Process in America: Toward More Democracy in the 21st Century* (Santa Barbara, CA: ABC-CLIO, 2010).

31. Fife, *Reforming the Electoral Process in America*, 128–33.

32. Secretary of State, State of North Dakota, "North Dakota ... The Only State without Voter Registration," https://vip.sos.nd.gov/pdfs/Portals/ votereg.pdf (accessed October 18, 2012).

33. Fife, *Reforming the Electoral Process in America*, 129.

34. Fife, *Reforming the Electoral Process in America*, 129.

35. Fife, *Reforming the Electoral Process in America*, 39–42.

36. Fife, *Reforming the Electoral Process in America*, 39–42.

37. Fife, *Reforming the Electoral Process in America*, 42.

38. See Justice David Souter's dissent in *Crawford v. Marion County Election Board*, 128 S.Ct. 1610 (2008).

39. Fife, *Reforming the Electoral Process in America*, 131.

40. William E. Hudson, *American Democracy in Peril: Eight Challenges to America's Future*, 7th ed. (Washington, DC: CQ Press, 2013).

41. Hudson, *American Democracy in Peril*, 133.

42. George Washington University, "Amitai Etzioni," http://elliott.gwu .edu/faculty/etzioni.cfm (accessed October 22, 2012).

43. Amitai Etzioni, "Communitarianism," in *Encyclopedia of Community: From the Village to the Virtual World*, ed. Karen Christensen and David Levinson (Thousand Oaks, CA: Sage, 2003), 224.

44. Hudson, *American Democracy in Peril*, 133–34.

45. Using Indiana as an illustration, during the 2012–2013 fiscal year, 46.8 percent of general fund appropriations were allocated to K–12 education and 12.1 percent to higher education. Thus, 58.9 percent of the general fund was allocated to education at all levels. See State of Indiana, "List of Appropriations," http://www.in.gov/sba/files/ap_2011_0_x.pdf (accessed October 23, 2012).

46. U.S. Department of Education, "Fiscal Year 2013 Budget," http:// www2.ed.gov/about/overview/budget/budget13/summary/13summary .pdf (accessed October 23, 2012).

47. National Priorities Project, "President Obama's Fiscal Year 2013 Budget," http://nationalpriorities.org/analysis/2012/presidents-budget -fy2013 (accessed October 24, 2012).

48. The SIPRI definition of military expenditure includes all current and capital expenditures for the armed forces, including peacekeeping forces, defense ministries, and other government agencies engaged in defense projects; paramilitary forces when judged to be trained, equipped, and available for military operations; and military space activities. Military expenditures include personnel, operations and maintenance, procurement, military research and development, military construction, and military aid. Excluded military expenditures include civil defense, benefits for veterans, demobilization, conversion of arms production facilities, and destruction of weapons. See SIPRI, "The SIPRI Definition of Military Expenditure," http://www .sipri.org/research/armaments/milex/resultoutput/sources_methods/ definitions (accessed October 24, 2012).

49. SIPRI, "The 15 Countries with the Highest Military Expenditure in 2011," http://www.sipri.org/research/armaments/milex/resultoutput/ milex_15/the-15-countries-with-the-highest-military-expenditure-in-2011 -table/view (accessed October 24, 2012).

50. American Presidency Project, "William J. Clinton: Address before a Joint Session of the Congress on the State of the Union, January 19, 1999," http://www.presidency.ucsb.edu/ws/index.php?pid=57577 (accessed October 24, 2012).

51. Center for Education Policy, Applied Research and Evaluation, University of Southern Maine, "Extended School Year Facts," http://www2 .umaine.edu/mepri/sites/default/files/Extended_%20Facts.pdf (accessed October 24, 2012).

52. *Columbus Dispatch*, "Strickland Wants Major Education Reform: More State Funds, Longer School Year—But No New Taxes," http://www .dispatch.com/content/stories/local/2009/01/28/astateofthestateap.html (accessed October 26, 2012).

53. Center for Education Policy, Applied Research and Evaluation, University of Southern Maine, "Extended School Year Facts."

54. NBC News, "Obama: Money without Reform Won't Fix School System," http://today.msnbc.msn.com/id/39378576/ns/today-parenting _and_family/t/obama-money-without-reform-wont-fix-school-system (accessed October 29, 2012).

55. *New York Times*, "To Increase Learning Time, Some Schools Add Days to Academic Year," http://www.nytimes.com/2012/08/06/education/ some-schools-adopting-longer-years-to-improve-learning.html?pagewanted =all&_r=0 (accessed October 29, 2012).

56. U.S. Secretary of the Interior, *Report of the Secretary of the Interior; Being Part of the Message and Documents Communicated to the Two Houses of Congress at the Beginning of the Second Session of the Fifty-Second Congress, in Five Volumes*, vol. 5—in two parts (pt. 2) (Washington, DC: Government Printing Office, 1895). William T. Harris was commissioner of education from 1889 to 1906.

The Bureau of Education was housed in the Department of the Interior from 1869 to 1930, and that is why the report was issued by the secretary of the interior. For more history on the Bureau of Education, see U.S. National Archives and Records Administration, "Records of the Office of Education," http://www.archives.gov/research/guide-fed-records/groups/012.html (accessed October 30, 2012).

57. U.S. Secretary of Interior, *Report of the Secretary of the Interior*, 665.

58. National Education Commission on Time and Learning, *Prisoners of Time: What We Know and What We Need to Know* (Washington, DC: Government Printing Office, 1994); Dave E. Marcotte and Benjamin Hansen, "Time for School?," *Education Next* 10, no. 1 (2010), http://educationnext .org/time-for-school (accessed October 29, 2012).

59. Michael Colasanti, "Minimum Number of Instructional Minutes/ Hours in a High School Day," http://www.ncsl.org/documents/educ/ ECSMinInstructionDays2007.pdf (accessed October 24, 2012).

60. Joy Elmer Morgan, *Horace Mann: His Ideas and Ideals* (Washington, DC: National Home Library Foundation, 1936), vii.

61. Joy Elmer Morgan, *Horace Mann at Antioch* (Washington, DC: National Education Association, 1938), 2.

Bibliography

ABC News. July 3, 2009. Duncan Promotes Charter School Debate. Accessed August 20, 2012, from http://abcnews.go.com/Politics/story?id =7977326&page=1.

Alterman, Eric, and Mark Green. 2004. *The Book on Bush: How George W. (Mis) Leads America*. New York: Viking.

American Historical Association. 1906. Papers of Dr. James McHenry on the Federal Convention of 1787. *American Historical Review* 11, no. 3: 595–624.

American Presidency Project. 2011. Election of 1840. Accessed June 28, 2011, from http://www.presidency.ucsb.edu/showelection.php?year=1840.

American Presidency Project. 2012. John F. Kennedy: Inaugural Address, January 20, 1961. Accessed August 22, 2012, from http://www .presidency.ucsb.edu/ws/index.php?pid=8032.

American Presidency Project. 2012. Theodore Roosevelt: Fifth Annual Message, December 5, 1905. Accessed August 4, 2012, from http://www .presidency.ucsb.edu/ws/index.php?pid=29546.

American Presidency Project. 2012. Theodore Roosevelt: Seventh Annual Message, December 3, 1907. Accessed August 4, 2012, from http:// www.presidency.ucsb.edu/ws/index.php?pid=29548.

American Presidency Project. 2012. Whig Party Platform of 1844. Accessed March 5, 2012, from http://www.presidency.ucsb.edu/ws/?pid=25852.

American Presidency Project. 2012. Whig Party Platform of 1848. Accessed March 5, 2012, from http://www.presidency.ucsb.edu/ws/?pid=25855.

American Presidency Project. 2012. Whig Party Platform of 1852. Accessed March 5, 2012, from http://www.presidency.ucsb.edu/ws/?pid=25856.

American Presidency Project. 2012. Whig Party Platform of 1856. Accessed March 5, 2012, from http://www.presidency.ucsb.edu/ws/?pid=25857.

American Presidency Project. 2012. William J. Clinton: Address before a Joint Session of the Congress on the State of the Union, January 19, 1999. Accessed October 24, 2012, from http://www.presidency.ucsb.edu/ws/index.php?pid=57577.

American Rhetoric. 2012. *Hubert Humphrey: Democratic National Convention Address, July 14, 1948.* Accessed January 9, 2012, from http://www.americanrhetoric.com/speeches/huberthumphey1948dnc.html.

American Rhetoric. 2012. *Ronald Reagan: Farewell Address to the Nation, January 11, 1989.* Accessed February 6, 2012, from http://www.americanrhetoric.com/speeches/ronaldreaganfarewelladdress.html.

American Rhetoric. 2012. *Ted Kennedy: 1980 Democratic National Convention Address, August 12, 1980.* Accessed June 6, 2012, from http://www.americanrhetoric.com/speeches/tedkennedy1980dnc.htm.

American Tradition Partnership, Inc. v. Bullock, 567 U.S. ___ (2012).

Avalon Project: Documents in Law, History and Diplomacy. 2011. Northwest Ordinance: July 13, 1787. Accessed March 25, 2011, from http://avalon.law.yale.edu/18th_century/nworder.asp.

Avalon Project: Documents in Law, History and Diplomacy. 2012. The Alien Act: An Act Respecting Alien Enemies: July 6, 1798. Accessed February 24, 2012, from http://avalon.law.yale.edu?18th_century/alien.asp.

Avalon Project: Documents in Law, History and Diplomacy. 2012. The Federalist Papers: No. 10, November 23, 1787. Accessed July 30, 2012, from http://avalon.law.yale.edu/18th_century/fed10.asp.

Avalon Project: Documents in Law, History and Diplomacy. 2012. The Federalist Papers: No. 46, January 29, 1788. Accessed February 21, 2012, from http://avalon.law.yale.edu/18th_century/fed46.asp.

Avalon Project: Documents in Law, History and Diplomacy. 2012. Kentucky Resolution—Alien and Sedition Acts: December 3, 1799. Accessed February 24, 2012, from http://avalon.law.yale.edu/18th_century/kenres.asp.

Avalon Project: Documents in Law, History and Diplomacy. 2012. The Sedition Act: An Act in Addition to the Act, Entitled "An Act for the Punishment of Certain Crimes Against the United States": July 14, 1798. Accessed February 24, 2012, from http://avalon.law.yale.edu/18th_century.sedact.asp.

Avalon Project: Documents in Law, History and Diplomacy. 2012. Virginia Resolution—Alien and Sedition Acts: December 24, 1798. Accessed February 24, 2012, from http://avalon.law.yale.edu/18th_century/virres.asp.

Avalon Project: Documents in Law, History and Diplomacy. 2012. Washington's Farewell Address: 1796. Accessed February 22, 2012, from http://avalon.law.yale.edu/18th_century.washing.asp.

Bailey, Stephen K., and Edith K. Mosher. 1968. *ESEA: The Office of Education Administers a Law.* Syracuse, NY: Syracuse University Press.

Ball State University. 2012. Center for Middletown Studies. Accessed March 26, 2012, from http://cms.bsu.edu/Academics/Centersand Institutes/Middletown.aspx.

Bartlett, Bruce. 2006. *Impostor: How George W. Bush Bankrupted America and Betrayed the Reagan Legacy.* New York: Doubleday.

Baugh, Joyce A. 2011. *The Detroit School Busing Case: Milliken v. Bradley and the Controversy over Desegregation.* Lawrence: University Press of Kansas.

Beer, Samuel H. 1978. Federalism, Nationalism, and Democracy in America. *American Political Science Review* 72, no. 1: 9–21.

Beer, Samuel H. 1993. *To Make a Nation: The Rediscovery of American Federalism.* Cambridge, MA: The Belknap Press of Harvard University Press.

Behnegar, Nasser. 2003. *Leo Strauss, Max Weber, and the Scientific Study of Politics.* Chicago: University of Chicago Press.

Bellah, Robert N., Richard Madsen, William M. Sullivan, Ann Swidler, and Steven M. Tipton. 1985. *Habits of the Heart: Individualism and Commitment in American Life.* Berkeley: University of California Press.

Berger, Raoul. 1987. *Federalism: The Founders' Design.* Norman: University of Oklahoma Press.

Biden, Joseph R. 1989. The Constitution, the Senate, and the Court. *Wake Forest Law Review* 24: 951–58.

Board of Education of Oklahoma City v. Dowell, 498 U.S. 237 (1991).

Bradwell v. Illinois, 83 U.S. 130 (1873).

Breyer, Stephen. 2005. *Active Liberty: Interpreting Our Democratic Constitution.* New York: Alfred A. Knopf.

Broome, Edwin C. 1929. *Report of the Committee on Propaganda in the Schools.* Washington, DC: National Education Association.

Brown v. Board of Education of Topeka, Kansas 347 U.S. 483 (1954).

Brown v. Board of Education of Topeka, Kansas 349 U.S. 294 (1955).

Buckley v. Valeo, 424 U.S. 1 (1976).

Bullough, Robert V. 1988. *The Forgotten Dream of American Public Education.* Ames: Iowa State University Press.

Burger, Warren E. 1988. "A Republic, If You Can Keep It": A Bicentennial Commentary. *Presidential Studies Quarterly* 18, no. 3: 467–73.

Burnham, Walter Dean. 1986. Those High Nineteenth-Century American Voting Turnouts: Fact or Fiction? *Journal of Interdisciplinary History* 16, no. 4: 613–44.

Bush, George W. 1999. *A Charge to Keep.* New York: William Morrow.

Bush v. Gore, 531 U.S. 98 (2000).

Bushaw, William J., and Shane J. Lopez. 2010. A Time for Change: The 42nd Annual Phi Delta Kappa/Gallup Poll of the Public's Attitudes toward the Public Schools. *Phi Delta Kappan* 92, no. 1: 9–26.

Butterfield, L. H. 1951. *Letters of Benjamin Rush, Volume I: 1761–1792.* Princeton, NJ: Princeton University Press.

C-SPAN. 2012. The Alexis de Tocqueville Tour: Exploring Democracy in America, May 9, 1997–February 20, 1998. Accessed July 29, 2012, from http://www.tocqueville.org.

C-SPAN. 2012. C-SPAN 2009 Historians Presidential Leadership Survey. Accessed July 10, 2012, from http://legacy.c-span.org/Presidential Survey/presidential-leadership-survey.aspx.

C-SPAN Video Library. 2012. Education Bill Signing Ceremony, January 8, 2002. Accessed March 14, 2002, from http://www.c-spanvideo.org/program/168090-1.

Campbell, Jodi. 2000. Benjamin Rush and Women's Education: A Revolutionary's Disappointment, A Nation's Achievement. *John & Mary's Journal* 13. Accessed March 9, 2011, from http://chronicles.dickinson.edu/johnandmary/JMJVolume13/campbell.htm.

Capaldi, Nicholas. 2004. The Ethical Foundations of Free Market Societies. *Journal of Private Enterprise* 20, no. 1: 30–54.

Cato Institute. June 23, 1995. Public Schools: Make Them Private (Briefing Paper No. 23). Accessed September 6, 2012, from http://cato.org/pubs/briefs/bp-023.html.

Center for Child and Family Policy, Duke University. 2012. A Brief History of the United States Department of Education: 1979–2002. Accessed August 19, 2012, from http://www.childandfamilypolicy.duke.edu/pdfs/pubpres/BriefHistoryofUS_DOE.pdf.

Center on Education Policy. 1999. A Brief History of the Federal Role in Education: Why It Began and Why It's Still Needed. Washington, DC: Center on Education Policy (ERIC Document ED 438335).

Center on Education Policy. 2007. Why We Still Need Public Schools: Public Education for the Common Good. Accessed August 27, 2012, from http://www.cep-dc.org/publications/index.cfm?selectedYear=2007.

Center for Education Policy, University of Southern Maine. 2009. Extended School Year Facts. Accessed October 24, 2012, from http://www2.umaine.edu/mepri/sites/default/files/Extended_%20Facts.pdf.

Center for Education Reform. 2012. Choice and Charter Schools: Facts. Accessed May 15, 2012, from http://www.edreform.com/issues/choice-charter-schools/facts.

Center for Education Reform. 2012. Choice and Charter Schools: Just the FAQS. Accessed May 15, 2012, from http://www.edreform.com/2012/03/15/just-the-faqs-charter-schools.

Center for Education Reform. 2012. School Choice Programs across the Nation. Accessed May 15, 2012, from http://www.edreform.com/in-the-states/explore-choice-programs.

Center for Research on Education Outcomes, Stanford University. June 2009. Multiple Choice: Charter School Performance in 16 States. Accessed May 20, 2012, from http://credo.stanford.edu.

Centers for Disease Control and Prevention. 2011. Data and Statistics: Obesity Rates among All Children in the United States. Accessed August 14, 2011, from http://www.cdc.gov/obesity/childhood/data.html.

Chernow, Ron. 1998. *Titan: The Life of John D. Rockefeller, Sr.* New York: Random House.

Church & State. November 1997. Catholic Official Attacks Education Secretary over School Vouchers. 50, no. 10: 16–17.

Citizens United v. Federal Election Commission, 550 U.S. 50 (2010).

Claremont Institute for the Study of Statesmanship and Political Philosophy. 2012. William J. Bennett. Accessed August 17, 2012, from http://www.claremont.org/scholars/id.37/scholar.asp.

Colasanti, Michael. 2007. Minimum Number of Instructional Minutes/Hours in a High School Day. Accessed October 24, 2012, from http://www.ncsl.org/documents/educ/ECSMinInstructiondays2007.pdf.

Collier, Christopher, and James Lincoln Collier. 2007. *Decision in Philadelphia: The Constitutional Convention of 1787.* New York: Ballantine.

Collins, Robert M. 2007. *Transforming America: Politics and Culture in the Reagan Years.* New York: Columbia University Press.

Columbus Dispatch. January 28, 2009. Strickland Wants More Education Reform: More State Funds, Longer School Year—But No New Taxes. Accessed October 26, 2012, from http://www.dispatch.com/content/stories/local/2009/01/28/astateofthestateap.html.

Conlan, Timothy. 1998. *From New Federalism to Devolution: Twenty-Five Years of Intergovernmental Reform.* Washington, DC: Brookings Institution Press.

Conlan, Tim, and John Dinan. 2007. Federalism, the Bush Administration, and the Transformation of American Conservatism. *Publius: The Journal of Federalism* 37, no. 3: 279–303.

Cooke, Jacob E., ed. 1961. *The Federalist.* Middletown, CT: Wesleyan University Press.

Cornell University Library. 2011. The United States Democratic Review. Accessed September 21, 2011, from http://ebooks.library.cornell.edu/u/usde/index.html.

Corrado, Anthony, Thomas E. Mann, Daniel R. Ortiz, and Trevor Potter. 2005. *The New Campaign Finance Sourcebook.* Washington, DC: Brookings Institution Press.

Corwin, Edward S. 1934. *The Twilight of the Supreme Court: A History of Our Constitutional Theory.* New Haven, CT: Yale University Press.

Corwin, Edward S. 1950. The Passing of Dual Federalism. *Virginia Law Review* 36: 1–24.

Crawford v. Marion County Election Board, 128 S.Ct. 1610 (2008).

Cremin, Lawrence A., ed. 1957. *The Republic and the School: Horace Mann on the Education of Free Men*. New York: Teachers College Press.

Culver, Raymond B. 1929. *Horace Mann and Religion in the Massachusetts Public Schools*. New Haven, CT: Yale University Press.

Dahl, Robert A. 1961. *Who Governs? Democracy and Power in an American City*. New Haven, CT: Yale University Press.

Dartmouth College v. Woodward, 17 U.S. 518 (1819).

Dave Leip's Atlas of U.S. Presidential Elections. 2012. 1836 Presidential General Election Results. Accessed March 5, 2012, from http://uselectionatlas.org/RESULTS.

Dave Leip's Atlas of U.S. Presidential Elections. 2012. 1840 Presidential General Election Results. Accessed March 5, 2012, from http://uselectionatlas.org/RESULTS.

Dave Leip's Atlas of U.S. Presidential Elections. 2012. 1844 Presidential General Election Results. Accessed March 5, 2012, from http://uselectionatlas.org/RESULTS.

Dave Leip's Atlas of U.S. Presidential Elections. 2012. 1848 Presidential General Election Results. Accessed March 5, 2012, from http://uselectionatlas.org/RESULTS.

Dave Leip's Atlas of U.S. Presidential Elections. 2012. 1852 Presidential General Election Results. Accessed March 5, 2012, from http://uselectionatlas.org/RESULTS.

Dave Leip's Atlas of U.S. Presidential Elections. 2012. 1856 Presidential General Election Results. Accessed March 5, 2012, from http://uselectionatlas.org/RESULTS.

Dave Leip's Atlas of U.S. Presidential Elections. 2012. 1964 Presidential General Election Results. Accessed January 9, 2012, from http://uselectionatlas.org/RESULTS.

Dave Leip's Atlas of U.S. Presidential Elections. 2012. 1980 Presidential General Election Results. Accessed January 24, 2012, from http://uselectionatlas.org/RESULTS.

Dave Leip's Atlas of U.S. Presidential Elections. 2012. 1984 Presidential General Election Results. Accessed January 24, 2012, from http://uselectionatlas.org/RESULTS.

Dave Leip's Atlas of U.S. Presidential Elections. 2012. 1988 Presidential General Election Results. Accessed February 6, 2012, from http://uselectionatlas.org/RESULTS.

Dave Leip's Atlas of U.S. Presidential Elections. 2012. 1992 Presidential General Election Results. Accessed February 6, 2012, from http://uselectionatlas.org/RESULTS.

Dave Leip's Atlas of U.S. Presidential Elections. 2012. 1996 Presidential General Election Results. Accessed February 6, 2012, from http://uselectionatlas.org/RESULTS.

Dave Leip's Atlas of U.S. Presidential Elections. 2012. 2000 Presidential General Election Results. Accessed February 6, 2012, from http://uselectionatlas.org/RESULTS.

Dave Leip's Atlas of U.S. Presidential Elections. 2012. 2004 Presidential General Election Results. Accessed February 6, 2012, from http://uselectionatlas.org/RESULTS.

Dean, John W. 2004. *Worse Than Watergate: The Secret Presidency of George W. Bush*. New York: Little, Brown.

Dean, John W. 2006. *Conservatives without Conscience*. New York: Viking.

Delli Carpini, Michael X. 2005. An Overview of the State of Citizens' Knowledge About Politics. Annenberg School for Communication Departmental Papers, University of Pennsylvania. Accessed July 9, 2012, from http://repository.upenn.edu/asc_papers/53.

Derthick, Martha. 1974. *Between State and Nation: Regional Organizations of the United States*. Washington, DC: Brookings Institution.

Dollars & Sense: Real World Economics. 1998. Charter Schools Expand: Will They Encourage Public School Reform? Accessed August 19, 2012, from http://www.dollarsandsense.org/archives/1998/0398rofes.html.

Downs, Robert B. 1974. *Horace Mann: Champion of Public Schools*. New York: Twayne.

Drake, Frederick D., and Lynn R. Nelson, eds. 1999. *States' Rights and American Federalism: A Documentary History*. Westport, CT: Greenwood Press.

Dray, Philip. 2005. *Stealing God's Thunder: Benjamin Franklin's Lightning Rod and the Invention of America*. New York: Random House.

Dredd Scott v. Sandford, 60 U.S. 393 (1857).

Drury, Shadia B. 1997. *Leo Strauss and the American Right*. New York: St. Martin's Press.

Easton, David. 1953. *The Political System: An Inquiry into the State of Political Science*. New York: Alfred A. Knopf.

Easton, David. 1957. An Approach to the Analysis of Political Systems. *World Politics* 9, no. 3: 383–400.

Easton, David. 1965. *A Framework for Political Analysis*. Englewood Cliffs, NJ: Prentice Hall.

Education Week. August 11, 2011. Vouchers. Accessed March 15, 2012, from http://www.edweek.org/ew/issues/vouchers.

Education Week. September 19, 2011. No Child Left Behind. Accessed March 14, 2012, from http://www.edweek.org/ew/issues/no-child-left-behind.

Education Week. June 19, 2012. Duncan: Administration's Position Hasn't Changed on D.C. Vouchers. Accessed August 20, 2012, from http://blogs.edweek.org/edweek/campaign-k-12/2012/06/duncan_administrations_positio.html.

Eidenberg, Eugene, and Roy D. Morey. 1969. *An Act of Congress: The Legislative Process and the Making of Education Policy*. New York: Norton.

Elazar, Daniel J. 1962. *The American Partnership: Intergovernmental Co-operation in the Nineteenth-Century United States.* Chicago: University of Chicago Press.

Elazar, Daniel J., ed. 1969. *The Politics of American Federalism.* Lexington, MA: D. C. Heath.

Etzioni, Amitai. 2003. Communitarianism. In *Encyclopedia of Community: From the Village to the Virtual World,* edited by Karen Christensen and David Levinson. Thousand Oaks, CA: Sage, 224–28.

Evans, Thomas W. 2006. *The Education of Ronald Reagan: The General Electric Years and the Untold Story of His Conversion to Conservatism.* New York: Columbia University Press.

Everson v. Board of Education of Ewing, 330 U.S. 1 (1947).

Famous Poetry Online. 2012. *Ulysses*—A Poem by Alfred Lord Tennyson. Accessed June 22, 2012, from http://www.poetry-online.org/tennyson_ulysses.htm.

Farber, David R. 2010. *The Rise and Fall of Modern Conservatism: A Short History.* Princeton, NJ: Princeton University Press.

Farrand, Max, ed. 1911. *The Records of the Federal Convention of 1787.* 3 vols. New Haven, CT: Yale University Press.

Farrand, Max. 1921. *The Fathers of the Constitution: A Chronicle of the Establishment of the Union.* New Haven, CT: Yale University Press.

Federal Election Commission. 2012. Contribution Limits for 2011–2012. Accessed August 6, 2012, from http://www.fec.gov/info/contriblimits1112.pdf.

Fife, Brian L. 1996. The Supreme Court and School Desegregation since 1896. *Equity and Excellence in Education* 29, no. 2: 46–55.

Fife, Brian L. 1997. *School Desegregation in the Twenty-First Century: The Focus Must Change.* Lewiston, NY: Edwin Mellen Press.

Fife, Brian L. 2004. The Supreme Court and the Politics of Vouchers. *International Journal of Educational Reform* 13, no. 1: 74–83.

Fife, Brian L. 2008. The Anatomy and Ideology of a Charter. ERIC Document ED501289.

Fife, Brian L. 2010. *Reforming the Electoral Process in America: Toward More Democracy in the 21st Century.* Santa Barbara, CA: ABC-CLIO.

Fife, Brian L. 2012. Federalism, Education, and Citizenship in an Era of Democratic Deliberation. In *The Hope for Audacity: From Cynicism to Hope in Educational Leadership and Policy,* edited by Stella C. Batagiannis, Barry Kanpol, and Anna V. Wilson. New York: Peter Lang, 115–39.

Fife, Brian L., and G. M. Miller. 2002. *Political Culture and Voting Systems in the United States: An Examination of the 2000 Presidential Election.* Westport, CT: Praeger.

Fisanick, Christina, ed. 2008. *At Issue: Has No Child Left Behind Been Good for Education?* Detroit: Greenhaven Press.

Fisher, Gordon M. The Development and History of the U.S. Poverty Thresholds—A Brief Overview. Accessed April 12, 2012, from http://aspe.hhs.gov/poverty/papers/hptgssiv.htm.

Fox, Richard Wrightman. 1983. Epitaph for Middletown: Robert S. Lynd and the Analysis of Consumer Culture. In *The Culture of Consumption: Critical Essays in American History, 1880–1980*, edited by Richard Wrightman Fox and T. J. Jackson Lears. New York: Pantheon, 101–41.

Fox, Richard Wrightman, and T. J. Jackson Lears, eds. 1983. *The Culture of Consumption: Critical Essays in American History, 1880–1980*. New York: Pantheon.

Freeman v. Pitts, 503 U.S. 467 (1992).

Friedman Foundation for Educational Choice. 2012. Indiana Gov. Mitch Daniels Signs Historic Voucher Bill into Law. Accessed May 22, 2012, from http://www.edchoice.org/Newsroom/News/Indiana-Gov—Mitch-Daniels-Signs-Historic-Voucher-Bill-into-Law.aspx.

Friedman Foundation for Educational Choice. 2012. Milton Friedman's Bio. Accessed January 16, 2012, from http://www.edchoice.org/The-Friedmans/Milton-Friedman-s-Bio.aspx.

Friedman Foundation for Educational Choice. 2012. Types of School Choice. Accessed May 24, 2012, from http://www.edchoice.org/School-Choice/Types-of-School-Choice.aspx.

Friedman, Milton. 1953. *Essays in Positive Economics*. Chicago: University of Chicago Press.

Friedman, Milton. 1962. *Capitalism and Freedom*. Chicago: University of Chicago Press.

Friedman, Milton, and Rose Friedman. 1973. *Free to Choose: A Personal Statement*. New York: Harcourt Brace Jovanovich.

Gallup Poll. October 21, 2003. How Many Americans Know U.S. History? Part I. Accessed July 10, 2012, from http://www.gallup.com/poll/9526/how-many-americans-know-us-history-part.aspx.

Gallup Poll. September 26, 2011. Americans Express Historic Negativity toward U.S. Government. Accessed June 25, 2012, from http://www.gallup.com/poll/149678/Americans-Express-Historic-Negativity-Toward-Government.aspx.

Gallup Poll. 2012. Presidential Approval Ratings—Gallup Historical Statistics and Trends. Accessed February 7, 2012, from http://www.gallup.com/poll/116677/presidential-approval-ratings-gallup-historical-statistics-trends.aspx.

Galston, William A. 2001. Political Knowledge, Political Engagement, and Civic Education. *Annual Review of Political Science* 4, no. 1: 217–34.

Garrison, Mark J. 2009. *A Measure of Failure: The Political Origins of Standardized Testing*. Albany: State University of New York Press.

Garvey, Ellen Gruber. 1996. *The Adman in the Parlor: Magazines and the Gendering of Consumer Culture, 1880s to 1910s*. New York: Oxford University Press.

Gawthrop, Louis C. 1998. *Public Service and Democracy: Ethical Imperatives for the 21st Century*. New York: Chatham House.

George Washington University. 2012. Amitai Etzioni. Accessed October 22, 2012, from http://elliott.gwu.edu/faculty/etzioni.cfm.

Giroux, Henry A. 1999. *The Mouse That Roared: Disney and the End of Innocence*. Lanham, MD: Rowman & Littlefield.

Giroux, Henry A. 2000. *Stealing Innocence: Corporate Culture's War on Children*. New York: Palgrave.

Glick, Wendell, ed. 1973. *The Writings of Henry D. Thoreau: Reform Papers*. Princeton, NJ: Princeton University Press.

Goldwater, Barry. 1960. *The Conscience of a Conservative*. New York: Hillman Books.

Goldwin, Robert A., ed. 1963. *A Nation of States: Essays on the American Federal System*. Chicago: Rand McNally.

Gore, Al. 1993. *Creating a Government That Works Better and Costs Less: Report of the National Performance Review*. Washington, DC: Government Printing Office.

Grant, Jane A. 2008. *The New American Social Compact: Rights and Responsibilities in the 21st Century*. Lanham, MD: Lexington Books.

Green v. County School Board of New Kent County, 391 U.S. 430 (1968).

Greenwood, David A. 2010. Chocolate, Place, and a Pedagogy of Consumer Privilege. In *Critical Pedagogies of Consumption: Living and Learning in the Shadow of the "Shopocalypse,"* edited by Jennifer A. Sandlin and Peter McLaren. New York: Routledge, 193–200.

Grodzins, Morton. 1960. The Federal System. In U.S. President's Commission on National Goals, *Goals for Americans*. New York: Prentice Hall, 265–82.

Grodzins, Morton. 1963. Centralization and Decentralization in the American Federal System. In *A Nation of States: Essays on the American Federal System*, edited by Robert A. Goldwin. Chicago: Rand McNally, 1–23.

Groen, Mark. 2008. The Whig Party and the Rise of Common Schools, 1837–1854. *American Educational History Journal* 35, no. 2: 251–60.

Hall, G. Stanley. 1911. *Educational Problems*. 2 vols. New York: D. Appleton and Company.

Hanna, Julia. 2005. The Elementary and Secondary Education Act: 40 Years Later. Accessed March 9, 2012, from http://www.gse.harvard.edu/news_events/features/2005/08/esea0819.html.

HAPLR Index. 2011. Hennen's American Public Library Ratings. Accessed June 26, 2011, from http://www.haplr-index.com/haplr100.htm.

Harty, Sheila. 1979. *Hucksters in the Classroom: A Review of Industry Propaganda in Schools*. Washington, DC: Center for Study of Responsive Law.

Hayek, Friedrich A. 1944. *The Road to Serfdom*. Chicago: University of Chicago Press.

Hayek, Friedrich A. 1960. *The Constitution of Liberty.* Chicago: University of Chicago Press.

Hayes, William. 2006. *Horace Mann's Vision of the Public Schools: Is It Still Relevant?* Lanham, MD: Rowman & Littlefield Education.

Hess, Frederick M., and Chester E. Finn Jr., eds. 2004. *Leaving No Child Behind? Options for Kids in Failing Schools.* New York: Palgrave Macmillan.

Hochschild, Jennifer L. 1984. *The New American Dilemma: Liberal Democracy and School Desegregation.* New Haven, CT: Yale University Press.

Hoechsmann, Michael. 2010. Rootlessness, Reenchantment, and Educating Desire: A Brief History of the Pedagogy of Consumption. In *Critical Pedagogies of Consumption: Living and Learning in the Shadow of the "Shopocalypse,"* edited by Jennifer A. Sandlin and Peter McLaren. New York: Routledge, 23–35.

Holmes, Oliver Wendell. 1897. The Path of the Law. *Harvard Law Review* 10, no. 8: 457–78.

Holt, Michael F. 1999. *The Rise and Fall of the American Whig Party: Jacksonian Politics and the Onset of the Civil War.* New York: Oxford University Press.

Horowitz, Daniel. 1980. Consumption and Its Discontents: Simon N. Patten, Thorstein Veblen, and George Gunton. *Journal of American History* 67, no. 2: 301–17.

Houston Chronicle. February 13, 2007. Paige Pushes School Voucher Program. Accessed August 19, 2012, from http://www.chron.com/news/houston-texas/article/Paige-pushes-school-voucher-program-1795047 .php.

Hoxby, Caroline M. 2006. Do Vouchers and Charters Push Public Schools to Improve? In *Choice and Competition in American Education,* edited by Paul E. Peterson. Lanham, MD: Rowman & Littlefield, 194–205.

Hubbell, George Allen. 1910. *Horace Mann: Educator, Patriot and Reformer: A Study in Leadership.* Philadelphia: Wm. F. Fell Company.

Hudson, William E. 2008. *The Libertarian Illusion: Ideology, Public Policy, and the Assault on The Common Good.* Washington, DC: CQ Press.

Hudson, William E. 2013. *American Democracy in Peril: Eight Challenges to America's Future.* 7th ed. Washington, DC: CQ Press.

Human Events: The National Conservative Weekly. April 16, 2007. Secretary Spellings Wants More Vouchers. 63, no. 13: 1, 6.

Indiana Department of Education. 2012. Indiana's Diploma Requirements. Accessed July 11, 2012, from http://www.doe.in.gov/achievement/curriculum/indianas-diploma-requirements.

Indiana State University Library. 2012. Floyd Family Collection: *McGuffey Readers and Spellers* (Arranged by Brother & Date). Accessed March 20, 2012, from http://library.indstate.edu/about/units/rbsc/floyd/mcguffey.html.

International Association for K–12 Online Learning. 2012. Fast Facts about Online Learning. Accessed May 24, 2012, from http://www.inacol.org.

Jacobson, Lisa. 2004. *Raising Consumers: Children and the American Mass Market in the Early Twentieth Century.* New York: Columbia University Press.

Jeffrey, Julie Roy. 1978. *Education for Children of the Poor: A Study of the Origins and Implementation of the Elementary and Secondary Education Act of 1965.* Columbus: Ohio State University Press.

Kaestle, Carl F. 1983. *Pillars of the Republic: Common Schools and American Society, 1780–1860.* New York: Hill and Wang.

Kallhoff, Angela. 2011. *Why Democracy Needs Public Goods.* Lanham, MD: Rowman & Littlefield.

Kaplan, Esther. 2004. *With God on Their Side: How Christian Fundamentalists Trampled Science, Policy, and Democracy in George W. Bush's White House.* New York: New Press.

Kendall, Willmoore. 1963. *The Conservative Affirmation.* Chicago: Henry Regnery.

Keyes v. School District No. 1, 413 U.S. 189 (1973).

Keynes, John Maynard. 1935. *The General Theory of Employment, Interest, and Money.* New York: Harcourt, Brace & World.

Kluger, Richard. 2004. *Simple Justice: The History of Brown v. Board of Education and Black America's Struggle for Equality.* New York: Vintage Books.

Kozol, Jonathan. 1991. *Savage Inequalities: Children in America's Schools.* New York: Crown.

Kozol, Jonathan. 2005. *The Shame of the Nation: The Restoration of Apartheid Schooling in America.* New York: Crown.

Krugman, Paul. 2007. Who Was Milton Friedman? *New York Review of Books,* February 15, 2007. Accessed January 16, 2012, from http://www.nybooks.com/articles/archives/2007/feb/15/who-was-milton-friedman.

Larson, Edward J. 2007. *A Magnificent Catastrophe: The Tumultuous Election of 1800, America's First Presidential Campaign.* New York: Free Press.

Larson, Edward J., and Michael P. Winship. 2005. *The Constitutional Convention: A Narrative History from the Notes of James Madison.* New York: Modern Library.

Leach, Richard H. 1970. *American Federalism.* New York: Norton.

Library of Congress. 2012. Campaign Finance: Comparative Summary. Accessed August 4, 2012, from http://www.loc.gov/law/help/campaign-finance/comparative-summary.php.

Library of Congress. 2012. Creating the United States: "Monarchy or a Republic?" Accessed July 4, 2012, from http://myloc.gov/Exhibitions/creatingtheus/Constitution/Ratification/ExhibitObjects/Monarchyor Republic.aspx.

Library of Congress. 2012. Jefferson's Letter to the Danbury Baptists, January 1, 1802. Accessed May 23, 2012, from http://www.loc.gov/loc/lcib/9806/danpost.html.

Library of Economics and Liberty. 2011. Friedrich August Hayek (1899–1992). Accessed September 8, 2011, from http://www.econlib.org/library/Enc/bios/Hayek.html.

Library of Economics and Liberty. 2011. John Maynard Keynes (1883–1946). Accessed September 8, 2011, from http://www.econlib.org/library/Enc/bios/Keynes.html.

Library of Economics and Liberty. 2012. Privatization. Accessed September 10, 2012, from http://www.econlib.org/library/Enc/Privatization.html.

License Cases, 46 U.S. 504 (1847).

Lipscomb, Andrew A., and Albert E. Bergh, eds. 1903. *The Writings of Thomas Jefferson*. 20 vols. Washington, DC: Thomas Jefferson Memorial Association.

Livermore, Shaw, Jr. 1962. *The Twilight of Federalism: The Distintegration of the Federalist Party, 1815–1830*. Princeton, NJ: Princeton University Press.

Lockard, Duane. 1969. *American Federalism*. St. Louis, MO: McGraw-Hill.

Lowe, Carl, ed. 1984. *Reaganomics: The New Federalism*. New York: H. W. Wilson.

Lowi, Theodore J. 1969. *The End of Liberalism: Ideology, Policy, and the Crisis of Public Authority*. New York: Norton.

Lynd, Robert S., and Helen M. Lynd. 1929. *Middletown: A Study in Contemporary American Culture*. New York: Harcourt Brace and Company.

Lynd, Robert S., and Helen M. Lynd. 1937. *Middletown in Transition: A Study in Cultural Conflicts*. New York: Harcourt Brace and Company.

Maggs, Gregory E. 2007. A Concise Guide to the Federalist Papers as a Source of the Original Meaning of the United States Constitution. *Boston University Law Review* 87: 801–47.

Maier, Pauline. 2010. *Ratification: The People Debate the Constitution, 1787–1788*. New York: Simon & Schuster.

Mann, Horace. 1891. *The Life and Works of Horace Mann*. 5 vols. Boston: Lee and Shepard.

Manna, Paul. 2006. *School's In: Federalism and the National Education Agenda*. Washington, DC: Georgetown University Press.

Marbury v. Madison, 5 U.S. 137 (1803).

Marcotte, Dave E., and Benjamin Hansen. 2010. Time for School? *Education Next* 10, no. 1. Accessed October 29, 2012, from http://educationnext.org/time-for-school.

Massey, Douglas S., and Robert J. Sampson, eds. 2009. *The Moynihan Report Revisited: Lessons and Reflections after Four Decades*. Special issue of the *Annals of the American Academy of Political and Social Science* 621.

Matt, Susan J. 2003. *Keeping Up with the Joneses: Envy in American Consumer Society, 1890–1930*. Philadelphia: University of Pennsylvania Press.

McConnell v. Federal Election Commission, 540 U.S. 93 (2003).

McCulloch v. Maryland, 17 U.S. 316 (1819).

McGerr, Michael. 2003. *A Fierce Discontent: The Rise and Fall of the Progressive Movement in America, 1870–1920*. New York: Free Press.

McGovern, Charles F. 2006. *Sold American: Consumption and Citizenship, 1890–1945*. Chapel Hill: University of North Carolina Press.

McGuffey, William H. 1879. *McGuffey's First Eclectic Reader*. Rev. ed. Cincinnati: Van Antwerp, Bragg & Co.

McGuffey, William H. 1879. *McGuffey's Second Eclectic Reader*. Rev. ed. Cincinnati: Van Antwerp, Bragg & Co.

McGuffey, William H. 1879. *McGuffey's Third Eclectic Reader*. Rev. ed. Cincinnati: Van Antwerp, Bragg & Co.

McGuffey, William H. 1879. *McGuffey's Fourth Eclectic Reader*. Rev. ed. Cincinnati: Van Antwerp, Bragg & Co.

McGuffey, William H. 1879. *McGuffey's Fifth Eclectic Reader*. Rev. ed. Cincinnati: Van Antwerp, Bragg & Co.

McGuffey, William H. 1879. *McGuffey's Sixth Eclectic Reader*. Rev. ed. Cincinnati: Van Antwerp, Bragg & Co.

McGuinn, Patrick J. 2006. *No Child Left Behind and the Transformation of Federal Education Policy, 1965–2005*. Lawrence: University Press of Kansas.

Meier, Deborah, et al., eds. 2004. *Many Children Left Behind: How the No Child Left Behind Act Is Damaging Our Children and Our Schools*. Boston: Beacon Press.

Meinke, Samantha. 2011. *Milliken v. Bradley*: The Northern Battle for Desegregation. *Michigan Bar Journal*, September, 20–22.

Messerli, Jonathan. 1972. *Horace Mann: A Biography*. New York: Alfred A. Knopf.

Miami University Libraries. 2012. About the William Holmes McGuffey Collection. Accessed March 20, 2012, from http://doyle.lib.muohio.edu/cdm4/about.php?CISOROOT=%2Fmcguffey.

Micklethwait, John, and Adrian Woolridge. 2004. *The Right Nation: Conservative Power in America*. New York: Penguin.

Milliken v. Bradley, 418 U.S. 717 (1974).

Minnich, Harvey C. 1936. *William Holmes McGuffey and His Readers*. New York: American Book Company.

Miron, Gary. 2012. Time to Stop and Rethink Charter Schools. Testimony Prepared for June 1, 2011 Hearing of the House Committee on Education and the Workforce. Accessed May 17, 2012, from http://edworkforce.house.gov/UploadedFiles/06.01.11_miron.pdf.

Missouri v. Jenkins, 515 U.S. 70 (1995).

Molnar, Alex. 1996. *Giving Kids the Business: The Commercialization of America's Schools*. Boulder, CO: Westview Press.

Molnar, Alex. 2006. The Commercial Transformation of Public Education. *Journal of Education Policy*, 21, no. 5: 621–40.

Molnar, Alex, and David R. Garcia. 2007. The Expanding Role of Privatization in Education: Implications for Teacher Education and Development. *Teacher Education Quarterly* 34, no. 2: 11–24.

Morgan, Joy Elmer. 1936. *Horace Mann: His Ideas and Ideals*. Washington, DC: National Home Library Foundation.

Morgan, Joy Elmer. 1938. *Horace Mann at Antioch*. Washington, DC: National Education Association.

Morrison and Foerster, LLP. 2012. Attorney Bio: Shirley M. Hufstedler. Accessed August 17, 2012, from http://www.mofo.com/shirley -hufstedler.

Morse, Suzanne W. 1999. Ward Republics: The Wisest Invention for Self-Government. In *Thomas Jefferson and the Education of a Citizen*, edited by James Gilreath. Hanover, NH: University Press of New England, 264–77.

Mosier, Richard D. 1947. *Making the American Mind: Social and Moral Ideas in the McGuffey Readers*. New York: King's Crown Press.

Mueller v. Allen, 463 U.S. 388 (1983).

Murley, John A., and John E. Alvis, eds. 2002. *Willmoore Kendall: Maverick of American Conservatives*. Lanham, MD: Lexington Books.

Nasaw, David. 2006. *Andrew Carnegie*. New York: Penguin.

National Commission on Excellence in Education. 1983. *A Nation at Risk: The Imperative for Educational Reform*. Washington, DC: Government Printing Office.

National Conference of State Legislatures. 2011. Compulsory Education. Accessed August 21, 2011, from http://www.ncsl.org/IssuesResearch/ Education/CompulsoryEducationOverview/tabid/12943/Default .aspx.

National Conference of State Legislatures. 2012. Publicly Funded School Voucher Programs. Accessed March 15, 2012, from http://www.ncsl .org/issues-research/educ/school-choice-vouchers.aspx.

National Education Association. 2012. Charter Schools. Accessed March 15, 2012, from http://www.nea.org/home/16332.htm.

National Education Commission on Time and Learning. 1994. *Prisoners of Time: What We Know and What We Need to Know*. Washington, DC: Government Printing Office.

National Federation of Independent Business v. Sebelius, 567 U.S. ___ (2012).

NBC News. September 27, 2010. Obama: Money without Reform Won't Fix School System. Accessed October 29, 2012, from http://today.msnbc .msn.com/id/39378576/ns/today-parenting_and_family/t/obama-money -without-reform-wont-fix-school-system.

Newberry v. United States, 256 U.S. 232 (1921).

New York Times. October 20, 1988. Washington Talk/Working Profile: Lauro F. Cavazos; In Search of a National Commitment to Education. Accessed August 19, 2012, from http://nytimes.com/1988/10/20/us/washington

-talk-working-profile-lauro-f-cavazos-search-national-commitment.html ?pagewanted=print&src=pm.

New York Times. December 13, 1990. Cavazos Quits as Education Chief amid Pressure from White House. Accessed August 19, 2012, from http:// www.nytimes.com/1990/12/13/us/cavazos-quits-as-education-chief -amid-pressure-from-white-house.html?pagewanted=all&src=pm.

New York Times. June 24, 1996. Terrel H. Bell, 74, Education Chief in Reagan Years. Accessed August 17, 2012, from http://nytimes.com/1996/06/ 24/us/terrel-h-bell-74-education-chief-in-reagan-years.html.

New York Times. August 18, 2004. Education Secretary Defends Charter Schools. Accessed August 19, 2012, from http://www.nytimes.com/ 2004/08/18/education/18charter.html?pagewanted=print.

New York Times. October 31, 2010. Theodore C. Sorensen, 82, Kennedy Counselor, Dies. Accessed August 20, 2012, from http://www.nytimes.com/ 2010/11/01/us/01sorensen.html?_r=1&pagewanted=all.

New York Times. August 5, 2012. To Increase Learning Time, Some Schools Add Days to Academic Year. Accessed October 29, 2012, from http:// www.nytimes.com/2012/08/06/education/some-schools-adopting -longer-years-to-improve-learning.html?pagewanted=all&_r=0.

Nobel Prizes. 2011. All Nobel Prizes. Accessed September 28, 2011, from http://www.nobelprizes.org/nobel_prizes/lists/all.

Noddings, Nel. 2000. Education as a Public Good. In *Not for Sale: In Defense of Public Goods*, edited by Anatole Anton, Milton Fisk, and Nancy Holm-strom. Boulder, CO: Westview Press, 279–94.

Office of Management and Budget. 2012. Budget of the United States Government, Fiscal Year 2013. Accessed October 23, 2012, from http:// www.whitehouse.gov/omb/budget/Overview.

Ohio History Central. 2012. William H. McGuffey. Accessed March 23, 2012, from http://www.ohiohistorycentral.org/entry.php?rec=263.

Olson, Mancur. 1965. *The Logic of Collective Action: Public Goods and the Theory of Groups.* Cambridge, MA: Harvard University Press.

OnTheIssues.org. 2012. Lamar Alexander on Education. Accessed August 19, 2012, from http://www.ontheissues.org/celeb/Lamar_Alexander _Education.htm.

Orfield, Gary. 2009. *Reviving the Goal of an Integrated Society: A 21st Century Challenge.* Los Angeles: Civil Rights Project/Proyecto Derechos Civiles at UCLA.

Orfield, Gary, Mark D. Bachmeier, David R. James, and Tamela Eide. 1997. Deepening Segregation in American Public Schools. *Southern Changes* 19, no. 2: 11–18.

Orfield, Gary, Susan E. Eaton, and the Harvard Project on School Desegrega-tion. 1996. *Dismantling Desegregation: The Quiet Reversal of Brown v. Board of Education.* New York: New Press.

Orthner, Dennis K. 2007. Public Schools: Building Capacity for Hope and Opportunity. In *Ending Poverty in America: How to Restore the American Dream*, edited by John Edwards, Marion Crain, and Arne L. Kalleberg. New York: New Press, 218–29.

Padover, Saul K., ed. 1965. *The Forging of American Federalism: Selected Writings of James Madison*. New York: Harper & Row.

Parents Involved in Community Schools v. Seattle School District No. 1, 551 U.S. 701 (2007).

Parker, Howard L. 1932. A Plan for Sifting Propaganda in the Schools. *Elementary School Journal* 33, no. 4: 277–82.

Patten, Simon N. 1968. *The New Basis of Civilization*. Edited by Daniel M. Fox. Cambridge, MA: The Belknap Press of Harvard University Press.

Peterson, Bob, and Barbara Miner. 2000. The Color of "Choice." In *Not for Sale: In Defense of Public Goods*, edited by Anatole Anton, Milton Fisk, and Nancy Holmstrom. Boulder, CO: Westview Press, 295–97.

Peterson, Paul E. 2006. The Use of Market Incentives in Education. In *Choice and Competition in American Education*, edited by Paul E. Peterson. Lanham, MD: Rowman & Littlefield, 3–12.

Pew Research Center for the People and the Press. April 11, 2012. What the Public Knows about the Political Parties. Accessed July 9, 2012, from http://www.people-press.org/2012/04/11/what-the-public-knows-about-the-political-parties/?src=iq-quiz.

Plessy v. Ferguson, 163 U.S. 537 (1896).

Progressive National Committee. 1912. *A Contract with the People: Platform of the Progressive Party Adopted at Its First National Convention, Chicago, August 7th, 1912*. New York: Progressive National Committee.

Project Vote. 2012. Election Day Registration. Accessed July 1, 2012, from http://projectvote.org/electon-day-reg.html.

Public Law 85-864. September 2, 1958. National Defense Education Act of 1958. Accessed March 9, 2012, from http://www.constitution.org/uslaw/sal/072_statutes_"at_large.pdf.

Public Law 89-10. April 11, 1965. Elementary and Secondary Education Act of 1965. Accessed March 8, 2012, from http://www.eric.ed.gov/PDFS/ED017539.pdf.

Public Law 89-329. November 8, 1965. Higher Education Act of 1965. Accessed March 9, 2012, from http://ftp.resource.org/gao.gov/89–329/00004C57.pdf.

Public Law 96-88. October 17, 1979. Department of Education Organization Act of 1979. Accessed August 19, 2012, from http://history.nih.gov/research/downloads/PL96–88.pdf.

Public Law 103-227. March 31, 1994. Goals 2000: Educate America Act. Accessed March 8, 2012, from http://www2.ed.gov/legislation/GOALS2000/TheAct/index.html.

Public Law 104-193. August 22, 1996. Personal Responsibility and Work Opportunity Reconciliation Act of 1996. Accessed October 14, 2012, from http://www.gpo.gov/fdsys/pkg/PLAW-104publ193/html/PLAW-104 publ193.htm.

Public Law 107-110. January 8, 2002. No Child Left Behind Act of 2001. Accessed March 8, 2012, from http://www2.ed.gov/policy/elsec/leg/ esea02/107–110.pdf.

Public Law 110-315. August 14, 2008. Higher Education Opportunity Act. Accessed March 9, 2012, from http://www2.ed.gov/policy/highered/ leg/hea08/index.html.

Public Law 111-148. March 23, 2010. Patient Protection and Affordable Care Act. Accessed October 18, 2012, from http://www.gpo.gov/fdsys/pkg/ PLAW-111publ148/pdf/PLAW-111publ148.pdf.

Ravitch, Diane. 2010. *The Death and Life of the Great American School System: How Testing and Choice Are Undermining Education*. New York: Basic Books.

Reagan, Michael D. 1972. *The New Federalism*. New York: Oxford University Press.

redefinED: The New Definition of Public Education. August 13, 2012. Margaret Spellings: Status Quo Benefits if Feds Don't Push Ed Reform, School Choice. Accessed August 19, 2012, from http://www.redefinedonline .org/2012/08/spellings-status-quo-benefits-if-feds-dont-push-ed-reform -more-school-choice.

Richardson, Leon B. 1932. *History of Dartmouth College*. 2 vols. Hanover, NH: Dartmouth College Publications.

Riker, William H. 1964. *Federalism: Origin, Operation, Significance*. Boston: Little, Brown.

Robin, Corey. 2011. *The Reactionary Mind: Conservatism from Edmund Burke to Sarah Palin*. New York: Oxford University Press.

Rockefeller, Nelson A. 1962. *The Future of Federalism*. Cambridge, MA: Harvard University Press.

Rudolph, Frederick. 1962. *The American College and University: A History*. New York: Vintage Books.

Rudolph, Frederick, ed. 1965. *Essays on Education in the Early Republic*. Cambridge, MA: Harvard University Press.

Scalia, Antonin. 1997. *A Matter of Interpretation: Federal Courts and the Law*. Princeton, NJ: Princeton University Press.

Schattschneider, E. E. 1960. *The Semi-Sovereign People: A Realist's View of Democracy in America*. Hinsdale, IL: Dryden Press.

Schlozman, Kay L. 2010. Who Sings in the Heavenly Chorus? The Shape of the Organized Interest System. In *The Oxford Handbook of American Political Parties and Interest Groups*, edited by L. Sandy Maisel and Jeffrey M. Berry. New York: Oxford University Press, 425–50.

School Choice Indiana. 2012. Indiana Choice Scholarship Program. Accessed May 22, 2012, from http://www.schoolchoiceindiana.com/w-content/uploads/2011/05/ProgramSummaries5.11.pdf.

Schor, Juliet B. 1993. *The Overworked American: The Unexpected Decline of Leisure*. New York: Basic Books.

Schor, Juliet B. 1999. *The Overspent American: Upscaling, Downshifting, and the New Consumer*. New York: Harper Perennial.

Schor, Juliet B. 2004. *Born to Buy: The Commercialized Child and the New Consumer Culture*. New York: Scribner.

Secretary of State, State of North Dakota. 2012. North Dakota … The Only State without Voter Registration. Accessed October 18, 2012, from https://vip.sos.nd.gov/pdfs/Portals/votereg.pdf.

Shipler, David K. 2007. Connecting the Dots. In *Ending Poverty in America: How to Restore the American Dream*, edited by John Edwards, Marion Crain, and Arne L. Kalleberg. New York: New Press, 13–22.

Sivulka, Juliann. 2001. *Stronger Than Dirt: A Cultural History of Advertising Personal Hygiene in America, 1875 to 1940*. Amherst, NY: Humanity Books.

Sivulka, Juliann. 2012. *Soap, Sex, and Cigarettes: A Cultural History of American Advertising*. 2nd ed. Boston: Wadsworth, Cengage Learning.

Smith, Adam. 1910. *The Wealth of Nations*. 2 vols. New York: E. P. Dutton.

Smith, Samuel J. 2010. New England Primer. In *Encyclopedia of Educational Reform and Dissent*, vol. 2, edited by Thomas C. Hunt, James C. Carper, Thomas J. Lasley, and C. Daniel Raisch. Thousand Oaks, CA: Sage, 661–62.

Smith, Tanya M., Paul Tafforeau, Donald J. Reid, Rainer Grün, Stephen Eggins, Mohamed Boutakiout, and Jean-Jacques Hublin. 2007. Earliest Evidence of Modern Human Life History in North African Early *Homo Sapiens*. *Proceedings of the National Academy of Sciences* 104, no. 15: 6128–33.

South Caroliniana Library, Books Division. 1829. *Exposition and Protest, Reported by the Special Committee of the House of Representatives, on the Tariff; Dec. 19th, 1828*. Columbia, SC: D. W. Sims. Accessed February 24, 2012, from http://www.teachingushistory.org/lessons/expositionand protest1828.htm.

Spring, Joel. 2003. *Educating the Consumer-Citizen: A History of the Marriage of Schools, Advertising, and Media*. Mahwah, NJ: Lawrence Erlbaum Associates.

Spring, Joel. 2010. Schooling for Consumption. In *Critical Pedagogies of Consumption: Living and Learning in the Shadow of the "Shopocalypse,"* edited by Jennifer A. Sandlin and Peter McLaren. New York: Routledge, 69–82.

Spring, Joel. 2011. *The American School: A Global Context from the Puritans to the Obama Era*. 8th ed. New York: McGraw-Hill.

Standerfer, Leslie. 2006. Before NCLB: The History of ESEA. *Principal Leadership* 6, no. 8: 26–27.

Stanford Encyclopedia of Philosophy. 2011. Leo Strauss. Accessed October 3, 2011, from http://plato.stanford.edu/entries/strauss-leo.

State of Indiana. 2012. List of Appropriations. Accessed October 23, 2012, from http://www.in.gov/sba/files/ap_2011_0_x.pdf.

Stewart, David O. 2007. *The Summer of 1787: The Men Who Invented the Constitution*. New York: Simon & Schuster.

Stiles, T. J. 2009. *The First Tycoon: The Epic Life of Cornelius Vanderbilt*. New York: Alfred A. Knopf.

Stockholm International Peace Research Institute. 2012. The 15 Countries with the Highest Military Expenditure in 2011. Accessed October 24, 2012, from http://www.sipri.org/research/armaments/milex/resultoutput/milex_15/the-15–countries-with-the-highest-military-expenditure-in-2011–table/view.

Stockholm International Peace Research Institute. 2012. The SIPRI Definition of Military Expenditure. Accessed October 24, 2012, from http://www.sipri.org/research/armaments/milex/resultoutput/sources_methods/definitions.

Strasser, Susan. 1989. *Satisfaction Guaranteed: The Making of the American Mass Market*. Washington, DC: Smithsonian Books.

Strauss, Leo. 1957. What Is Political Philosophy? *Journal of Politics* 19, no. 3: 343–68.

Strauss, Leo. 1963. *On Tyranny*. New York: Free Press of Glencoe.

Stuckler, David, Andrea B. Feigl, Sanjay Basu, and Martin McKee. 2010. The Political Economy of Universal Health Coverage. Background Paper for the Global Symposium on Health Systems Research. Accessed October 17, 2012, from http://www.pacifichealthsummit.org/downloads/UHC/the%20political%20economy%20of%20uhc.PDF.

Sunderman, Gail L., ed. 2008. *Holding NCLB Accountable: Achieving Accountability, Equity, and School Reform*. Thousand Oaks, CA: Corwin Press.

Swann v. Charlotte-Mecklenberg Board of Education, 402 U.S. 1 (1971).

Tambo, David, Dwight Hoover, and John D. Hewitt. 1988. *Middletown: An Annotated Bibliography*. New York: Garland.

Taylor, Thomas C. 1981. *The Fundamentals of Austrian Economics*. London: Adam Smith Institute.

Thomas Jefferson's Monticello. 2011. Research and Collections. Accessed September 21, 2011, from http://www.monticello.org/site/research-and-collections.

Tiefer, Charles. 2004. *Veering Right: How the Bush Administration Subverts the Law for Conservative Causes*. Berkeley: University of California Press.

Tocqueville, Alexis de. 2000. *Democracy in America*. Chicago: University of Chicago Press.

Toobin, Jeffrey. 2012. Money Unlimited: How Chief Justice Roberts Orchestrated the Citizens United Decision. *The New Yorker*, May 21, 2012.

Accessed August 7, 2012, from http://www.newyorker.com/reporting/ 2012/05/21/120521fa_fact_toobin.

Tyack, David. 2003. *Seeking Common Ground: Public Schools in a Diverse Society.* Cambridge, MA: Harvard University Press.

United Nations Children's Defense Fund. May 2012. *Measuring Child Poverty: New League Tables of Child Poverty in the World's Rich Countries.* Accessed October 12, 2012, from http://www.unicef.org.uk/Documents/ Publications/RC10-measuring-child-poverty.pdf.

United Nations Educational, Scientific and Cultural Organization, International Institute for Educational Planning. 2002. Education Privatization: Causes, Consequences, and Planning Implications. Accessed September 6, 2012, from http://unesdoc.unesco.org/images/0013/001330/ 133075e.pdf.

U.S. Census Bureau. 2012. Highlights. Accessed April 12, 2012, from http:// www.census.gov/hhes/www/poverty/about/overview/index.html.

U.S. Congress. 2012. *Biographical Directory of the United States Congress, 1774– Present: Barry Morris Goldwater.* Accessed January 9, 2012, from http:// bioguide.congress.gov.

U.S. Congress. 2012. *Biographical Directory of the United States Congress, 1774– Present: Hubert Horatio Humphrey, Jr.* Accessed January 9, 2012, from http://bioguide.congress.gov.

U.S. Congress, Office of Technology Assessment. 1992. *Testing in American Schools: Asking the Right Questions.* Washington, DC: Government Printing Office.

U.S. Department of Education. 2012. ESEA Flexibility. Accessed October 9, 2012, from http://www.ed.gov/esea/flexibility.

U.S. Department of Education. 2012. ESEA Flexibility Requests and Related Documents. Accessed October 9, 2012, from http://www.ed.gov/esea/ flexibility/requests.

U.S. Department of Education. 2012. Fiscal Year 2013 Budget. Accessed October 23, 2012, from http://www2.ed.gov/about/overview/budget/ budget13/summary/13summary.pdf.

U.S. Department of Education. 2012. No Child Left Behind: 10 Facts about K– 12 Education Funding. Accessed March 7, 2012, from http://www2.ed .gov/about/overview/fed/10facts/10facts.pdf.

U.S. Department of Education. 2012. Overview: The Federal Role in Education. Accessed March 7, 2012, from http://www2.ed.gov/about/ overview/fed/role.html?src=ln.

U.S. Department of Education, National Center for Education Statistics. 2011. *The Condition of Education 2011.* Accessed June 7, 2011, from http://nces .ed.gov/pubs2011/2011033.pdf.

U.S. Department of Education, National Center for Education Statistics. 2012. Fast Facts: Homeschooling. Accessed May 24, 2012, from http://nces.ed .gov/fastfacts/display.asp?id=91.

U.S. Department of Health and Human Services. 2013. 2013 HHS Poverty Guidelines. Accessed April 2, 2013, from http://aspe.hhs.gov/poverty/13poverty.cfm.

U.S. Department of Labor, Office of Policy Planning and Research. March 1965. *The Negro Family: The Case for National Action.* Accessed October 12, 2012, from http://www.dol.gov/oasam/programs/history/webid-meynihan.htm.

U.S. Department of Treasury, Bureau of the Public Debt. 2013. The Debt to the Penny and Who Holds It. Accessed April 2, 2013, from http://www.treasurydirect.gov/NP/BPDLogin?application=np.

U.S. Equal Employment Opportunity Commission. 2011. The Equal Pay Act of 1963. Accessed August 22, 2011, from http://www.eeoc.gov/laws/statutes/epa.cfm.

U.S. House of Representatives. 2012. U.S. House of Representatives Roll Call Votes 107th Congress—1st Session (2001). Vote 497 (December 13, 2001). Accessed March 13, 2012, from http://clerk.house.gov/evs/2001/roll497.xml.

U.S. National Archives and Records Administration. 2012. Morrill Act—Public Law 37-108, July 2, 1862. Accessed March 9, 2012, from http://www.ourdocuments.gov/doc.php?doc=33.

U.S. National Archives and Records Administration. 2012. Records of the Office of Education. Accessed October 30, 2012, from http://www.archives.gov/research/guide-fed-records/groups/012.html.

U.S. National Archives and Records Administration. 2012. Remarks in Johnson City, Texas, upon Signing the Elementary and Secondary Education Bill, April 11, 1965. Accessed March 12, 2012, from http://www.lbjlib.utexas.edu/johnson/archives.hom/speeches.hom/650411.asp.

U.S. National Archives and Records Administration. 2012. Servicemen's Readjustment Act Public Law 78-346, June 22, 1944. Accessed March 9, 2012, from http://www.ourdocuments.gov/doc.php?doc=76.

U.S. President's Commission on National Goals. 1960. *Goals for Americans.* New York: Prentice Hall.

U.S. Secretary of the Interior. 1895. *Report of the Secretary of the Interior; Being Part of the Message and Documents Communicated to the Two Houses of Congress at the Beginning of the Second Session of the Fifty-Second Congress in Five Volumes.* Volume 5—in two parts (Part 2). Washington, DC: Government Printing Office.

U.S. Senate. 2012. The Expulsion Case of Truman H. Newberry of Michigan (1922). Accessed August 6, 2012, from http://www.senate.gov/artandhistory/history/common/expulsion_cases/102TrumanNewberry_expulsion.htm.

U.S. Senate. 2012. U.S. Senate Roll Call Votes 107th Congress—1st Session (2001). Vote 371 (December 18, 2001). Accessed March 13, 2012, from

http://www.senate.gov/legislative/LIS/roll_call_lists/roll_call_vote
_cfm.cfm?congress=107&session=1&vote=00371.

United States v. Classic, 313 U.S. 299 (1941).

Urban, Wayne, and Jennings Wagoner Jr. 2000. *American Education: A History.* Boston: McGraw-Hill.

Vail, Henry H. 1911. *A History of the McGuffey Readers.* Cleveland, OH: Burrows Brothers Co.

Verkuil, Paul R. 2007. *Outsourcing Democracy: Why Privatization of Government Functions Threatens Democracy and What We Can Do about It.* New York: Cambridge University Press.

Viguerie, Richard A. 2006. *Conservatives Betrayed: How George W. Bush and Other Big Government Republicans Hijacked the Conservative Cause.* Los Angeles: Bonus Books.

Vinovskis, Maris A. 2009. *From a Nation at Risk to No Child Left Behind: National Education Goals and the Creation of Federal Education Policy.* New York: Teachers College Press.

Waldman, Paul. 2004. *Fraud: The Strategy Behind the Bush Lies and Why the Media Didn't Tell You.* Naperville, IL: Sourcebooks.

Walker, David B. 1981. *Toward a Functioning Federalism.* Cambridge, MA: Winthrop Publishers.

Warfel, Harry. 1936. *Noah Webster: Schoolmaster to America.* New York: Macmillan.

Watts, Steven. 2005. *The People's Tycoon: Henry Ford and the American Century.* New York: Alfred A. Knopf.

Webster, Noah. 1809. *American Spelling Book; Containing, the Rudiments of the English Language for the Use of Schools in the United States.* Hartford, CT: Hudson & Goodwin.

Westminster Assembly. 1797. *The New-England Primer; Much Improved. Containing, a Variety of Easy Lessons, for Attaining the True Reading of English.* Philadelphia: T. Dobson, at the Stone House, No. 41, S. Second Street.

Whig Party Campaign Literature. 1856. *The Great Fraud upon the Public Credulity in the Organization of the Republican Party upon the Ruins of the "Whig Party": An Address to Old-Line Whigs of the Union.* Washington, DC: Printed at the Union Office.

Wilkinson, Gary. 2006. McSchools for McWorld? Mediating Global Pressures with a McDonaldizing Education Policy Response. *Cambridge Journal of Education* 36, no. 1: 81–98.

Will, George F. 1983. *Statecraft as Soulcraft: What Government Does.* New York: Simon & Schuster.

Wilson, Woodrow. 1887. The Study of Administration. *Political Science Quarterly* 2, no. 2: 197–222.

Witters v. Washington Department of Services for the Blind, 474 U.S. 481 (1986).

Wolfson, Adam. 2004. Conservatives and Neoconservatives. *The Public Interest* 154: 32–48.

World Bank. 2012. Gross Domestic Product 2011. Accessed October 11, 2012, from http://databank.worldbank.org/databank/download/GDP.pdf.

Worthington, C. Ford, et al., eds. 1904–1937. *Journals of the Continental Congress, 1774–1789*. 34 vols. Washington, DC: Government Printing Office.

York, J. G. 2008. Neoconservatism and Leo Strauss: The Place of a Liberal Education. *Critical Studies in Education* 49, no. 1: 67–80.

Zelizer, Julian E., ed. 2010. *The Presidency of George W. Bush: A First Historical Assessment*. Princeton, NJ: Princeton University Press.

Zelman v. Simmons-Harris, 536 U.S. 639 (2002).

Zobrest v. Catalina, 509 U.S. 1 (1993).

Index

About the Author

BRIAN L. FIFE, PhD, is professor of public policy at Indiana University–Purdue University Fort Wayne. His published works include Praeger's *Reforming the Electoral Process in America: Toward More Democracy in the 21st Century, Political Culture and Voting Systems in the United States: An Examination of the 2000 Presidential Election, Higher Education in Transition: The Challenges of the New Millennium,* and *Desegregation in American Schools: Comparative Intervention Strategies.* He holds a doctorate in political science from the State University of New York at Binghamton.